THE 100

GREATEST WOMEN IN AVIATION

by LIZ MOSCROP and SANJAY RAMPAL

SUPPORTED BY

AERO TOY STORE

pininfarina

Published in 2008 by Aerocomm Ltd.

Aerocomm Ltd
The Gatehouse
104, Lodge Lane
Grays
Essex RM16 2UL
United Kingdom

www.aerocomm.aero <http://www.aerocomm.aero/>

Tel: (+44) 1375 427014

ISBN 978-0-9554195-3-9 CATEGORY Transport

Designed in the UK by Chris Murray of Allsortz Ltd, Bramfield, England.
Printed and bound by Newnorth, Bedford, England.
Marketing sales support by Acapella Publishing Resources

AEROCOMM

Contents

Prologue

We are aware that this book's title throws down the gauntlet. Choosing the '100 Greatest' anything is always going to be a subject of hot debate and we are extremely grateful to everyone who has pitched in to help us make our selection, which encompasses a century of flight of all kinds across several continents.

So why do it? Over the last few years there have been various 'century of flight' celebrations, but as yet, nothing of significance about women's contribution. That got me thinking about how little I knew about female aviators. A little investigation revealed that in 1908 there were at least two documented instances of women flying as passengers: Therese Peltier, who flew with Leon Delagrange and Mrs Hart O Berg, who jumped in with Wilbur Wright. By climbing into the rickety contraptions, they did more than hitch a lift – they defied the social conventions of the day and showed the world that women could fly.

It was then only a matter of months before women actually took the controls of powered aircraft. In the grand scheme of things aviation is a young industry. It is astonishing to see what a difference a decade makes in terms of airframe and systems knowledge. One thing that has not changed much, however, is the ratio of women to men in the field. Even in a growing world-wide market a 15% intake of female trainees (in India) is considered a high number. There are still several military forces that do not put women into their fighter jets and I have yet to meet a female police helicopter pilot.

We drew up an initial list of "possibles" and diverted from our plan several times as new stories were presented to us. We wanted to highlight excellent aviators, for sure, but also women who have made or are making a huge difference in terms of getting other people flying, such as Chanda Budhabhatti, Nancy Bird and Mandy Pantall. We have also included pioneers, like the first space travellers.

Initially several people thought we would have a hard job finding 100. That has not proved to be the case; rather it has been harder to leave people out. It has been a great adventure unearthing some ripping yarns that bear re-telling, such as the two Chinese barn-stormers who toured America in wartime. Then there was Pancho Barnes, a totally unsuitable wife for her clergyman husband, who would 'buzz' her husband's congregation on Sundays.

What has been a terrific boost is the enormous amount of support we have received to get this mammoth project off the ground in a short space of time. Many people have helped, in particular Captain Lucy Lupia and Fiorenzi de Bernadi who assisted with the Brazilian and Italian stories. Chanda Budhabhatti for her input on India. David Lam, who gave us excellent insights into the early fliers. Col. Marietta Hartley and Major Elize Beukes of the South African Air Force were hugely helpful and Olav Gynnild, Patti Gully and Helen Krasner were kind enough to share their own research with us. Sonja Veljanovska pulled out all the stops to get pictures, as well as translating information on Katarina Kulenevic. We owe particular thanks to Alan Peaford and Marcelle Nethersole at Aerocomm and Chris Murray at Allsortz for taking a chance and getting the book edited, designed and published in double quick time. I am also personally deeply indebted to my partner Sanjay for his writing, help and support.

The story is not over yet. There are young women flying into history today as they start their careers. UAE-based Aisha Al Mansoori and Salma Al Balooshi are the first two female cadets in Etihad. Britain's Jo Kelland is aiming to be the youngest female airline pilot in the world and, at 20 years old has a good shot at it.

We do hope you enjoy our selection. If you completely disagree with us and feel we have missed out someone hugely important, please hurl this book across the room and stomp off to tell her story to your daughter. You never know, you might just inspire her to fly.

LIZ MOSCROP

UAE-based Aisha Al Mansoori and Salma Al Balooshi are the first two female cadets in Etihad.

Jo Kelland is aiming to be the youngest female airline pilot in the world.

Before writing this book I had little inkling as to the trials and tribulations faced by the intrepid women who dared to venture into the world of flying. For the earliest of pioneers it wasn't just a case of donning a leather flying helmet and shouting 'contact' and waiting for the engine to cough to life. For a woman to be sitting in that cockpit in the first place was always going to be a challenge. But that was yester year, today in a more equitable world things have changed or at the very least are moving in the right direction.

With my father a former jet fighter pilot I've long harboured an avid interest in anything that possessed wings and could fly. I imagined myself as clued up as the next historical aviation enthusiast.

However when the idea of the book for 'The 100 Greatest Women In Aviation was broached by my partner Liz, I frowned my confusion. Were there that many women pioneers? Only a paltry few legendary names spewed forth from ignorant lips. 'Amy Johnson' and 'Amelia Earhart' I stuttered followed by the embarrassing silence to contemplate the question to my navel. 'Was there anyone else?'

Oh yes indeed there was, and are, and will always be. In fact there are a lot more and the numbers are growing. Women have played a pivotal yet silent role as unsung heroines of flight ever since the Wright Brothers had started the new powered flight craze back in 1903. Immersing myself in each of their stories I came away with a sense of belief that these women were resolute in both mind and soul yielding to nothing that would prevent them from embracing the freedom of the skies. Facing their detractors and enduring much hardship to achieve their lofty goals the steely aviatrixes were in a different league than the average 'Joe' with pilots' wings. This is not to denigrate the contribution of men to aviation, however the astonishing wealth of aviation firsts attained by women is long overdue on the celebratory front.

I have had the pleasure of communicating directly with some of the women featured in this book and they all belong to a sisterhood sharing a common bond through adversity and the love of flying. Each and every account is inspirational to the extent you start to think that their ability to fly is hard coded into their DNA. Almost all without exception were convinced of their calling to climb into a cockpit be it in a modern fighter or a contraption hewn from canvas, a few pieces of strategically glued wooden spars and much prayer.

Harriet Quimby, Jackie Cochran, Jean Batten, Pauline Gower, Jerrie Cobb, Elinor Smith, Patty Wagstaff, Nicole Malachowski and Michelle Goodman represent a few names and the rolling eras comprising the first centenary of women in aviation.

I just hope that I and the amazing Liz have done justice to the legendary women featured in this publication. From my heart I respectfully salute each and everyone one of them. Perhaps readers will be able to utter a few more names of the women who deserve to be remembered for the invaluable contributions they have made in shaping the world of flying. Roll on the next 100 pioneering women in this exciting new century of flight!

SANJAY RAMPAL

THE 100

GREATEST WOMEN IN AVIATION

1910

ELISE RAYMONDE DEROCHE – AKA 'BARONESS' RAYMONDE DE LAROCHE (FRANCE) 1886 – 1919

Defied broken bones to become the first woman in the world with a pilot's licence

N o matter how many bones she broke, the self-styled "Baroness de Laroche" was always determined to climb back into the sky. Born Elise Raymonde Deroche, the flamboyant avia-trix was the first woman in the world to win her pilot's licence from the International Aeronautics Federation (FAI) on 8 March 1910, when she was 24. She was awarded licence number 36, swiftly followed by other international female pioneers: Lydia Zvereva in Russia, Melli Beese in Germany, Hilda Hewlett in the UK, and Harriet Quimby in the US.

Born on the 22 August 1886 in France, Elise's father was a plumber. As a young woman she became a stage performer and used the name "Raymonde de Laroche". Exact details of her previous career are hazy, but most accounts describe her as some kind of actress or comedian.

In 1908, the Wright Brothers were offering demonstration flights at a racetrack near Le Mans, in France. De Laroche, then 22, had heard about Santos-Dumont's first flight in France two years earlier and was keen both to see and ride in an aircraft herself. Historian Eileen Lebow recounts that de Laroche visited aircraft manufacturer Charles Voisin and asked him to teach her to fly. Voisin fell under her spell and the pair became good friends.

On 22 October 1909 Elise flew 300 yards at Chalons, 90 miles east of Paris at the Voisin brothers' plant. She may have been the first woman to fly a powered heavier-than-air craft. That is debatable as some accounts report that trophy may belong to her contemporary Thérèse Peltier who may have taken the controls in 2008.

Flight magazine reported on her flight: "For some time the Baroness has been taking lessons from M. Chateau, the Voisin instructor, at Chalons, and on Friday of last week she was able to take the wheel for the first time. This initial voyage into the air was very short – terra firma was regained after 300 yards." Biographer Eileen Lebow wrote: "On her first try, she revved up the fifty-horsepower motor and taxied across the field, turned into the wind, and with full power raced back across the field. Suddenly her wheels left the ground, and she continued in the air for three hundred meters before gently settling down."

The New York Times also published an account of the historic event on December 19, 2009 under the headline "Woman aviator makes two flights." The story went on to say: "Baroness de la Roche is the first woman to make unaided a flight in an aeroplane. In her first effort at Chalons Camp, France, the Baroness flew some 300 yards in her Voison (sic) biplane. Her second attempt resulted in a flight of two circuits of the aerodrome, a distance of about four miles, which she accomplished with all the a assurance of a Paulham, Wright, Curtiss or Farnam, in spite of gusty winds." According to the newspaper she was not frightened by making midair turns and said: "I found that the jolliest part of the flight. The gusts bothered me when they caught me unawares and aeroplane tilted over, but I got used to that after the first two corners."

Ten weeks later she knocked into a tree and crashed landed horribly at an Air Meet in Rheims, suffering concussion and a broken collarbone. She was unfazed and off to an air show in Egypt as soon as she healed. On her return, she earned her pilot's license for flying four times around the aviation course mapped at Heliopolis, a distance of twelve miles.

She went on to take part in air meets at Heliopolis, Budapest, Rouen, and Saint Petersburg. In Russia Czar Nicholas singled her out to praise her bravery and audacity. She wrote an article about the trip for Colliers Magazine entitled "Flying in the Presence of the Czar." It was printed in French on 30 September 1911. Historian Dave Lam has translated it.

"I had hardly recovered from my accident, but I felt no apprehension on mounting my machine once more. What can I tell you of this first meeting, except that as soon as we took the air we were all seized by treacherous currents, which flopped us about at the wind's pleasure, although the atmosphere seemed perfectly calm? From there I went to Saint Petersburg.
"The aviation ground was small. None of us was willing to fly, and yet we all decided to do so. On the occasion of one of my

flights I mounted to a height of 150 meters, being enveloped by the smoke from the factory chimneys, which surrounded the ground. I flew over houses, then above forests, and turned three times. In order to reach the ground at the end of the fourth turn I made a little curve, tacked, and stopped my motor at a height of 100 meters. It was my first volplane, so I was somewhat excited. To my great astonishment nothing broke. The Czar, who was present at this meeting, wished to congratulate me. He asked what my feelings had been, and I was able to assure him that his presence in the first place, and the houses and the landing ground, which was only 30 meters wide, in the second, had brought my heart into my mouth."

On 8 July 1910 she was flying a Voisin biplane at the Rheims Air Meet when she flew into air disturbed by another aircraft, suffering wake turbulence. She lost control of her aeroplane, was knocked into a 160ft dive and crashed, fracturing her arms and legs. The New York Times reported the "second distressing incident of the aviation meeting" It continued: "The Baroness had flown once around the big field a at height of 80 meters or about 200 feet...Suddenly, just in front of the stand, she appeared to become frightened at the approach of two other aeroplanes, one of which, a Sommer, driven by M Lindpainter, passed directly over her." She cut the ignition, but the plane "turned over and fell like a stone to the ground, where it lay in a tangle of wreckage with the woman who had just been the object of the plaudits of the crowd crushed and mangled beneath it." The spectators threatened to lynch Lindpainter, although he was subsequently proved to be blameless. The same meeting had seen the death of Charles Wachter, flying an Antoinette, which had "crumpled up at a height of 500 feet, lost its wings and dropped like a stone, instantly killing Wachter, whose wife and children were among the crowd looking on."

Again she made a full recovery and returned to flying, despite the fact it had nearly killed her. Soon afterwards she set new women's records, including distance (323 km) and altitude (4500 m). She won the Coupe Femina in 1913, with a flight on 25 November of 323 km, which was curtailed only when she ran into mechanical problems.

She then suffered a third near-fatal accident a year later when she and Voisin had an horrific car accident. Voisin was killed in that crash and de Laroche was once again seriously injured. She recovered, and kept on flying until the start of World War I. Like all female pilots of the era, she was grounded for the duration of the war. Instead she worked as a chauffeur for the French army, driving officers through showers of bullets.

In June 1919 she took to the air again and set two women's altitude records, one at 15,700 feet; and also the women's distance record, at 201 miles. The same year she reported to the airfield at Le Crotoy to co-pilot a new aircraft in hopes of becoming the first female test pilot. Unfortunately the aircraft went into a dive on landing and she suffered her final crash. This time it was fatal.

Although she died at a young age, she did so doing what she loved. "The Baroness" earned her place in history because of her fearlessness and absolute delight in pushing the barriers of aviation. She was unequivocal about her passion and said: "Flying is the best possible thing for women."

Events in 1910

- Japan annexes Korea.
- Boy Scouts of America founded.
- Eugene Ely takes off from a temporary platform erected over the bow of the light cruiser USS Birmingham, the first take-off from a ship.
- French Air Force is formed as its own command, with a total of five aircraft.
- Blanche Stuart Scott and Bessica Raiche solo in the USA.

1910

HELENE DUTRIEU (BELGIUM/FRANCE) "THE SPARROW HAWK" 1877 – 1961

Hélène Dutrieu was dubbed the 'Female Sparrow Hawk' or 'La Femme Epervier' because, like the swift predatory bird, she swooped in to claim a number of firsts in aviation. Prolific and energetic, Hélène's competitive spirit brushed aside worthy challengers, buffeted by the wake of her sleek wings.

élène was born in Tournai, Belgium on July 10th 1877. Her father was an officer in the Belgian army. She left school early to support her family, who had fallen on hard times. Working in domestic settings did not appeal to Hélène who turned to outdoor pursuits for income generation. At first glance her waif-like frame would have dismissed her from achieving anything in the sport of competitive cycling. But the many hours she spent training alongside her brother had transformed her into a diminutive powerhouse. She went on to set the first Belgian record for distance covered in one hour on a bicycle in 1895, and repeated the feat in 1897.

Successively in 1897 and 1898 she won the women's speed track cycling championship in Ostend, adding further records to her name. Her increased public recognition garnered her the first of many nicknames: "La Fleche Humanine" (The Human Arrow). She conquered the Grand Prix d'Europe in August 1898. Emboldened by a string of victories, the unstoppable Hélène triumphantly claimed the "Course de 12 Jours" title, riding from Paris to London in twelve days. In recognition of her achievements, Leopold II awarded her the Cross of St Andre.

Hélène then performed as comedic stunt cyclist throughout Europe, delighting crowds in both France and England. Transferring her act to motorcycles allowed her to thrill audiences with her "looping the loop" performance in the larger European cities. Her fearless and daredevil antics moved up a gear when she used automobiles for the same stunts. Explosions and spectacular crashes were a mainstay of this death-defying heroine's epic displays. During one performance she crashed and was badly injured whilst she was looping a car. A protracted period in hospital followed, giving her time to contemplate less hazardous ways of making a living.

In 1908 Hélène was approached by the Clement Bayard Company to fly its Santos Dumont designed ultra lightweight "Demoiselle" ("Young Lady") monoplane. Clement Bayard felt that using a woman would be good publicity and the elfin Hélène was ideal for the small plane. With little or no instruction she flew the fragile and unstable Demoiselle, only to crash on her first flight. Emerging from the shattered wreckage she persevered with the unpredictable airframe, managing to survive further mishaps. However, fresh memories of her car stunt accident and languishing for six months in a hospital prompted her to stop the Demoiselle flight tests. She was suitably intrigued by the experience, though, and wished to explore the world of flying further.

Hélène's next aerial jaunt was in 1909 in the Sommer biplane, designed and built by Roger Sommer of the Ardennes. Her limited flying experience notwithstanding, she flew the heavier aircraft without incident; although she confessed later that she was terrified because she knew inevitably she would have to land the unfamiliar machine. Following her successful solo flight, she carried a passenger in the Sommer, becoming the first woman in the world to do so. But her association with Sommer was to cease abruptly, when she crashed and wrecked the plane at a flying meet in Odessa. An irate Sommer dismissed the contrite aviatrix as she clambered out from the ruins of his valuable biplane.

Bruised, battered and rejected, Hélène decided it was time for a few flying lessons and gain an official flying licence. At the same time she struck up a new partnership with Henry Farman, another pioneering airframe manufacturer. Receiving direct instruction from Henry, she familiarised herself with his aircraft, the Farman III. Her first attempt at qualifying for a license was deemed a failure by the French judging panel that insisted she repeat the test. A steadfast Hélène refused, citing a scheduled appearance at an exhibition in Belgium. She went on to make a non-stop flight from Ostend to Bruges in September 1910.

She eventually gained the coveted licence on 25th November 1910 in Belgium, and is credited as the first Belgian woman, and the fourth woman in the world to secure an official pilot qualification. The Aero Club De Belgique issued her licence number #27. The steely wings of the 'Female Sparrow Hawk' or 'Girl Hawk' were to ruffle more than a few feathers in the competitive circuit, and cause a great deal of controversy.

Hélène scooped another first by winning the Femina Cup (Coupe Femina) in December 1910 by setting the longest flight endurance record of two hours and 35 minutes, covering a distance of 167 kilometres (104 miles). In 1911 she retained the Femina Cup temporarily with a flight of 254 kilometres (158 miles) in two hours 58 minutes.

The year 1911 was a busy time for the La Femme Epervier as she jumped from one competitive event to another. In May she participated in Florence, Italy for the King's Cup (Coppa del Re), beating fourteen male competitors to take the title. Hélène then scooted between other meets in Spain, Germany and France.

One notable event at Le Mans caused much consternation amongst those of a sensitive and orthodox ilk. Hélène was the centre of a scandal, which caused a few onlookers to bring out reviving pungent smelling salts. She had a slight mishap at an air meet. Her plane crashed into a grandstand, and she inadvertently hospitalised several spectators. Incredibly, the welfare of these hapless members of the public was secondary to the revelation that Hélène was not wearing a corset. The non-conforming aviatrix was frowned upon for her audacious lack of proper attire. The media had a feeding frenzy at the expense of a red faced Hélène. She protested that she had not worn the restrictive garment for comfort reasons.

In September 1911 she travelled to the United States with her trusty Henry Farman III biplane to compete against the formidable Americans. Popular with the US public, she soon broke the US record for endurance set by a woman. She then vied for the Rodman-Wanamaker Trophy, awarded to the woman achieving the highest altitude. However, despite her spirited performance at the Nassau Boulevard airfield in New York, Matilde Moisant won the event and title.

Returning home, Hélène notched another first by being the first to pilot a seaplane in 1912, designed and manufactured by Henry Farman. She also entered into seaplane trial competitions and accrued further title wins.

In 1913 Hélène was showered with honours. She was awarded the Medaille d'Or from the Aero Club of France. King Albert presented her with the Grand Plaque of the Belgium Aero Club. The same year the French government bestowed her with membership of the Légion d'honneur. She was the first female aviator to achieve this - one of France's highest accolades.

The onset of war and simmering tensions in Europe curtailed any further competitive appearances by Hélène. She volunteered as an ambulance driver during the conflict, like many of her contemporaries. For example, Katherine Stinson drove for the Red Cross. Hélène later became director of a military hospital. Following the war, research suggests that she became a journalist. She married in 1922 in her adopted France, becoming a French citizen.

In 1956 she established the Coupe Hélène Dutrieu Mortier prize of 200,000 francs to the female aviator achieving the longest distance flight without landing. She also held the position of vice president of the women's section of the Aero Club of France.

Hélène Dutrieu passed away in Paris, aged 84 on 26th June 1961. It was a quiet passing compared to the frenetic pace with which the Girl Hawk took centre stage in the world of competitive aviation. Regarded as one of the French greats, it is ironic that she gravitated towards flying because of her overriding need to extricate her family from poverty. Pioneering spirit and resolve is independent of wealth and opulence. Hélène was always destined for great things because a sparrow hawk will instinctively prey upon that final prize…

More events in 1910

- **Raymonde de Laroche gains first licence awarded to a woman.**
- **Union of South Africa established.**
- **Blanche Stuart Scott makes the first non-accredited solo flight by a US woman.**
- **Bessica Raiche makes the first solo accredited flight by a woman in the US.**

1910
BLANCHE STUART SCOTT (USA) 1885–1970

Blanche Stuart 'Betty' Scott is credited by many as being the first American woman to achieve a solo hop in an aircraft.

Born April 8th 1885 in Rochester, New York Blanche's father was a successful businessman dealing in patented medicines. From a very early age Blanche was keen to demonstrate her pioneering, almost daredevil spirit. She was an accomplished ice skater and won several medals; however the young girl was less successful as a bicycle stunt artist. This prompted her father to steer her towards her first Cadillac. At the tender age of thirteen, a precocious Blanche skittered around the streets of Rochester in her new car when many of her contemporaries would have been learning to ride bicycles. Local authority figures frowned upon her activities, yet were powerless to stop her from continuing her motoring escapades since the minimum legal age for driving had yet to be established.

Her tomboy pursuits landed her a stint at a finishing school, after which she drew the media spotlight when in 1910 she became the first woman to drive a car coast to coast across America. She convinced the Willys-Overland company to sponsor her trip from New York to San Francisco on the provision that she alight at each Overland dealership. After a quick instruction in car mechanics she set off in her car nicknamed "Lady Overland" on the 6,000 mile journey with a female journalist, Gertrude Buffington Phillips, as her travelling companion. The dearth of a suitable road infrastructure outside the cities in the United States at the time made for a hair raising transcontinental crossing. In 1910 it was estimated that there were only 218 miles of paved roads in North America. En route Blanche caught sight of a few airplanes lumbering through the skies, which captivated her interest.

The success of her lucrative road trip gave her the fame she so coveted and whetted her appetite for greater adventures. Fortune smiled again when she attracted the attention of Jerome Fanciulli and Glenn Curtiss of the Curtiss Exhibition team. At Fanciulli's insistence, Curtiss agreed to give the budding aviatrix flying lessons making Blanche the first and only student to receive instruction from him. Her flight training took place in Hammondsport, New York in September 1910 with her first flight in a Curtiss pusher-type plane. She was entrusted with practicing taxi runs on the ground alone. The throttle of her aircraft had been restricted with a limiter to prevent the machine from becoming airborne. On one fateful day the limiter failed, or a sudden gust of wind lifted her into the sky. Either way she levitated into the history books by becoming the first woman to solo - albeit accidentally.

The exact date of her inadvertent solo hop is unclear, but the "Early Birds of Aviation" organisation credits Blanche with the date of 6th September. However, another organisation, "The Aeronautical Society of America," says that the honour went to another aviatrix, Bessica Medlar Raiche, who achieved her first solo flight on 16th September 1910. Raiche was unconcerned, seeing the advancement of women fliers as being for the greater good, rather than who took-off first.

More events in 1910

- Leon Delagrange, the man who helped Therese Peltier and Raymonde de Laroche gain their wings is killed at Pau after wings on Bleriot collapse.

- Raymonde de Laroche becomes the first woman in the world to receive a pilot's licence.

- First Hollywood film released; *Griffith's In Old California*.

- Halley's Comet appears.

Blanche soon earned her wings, graduating to become a fully-fledged member of the Curtiss Exhibition team. Her maiden flight as part of this aerial troupe took place on October 24th 1910 in Fort Wayne, Indiana. She was the first woman to fly at such airshow events and her subsequent exploits earned her the nickname "*The Tomboy of the Sky.*"

She often received front billing on airshow posters and newspapers around the country. The extra publicity enhanced the popularity of the Curtiss team and drew in the crowds. Her flying prowess transformed Scott into a daredevil stunt pilot with her trademark inverted flying and "death dives." The latter involved pushing her aircraft to its very design envelope by plummeting from 4,000 feet to pull up a mere 200 feet from the ground. Her public recognition earned her a fortune. She was coining in $5,000 a week and rubbing shoulders with other industry doyennes, such as Harriet Quimby.

Ever the passive record breaker, in 1911 Blanche became the first woman to achieve a long distance flight, which she accomplished on a whim. Taking off from Minneola, New York for a 60-mile jaunt, she returned to the airfield to establish the unintentional record. In 1912, Glenn Curtiss recruited her as a test pilot for his prototype airframes - she flew them before the ink had even dried on the final production blueprints. In 1913 she joined the Ward Exhibition team and finally retired from flying in 1916. Furiously disgusted by the lack of opportunities for women in the aviation industry and the public's insatiable appetite for air crashes she left the arena altogether.

The 1930s saw her transition to the glittering world of media and print. Drawing upon her earlier theatrical experiences, Blanche became a Hollywood scriptwriter, writing for such big name studios as Universal, Warner Brothers and RKO pictures. She also wrote, produced and performed in a number of radio shows broadcast in her native New York. In addition, she had a stint on stage and wrote short stories. In 1954, Blanche began working for the Air Force Museum at Wright Patterson in Ohio as a public relations representative, tasked with amassing historical information for the museum. She was also member of the Early Bird, OX-5 and the Long Island Early Flier's Clubs.

The lure of aviation and unintentional record setting never left her. In 1948 she became the first women to fly in a fast jet as a passenger in a TF-80C Shooting Star, piloted by the legendary Chuck Yeager. Chuck was the first person to break the sound barrier and knew about Blanche's stunt flying past, so treated her to a 14,000 feet power dive and a succession of snap rolls.

Blanche Stuart 'Betty' Scott died aged 84 on January 12 1970 in Rochester, New York. She is gone, but not forgotten. Author Julie Cummins wrote an account of her life: "Tomboy of the Air: Daredevil Pilot Blanche Stuart Scott." As a fitting tribute to this remarkable aviatrix, the United States Postal Service celebrated her achievements by issuing commemorative stamps in her honour during the 1980s.

1911
AMELIA 'MELLI' BEESE (GERMANY) 1886 – 1925

"Flying is everything; Living is nothing."
Melli Beese meant what she said and gave up her life for her passion.

O n September 8 1911, 25-year old Melli Beese gave her aircraft a final check. She was about to take off for the flight that would turn her into Germany's first licensed female pilot. She discovered the fuel had been drained from her tank, control wires had been loosened, and the fresh spark plugs she had installed had been switched with contaminated ones. Apparently her male classmates were none too happy about her success as a pilot. One of the men responsible reputedly said: "A woman who flies would take our glory from us."

Melli's story is a sad one. She was born Amelie Hedwig Boutard-Beese on September 13, 1886 in Laubegast, near Dresden to a wealthy family. She opted for a career as a sculptor. However, German art schools did not admit female students at the time. So the young Melli travelled to Stockholm and took a three-year course at the Royal Academy there between 1906 and 1909. At college she learned to sail and also became a competent skier. She returned to Dresden in 1909 and attended lectures in mathematics, shipbuilding, and aeronautical engineering. This fuelled her desire to become a pilot.

By this time, French sculptress Therese Peltier had hit headlines as probably the first woman to fly as a passenger in 1908 with pioneering aviator and artist Leon Delagrange. Peltier had subsequently taken up flying lessons. Another Delagrange, protégée, Frenchwoman Raymonde de Laroche, had earned the first licence awarded to a female in 1910, and all over the world bright young women were attempting to spread their wings and fly. Melli's father was supportive of his daughter's plans to become a pilot. However, as was the case with many of her contemporaries worldwide, many airmen refused to teach her.

In November 1910 she travelled to Johannisthal, Berlin's first airfield, where pioneering pilots from all over the world were congregating. In December of that year Robert Thelens agreed to help her, but abandoned his tuition soon afterwards when Melli crashed her aircraft and sustained multiple injuries, including broken ribs and nose and fractured leg bones. In 1911, flight test regulations were toughened and Melli found it increasingly difficult to find someone to teach her. However, she managed to persuade another instructor and learned her skills on a Wright Flyer at the "Ad Astra" school. In 1911 a pilot named von Mossner agreed to let her take complete control of an aeroplane for the first time. Melli then appealed to Major von Tschudi, the director of Johannisthal airfield, to let her try for her license. Von Tschudi realised he would attract huge publicity if he allowed a woman to participate in his next flying display, so at the end of July, Melli was allowed to fly solo.

Although other candidates sabotaged her aircraft the day she took her pilot's test, she passed. She earned her license on 13 September 1911. Not content with being the first woman with an official ticket in her home country, the next day she capped pioneering Belgian aviatrix Helen Dutrieu's altitude record of 1,476 feet (450 meters), soaring to a height of 2,707 feet (825 meters). On her 25th birthday she received license number 115 from the International Aeronautics Federation (FAI). Melli's persistence paid off. After finally getting her license, she set a succession of endurance and altitude records.

In 1912 Melli's father died and her mother loaned her money to open a flying school at Johannisthal. The same year she designed and patented a collapsible aircraft. One of her early pupils, Charles Boutard, showed aptitude for aircraft design, and the pair worked together on plans for a flying boat. They grew close and married in 1913.

They were evidently unaware of how close war was. Fighter ace Karl Hackstetter was witness at the ceremony. Adelbert Norden's biography of Melli "Fluegel am Horizont," published in 1939, describes the Justice of the Peace officiating at wedding as saying words to the effect of: "Ms Beese, if war breaks out, you may have a problem with marrying Charles Boutard as he is a French national." Hackstetter replied: "Well war won't break out just for them."

Melli and Charles continued to design and build aircraft. Between 1912 and 1914 Melli applied for several patents, including a floatplane and a light plane. During her experiments she crashed several times and was severely injured. However, she was undeterred and always went flying again as soon as she recovered. Despite her own injuries, her own flying school was known to be one of the safest, with no serious accidents or fatalities occurring during training. She built her own trainer the "Melli Beese Colombe" (Melli Beese's Dove), which she used to teach students.

Melli's marriage meant that she was regarded as a French citizen during the First World War, so her teaching license was revoked; her business confiscated and her planes seconded to the military. Both she and Boutard were arrested and tried as "undesirable aliens" and Boutard was imprisoned. They moved to Wittstock to sit out the war. Boutard was constantly interned then freed. Melli was not allowed to fly, teach, or build aircraft, neither was she allowed to enter an aerodrome.

They were ruined financially.

When the war ended, they tried to get back into their business. After the armistice the Boutards filed compensation claims for their confiscated goods. These lawsuits lasted throughout the rest of Melli's life. The value of the aircraft had dwindled thanks to the extreme inflation in Germany immediately after World War I. At this point Melli started to make a film about her flying. Some surviving footage was included in a 1940 film by Walter Jerven. The couple attempted to raise funds for a round-the-world flight in 1921, but were unable to find sponsors.

The pressures put a terrible strain on their relationship and the marriage foundered. By 1925 she had separated from her husband and was living alone in Schmargendorf, Berlin. She made a last attempt to renew her pilot's license, but unfortunately crashed her aircraft during the test. The total loss of her flying privileges sent her into a tailspin from which she was unable to recover. Alone in her small flat at Christmastime, she was desperate. On December 22, 1925, she summoned the last shreds of her courage, put a gun to her temple and pulled the trigger.

She is buried in Berlin-Schmargendorf cemetery. Germany has not forgotten its pioneering daughter. In 1992, Strasse 19 in Teptow was renamed Melli-Beese-Strasse. There is an exhibition dedicated to her in the Heimatmuseum in the eastern suburbs of Berlin, forever linking her with the aviation she so loved.

Events in 1911

- Eugene Ely lands on the deck of USS Pennsylvania, marking the first time an aircraft landed on a ship.

- Hilda Hewlett becomes the first British woman to receive a pilot's licence.

- Harriet Quimby is first licensed female pilot in US.

1911

Hilda Hewlett
(UK) 1864 – 1943

"Women will never be as successful in aviation as men. They have not the right kind of nerve."
Maurice Hewlett, husband of Britain's first licensed female pilot and aircraft manufacturer.

n April 2008 the world's press reported on Britain's Prince William earning his wings. He was the latest in a long line of military pilots to graduate in the UK. His training may have been tough, but possibly not as tough as that of young Francis Hewlett almost a century earlier in 1911. Not only was Francis a pioneer –he was the first and possibly the only - military airman to have been trained by his mother.

His mother was, of course, Hilda Hewlett. She was the daughter of an Anglican vicar, and born Hilda Beatrice Herbert in Vauxhall, London, England, on 17 February 1864, one of nine children. She was an artistic soul and went to the National Art Training School in South Kensington. Whilst there she specialised in: woodwork, metalwork, and needlework.

At 19 she went to Egypt with her parents and at 21 spent a year training as a nurse in Berlin. She learned to ride a bicycle and drive a car and entered automobile rallies, both activities that were highly daring for a woman in her day.

On 3 January 1888, she married Maurice Henry Hewlett in St. Peter's Church, Vauxhall. Her father officiated at the ceremony. The couple had a son and a daughter, Francis and Pia. Maurice had been a partner in his family's law firm, but gave up the law in 1901 and became a successful romantic novelist. His wife continued to develop her passion for cars and in about 1909 attended an automobile meeting where she met Gustave Blondeau. He was a French engineer who had worked for the Farman brothers on their aeroplanes. The pair had a great deal in common and become fast friends. In October 1909 they went to the UK's first aviation meeting in Blackpool. Hilda watched Hubert Latham fly an Antoinette monoplane and decided she wanted to do the same herself. Blondeau also decided to dedicate himself totally to aeronautical engineering.

Within a few months, Hilda had saved enough money to buy a Farman airplane. She and Blondeau headed to Camp de Chalons in France to learn how to fly and maintain it. Hilda travelled under the pseudonym "Mrs Grace Bird." She became fluent in French and worked alongside the men in the engineering shops to build her new machine. She was in the right place. According to biographer Eileen Lebow's excellent account of aviatrixes in that era: "Before Amelia," female pilots in France "were treated with respect as members of the flying community. In England there was mistrust and even open hostility." Blondeau took his flying test and earned his license from the Aero Club in France on June 10, 1910.

In July the pair returned to England with the aircraft, nicknamed the "Blue Bird." Maurice Hewlett was deeply unsympathetic to his wife's aspirations and is widely quoted as having said: "Women will never be as successful in aviation as men. They have not the right kind of nerve."

His wife blithely ignored him. In the summer of 1910 she and Blondeau opened the first British flight training school at the disused Brooklands car-racing track in Surrey, which ran for 18 months. Many famous pilots and engineers had their first taste of aviation at the school, including Thomas Sopwith. In total thirteen pilots graduated from Brooklands. Like Melli Beese's school in Berlin, there were no accidents at Hilda's establishment, which was remarkable for the time.

Then on the 29 August 1911 47-year old Hilda earned her own pilot's ticket at Brooklands, flying into history as the first British woman to earn a licence. She was awarded certificate No.122 from the Royal Aero Club. She also taught her son Francis to fly. He got his licence on 14 November 1911 and subsequently had a distinguished aviation career in the military in both the UK and New Zealand, reaching the rank of group captain. He was awarded the Distinguished Service Order in 1915. Hilda became a well-known figure on the aviation circuit in the UK and regularly flew her Farman biplane in airshows and competitions. In 1912 she won a quick-start competition.

Hilda and Blondeau worked together for a decade. They established a successful manufacturing business, Hewlett & Blondeau Limited (H&B), building aircraft under licence. Hilda managed the plant, which built Farman, Caudron and Hanriot aeroplanes. She became a familiar sight locally, driving up to the plant in a large car with her Great Dane sitting on the back seat. She dressed eccentrically and by that time had her hair cropped short in a masculine hairstyle.

However, the firm had a good reputation and was successful. By August 1914 it employed 700 workers and was producing 10 different types of planes. During the First World War it supplied over 800 military aircraft. The business started at Brooklands, decamped to London and finally grew into a 10-acre site in Bedfordshire in May 1914. At around this point she "politely" separated from her husband. He died in 1923. During the First World War, H&B built more than 800 military aircraft, and employed 700 people. After the war they added farming equipment to their product list. However, the huge productivity necessary to supply the war effort was no longer needed and the factory shut its doors for the last time in October 1920. They put the site on sale.

Hilda then spent nine months touring New Zealand and the United States. She finally sold the old H&B site to Electrolux in 1926. That year she moved to Tauranga in New Zealand with her daughter Pia and her family. She said of her move: "The urge to escape from the 'three Cs:' crowds, convention, and civilization, became strong." She loved being outdoors, and developed a strong taste for camping and fishing. Her family nicknamed her "Old Bird."

Two years after she emigrated, Hilda bought land in Tauranga, overlooking the Waikareao tidal estuary, which had served as the local airfield for eight years. It was a tricky location since landing and take-off could only take place for a short period either side of low tide. By June 1932 she had helped establish the Tauranga Aero and Gliding Club and was elected president the following month. The aero club expanded and Hilda searched for a permanent non-tidal home. Her son, Francis, helped to choose the club's next 140-acre airport site at Whareroa.

Hilda regularly travelled between New Zealand and England and in 1932, she became the first female passenger to make a "through flight" from London to New Zealand. She stopped off in Jakarta in Indonesia. The trip took eleven days, with KLM Airlines in a Fokker FVIIb/3m. This would have been the same airline that Hilda's Irish contemporary Lady Mary Heath had hoped to fly for. Heath had flown for the company unpaid for a time, aiming to be hired for its long-distance route. That did not happen. However, Hilda's trip had put her in the spotlight again. Four years earlier Amelia Earhart had been lauded for becoming the first female passenger to cross the Atlantic as a passenger. Although Earhart established her own solo flight in 1932, this was still an era when long distance air travel was considered risky. Two years later in 1934 Hilda played host to the famous New Zealand aviatrix Jean Batten, who was touring the country after her feted solo flight from England to Australia.

Hilda was widely respected in her adopted homeland and in January 1939 Frederick Jones, New Zealand's minister of defence, named a road after Hilda and her son Francis. She died in 1943 aged 79 in Tauranga and was buried at sea as she had requested.

In addition to her famous 'firsts' she left behind the start of flight training in two countries, paving the way for a women and princes to realise their aerial dreams.

More events in 1911

- ■ **The Spanish Air Force is created as the Aeronáutica**
- ■ **Harriet Quimby becomes the first licensed female pilot in the US**
- ■ **Melli Beese becomes the first licensed female pilot in Germany**
- ■ **Marie Curie won her second Nobel Prize**

HARRIET QUIMBY (USA)
1875 – 1912

On July 12th 1912 Harriet Quimby lost control of her plane and fell to her death before thousands of horrified spectators. It was an untimely and tragic end to a remarkable life in the limelight.

uimby introduced a sense of flamboyant chic when she took to the air in her couture purple flying suit to thrill an enthralled crowd. Apart from her striking beauty and panache, she is credited with being the first woman in the United States to gain a pilot's licence. She achieved another first by becoming the first woman to fly across the English Channel.

Born on May 11th 1875 in Coldwater, Michigan, the early 1900s saw her family move to San Francisco, where she embarked on a career in journalism. She aspired to become an actress so used her journalistic talents to write theatrical reviews in addition to her stories for the San Francisco Bulletin.

She moved to New York in 1903 where she wrote for Leslie's Illustrated Weekly. The prestigious publication printed over 250 of her articles over a period of nine years. She wrote about a variety of subjects from house and home to car mechanics. As a photojournalist she became famous for travelling to Europe, Iceland, Egypt and Cuba. Quimby embodied an independent spirit and strength, which thrived in a world so closed to enterprising women. In addition to her journalistic career she found the time to write five romantic screenplays, each brought to the silver screen as silent shorts.

But there was an adventurer's heart beating in her elegant form, and Quimby desired a greater adrenaline rush. She developed a taste for fast cars following an assignment at a racetrack. This inspired the plucky newshound to purchase her own automobile at a time when it was exclusively a male dominated pursuit.

By 1910 she was drawn towards the exciting emerging world of aviation. Her interest was spawned when she attended the 1910 Belmont Park International Aviation Tournament held in Long Island New York in late October. It was there that she met an aspiring aviatrix named Matilde Moisant and her brother John, also a pilot. John was the archetypical all-American hero and a daring air race pilot who, along with brother Alfred, ran a flying school out of Long Island. Both Quimby and Moisant were accepted as pupils at the flying school, although Quimby kept the flying lessons under a shroud of secrecy.

However it was not long before the media picked up the scent of her endeavours, and, whether by accident or design, both she and Matilde Moisant were thrust into the limelight. Quimby took advantage of her heightened fame to write a progressive set of articles for Leslie's on her flying training experiences. Having the right stuff, she proved to be a natural flyer when on August 1st 1911 she became the first woman in the US to achieve an official pilot's licence. She wrote: "The men flyers have given out the impression that aeroplaning is very perilous work, something that an ordinary mortal should not dream of attempting. But when I saw how easily the man flyers manipulated their machines I said I could fly." Moisant soon followed in her dainty footsteps, and became America's second woman certified to fly.

Freshly qualified, Quimby made her public debut at the Richmond County Fair on September 4th 1911, flying a Moisant-built version of the French Bleriot monoplane. It was at the fair that she established another record and achieved the first night flight by a woman. Shunning the bulky garments worn by male aviators, she sought the expertise of a renowned tailor to design a more elegant flying costume made from purple satin. She said: "If a woman wants to fly, first of all, she must, of course, abandon skirts and don a knickerbocker uniform." She cut a strikingly beautiful figure in her practical form fitting flying suit with jewellery completing the fetching look. Quimby courted publicity and basked in public adulation, so was an instant hit with the crowds, earning the nickname "Dresden China Aviatrix of New York." Her exposure was good for Leslie's circulation, since her fame sold many thousands of issues to readers eagerly anticipating her stories.

In November 1911 both Quimby and Moisant became performers with the Moisant exhibition team, flying at various air meet gatherings and official events, both in the United States and Mexico. It was whilst on the exhibition circuit that Quimby became inspired by Louis Bleriot's earlier flight of 1909 when he crossed the English Channel in his Bleriot monoplane. She wanted to become the first woman to make the crossing, but in reverse from Dover, Great Britain to Calais in France.

A determined Quimby sailed to England from New York on March 1912, keeping her ambition a secret in case another aviatrix learned of her intentions and beat her to it. She had convinced London's Daily Mirror newspaper to fund her record attempt in return for exclusive rights to cover the story. Her furtive attempts at trying to purchase a two-seater Bleriot were unsuccessful; however Bleriot himself came to the rescue and loaned her an aircraft.

The sinking of the RMS Titanic two days before the morning of the 16th of April cast a sombre cloud over the day of her record-breaking attempt. A close friend and advisor Gustav Hamel tried to dissuade her from making the hazardous flight where others more experienced had perished. He volunteered to take her place, offering to disguise himself in her trademark satin flight suit and make the treacherous journey on her behalf. But an unfazed Harriet steadfastly refused; resolute and committed to the perilous undertaking, seeking only his advice on how to read a compass.

She took to the skies, only to be greeted by a thick cloud bank that tested her natural instrument flying skills. Just shy of 59 minutes later, the spirited and determined aviatrix touched down thirty miles from her destination of Calais to end up in the fishing village of Hardelot-Plage, Pas-de-Calais. The locals, aware of her monumental feat, greeted Quimby with the rapturous welcome fit for the first woman to cross the English Channel. But her achievement was overshadowed by the still raw tragedy of the Titanic and the loss of life, which dominated the headlines both in the United States and Great Britain. The newspapers largely overlooked her story with very little column space dedicated to her achievement. Her comments at the time give a clue to her psyche: "I was annoyed from the start by the attitude of doubt on the part of the spectators that I would never really make the flight. They knew I had never used the machine before, and probably thought I would find some excuse at the last moment to back out of the flight. This attitude made me more determined than ever to succeed."

Following the muted success of her channel crossing, she resumed her flying at air meets in the US. A tragic accident on July 12th 1912 cut short a remarkable life. Quimby was flying her factory-fresh two seat Bleriot monoplane at the third annual Boston Aviation Meet in Squantum, Massachusetts. Her passenger was the event's organiser William Willard. Inexplicably the plane pitched forward, ejecting both of them. Quimby and Willard then plunged to their deaths before a shocked crowd into the shallow mud flats of Dorchester Bay.

During her short and eventful life Quimby was also a visionary, commenting on the future of passenger flights and the commercial use of aircraft. Ironically and rather poignantly, she was also vocal in her articles concerning flying safety and the dangers of complacency. Her legacy was to inspire other women, especially one Amelia Earhart, who drew inspiration from her pioneering and fearless exploits.

In 1991 a United States postal service stamp was issued in her honour. During the 1960's the Old Rheinback Aerodrome museum dedicated to the resurrection of historically significant aircraft allegedly restored her wrecked Bleriot to flying condition.

More events in 1911

- First Monte Carlo races.
- Glenn H. Curtiss flies the first successful seaplane.
- First official air mail flight took place in Allahabad, India to Naini, India, when Henri Pequet carried 6,500 letters a distance of 13 km.

1912

MARIE MARVINGT (FRANCE) 1875 – 1963

Superwoman. "Danger's fiancée" Marvingt is less well-known today than her famous contemporaries such as Amelia Earhart and Amy Johnson, but her contribution to aviation is arguably the most important ever made by a woman.

ot many octogenarians celebrate their birthdays by breaking the sound barrier – allegedly. It is rumoured that on 20 February 1955, the day she turned 80, Marie Marvingt was flown over Nancy by a US Air Force officer from Toul-Rosières Air Base in a F-101 Voodoo fighter jet. It does seem highly possible, since in the same year she started to take her helicopter lessons. Five years later, aged 86, she cycled 219 miles (352 km) from Nancy to Paris. Such was the measure of France's greatest aviatrix. She was the most decorated woman in French history, earning more than 34 official medals and decorations.

Born on the 20 February 1875 in Aurillac, Marvingt was a superb athlete, mountaineer and aviator. She won countless prizes for her sporting achievements. She was the first woman to conquer several of the mountains in the French and Swiss Alps. A record-breaking balloonist, and pioneering pilot, she won the Croix de Guerre during World War I for flying sorties as a bomber pilot - the first woman to fly in active combat. She was a qualified surgical nurse, and made the establishment of worldwide air ambulance services her lifelong mission.

Her father encouraged her to take up sports, and she is known to have excelled in swimming, fencing, shooting, ski jumping, speed skating, bobsledding and mountaineering. She also learned circus skills. At 15 she canoed 250 miles (400 km) from Nancy to Koblenz and in 1905 became the first woman to swim the length of the Seine through Paris. She was nicknamed "l'amphibie rouge" ("the red amphibian") because of the colour of her swimming costume. Two years later she won an international military shooting competition with a French army carbine, becoming the only woman ever awarded the palms du Premier Tireur (First Gunner palms) by a French minister of war. Between 1908 and 1910 she won first place in more than twenty sports events at Chamonix, Gérardmer, and Ballon d'Alsace, including the Leon Auscher Cup in the women's bobsledding world championship. She had limitless energy and reportedly needed fewer than four hours of sleep a night.

An avid cyclist, she once rode 825 miles (1,327 km) from Nancy to Naples, Italy to watch Vesuvius erupting. Refused permission to participate in the 1908 Tour de France because of her gender, Marvingt cycled the 1,865-mile (3,500 km) course after the race. She managed the arduous journey, unlike 88 of the 114 male entrants to compete. She was such a great all-rounder that on 15 March 1910 the French Academy of Sports awarded her a gold medal "for all sports", the only multi-sport medal it has ever awarded.

Marvingt first piloted a balloon in July 1907. She soloed in September 1909, the same month she experienced her first flight as a passenger in an aeroplane. On 26 October 1909 she became the first woman to fly a balloon across the English Channel to England. She took up fixed-wing flying in an Antoinette aeroplane in 1910. The same year she earned her balloon pilot's ticket in June, followed by her fixed wing licence in November, making her the third woman in the world licensed to fly aeroplanes. She was particularly proud of the fact that in her first 900 flights she never "broke wood" in a crash, a record unequalled at that time. She loved to fly in airshows and in December 1910, set the first official women's flight records for duration and distance at 53 minutes and 26 miles (42 km) while competing in Turin for the Femina Cup, which was won by Belgian Helene Dutrieu.

She saw the potential for aviation in medical evacuation and in 1912 designed and ordered a prototype air ambulance from the Deperdussin factory. She explained her passion: "I have been for a very long time a diploma'd nurse of the Red Cross and the hospitals. My dream is to place the aeroplane in the service of military casualties. My aircraft would be a Deperdussin monoplane with three places, powered by a 100 hp Gnome motor, and equipped with radio: It would provide information to the senior doctors, and would be able to resupply aid posts. I have studied, with a view toward the colonies, a type of flying litter, very comfortable, which could be adapted to my

machine…. Piece by piece, I will accumulate what seems to be necessary, and I will realize my greatest desire for France. It will be one of the greatest joys of my life" Sadly her project was never realised because the owner, Armand Deperdussin, embezzled company funds and the manufacturer went bust.

Marvingt was highly courageous. She disguised herself as a man during the First World War and served on the front line until she was discovered and sent home. However, Marshal Foch then asked her to participate in military operations with the Alpine regiment in Italy, where she served as a Red Cross nurse. In 1915 she flew bombing missions over the German military base in Metz. Between the two World Wars she worked as a journalist, war correspondent, and medical officer in North Africa.

She was passionate about medical evacuation, and gave thousands of lectures at conferences and seminars on the subject worldwide. She was co-founder of the French organisation Les Amies De L'Aviation Sanitaire (Friends of Aviation Medicine). In 1931 she implemented the Challenge Capitaine-Écheman (Captain Écheman Challenge) to solicit the best designs for converting planes to air ambulances. In 1934 she established Morrocco's first civil air ambulance service and was subsequently awarded the Moroccan Peace Medal. She also created training courses for the Infirmières de l'Air (Nurses of the Air) and in 1935 became the first licensed aviation paramedic.

In addition to her sporting prowess, she was creative and wrote and directed two documentaries about the use of air ambulances: "Les ailes qui sauvent" (Wings which save) and "Sauvés par la colombe" (Saved by the Dove). She published two articles such as: "La fiancée du danger" and "Ma traversée de la Mer du Nord en ballon" (My balloon journey across the North Sea). She also penned fiction and prize-winning poetry under the pseudonym Myriel. On January 24, 1935 she was made a Chevalier de la Légion d'honneur (Chevalier of the Legion of Honour).

During World War II she established a care centre for pilots injured in battle. She also worked as a nurse. On 30 January 1955 she received the Deutsch de la Meurthe grand prize from the French National Federation of Aeronautics at the Sorbonne for her work in aviation medicine.

She died on 14 December 1963, aged 88. The French are justifiably proud of their most famous aviatrix and have named streets, schools and flying clubs after her.

France also issued an airmail stamp in her honour in 2004. Several annual awards are given in her memory. Many historians have documented her life. Two of the best accounts come from David M.Lam, who has written extensively about Marvingt and the development of aeromedical evacuation and Marvingt's biographers Marcel Cordier and Rosalie Maggio.

In 1922 Marvingt bet $10,000 that nobody could better her list of prizes in sport, art, science and travel. She re-issued her bet in 1936 and in 1948. No one ever took up the challenge.

Events in 1912

- Anthony Fokker establishes Fokker Aeroplanbau in Germany, predecessor to Fokker Aircraft Company.

- Harriet Quimby becomes the first woman to fly the English Channel.

- Sun Yat-sen made first provisional President of Chinese Republic. Boy Emperor, Xuan Tong ("Pu Yi") abdicates

- RMS Titanic hits an iceberg and sinks on maiden voyage from Southampton to New York. More than 1,500 passengers are killed.

1913

ROSINA FERRARIO (ITALY) 1888 – 1959

Forgotten trailblazer who entertained thousands in her heyday

Take a look at the picture of the Caproni Ca 1 aircraft. Now imagine standing in a crowd in a field on a hot day watching this contraption fly above you piloted by a small figure in a leather cap and goggles. Suddenly a host of red carnations falls from the machine and the aircraft turns to do a circuit of the field. Now imagine the pilot is a child.

Extreme perhaps, but that was how many of the pioneering female aviators were viewed initially – as highly precocious oddities. Audiences loved them. It is hard today to grasp the enormous impact Italy's first licensed female pilot Rosina Ferrario would have had on the spectators at the 1913 Naples Air Meet. She had earned FAI licence number 203 on January 3 1913, becoming the eighth woman in the world to be licensed as a pilot.

Born on the 28 July 1888 into a wealthy bourgeois family, in her youth she developed a passion for sports and mountaineering. Rosina was young in an era when women were fighting for the same privileges as men, and women worldwide were challenging established conventions. Her contemporaries in Europe and in the US were learning to drive cars, or, even more thrillingly, climbing into aeroplanes and flying. Frenchwoman Raymonde de Laroche was first to earn her wings in 1910 and was now competing in air races against compatriot Marie Marvingt and Belgian Helene Dutrieu.

Rosina attended a flying exhibition in Milan in 1910, which had whetted her appetite to fly. The following year she presented herself to Giovanni Caproni's flight school to take lessons, travelling there by bicycle. Caproni was a celebrated aviator who had set up a flying school at Vizzola Ticino in 1911. He had designed and built a single-engine, twin propeller biplane, the Ca.1 and combined this with teaching students to learn to fly. He also took part in several events and demonstration flights throughout Italy. The Caproni organisation went on to build 180 different types of aircraft over the next half a century.

There is evidence to suggest that there was another woman named Ester Vietta at the school at the same time Rosina was studying. However, there is little additional information about Vietta. The two women would have had to overcome huge hurdles to realise their dreams. At the time most women remained at home. Even going to work or driving a car was a sign of emancipation, and only the most eccentric women would dare fly an aeroplane. Rosina had to fight against her family's hostility and deep-rooted prejudices even among her flying colleagues. The political climate in Italy at that time was repressive and eventually, her aerial dreams were quashed by the First World War, which abolished all civil flying.

It is worth considering the other practical difficulties the early pilots faced. The machines they flew were monoplanes made out of wood with only one seat. This meant students necessarily had to practice on their own, with their instructors shouting instruc-

tions from the ground. Physically, it would have been uncomfortable. The aviator's body was exposed from the waist up, with her head protected only by a leather helmet. Landing fields were usually improvised. Accidents were commonplace and rough weather could cause many extra problems.

Add to this the sheer physical strength needed to fly an airplane, and many women were defeated even before starting out. In that era athletics would have been considered "unladylike," with acceptable women's sport confined to gentler activities, such as croquet and tennis. Several journalists were openly hostile towards female pilots and publicly reviled them. However that changed as writers saw the huge courage required to get airborne, especially given the high accident rate. None of this troubled Rosina.

The details that remain tell of a pioneer who loved to fly. Her fame was at its height between 1913 and 1914, when she participated in several events and demonstration flights. She was invited to perform with Achilles Landini, another stunt pilot at an event celebrating the centenary of the birth of Giuseppe Verdi. The pair had to land in thick fog in a field of corn, especially prepared for the occasion around Busseto. Reports indicate that she also flew to Rome for the visit of the king and flew a circuit around the lake. She was invited to participate in a promotional flying tour around Latin America, but was forced to give up the idea because of the war.

Events in 1913

- Igor Sikorsky becomes the first person to pilot a four engine aircraft.
- Emily Davison, a suffragette, runs out in front of the king's horse at the Epsom Derby. She was trampled and died four days later.
- Ford Motor Company introduces the first moving assembly line
- Mohandas Gandhi is arrested while leading a march of Indian miners in South Africa.

Rosina tried to enlist to fly aircraft to help rescue wounded soldiers on behalf of the Red Cross. She offered her services, but was rebuffed with the explanation: "We have no plans to recruit ladies in the Army."

After the war Rosina was a regular attendee of the "Pioneers dell'Aeronautica," meetings. However she never flew again since she did not have the skills to fly the new aircraft designs that had hit the skies. She called them "buses," preferring the days when flying was a romantic adventure, putting the pilot in direct contact with the elements.

In 1921 she married entrepreneur Henry Grugnola, whom she met on a mountain hike at the Italian Alpine Club.

The pair opened the Hotel Italia in Piazzale River in Milan and had two children. Rosina devoted herself to family life. Her last link to aviation was her involvement with members of the Pioneers.

She died in 1959 and is buried in Sesto San Giovanni. The only sign of her aeronautical past on her grave is the notice that she was a member of the Pioneers.

There are two streets named in her honour in Palermo and Milan. Like many of the pioneer aviatrixes, her story is not as well-documented as those of her male contemporaries. However, the sheer life force of a woman who managed to become one of the world's first ten licensed female pilots has lasted down the years.

1915

KATHERINE STINSON (USA) 1891 – 1977

The "Flying Schoolgirl" who broke many records

Long before the modern day airshow re-enactments of famous World War One aerial battles, Katherine Stinson was enthralling crowds with her dogfight manoeuvres and the dropping of flour bombs on simulated trenches of the Somme.

Born February 14th 1891, Stinson aspired to have a career in music and intended to study in Europe. Her goal was to hone her nimble and dextrous hands to perfection in order to teach piano. However the cost was prohibitive, so a resourceful Katherine sought other avenues to fund her future musical studies.

Hearing of the lucrative earnings that a new breed of stunt flyers could readily command, Katherine soon caught the flying bug. A balloon ride further fuelled her desire to gain a pilot's licence, so she took a sabbatical in a profession fraught with mortal danger. It was only seven years since the Wright Brothers had first flown and advances in reliable airframe design were still in their infancy.

The hazards and risks did not sway a determined Katherine, who pestered famed stunt flyer and pioneer Max Lillie for flying lessons. Lillie eventually relented and reluctantly agreed to offer her instruction. His initial doubts were soon swept aside, as, despite her small stature, Katherine proved adept in handling an aeroplane. She was a natural pilot, soloing with ease after just four hours of lessons.

Funding her flying lessons also tested Katherine's powers of persuasion. Her mother was easier to convince than her father, who eventually conceded defeat and financed half the cost. Katherine explained: "When I began to talk about flying, she (my mother) already had confidence in me. My mother never warned me not to do this or that for fear of being hurt, Of course I got hurt, but I was never afraid." Smitten by her new ambition, Katherine sold the family piano to make up the shortfall.

On July 24th 1912, age 21, Katherine became the fourth woman in the US to obtain a flying licence. Her licence issue number was FAI #148. Following in the footsteps of such luminaries as Harriet Quimby and Blanche Stuart Scott, the diminutive Katherine entered the exhibition flying circuit. Physically younger in appearance than her actual years, she claimed to be 16 and was billed as the "flying schoolgirl." Touring across the US to perform at County and State fairs she was making $500-$1,000 for each appearance. The financial rewards from such flying were enough for the plucky barnstormer to abandon all her notions about studying music.

Lillie also tutored her in the art of stunt flying and soon she was thrilling the crowds using routines she devised herself. Katherine also wanted her own tailor-made plane and obtained the engine from the wreckage of legendary stunt pilot Lincoln Beachey's doomed machine. Her newly acquired Partridge and Keller aircraft allowed her death-defying aerobatics to flourish and astound. She was the first woman to perform a loop in 1915 at Cicero Field in Chicago. She went on to perform the same manoeuvre 500 times without incident. Stinson also came up with her very own trick called the "Dippy Twist Loop," which was essentially a loop topped with a snap twist roll.

Katherine was blessed with a natural engineering acumen and her eye for detail and fastidious approach to maintenance ensured that in all her stunt flying years she only suffered one minor crash landing accident. She was the first pilot to introduce the 'walk around,' checking her aircraft each time before she took off. She understood the risks of flying, though, and wrote: "When you are flying toward a cloud, it does not seem as if you yourself are moving. The cloud seems to be rushing at you. And when you enter it, you are in the thickest fog you ever imagined.. I have been in clouds so dense I couldn't see my own hands operating the controls."

Although renowned as an aerobatics aviatrix, her daredevil spirit and inventiveness delivered a few other world firsts. She became the first

woman to fly at night, performing with magnesium flares strapped to her wingtips. She was also the first to introduce the art of night skywriting by spelling out the word 'CAL' in the skies above Los Angeles in 1915. Later she was the first US woman ever to tour and perform in both China and Japan. Thrilling the crowds with her precise routines she was both revered and celebrated as the "Air Queen." In 1917, she broke the long distance flight record previously held by Ruth Law from San Diego to San Francisco. She was also the first woman to be officially appointed as an airmail carrier.

Inspired by her achievements, Katherine's siblings – younger sister Marjorie and brothers Jack and Eddie – embarked upon careers in aviation. With her mother's consent Marjorie trained at the Wright School in Dayton. She became the ninth US women to gain a licence on August 12th 1914. Both sisters were part of the "Early Bird Association," having soloed before September 1916, which was the condition for membership.

The entire Stinson family migrated to San Antonio, Texas in 1915 where the weather was more favourable for stunt flying. It was here that Katherine introduced more gut-wrenching manoeuvres to entertain the masses. Soon after they established the Stinson School of Flying. A family enterprise, Marjorie and Katherine instructed the fledgling pilots and brothers Eddie and Jack served as mechanics. Their matriarchal mother was business manager, and research suggests very little participation on the part of their father in the venture.

As a regular performer at the Edmonton Exhibition fair in Canada, Katherine in 1917 demonstrated some of the flying tactics used by the aces fighting in Europe.

She showed captivated crowds the concept of aerial dogfights and used her airplane to simulate bombing runs on specially dug out trenches for the show. It was her scheduled return to the Edmonton Exhibition in 1918 that led her to make the second airmail delivery flight in Canada. En route to the air fair she diverted to Calgary due to mechanical problems. A quick repair later and loaded with a sack of first class "Aeroplane Mail" she made an inadvertent postal delivery flight to Edmonton on July 9th 1918.

With the outbreak of war the Stinson flying school trained many

Events in 1915

- ■ Automobile speed record of 102.6 m.p.h. set at Sheepshead Bay, N.Y. by Gil Anderson driving a Stutz.

- ■ The first prototype tank is tested for the British Army for the first time.

- ■ British and German forces have a Christmas free-for-all kick-around football game in no-man's land.

of the Canadian Air Corp pilot cadets. Graduates from the school were dubbed the "Texas Escadrille." Katherine herself was inducted into the US Aviation Reserve Corp, the only woman to be accepted. Her application to serve in actual combat missions was denied twice on the grounds she was female. She sought to play her part for the war effort by raising $2 million for the Red Cross through the air show circuit and by delivering airmail.

With the war in full swing the Stinson Flying School was forced to close because of government restrictions on private flying. Katherine then volunteered as an ambulance driver for the Red Cross in Europe. But the combination of harsh winters and testing battle conditions took their toll and she succumbed to influenza. In 1920 she was hospitalised in France for a year after contracting tuberculosis and it was only on return to Santa Fe, New Mexico that she made a full recovery. As she recuperated she met Miguel Otero, who was also a flyer. She married him in 1928. Following her debilitating illness, Katherine gave up flying altogether to become an architect after a stint of technical drafting for the army.

Marjorie, possibly encouraged again by her older sister, worked for the navy undertaking aeronautical drafting. Her brothers Eddie and Jack moved on to manufacture light aircraft and established the Stinson Aircraft Company.

Katherine Stinson's pioneering torch illuminated the path that allowed her siblings and others to follow in her successful wake. Her pushy, altruistic and entrepreneurial spirit surmounted many of the obstacles that traditionally prevented women from flying and realising their dreams. She said: "I have found that women are not only just as much interested as men are in flying, but apparently have less fear than the men have. At least, more women than men asked to go up with me. And when I took them up, they seemed to enjoy it."

Following a long illness, Katherine passed away in 1977 aged 86 after a successful and award-winning career as an architect. There are several excellent books about her, including: "Katherine Stinson, the Flying Schoolgirl" by Debra L Winegarten. The Stinson family's contribution to aviation was recognised in their home state of Texas with an airport in San Antonio named after them.

1921

BESSIE COLEMAN (USA) 1892 - 1926

The girl who wanted to 'amount to something'

n the 1920s US as Ku Klux Klan membership reached a height of 4.5 million and women were fighting for equal rights to men, a young black girl from Texas proved to the world that she could "amount to something." Bessie Coleman triumphed against incredible odds to became the world's first licensed black pilot.

Bessie was born in Atlanta, Texas, on January 26, 1892, the tenth of thirteen children. Her parents were sharecroppers who worked arduous long hours on tenant farms. Her father George moved the family to Waxahachie, hoping for greater opportunities for work. He bought a quarter acre plot in the black section of town and built a three-room house. Bessie looked after her sisters and helped her mother in the garden. At aged six, she began school and had to walk four miles each day to get there. She was an outstanding maths student. Bessie managed to finish high school by using the travelling library that came through two or three times a year, which was no mean feat considering her circumstances.

In 1901 George Coleman had had enough of the racism in Texas and went to Oklahoma to look for a better life. His wife and children stayed in Waxahachie and soon afterwards Bessie's older brothers also left home. Susan Coleman had to struggle alone with four girls under the age of nine and took in laundry to make ends meet. At twelve Bessie was accepted into the Missionary Baptist Church school, where she completed all eight grades. She saved any money she earned and in 1910 enrolled in the Colored Agricultural and Normal University in Langston, Oklahoma. She lasted one term before she ran out of money and was forced to return to Waxahachie.

In 1915 Bessie went to stay with her brothers Walter and John in Chicago. The pair had served as soldiers in France and escaped without injury, returning to witness the worst race riot in Chicago's history in 1919. All Bessie wanted was a chance to "amount to something". She had escaped the oppressive south and had high hopes

for a new life. She decided to learn the beauty trade and became a manicurist in a barbershop. She still thirsted for education and met many influential men from Chicago's black community in the salon, including Robert S. Abbott, founder and publisher of the Chicago Defender newspaper, and Jesse Binga, a real estate promoter. Abbott was the wealthy son of a former slave who became one of America's first self-made millionaires of African American descent. He was a passionate campaigner against racial prejudice.

John teased his sister about French women flying and having careers, so Bessie decided to become an aviator. She read everything she could on the subject and applied to one flying school after another. She was constantly rebuffed. It is impossible to overestimate the courage and determination this must have taken. In 1919 women were definite underdogs and still fighting for the vote. Bessie would have encountered horrific prejudice wherever she went, because of her gender and her ethnicity. But she was determined to get ahead, and lead the way for others blighted by the effects of racism, poverty and ignorance. Her yearning to "amount to something" was now a driving force in her mission to become a pilot.

When she could not find anyone to teach her to fly, she took Abbott's advice and prepared to attend aviation school in France. This meant that she had to learn to speak French – again, a considerable achievement for someone with such a small amount of schooling. She had savings from her manicurist's job, supplemented by working in a chilli parlour, and managed to secure additional funding from Binga, and from the Chicago Defender. Abbott capitalised on her flamboyant personality and her beauty both to promote his newspaper, and to promote her cause.

Bessie left for France in November 1920 and finished a ten-month course in only seven months at the Ecole d'Aviation des Freres Caudon at Le Crotoy in the Somme. She learned to fly in a French Nieuport Type 82, mastering "tail spins, banking and looping the loop." She received her licence

Events in 1921

- Boeing wins a $1,448,000 contract to build 200 Thomas-Morse MB-3 fighters for the US Army, allowing the company to abandon furniture-making.

- The Spanish airline Compania Española de Trafico Aereo is established - it will eventually form part of Iberia Airlines.

- First birth control clinic opened in London by Marie Stopes.

from the renowned Federation Aeronautique Internationale (FAI) on June 15, 1921. Her age was listed as 25 (which was on her passport) although she was 29. Bessie was the first black woman ever to earn a licence, and she was the only woman among sixty-two candidates who earned their licenses during that period.

She sailed to New York on September 16, 1921 on the SS. Manchuria and was greeted by massive media attention. Since she did not have the aerobatic skills required to fly as an entertainer, she had to return to France in 1922 for extra training. Her first US appearance at an air show was sponsored by the Chicago Defender and took place on September 3, 1922 at Curtiss Field near New York City. For five years she toured the country, barnstorming, organizing exhibition flights and speaking in churches and schools about the potential both of flight and of her race. She flew World War I "Jennies" (U.S. Army Curtiss JN-4) and De Havillands. The Defender dubbed her "Queen Bess."

Bessie was determined to open a school for black aviators. She earned enough money to buy a plane, but unfortunately crashed it almost immediately. Undeterred, she went to Orlando where she invested in beauty salons to raise the cash for her venture. She also lined up a series of lectures and exhibition flights in Texas. She borrowed aircraft to continue her exhibition flying and even para-chuted out of an aircraft on one occasion when the performer failed to show. She fought tirelessly against racism and refused to fly unless the audiences were desegregated and everyone attending a show used the same gates. Although she actively courted fame, she turned down the chance to star in a Hollywood film when she was presented with a scene to play that portrayed black people in a negative light.

She finally raised enough to buy her own Curtiss Jenny. On the evening of April 30th 1926 she and her mechanic took it up for a test flight. There was a problem, and the mechanic who was piloting the aircraft from the front seat lost control. Bessie fell from the open cockpit several hundred feet to her death.

Five thousand mourners attended a memorial service for her before her body travelled by train from Orlando to Chicago. Ten thousand others filed past her coffin to pay their final respects. Still more attended her funeral. After her death William J. Powell estab-lished the Bessie Coleman Aero Club in Los Angeles, California in 1929 for African Americans. The school went on to spawn other great aviators, such as the Five Blackbirds, the Flying Hobos (James Banning and Thomas Allen), the Tuskegee Airmen, Cornelius Coffey, John Robison, Willa Brown and Harold Hurd. Numerous books have been written about her, including Doris Rich's excellent" "Queen Bess: Daredevil Aviator."

So whilst the majority of the odious KKK racists of the era sank into individual obscurity, Bessie Coleman added her strength and beauty to the age that coined the phrase "Black is Beautiful," and witnessed the growth of the National Association for the Advancement of Colored People, plus the success of stars like Louis Armstrong, Josephine Baker and Bessie Smith. Her star shines on.

1922

THEREZA DE MARZO (BRAZIL) 1903 – 1986

**Pioneering
pilot who
held her own
amongst the
Boys from
Brazil**

Thereza de Marzo passed many goalposts to get airborne, including those on a football field in the middle of San Paolo. On one occasion, she narrowly escaped death during an exciting soccer match, at which she was performing a display and was forced to start an emergency landing in front of hundreds of people.

She was not brought up to be a pilot. Thereza de Marzo was born in São Paulo on August 04, 1903, one of seven children. Her father Affonso de Marzo, was an affluent Italian immigrant from Napoli. Her mother, Maria Riparullo tended to defer to her husband, as was the social norm of the day. When Thereza was 17, she saw her first aeroplane. She was enchanted and knew that some day she, too, would have to try flying. However, her family had other notions. Her father, in particular was furious. He said that his daughter "ought to think about getting married, not about flying a plane"

Young Thereza refused to be cowed. Instead, she walked all the way to Jardim Paulista, the Brazil Airfield, where two Italian brothers were giving flying lessons. They told Thereza it would cost her 600 réis for ten lessons of an hour apiece. Knowing that her father would not give her the money to learn, she decided to raffle her phonograph. On the first attempt nobody won the prize. However, two cards remained unsold and so she re-drew the lots among her family's friends. She had raised the cash she needed. Now she was truly able to start her classes.

Until she started flying, her only vanity was her shoes, but even this frivolity was cast aside in favour of spending time and money flying. She started her lessons in March 1921. Her instructors João and Enrico Robba were constantly travelling, disrupting their pupils' schooling.

Things looked up when Thereza met aviator and mechanic Fritz Roesler, a World War II fighter pilot and native of Strasbourg. She asked him to become her instructor. With a new instructor and regular classes, she progressed rapidly. On March 17, 1922, she soloed, a year after she had started flying. On April 8th she took her exam in a French aircraft, the Caudron G-3 with a 120 hp revolving engine. She remained airborne for 40 minutes, executing the required manoeuvres perfectly. She flew accurately and landed with flair and natural ability on the short landing strip, which was only 150 meters long and 60 meters wide. This drew the admiration and respect of the people gathered to assess her performance. Her examiners were Dr. Luiz Ferreira Guimarães, the director of the Brazil Aeroclub, who had travelled to São Paulo especially to test her. State representatives Manoel Lacerda Franco, Amadeu Saraiva and João Robba and her instructor Fritz Roesler joined him.

Thereza was awarded licence number 76 from the Aeroclube do Brasil, which was affiliated with the Federation Aeronautique Internationale (FAI). She was the first Brazilian woman to fly solo and the first to receive an international pilot's licence. She attracted a great deal of positive publicity for her achievement. A few days later, she did her first trop to the city of Santos, where she flew over the Bartolomeu de Gusmão's statues. Along with other illustrious aviators, she played host to the celebrated Portuguese pilots Gago Coutinho and Sacadura Cabral.

Thereza had fun with her passion. She created "Aviation Afternoons," offering joy rides for passengers. One day she and a colleague, Átila took off from Ypiranga Aeroclub. She flew as pilot in command, and he was to throw flowers over the soccer players, enjoying their game, as the pair made low flying passes above the Palestra Itália Stadium. As Átila drew his hand back into the aircraft, he accidentally knocked the fuel cut off knob, stopping the fuel flow and shutting down the engine. Thereza looked around for an emergency-landing site. She was ready to put the plane down, when she decided to try to restart the engine one last time. Barely a few feet from the ground, the motor started up again and the aircraft roared into action. Thankfully the flight continued without any further incident.

Thereza continued to fly for four more years. On the advice of friends she had bought, a Caudron G-3 for 800 réis, which she named "Sao Paulo". She also acquired an Oriole. She flew about 350 officially logged hours, but also many more that were not recorded as her instructor felt it was not necessary for her to do so. It was becoming increasingly difficult to maintain an aircraft and she asked President Luiz Washington if he would grant her access to fuel. He refused, saying he did not want to contribute to her suicide. Prejudice against women succeeding in traditionally male roles was rife. It became too expensive for Thereza to keep up with her flying.

In the meantime, Fritz Roesler had fallen in love with his former pupil. The pair were married on September 25th, 1926, much to the shock of respectable Brazilian society.

Fritz was against his wife's flying. She was heartbroken, but did not have money to pay for fuel and hoped he would change his mind. Although she supported him professionally, she no longer flew. She had elements of the aviation world in her life. She helped construct a hangar at Ypiranga by fundraising in Santos. In 1923, the Roeslers sold this hangar and moved to the Mars Camp. There she worked in the flight training school and gliders club, which Fritz had established to construct the first gliders EAY-101 (primaries and secondaries) in Brazil and also build the first five Ypiranga EAY-201.

Fritz helped found the Ypiranga Aeronautical Enterprise in 1931 in partnership with Henrique Santos Dumont and the American aviator Orton Hoover. The project was sold later to Francisco Pignatari, owner of the Paulista Aeronautical Company. The EAY-201 evolved into the CAP-4, Paulistinha, with 65 HP, and was widely used in basic instruction in Brazilian aero clubs for many years afterwards.

Fritz become a Brazilian citizen in 1932. In 1933 he helped to found the VASP with Henrique Santos Dumont and engineer Jorge Corbisier. Both Fritz and Thereza received several awards. Thereza was awarded an aeronautical pioneer medal by the Santos Dumont Foundation in 1961, as well as the aeronautical merit medal by the aeronautical m in 1976 and the Santos Dumont gold medal in 1980.

The Roeslers were married for 45 years until his death on July 02, 1971. He was buried on the Araçá's Cemetery, at São Paulo City. Thereza died on February 9, 1986 and was buried next to him. Although she had overcome many hurdles at the beginning of her aviation life, the obstacles were just too great for her to surmount in the end and she succumbed to society's pressure to become a dutiful wife. However, the legacy she left for other Brazilian aviatrixes shines on. Both Captain Lucy Lupia, the first female airline pilot in Brazil, and Ada Rogato benefited from Thereza's encouragement and support.

Lucy has dedicated a website to Thereza and other pioneers. For more information go to www.captain.lucyl.nom.br

Events in 1922

■ **The first midair collision, between a Daimler Airway de Havilland DH.18 and a Compagnie des Grands Express Aériens Farman Goliath, Amiens, France.**

1924

RUTH ROWLAND NICHOLS (USA) 1901 – 1960

Ruth Nichols would have made a cat cry. Hobbling away from the strewn and burning wreckage of several airframes, she easily used up more than nine lives, but her resolve never wavered. Splintered bones and horrendous injuries were merely inconvenient for this steely aviatrix. From dirigibles to jet fighters, Ruth had piloted them all, and perhaps would have travelled into the farthest reaches of space had the opportunity arisen.

Ruth Rowland Nichols was born on 23rd February 1901 in New York and came from affluent stock. Her father was a former member of Theodore Roosevelt's "Rough Riders" cavalry unit during the Spanish American War. Her mother was a staunch Quaker and socialite.

Ruth's first brush with flying came in 1919, following her graduation from high school. As a graduation present, her father surprised her with a plane ride with Eddy Stinson, famed First World War fighter ace and brother of pioneer stunt pilot Katherine Stinson. Terrified and exhilarated, Ruth emerged from her flying experience shaken, but stirred to act on her instincts. She relished the idea of learning to fly, albeit secretly so as not to attract the attention of her parents.

Ruth enrolled at Wellesley College on a pre-medical course to become a doctor. While studying she led a double life, furtively taking flying lessons under the tutelage of Harry Rogers, a flying boat pilot. When she graduated in 1924 her clandestine flying activities delivered a positive result. She became the first woman in the world to earn an international hydroplane license. The cat was certainly out of the bag and about to start testing her many lives.

Much to the disapproval of her parents, Ruth immersed herself in aviation. In 1927, she became one of the first two women to receive a Department of Commerce transport licence. Then, on the eve of

1928, she flew as co-pilot to her mentor Harry Rogers non-stop from New York to Miami. The epic flight brought her a great deal of attention. Because of her aristocratic ties she was dubbed "The Flying Debutante" by the media. She sorely despised the title, but the subsequent offer of a sales position with aircraft manufacturer Fairchild Aviation defused her annoyance.

She excelled in the position, which further fuelled her desire to participate in sports flying and set new world records. Ruth would often draw upon her celebrity status and high society connections to make an even greater name for herself. She was instrumental in the establishment of the Long Island Aviation Club and took part in a promotional touch-and-go tour taking her to all 48 states of America. In 1929 she, along with other luminaries, such as Amelia Earhart and Fay Gillis Wells, founded the Ninety Nines – a group dedicated to the cause of licensed women pilots. Ruth also took part in the 1929 Women's Air Derby. Although she didn't win any of the successive "Powder Puff Derbies," the experience of flying them convinced her that she needed a much faster plane to make an impact.

During the 1930's she established a number of aviation firsts. Ruth was the first woman to set speed, altitude and distance records simultaneously. In 1930, flying a souped-up Lockheed Vega, she set a new cross-country flight time record for a woman flying from New York to Los Angeles. On the return journey she managed to beat Charles Lindbergh's time for a transcontinental flight, making it in 13 hours and 22 minutes.

Flying the same Vega in March 1931 to test its high altitude performance she set a new altitude record for a woman, climbing to a recorded 28,743 feet. Then in April, with throttles pushed beyond their stops, she established a world speed record in the modified Vega, clocked at 210.7 miles per hour, faster than any women had flown before.

The succession of records tested Ruth's flying ability, compelling her to attempt the next monumental challenge, namely conquering the Atlantic. In June 1931 her transatlantic solo flight began in New York. But tragedy struck, as blinded by the sun on approach to New Brunswick, she crash landed. Surviving the accident with several shattered vertebrae, Ruth spent several months recovering in hospital.

Returning to full strength late in October 1931 she flew into the record books by flying from Oakland, California to Louisville, Kentucky - the longest distance flown by a woman. She flew 1,977 miles in the rebuilt Vega, and some commentators suggest she wore a metal corset to support her still healing back. But misfortune was to strike again when her plane caught fire while taxiing.

The setback of being without a plane was short-lived, Because of her celebrity status she was able to obtain another Vega on loan. However, her second attempt at a transatlantic flight was abandoned following Amelia Earhart's successful crossing in 1932, now credited as the first.

This diesel fuel-efficient version of the Vega would allow her to establish yet another record in 1932. Because the "Flying Furnace" was smoky and rather noisy, she flew to a height of 19,928 feet over New York, establishing a new altitude record over the city. The

same year she used the aeroplane as part of the "good will tour" promoting the International Congress of Women in Chicago, flying 3,000 miles for the cause.

In 1932 Ruth would become the first women pilot of a commercial passenger carrier by flying on behalf of New York and New England Airways. But in 1935 bad luck cast a shadow over her life. Wrestling with a crippled transport aircraft and declaring an emergency she crashed at Troy, New York. Her injuries were severe enough to put her back in hospital and she was unable to fly for almost a year.

The near fatal accident had forced a new perspective on Ruth, who then devoted some of her time to humanitarian causes. Back in the flying saddle and inspired by her mother she went to work for the Emergency Relief Campaign, a Quaker organisation. In 1939 she founded Relief Wings for emergency relief flights, which was absorbed into the Civil Air Patrol during World War II.

After the war Ruth used her influence to further the causes of UNICEF and Save The Children Federation, raising awareness through a round-the-world piloting tour in 1949. Throughout the fifties she served as director of the United Hospital Fund and promoted the National Nephrosis Foundation.

Over the years Ruth had the accolade of having flown every type of aircraft developed. She was rated to fly a dirigible, glider, autogyro, landplane, seaplane, amphibious planes, monoplanes, biplanes, tri-planes, twin and four engine transports and the final icing on the cake - supersonic jets. She fought for the last type - lobbying the US Air Force to allow her to fly a TF-102A Delta Dagger jet fighter. As co-pilot, Ruth flew the jet interceptor at Mach 1 and to an altitude of 51,000 feet. At 57 she was the only woman of her era to have established new records in a fast military jet.

In a testament to her courageous and pioneering spirit, Ruth then subjected herself to the same rigorous astronaut training conducted by the National Aeronautics and Space Administration (NASA) during the Gemini program in 1959. Research suggests that Ruth had performed well, although the results of her NASA training were never publicised. Her goal was to prove that women were both physically and mentally capable of being astronauts. Perhaps her participation had a positive impact, paving the way, albeit years later, for Eileen Collins and Sally Ride to be selected for space shuttle missions.

Ruth was inducted into the National Aviation Hall of Fame in 1992. She had dedicated her life to the cause she loved. In an interview during the fifties she was quoted as saying: "It takes special kinds of pilots to break frontiers, and in spite of the loss of everything, you can't clip the wings of their hearts."

On September 25th 1960, aged just 59, Ruth was found dead in her New York apartment, having allegedly overdosed on barbiturates. It was thought that she had taken her own life because of depression. The fearless cat had finally run out of lives.

Like many of her contemporaries, Ruth relished the chance to get back into the air, despite near loss of life or loss of plane. Driven and determined, she contributed more to the world in general than just laying claim to an astonishing number of flying records.

Events in 1924

- Pelletier d'Oisy flies from Paris to Tokyo in 120 hours

- Lenin dies. Stalin rules as Soviet dictator until death in 1953

- New York's Computer Tabulating Recording Company is renamed International Business Machines Corp. (IBM).

- Walt Disney creates his first cartoon, *Alice's Wonderland.*

1927

PHOEBE FAIRGRAVE OMLIE (USA) 1902 -1975

Phoebe Fairgrave Omlie introduced her own brand of daredevil spirit to the early barnstorming days of the twenties. She seemed impervious to fear. Her death defying aerial antics attracted hordes to gape at the aviatrix repeatedly tempting fate and the strength of her parachute silk.

Regarded as a pioneer of the same ilk as Amelia Earhart and Jackie Cochran, Phoebe Omlie would later find favour with President Roosevelt and embark on a crusade for promoting civilian aviation and support mechanisms across the United States.

Heralding from Des Moines, Iowa, Phoebe was born in 1902. She developed an infatuation for flying on witnessing a formation of military planes. Frequenting a local airfield, the enthralled teenager pestered the manager for a joyride until, exasperated, he instructed one of his pilots to give her the 'full works'.

Nosedives, loops, together with violent stomach-churning manoeuvres failed to dissuade the ebullient teenager, who was now even more smitten. Following her fourth flight she blew the $3,400 inheritance bequeathed to her by her grandfather to become the proud owner of a Curtiss JN-4 Jenny biplane.

Phoebe then delved into the perilous realms of acrobatic wing walking. The fast talking teenager even secured a contract with the Fox Moving Picture company to film her performing her wing walks and parachute jumps for their Saturday matinee serial- The Perils of Pauline.

For $25 an hour she hired a former World War 1 ace pilot and instructor, Vernon Omlie as her pilot for all the contractual motion picture and barnstorming stunt work. Clambering onto the top wing of the Curtiss Jenny held steady by Vernon, Phoebe taught herself to wing walk.

She danced the Charleston on the upper wing, and clamped her teeth to a special mouthpiece attached to a rope that allowed her to dangle from the aeroplane. Vernon would swoop low over the mesmerized crowd with Phoebe twisting and twirling in the plane's slipstream. Her finale was a double parachute jump. Leaping from the wing, she briefly deployed her first parachute, cutting away the straps of the life saving canopy to plummet earthward. Horrified gasps from spectators coincided with the unfurling of a second parachute saving her from instant death.

Her next deliberate brush with danger involved a mid-air trapeze act of transferring from the Curtiss Jenny to another plane. For this endeavour both Phoebe and Vernon teamed up with famed stunt pilot Glenn Messer. They worked out the practicalities of the stunt on the ground, using a horse drawn buggy to serve as the Curtiss Jenny, with Vernon at the reins. Glenn suspended himself from the rafters of a disused barn to snag Phoebe as she swept by on the galloping 'Jenny'. Handclasps were repeated to near perfection and an inverted Glenn was able to 'catch' Phoebe during each run.

Their first attempt in the air nearly ended in disaster with Phoebe's Curtiss Jenny jostled by turbulence and almost bumping into the plane carrying Glenn hanging precariously from its undercarriage axle. A quick-witted Phoebe narrowly avoided being decapitated by the propeller of the overhead recipient plane. The blades sliced harmlessly through the aileron of Vernon's plane, where only seconds earlier Phoebe had been poised. Given the close call, they modified the routine with the introduction of a twenty-foot rope ladder tied to the recipient plane. Glenn hooked himself to the lowest rung to clasp and lift Phoebe successfully away from Vernon's transfer plane.

The act became an instant sensation for the Phoebe Fairgrave/Messer Flying Circus drawing many thousands to gawp at the daring display. But the pickings were hardly rich given the derring-do and risks. Phoebe supplemented her income through speaking engagements at the Princess Theatre in Memphis, describing her life in aviation and in the movies.

Mutual admiration and respect between Vernon and Omlie soon turned into love and they married in February 1922. The name on the side of their trusty Curtiss Jenny now changed to the 'Phoebe Fairgrave Omlie Flying Circus'. On July 10th 1922 to attract further publicity for their ailing enterprise she made a high altitude parachute drop. Plummeting almost three miles, Phoebe established a new world record.

Their stunt flying escapades continued for a few more seasons, however Vernon wanted to start his own aviation business and wished for a permanent base in Memphis. The state of Memphis at the time was bereft of an airport infrastructure forcing the Omlies to set up shop first on a racetrack. Their subsequent eviction caused them to relocate again to an open field. Their operational activities included flying lessons, aircraft servicing and the odd barnstorming session.

The floods of 1927 led to the Omlies' performing an invaluable service to the citizens of Memphis by delivering medicines and mail. They flew round the clock for eight days, their contributions recognised to the extent that it resulted in the building of the first airport by the local authorities. Vernon would eventually move his charter operation to this new Memphis Municipal Airport.

Phoebe still yearned for adventure and already a pilot herself she was the first woman in 1927 to gain both a transport pilot's licence and a mechanic's licence. Her acrobatic and movie stunt fame landed her an association with the Mono Aircraft Company flying Monocoupe racing planes. Her exploits in the Monocoupe began with an altitude record of 25,400 feet in 1928 before she joined the air race circuit.

She was the first women to fly her Monocoupe, aptly named 'Miss Memphis' in the 6,000 mile National Reliability Air Tour for the Edsel Ford trophy. In August 1929 Phoebe competed in the first women's Transcontinental Air Race dubbed by the media as the 'Powder Puff Derby.' She raced with the likes of Amelia Earhart, Blanche Noyes and Pancho Barnes. Phoebe negotiated the 2,500 mile race to its

Events in 1927

- Trotsky is expelled from the Russian Communist Party
- Philo T. Farnsworth demonstrates the first all-electronic television.

finish, with the title going to Louise Thaden in the DW (heavy class). Louise was also first across the finishing line. According to Ann Lewis Cooper in "Stars of the Sky," Phoebe was actually the winner of the race, having come first in the CW (light class) category and accumulating the most points, which was how the race was scored. Phoebe later became a member of the Ninety Nines, the organisation initiated by Amelia Earhart, Bobbi Trout and Fay Gillis Wells.

Miss Memphis secured a decisive victory in the 1930 Dixie Derby. Phoebe then brushed aside a sizeable contingent of male competitors to win the 1931 Handicap Air Derby. Such was her prominence that Phoebe and her plane were seconded by the democratic entourage to promote the then US presidential candidate Franklin D. Roosevelt. Miss Memphis flew delegates a total of 5,000 miles with Phoebe canvassing her support on the campaign trail.

Her efforts were rewarded by the inaugurated President Roosevelt who appointed her Advisor for Air Intelligence to the National Advisory Committee for Aeronautics (NACA) in 1933. NACA was the precursor to NASA, today's National Space and Aeronautics Administration.

As the first woman to hold a position with the federal government in aviation she contributed significantly to the legislative and procedural foundations for both private and commercial aviation in America. Furthermore, she championed the cause of attempting to integrate women into all sectors of aviation including the pilot profession.

Her biggest undertaking was the navigational air-marking programme she instituted with the help of the Bureau of Air Commerce. Phoebe recruited and directed a band of five aviatrixes to oversee the painting of coordinates and markers upon barns, factories, warehouses and water tanks. The pilots were Louise Thaden (winner of the 1936 Bendix Trophy), Helen Richie, Blanche Noyes, Nancy Harkness Love (co-founder of the WASP), and Helen McCloskey.

In the midst of her tenure in Washington, tragedy struck a cruel blow as Vernon lost his life in a plane crash flying as a passenger. Distraught, she resigned and returned to Memphis to take the helm of her late husband's thriving aviation business. Phoebe never remarried but would later return to Washington to contribute to the war effort as an aviation bureaucrat. She set up flying schools with women serving as instructors.

Another significant milestone was her successful enacting of a law allocating a small amount of the aviation tax collected by the state of Tennessee to be directed to aviation instruction in schools. This was rolled out to other states, which led to the creation of the government sponsored Civilian Pilot Training Program. The latter helped Whirly Girl Jean Ross Howard gain her pilot's licence during the war years.

Phoebe resigned from the Civil Aviation Authority in 1952, disenchanted with the organisation and returned to Memphis. After unsuccessfully running a cattle ranch, a hotel and a restaurant she reportedly spiralled into seclusion and despair. Taking up residence in a nondescript hotel in Indianapolis she passed away after a long period of illness on July 25th 1975, aged 73. She was buried next to her husband at the Forest Hill cemetery in Memphis.

In honour of Phoebe and Vernon's tireless contribution to aviation, the new control tower at Memphis International airport was named after the pioneering couple in 1982.

1927

ELINOR PATRICIA SMITH (USA) 1911 –

Determined teenager with a taste for high adventure

Elinor Patricia Smith and Evelyn 'Bobbi' Trout were almost preordained to enter the world of competitive aviation. Their stories are similar. Smitten from an early age by aviation, they both turned into accomplished flyers. Inevitably their respective paths would cross, each vying to establish an unbeatable endurance record. Later a quirk of fate saw the indomitable pair jointly embark upon a gruelling voyage, testing their stamina and resolve. But this story is about Elinor who became the youngest person in the world to solo in an airplane. To this day the pioneering and gutsy aviatrix remains active in aviation and still flies.

She was born on August 17th 1911, the year that the glamorous Harriet Quimby became the first American woman to gain a pilot's licence. Aged six Elinor knew she was a pilot, it was just a matter of time before her feet would reach the rudder pedals. Her love of flying came from a Sunday afternoon jaunt in 1918 with her parents and brother. Cruising through Hicksville their father, comedian and flyer, Tom Smith spotted a sign advertising $10 aeroplane joyrides. In the middle of a potato field, six-year-old Elinor and her brother discovered themselves being strapped into a Farman Pusher by their father.

Elinor was overwhelmed by the magical ride, her bird's eye view giving her panoramic vistas of landscape and sky. From then on she decided that age (let alone gender) would not stall her ambitions of learning to fly. Fortunately a mother who felt that she should not be denied anything because of her sex, and a father who was passionate about planes made her passage into the cockpit easier.

Tom would take Elinor to Curtiss Field in Mineola, New York where other pilots would often indulge her with a joyride or two. Sensing her enthusiasm, the seasoned flyers would hand over the controls to the naturally gifted, freckled-faced eight-year old.

As a teenager her zeal was enough for her to rise early in the morning, and drive her father's car to a local airfield to catch a flying lesson before school. Flying from Wantagh to Curtiss Field she practised her take-offs and landings before the morning school bell rang.

Elinor's almost fanatical dedication earned her a place in history, when at just 15 years old she became the youngest woman in the world to fly solo in May 1927. This was the same year that Charles Lindbergh made his historic flight from New York to Paris.

Three months on, a determined Elinor was to set an unofficial altitude record of 11,889 feet in a Waco 9 biplane. A year later, September 1928, aged 16 she became the youngest woman in the United States to be granted an official pilot's licence. A month after she had earned her certificate she jeopardised her coveted licence by pulling a stunt, which made headline news across the globe.

Research suggests that on a dare from either a boisterous barnstormer or reporter she flew under four East River bridges, namely Queensboro, Willamsburg, Manhattan and Brooklyn.

Meticulously preparing for this perilous undertaking Elinor pored over tide tables for bridge clearances and practised low level flying. Then on 21st October 1928 the conditions were perfect for the risky venture.

She took off from Curtiss Field. Her hand gripped the throttle of her Waco 9, rocking from its OX5 radial engine in preparation for take-off. A tap on her shoulder startled her. To her surprise it was Charles Lindbergh grinning and shouting above the din to say: "Good luck kid, keep your nose down in the turns." Elinor later recalled that following that encounter she and the Waco "soared aloft like a couple of dry leaves in high wind."

Ducking under all four bridges without incident, Elinor landed back at Curtiss Field to face a legion of reporters. Basking in the limelight, she was snapped by the paparazzi nonchalantly adjusting her makeup at the end of the stunt. But her daredevil antics had drawn the ire of the Mayor of New York, Jimmy Walker. He let her off lightly with a ten-day suspension to her flying licence and a slap on the wrist.

An emboldened Elinor soon established further records. Just like Harriet Quimby, she preferred a tailored made flight suit. On January 31st 1929 she achieved her first endurance record in sub zero conditions. Flying an open cockpit Brunner-Winkle 'Bird' biplane she established a non-stop endurance record of thirteen hours and sixteen minutes.

But the cold, frozen controls and turbulent winds tested the teenager's innate skill, forcing her to abandon the feat. Having never landed at night, particularly in an unresponsive plane loaded with high-test volatile fuel, she squinted into the darkness for a suitable place to alight. Fortunately, another plane orbiting below caught her eye and deliberately guided her to a safe landing at Mitchell Field. The pilot of the plane was Jimmy Doolittle, who later during World War II established the famed 'Doolittle Raiders,' tasked with daring bombing raids into the Japanese mainland.

Her record flight time was smashed on February 10th by another aviatrix, one Evelyn "Bobbi'" Trout, who extended the endurance time by four hours. Not to be outdone, Elinor lobbied aviation doyen Giuseppe Maria Bellanca to loan her one of his sturdier airframes to crack Bobbi's record. Her persistence was rewarded with a Bellanca CH monoplane, complete with cosier enclosed cabin and a powerful 225 horsepower engine.

More events in 1927

- The Cessna company is established.
- Paul R. Redfern leaves Brunswick, Ga flying his Stinson Detroiter "Port of Brunswick" to attempt a solo non-stop flight to Rio de Janeiro, Brazil. He later crashes in the Venezuela jungle, the crash site never located.

At the controls of this heavier beast designed for a larger frame, the diminutive 17 year old took to the skies for a marathon flight one day in April. Despite the cockpit shielding her from the weather, Elinor wrestled with the heftier machine.

At the 24th hour the trimming mechanism failed, adding to her problems of controlling the aircraft. Signalling that she needed to land, Elinor managed to touch down safely at Curtiss field to establish a new record endurance time of twenty-six hours and sixteen minutes.

The year 1929 was proving to be an eventful one for the plucky teenager as she added more pages to the record books. In May she became the first and youngest women ever to fly a military Curtiss Falcon, setting a speed record of 190 mph in the process.

The same year aged 18 she became the youngest person to be granted a transport licence by the United States Department of Commerce. In June Elinor was contracted by the Irving Chute Company to fly a Bellanca Pacemaker for a 6,000-mile tour of the US. She debuted the first mass parachute drop at the Cleveland air races. In November she teamed up with former rival Bobbi Trout to establish an endurance flight record of forty-two hours. With a second plane acting as an in-flight tanker they became the first women to refuel in mid-air.

Elinor humbly recites that her finest achievement was receiving the accolade of the "Best Woman Pilot in America" in 1930. She had surpassed the likes of other equally accomplished flyers, such as Amelia Earhart to gain recognition at the age of 19. Soon after she served as test pilot for both Bellanca and the Fairchild Aviation Corporation.

In 1931 Elinor was the first women to fly above 30,000 feet. Her first attempt nearly ended in disaster and only instinctive quick thinking resulted in nothing more than a bent propeller. On the second attempt she set a new women's record of 30,500 feet above Roosevelt Field.

With the onset of the Great Depression, Elinor circumvented the economic gloom by flying as a stunt pilot for movies, air shows and charity events. In 1933 she married New York state attorney Patrick Sullivan and domesticity calmed her enough to take a sojourn from flying as she raised her four children.

In 1956, following the death of her husband, the thrill of flying came knocking again on her suburban door. The United States Air Force provided her the taste of fast jet flying by allowing her to co-pilot a T-33 Shooting Star from Mitchell Field. In the decades that followed to the present day, Elinor continues her involvement in aviation as a consultant and speaker to local and national museums. She recounted many of her experiences in her book "Aviatrix," published in 1981.

In March 2000, Elinor accepted the invitation to fly the space shuttle in a simulator. She successfully negotiated the simulated flight becoming the oldest pilot to do so. In April 2001 at the age of 90 she flew an experimental Beech Bonanza modified by NASA. Elinor resides in Santa Cruz, California and uses a local airport to maintain her flying hours. The adventure that began so innocently in a nondescript potato field in Hicksville so long ago still continues...

1928

LADY MARY HEATH (IRELAND) 1896 - 1939

Flamboyant adventurer who conquered Cape Town to Cairo route

A murderer's daughter and thrice-wed six-footer - Lady Mary Heath would have attracted attention even before she got started with flying. Married and widowed before she was 29, she was a celebrity before the term was invented; Mary loved the limelight and used her considerable intelligence to further the cause of women in society.

Sophie Catherine Theresa Mary Peirce-Evans was born in 1896 in Knockaderry, County Limerick. When she was a year old her father beat her mother to death. He was convicted of murder, but declared insane. Sophie went to live with her grandfather and two maiden aunts. She attended St Margaret's Hall school in Dublin, where she played hockey and tennis. When she graduated she enrolled at the Royal College of Science and was one of the few women in the entire college. She continued to play sport and played for the hockey team. She also contributed to a student magazine, copies of which are still held in Ireland's national library.

In early 1917 she signed up to the war effort, driving motorbikes and ambulances, in London. She moved nearer to the Front in France, where the artist Sir John Lavery painted her portrait. After the war she wished to return to her studies and applied for a grant to complete her science degree. It was turned down on the grounds that she was a married woman, so her husband was financially responsible for her. Besides she had "no need" for further skills. She had by then wed her first husband William Davies Eliott Lynn, a British army officer and was known as "Lady Hell-Of-Din," thanks to her assertive personality.

Mary spent little time with her husband, who was in East Africa, where he had bought a coffee farm. Instead she had become deeply involved with athletics and was a founding member of the Women's Amateur Athletic Association (WAAA). She was the first British women's javelin champion and flew to Prague as part of the WAAA deputation to lobby the 1925 International Olympic Committee to include women's track and field in its 1928 programme. They met with little sympathy. Women's athletics was reckoned to be "unladylike". Undeterred, Mary wrote "Athletics for women and girls: how to be an athlete and why." She also gave a speech on the topic that was broadcast by the BBC on 9th April 1925.

Determined to make her own money, she discovered the joys of flying, which promised to be lucrative. Air shows were attracting crowds of thousands. In 1925 she took her first flying lessons. As soon as she earned her private "A" licence, she competed in air races and often won. The International Commission for Air Navigation had revoked commercial, or "B" licenses, in 1924. She campaigned for the law to be changed and signed up powerful allies, such as the MP Lady Astor. The commission agreed that if she attended flight school and passed her test she would be granted a commercial licence. She did so and in 1926 the ban was lifted. Mary's lobbying had paid off and in 1926; she became the first women in Britain and Ireland to hold a commercial licence. Two other Irish women Sicele O'Brien and Lady Mary Bailey rapidly followed in her wake. Mary went on to set an altitude record of 17,000 feet (5,182 meters) in a light plane and a Short's seaplane, and was the first woman to make a parachute jump, landing in the middle of a football match.

In 1928 her first husband drowned in the river Thames. She married Sir James Heath, more than forty years her senior, and became Lady Mary Heath. He bought his bride a new plane, which they took to South Africa. From there in the three months from January to May 1928, she became the first person to fly a small open cockpit aeroplane from Cape Town to Cairo. She wrote about the experience later in a book "Woman and Flying," co-written with Stella Wolfe Murray. She also told the Jacksonville Journal that her luggage for the trip had been a Bible, a shotgun, a couple of tennis rackets, six tea gowns and a fur coat; in contrast to a male pilot's luggage of boiled eggs and ham sandwiches. After her record-breaking flight she established another world altitude record for light planes at 23,000 feet (7,010 meters).

Her fame was at its height and she earned a living giving demonstration flights and lectures. She frequently returned to her hometown of Ballybunion to visit her aunt Cis, who had brought her up. On her visits she would land her plane in a place called Larkin's Field, and, for a small fee, take spectators up for a quick spin.

When Amelia Earhart flew across the Atlantic as a passenger in 1928, Heath was at Croydon Airport to greet her. The pair took an instant shine to one another. Earhart was interested in the handling characteristics of the Avro Avian aircraft Mary had used in her record-breaking flight, so Mary sold her the machine, G-E BUG, for US$3,200. Earhart was still a social worker at the time, however Mary must have recognised her potential. When she presented the plane to the American, Mary had a plaque made: "To Amelia Earhart from Mary Heath. Always think with your stick forward." Later that year Earhart flew the small biplane across America.

Mary then flew as the first-ever female commercial airline pilot with Dutch company KLM Amsterdam

flying on all their European routes. She did this unpaid, with a view to getting a job with the company on its long-haul routes to Indonesia. This was not to be. It took another forty years before women were regularly hired as pilots by airlines.

Her ambitions thwarted, Mary headed to the USA, where she became the first female to obtain a mechanic's qualification. Charles Lindbergh and Amelia Earhart's flights had grabbed headlines in America, and Mary's African flight had made front-page news. She was nicknamed "Britain's Lady Lindy," and invited to take part in lectures, races and long distance flights.

A newspaper report from the era details a visit she made to Jacksonville. It reveals the awe in which pilots were held by that time "The Lady-Queen flew into Jacksonville at 3 pm on Jan. 4, 1929. Her tiny De Havilland Moth appeared as a dot in the far-off sky. Onlookers gaped from the field. Perfectly and mundanely the Moth met the grass; the Queen alighted every inch the British Olympian who had flown the length of darkest Africa." Mary was reported to have said: "Flying is so safe. A woman can fly across Africa wearing a Parisian frock and keeping her nose powdered all the way."

Mary's high-flying career smashed to an end when she crashed and got badly injured just before the Cleveland National Air Races in 1929. She wound up with a metal plate in her head and never flew competitively again. Time magazine reported the outcome of the accident in 1931. "Compensation. Lady Mary Heath, flying as a demonstrator for American Cirrus Engines, Inc., crashed with her plane through a factory roof during the National Air Races of 1929 in Cleveland. She sued her employers for $275,000, returned to England. Last week a referee in Jersey City, N. J. awarded Lady Heath $3,850 under the Workmen's Compensation Act, as out-of-court settlement."

She returned to Ireland and set up Dublin Air Ferries in Kildonan, with her third husband, Trinidadian pilot Jack Williams. She continued to promote aviation and founded the National Aero Club, the Irish Aero Club and the National Junior Aviation Club. She based her Gipsy Moth, G-ACBU, nicknamed "the Silver Lining" at the airfield.

Dublin Air Ferries folded and she managed Iona National Airways, from February 1935 until August 1938. However, her health was declining rapidly. She was drinking alcoholically and had run out of money. She died destitute in 1939 after a fall from a tram in London.

Mary's life may have ended badly, but her contribution to aviation was enormous. In 2004 journalist Lindie Naughton published an excellent biography entitled: "Lady Icarus." Mary's name lives on in her native Limerick, where she is affectionately referred to as "Sophie."

Events in 1928

- ■ Rev John Flynn founds the Royal Flying Doctor Service of Australia.
- ■ Umberto Nobile commands the Italian airship Italia on an ill-fated flight over the North Pole. The airship crashes, and Roald Amundsen is killed trying to rescue survivors.

1929

FLORENCE 'PANCHO' BARNES (USA) 1901 – 1975

Racy winner of first Women's Air Race, who put fun into flying, but pulled out the stops to help with the war effort

The legendary stunt pilot Florence "Pancho" Barnes is fondly remembered as the proprietor of the "Happy Bottom Riding Club" bordering Edwards Air Force Base. A popular haunt for military and civilian patrons deep in the Mojave Desert, it was also a shrine to some of the finest pilots in the world.

Born in 1901 in Pasadena, socialite and adventurer Florence 'Pancho Barnes' Lowe hailed from an affluent family. The Lowe family was hugely wealthy thanks largely to the entrepreneurial activities of Florence's grandfathers. Her paternal grandfather and mentor, Thaddeus Lowe commanded the US Army's Aeronautic Corps, and was honoured as the founding father of the United States Air Force. Her mother's father, Richard Dobbins, had amassed a fortune from architecture and real estate investments. Thaddeus left a lasting impression on the indomitable Florence. His powerful influence led her to embrace an adventurous and free spirited lifestyle.

Florence Lowe grew up in a lavish 35-room mansion in a well-heeled suburb of San Marino. From an early age she demonstrated an innate ability for anything she turned her hand to. Having mastered horseback riding by the age of three, she was soon winning medals at equestrian events. Wild as an unbroken mustang, Florence loved the freedom of long distance riding, much to her mother's disapproval. With a like-minded wayward companion she made several galloping excursions to Mexico.

After a number of such tomboy escapades, Florence's mother despatched her to a catholic convent school in a vain attempt at reigning in her rebellious daughter.

It was a fruitless exercise. Florence remained fiercely independent and stubborn.

When she turned eighteen in 1919, her mother introduced and hastily married her to Rankin Barnes, a respected local Episcopalian priest. The union appeared to tame the vivacious Florence, who gave the semblance of settling into the life as a clergyman's wife. Within nine months she had a son named William.

But a sedate and uneventful existence as a pastor's wife did not suit Florence. The tipping point came in 1924 with her mother's death and a substantial inheritance. The call of the wild proved too strong and she succumbed to her desire for adventure…and a little fun of course.

Abandoning husband and son, she travelled extensively throughout the USA and South America, staying away for long periods of time. In 1928 disguised as a man she joined a banana boat crew bound for South America. She discovered with delight that the freighter was actually smuggling arms to Mexican revolutionaries. It was whilst wandering around the Mexican countryside on a burro that a companion dubbed her "Pancho". Florence loved the name and for the remainder of her life she was affectionately known as "Pancho" Barnes.

Following a stint with the revolutionaries, Pancho returned to San Marino in the spring of 1928 to discover the exciting world of aviation. Her cousin Dean Banks was learning to fly and this ignited her interest in airplanes. She oiled the palm of her cousin's instructor, and had her first taste of flying. After just six hours' instruction Pancho soloed. Elated by her achievement, she immediately treated her friends to joyrides. She later found it difficult to resist a few buzzing passes over her husband's congregation on a Sunday.

Pancho purchased a brand new "Travel Air" biplane and toured the local countryside performing her barnstorming routine. She hired a parachutist and named her aerial stunt showcase "The Pancho Barnes Flying Mystery School." They treated the crowd to impressive aerobatics. Their daredevil antics included plucking unsuspecting ladies from the audience on the pretence of a joyride. Blissfully unaware, no one expected Pancho's parachuting assistant to push her into the aircraft's slipstream. Thankfully, the rip chord of her chute would be pulled in time, and none of the shrieking victims was ever hurt.

In 1929 Pancho discovered the frenetic world of high-speed racing. A gifted competitor, she won the first ever women's air race, which comprised an 80-mile stretch. Her triumph was all the more rewarding as she beat two well-known flyers: Bobbi Trout and Margaret Perry.

Although she was buoyed by the win, her debut in the 1929 transcontinental Women's Air Derby was not as successful. Her race ended early following an inadvertent collision with a truck in an early leg. Unfazed, she returned the following year, having secured sponsorship from the Union Oil Company. She subsequently won in her "Mystery Ship" Travel Air Model R biplane, slashing Amelia Earhart's speed record and setting a new benchmark of 196.19 miles per hour. The same month she won the 225-mile "Tom Thumb" race. Pancho was credited with a number of speed records in California, as well as being the first woman to fly into Mexico's interior in order to establish a new airline route.

With the help of other female pilots Pancho founded the Women's

Air Reserve (WAR). The humanitarian relief organisation schooled itself by conducting training exercises, parachute drops, and acquiring medical emergency skills. In 1934 members of WAR made a promotional cross-country flight tour to raise the organisation's profile.

Pancho turned her attention to Hollywood, where her flight jacket rubbed shoulders with both stars and powerful movie moguls alike. She was said to have consulted and flown as a stunt pilot in a number of films. She had allegedly been involved with a few flying sequences in Howard Hughes's action flick "Hells Angels." Dazzled by her dalliances with the stars, Pancho's party lifestyle was taking its toll on her dwindling wealth. The marathon parties at her inherited mansion were grandiose, and placed considerable strain on her family relationships.

Caught in the Great Depression, Pancho sold her dwindling assets and acquired eighty acres in the Mojave Desert in March 1935. She built a ranch in the desolate surroundings and she and son William ebbed out an existence supplying dairy and meat produce to the adjacent March Field Army Air Corps base.

Pancho expanded her desert residence, opening it as the "Rancho Oro Verde Fly-Inn Dude Ranch," aka "The Happy Bottom Riding Club." Pancho's motel, restaurant, rodeo and leisure pursuit operation was the destination of choice for military and civilian pilots alike. March Field became Edwards Air Force base dedicated to testing experimental aircraft. Many of the assigned test pilots of that era hung out at Pancho's sprawling resort from 1940 until 1952. A few notable patrons were Chuck Yeager who broke the sound barrier in the Bell X-1, General Doolittle and Buzz Aldrin. They all became Pancho's lifelong friends.

The Happy Bottom Riding Club flourished with three airstrips, hangars and an ornate swimming pool, together with dance halls and musical entertainment. It was an oasis of pleasure for the aviation community, holed up in an arid setting. In 1953 Pancho became the victim of her own success. The expansion of Edwards AFB involved the acquisition of her land. She fought tooth and rivet, refusing to be evicted. However, a mysterious fire razed her club to ashes. The destruction of her establishment also consumed the memorabilia, signed photos and souvenirs that had celebrated the world of her friends.

Edwards got Pancho's land, but entered into an acrimonious legal fight, which the legendary aviatrix won. In her last years she became a lecturer and was honoured by a number of aviation organisations. Pancho Barnes finally lost her only fight, which was to cancer, and passed away in April 1975.

Pancho Barnes is still celebrated and remembered for her pioneering 'have-a-go' spirit. In tribute to this remarkable aviatrix and loyal friend of the Air Force, the site of the Happy Bottom Riding Club at Edwards is the venue for an extravagant annual party laid in her honour. She was also depicted in the epic film adaptation of Tom Wolfe's 'The Right Stuff' in 1983 making her famous once again.

Events in 1929

■ First in-flight movie shown on an internal flight in USA.

■ Lufthansa uses a catapult to launch a Heinkel HE 12 mail plane from the passenger liner Bremen, 400 km (249 miles) out of New York, speeding the mail on its way before the ship reached port.

■ Wall Street Crash began with 13 million shares changing hands, in 4 days 5 billion dollars were wiped off stock and share values. This set off the great world-wide depression of the 30s.

1929

FAY GILLIS WELLS (USA) 1908 – 2002

First female to join the Caterpillar Club, the first president of the Ninety Nines lived an extraordinary life

ay Gillis Wells had to take a leap of faith when the experimental biplane she was flying broke apart in midair. Bailing out of the disintegrating airframe, she pulled the rip chord on her parachute to slow the frantic pace of her free fall to mother earth. Floating slowly down, she had a moment to take a deep breath, the only respite before she resumed the break neck speed of her life with gusto.

Pioneering aviatrix, foreign correspondent, suspected spy, adventurer and owner of exotic predatory cats, Fay Gillis Wells made a splash wherever she went. The ripples of her exploits are now etched in history. Celebrated to this day, she was justly recognised with many awards and honours. Strange to think it all began after her father chastised her for not having enough ambition.

Fay, a native of Minneapolis, was born on October 15th 1908. Her mining engineer father was always on the move, his family shifting with him. During the late twenties his daughter had a brief stint at Michigan State University, before dropping out to begin a flying career.

Her first flying lesson was on August 1st 1929 at the famous Curtiss Field in New York. Exactly a month later she soloed. Later that day her aircraft suffered major structural failures. Both she and her instructor bailed out of the stricken and crumbling aeroplane. The unexpected and rather necessary parachute jump made her the first women to join the ranks of the Caterpillar Club. The name is coined from the invertebrate responsible for producing parachute silk. Membership of this informal association is by the default act of jumping out of a disabled aircraft in an emergency. Just ten days before her 21st birthday, Fay was awarded her pilot's licence (number 9,497) on October 5th 1929.

Her inadvertent parachute jump made headline news and attracted the attention of the legendary aircraft manufacturer Glenn Curtiss. He hired her to sell and demonstrate his Curtiss Wright aeroplanes. Fay became the first women to perform such a job. Ironically she would also be tasked to promote aircraft as a safe form of travel during air show events. Such exhibition gatherings introduced Fay to other women pilots, notably Amelia Earhart, with whom she formed an instant friendship.

Fay was instrumental in establishing the Ninety Nines, an organisation for licensed US women pilots. The idea for such an organised network came towards the end of the first Women's Transcontinental Air Derby, or "Powder Puff Derby" in September 1929. Gathered under the bleachers of a public grandstand in Cleveland, Amelia Earhart, Bobbi Trout and a host of other female fliers came up with the concept of a club for women pilots. A month later Fay took up the challenge and wrote to the 117 licensed women pilots in the US, inviting them to become charter members. Ninety-nine responded by signing up to join. Thus the Ninety Nines came into existence, with Fay and Amelia as the first secretary and president respectively.

The next decade was chock full of dizzying twists of adventure and a whirlwind romance that quite literally gave her a new lease of life. It began in 1930 when Fay's father pursued a lucrative business opportunity in the Soviet Union. This necessitated moving the entire family to Russia, which gave Fay the chance to nurture a new career. She became a freelance aviation correspondent, writing for the New York Herald Tribune, and as a special reporter for the New York Times. She also became the first American women to pilot a Russian built aircraft, a Polikarpov U-2/ Po-2 trainer. She seized on the chance of being the first and only foreigner to own and fly a Soviet manufactured glider.

Fay would often indulge her own impulsiveness without thinking through the consequences of her actions. She wanted to experience the Palace of Weddings in Moscow, so married writer Ellery Walter on a whim. The subsequent annulment of the spontaneous union proved to be complicated.

Apart from rash behavioural traits, Fay had many talents. Pioneering aviator Wiley used her acumen for logistics. The Russian leg of his 1933 round the world record breaking solo flight took him through uncharted Siberia. Fay assisted his passage through the desolate region by identifying landing fields and arranging for fuel storage.

More events in 1929

■ **Lt Jimmy Doolittle makes a completely blind take-off, flight, and landing.**

■ **Penicillin is first used to fight an infection.**

In 1935 following his solo flight, Wiley Post invited Fay to accompany him on a long flight to Siberia via Alaska. However, the accomplished journalist fell for the charms of a dashing adventurer, pilot and foreign correspondent, Lintell Wells. She eloped with Lintell, so Wiley took satirist Will Rogers as her replacement. He had been flying an experimental nose heavy plane that crashed near Point Barrow, Alaska, killing the pair of them. Fay's unanticipated romantic interlude had saved her life.

Lintell became Fay's second husband and the newlyweds spent their honeymoon not on some romantic beach, but in the war torn landscape of Abyssinia (Ethiopia). The couple reported on the invasion by Italian forces of Abyssinia and the Syrian riots for the Herald Tribune. Some of the British tabloids speculated on the couples' journalistic presence as a cover for a spying mission.

Over the years the husband and wife foreign correspondent team reported from the most dangerous and war ravaged parts of the world. As globe trotting newshounds their by-lines would often appear on the same page of the newspapers they freelanced for.

Leaving Africa in 1936 with a menagerie of predatory cats- a lioness, cheetah and leopard, they headed to cover the glitz and glamour of Hollywood. Fay wrote for the Tribune and would often be accompanied by 'Snooks' her pet leopard during interviews.

The intrepid couple then took off to Latin America in 1938, where they pioneered radio show broadcasts from the region. Having founded the Ninety Nines, Fay's journalistic experiences prompted her to establish the Overseas Press Club.

Perhaps the British media were onto something with their spying angle, as both Fay and Lintell were recruited by President Roosevelt later in 1941 on a clandestine top secret mission. It may have proved impossible, but their mission was to scout around Africa in search of a suitable homeland for a Jewish populace displaced by the war. In the end they recommended Angola as a probable haven.

They stayed in Africa to oversee the procurement of strategic mate-

rials as part of the war effort until the birth of their son, Lintell II in 1946. Returning to America, the Wells' clan resided in a houseboat in Florida where Fay kept herself busy designing nautical furniture.

In 1963 she took over the Washington Bureau of the Storer Broadcasting Company, becoming a dedicated White House correspondent for thirteen years. Her stint at the White House covered three administrations and she was one of only three women to travel with President Nixon on his historic tour of China in 1972.

Fay strengthened her ties with aviation. She had already set up a scholarship fund in the name of Amelia Earhart and managed to get a postage stamp issued to honour the aviatrix in 1963. Fay also served as chairwoman of the first Ninety Nines international conference in 1967. She actively promoted the planting of trees and flying to foster international ties. This led to the formation of the International Forest of Friendship in Atchison, Kansas, Amelia Earhart's birthplace.

Numerous awards honoured her accomplishments in aviation and broadcasting. These include: the 1972 Woman of the Year by OX5 Aviation Pioneers, numerous accolades from the Ninety Nines such as "Most Valuable Pilot," and International Woman of the Year 1975. In 1984 she took the Women's Aerospace Achievement Award and in 2002 earned the Amelia Earhart Pioneering Achievement Award.

Fay even had an asteroid named after her. She died in 2002 aged 94, but remained active to the very last. In her final days she was part of the National Aeronautical and Space Administration advisory board to assist in the selection of the first journalist to fly on the space shuttle. Her pioneering spirit was such that she often lamented not being young enough to be an astronaut.

Fay Gillis Wells cavorted with danger without actively seeking it. From parachuting from a shattered plane to becoming a war correspondent in the middle of a battlefield, her guardian angels kept a close eye on her to the very end. That pep talk from her father had far reaching consequences when it came to her career choices.

1929

EVELYN 'BOBBI' TROUT (USA) 1906 – 2003

The girl with the cute hairstyle who had the stamina to set endurance records

Evelyn Trout was affectionately called "Bobbi" having cropped her hair to assume the same bobbed hairstyle popularised by film star Irene Castle. But there was more to her than just "hair today gone tomorrow." Bobbi Trout was unrivalled in her contribution to the world of aviation, and was later honoured as a living national treasure.

Born January 7th 1906, in Greenup, Illinois, her family moved to Los Angeles when she was young. The way she told it, her aviation story began in 1918 when just twelve, she spotted her first aircraft, lumbering overhead. "An airplane!" she exclaimed, recognising the noisy, gravity-defying construct hewn from wood and canvas. Dashing home she proclaimed to a family member that she, too, would fly airplanes one day. Serendipity and sheer determination would take care of the rest.

Her childhood dream neared reality when aged 16, she had her first ride in an aeroplane. Working in the family's service station business in Los Angeles she informed a customer of her ambition to fly, unaware that the gentlemen owned a Curtiss Jenny. On 22 December 1922 an elated Bobbi found herself aloft in that same Jenny, the ride cementing her desire to become a pilot. She diligently saved enough money to fund her $250 lessons with Burdett Airlines School of Aviation. Apart from a slight mishap, not of her doing, but serious enough to cause the destruction of a plane, an unscathed Bobbi soloed on 30th April 1928. Her proud yet apprehensive mother rewarded her with her very own biplane, a factory fresh International K-6. She acquired her official licence, numbered 2,613, from the Department of Commerce in September 1928. She ventured into the exhibition circuit and proved popular enough to obtain sponsorship from the Sunset Oil Company.

Gaining in recognition,

Bobbi had the opportunity of flying a new experimental plane, the Golden Eagle. The aircraft's creator, RO Bone, felt Bobbi fitted the bill for both flying and promoting his new monoplane airframe. The choice of pilot was a wise move, as Bobbi would use the aircraft to establish both endurance records and to win air races. Her first win occurred at a dedication race to inaugurate the Los Angeles Metropolitan Airport, today known as Van Nuys Airport. Next Bobbi achieved her first endurance record on 2nd January 1929, flying a total of twelve hours and thirteen minutes to break the previous record of eight hours held by Viola Gentry.

However, her endurance crown was soon snatched by Elinor Smith, who extended the aerial loitering record by one hour. Not to be outdone Bobbi returned to oust Elinor's record on February 10th establishing a new record of seventeen hours and twenty-four minutes. Following the marathon flight she was treated to a rapturous welcome from newsreel cameras and film stars alike. A local newspaper covered the events with a rather unflattering headline: "Tomboy stays in air 17 hours to avoid washing dishes". However, lured by the challenge, Elinor Smith managed to wrestle the endurance tiara from Bobbi for the second time. So the competitive tussle between the two aviatrixes continued, until eventually they were to join forces to set a joint endurance record. Bobbi's feats were gaining enough recognition for sponsorship deals to roll in and so financing future record-breaking ventures was getting easier. She then competed in the first-ever recorded women's pylon race to commemorate the opening of Glendale Central Airport on February 22nd 1929. Her underpowered Golden Eagle struggled to keep abreast with more powerful machines, but she crossed the finishing line in a respectable third place. The air race experience prompted R O Bone to offer Bobbi the new Golden Eagle Chief, mated to an 80 horsepower race tuned engine. On 16th June 1929, she

securing a win, but she did make it to the finishing line in Cleveland. Following the eventful race, Bobbi, Amelia and fellow women pilots gathered under the bleachers to moot the idea of an organisation dedicated to the interest of women pilots. The historic meeting led to the creation of the Ninety Nines' organisation.

The germ of an idea to set a new endurance record had taken root during the Air Derby. Bobbi formed an alliance with former rival Elinor Smith, and with the help of promoter Jack Shergill, a Sunbeam biplane was procured. After three aborted attempts, Bobbi and Elinor took to the skies on November 27th 1929 with the intention of remaining aloft for a month. Fuel and food needs would be provided by another aeroplane, a Curtiss Pigeon, serving as in-flight tanker. The fuel line was a weighted bag, which Bobbi would ensnare twice a day to insert into the tank of her thirsty plane.

On the 39th hour the Curtiss Pigeon sustained damage during refuelling and was forced to make an emergency landing. With limited fuel transferred the Sunbeam remained aloft until the early hours. However, tanks exhausted they were forced to land. The endurance record was pegged at forty-two hours, three minutes and thirty seconds - a first for women.

Bobbi went on to win several more races before revisiting the endurance record. She claimed title to the 1930 Women's Air Race held in honour of the new United Airport (known today as Burbank-Glendale-Pasadena Airport).

Flashguns popped and a media frenzy enveloped Bobbi, as the next endurance record was made in the company of Hollywood starlet Edna May Cooper. The plane of choice was a second hand Curtiss Robin Challenger monoplane. After a false start, the aviatrix and star ascended into the skies on 4th January 1931. Bobbi soon surpassed her original record and also celebrated her 25th birthday by eating chocolate cake lowered from the Curtiss Pigeon.

Battling stormy weather, more misfortune struck the intrepid pair on January 9th. Their engine coughed and spluttered, spewing oil into the slipstream and possibly dousing them.

Bobbi valiantly wrestled with the stricken plane for several hours until they were forced to land during the night. The new marathon endurance world record tallied to a final 122 hours and 50 minutes. For this Bobbi was showered with medals ranging from the Federation Aeronautique Internationale to the accolade of The Aviation Cross from King Carol of Romania.

The Great Depression of the 1930s bit, making financing further record attempts difficult. Undeterred, Bobbi remained active in aviation. She helped Pancho Barnes to establish the humanitarian relief unit, the Women's Air Reserve. Her tireless entrepreneurial spirit led her to establish aircraft related engineering companies and later still she ran a successful real estate and life insurance business. The legendary aviatrix was honoured in 1976 by the OX5 Pioneer Women of the Year Award and later inducted into the OX5 Aviation Pioneers Hall of Fame. Lt Eileen Collins also carried Bobbi's flying licence during her first space flight in the shuttle as pilot. In 1993 Bobbi became a member of the Women's Aviation Hall of Fame.

Evelyn 'Bobbi' Trout passed away on January 24th 2003. The memory of her achievements and contributions will endure for some time to come.

More events in 1929

■ Carl Spaatz, Ira Eaker, and Elwood Quesada set an endurance record of 151 hours aloft in a Fokker F.VIIa-3m

took the Chief up and shattered the world altitude record in the light plane class, setting a new benchmark of 15,200 feet. This stunt garnered both Bobbi and the Golden Eagle manufacturers high praise, celebratory banquets and recognition the world over.

Her thoughts now turned to the first Women's Transcontinental Air Derby in August 1929. However, the idea of an extended flight endurance record, suggested by the 156 mph speed record holder Louise Thaden, appealed to Bobbi. The concept would involve refuelling in-flight, however R O Bone expressly prohibited the use of his aircraft for the endeavour.

Unfazed by her employer's lack of interest, Bobbi mulled over trying to get another female pilot to sign up for the challenge. In the meantime she entered the Transcontinental Air Derby, or "Powder Puff Derby," competing with the likes of Amelia Earhart and Louise Thaden. During the derby she tried to recruit Amelia Earhart for the feat. Although Amelia was interested, she was fully booked.

Bobbi roared through the circuit in her Chief, beginning at Clover Field, Santa Monica on 18th August 1929. Despite an encouraging start, her plane crash-landed twice due to technical problems. Hasty repairs and protracted delays dashed any hopes of

1930

MRS VICTOR BRUCE (UK) 1895 – 1990

First person to fly from England to Japan - first to fly the Yellow Sea, and the first woman to fly around the world alone (crossing the oceans by ship)

The first record Mary Petre set was to be the first woman prosecuted at London's Bow Street police court for speeding in 1911. Speed was a theme that dominated her life. Aged 79 she clocked a personal best when she test-drove a Ford Ghia Capri at 110 mph (176 km/h) around a racetrack. Two years later she looped the loop in a two-seater De Havilland Chipmunk.

Mildred Mary Petre was born on 10 November 1895 in Essex, the daughter of wealthy landowner and his actress wife. She had five brothers and actively engaged in traditional male pursuits as she grew up. She had a motorbike with a sidecar, and later, sport cars. She adored speed and motor racing and married a soul mate in February 1926, the Hon. Victor Austin Bruce. He had won the Monte Carlo rally the year they were wed and introduced her to motor touring and racetracks. In 1927 Mary took the women's cup at the Monte Carlo rally, covering 1,700 miles in seventy-two hours.

The married couple shared the pain in December 1927, driving to set an endurance record of 15,000 miles in nine days. They also undertook a mammoth tour, taking in the western Mediterranean. Mary wrote a book about their adventure, called "Nine Thousand Miles in Eight Weeks."

She returned to Montlhéry in June 1929 and claimed a speed record for a solo 24-hour drive of 2,164 miles. In September 1928, she squeezed in the fastest time for a Dover–Calais channel crossing by motorboat. Around the same time she wrote a series of humorous short stories for Sketch magazine, which were collected in a book named "The Peregrinations of Penelope" in 1930.

In summer 1930 she passed a car showroom off Bond Street that was displaying a Blackburn Bluebird light aircraft for sale at £550. According to an article published in the UK's Daily Telegraph in November 2003 she said: "I had an urgent appointment in London at one o'clock on a typically wintry summer day: I found myself walking down Burlington Gardens, with an hour to spare and nothing to do. Such things nearly always lead to my spending money - if I have any. On this occasion it led to much more, for what did I see in a shop window but a full-sized aeroplane for sale?...I came to another shop with a very pretty dress in the window: it was easily the best I had seen for years, and soon I was inside trying it on. The dress sealed my fate, for it didn't suit me, and I wandered back towards the shop with the aeroplane, still with half an hour to spare before my appointment."

The aeroplane was billed as: "Bluebird: Honeymoon model: ready to go anywhere." That sealed the deal – the salesman told her since it had folding wings it could travel the world –via ship if necessary. So she bought it. She opened an atlas and drew a line through Europe and Asia, all the way to Japan. She visited the minister of aviation to let him know she was going to fly around the world. When he asked how long she had held her flying licence she told him she had not yet got one, but intended to get one before going. The Bluebird was sent back to the factory to have an extra fuel tank fitted on the passenger seat.

She learned to fly in a few weeks at Brooklands School of Flying and eight weeks later set off from Heston (now Heathrow) aerodrome on September 25 1930. Her father, husband, and son Anthony, waved her off. She had forty hours in her logbook and her luggage consisted of route maps provided by the Automobile Association and an American flag to be dropped on her mother's house. She also had a small shoulder bag containing her husband's compass, her passport, logbook, and a bottle of water, sun helmet, light cotton dresses and an evening frock. Four hours later, she was in Munich.

Over the next five months she covered 20,000 miles in forty-seven days of flying. She had a few close shaves en route. Near Belgrade she was navigating by tracking a train and almost followed it into a tunnel. She had to perform a steep turn to avoid smashing into a hillside. Over Turkey, she

Events in 1930

- **Ellen Church becomes first flight attendant, working for Boeing Air Transport.**

- **Amy Johnson flies from England to Australia in a de Havilland Gipsy Moth.**

was wiping oil from the windscreen when she accidentally kicked one of the rudder pedals, sending the aeroplane into a spin. She recovered less than 500 feet above the ground.

She had engine failure over the Gulf of Persia caused by an oil leak. Although she reached the coast, she landed on a salt lake and nosed into the mud, breaking the aircraft's propeller. She escaped uninjured and was reportedly rescued by tribesmen. Three days later British officers stationed in Iran arrived and helped her pull Bluebird from the lake, replace the propeller and repair the faulty oil line.

She carried on and was lauded in Indo-China, Hanoi and Hong Kong, before stopping in Amoy and Shanghai. Although she had intended to go directly to Tokyo, she had to divert to Seoul in Korea, since it was illegal in Japan to look down on the Emperor, who was attending military manoeuvres in the area. When these finished she resumed her flight.

From Japan she sailed to the US with Bluebird in stowage. Once there she flew across the States, dropping the flag on her mother's house as promised. In Baltimore she took off from a too-short runway, stalled and spun into the ground. The plane flipped and landed on its back. Luckily the Glen Martin Aircraft Factory was across the road, so she was immediately able to have her aeroplane repaired. In New York she flew along Broadway, over the Statue of Liberty and on to the Empire State Building, which she circled several times. For that stunt she had a welcome party of police waiting for her when she landed at Glenn Curtiss Airfield.

She then sailed the Atlantic and was honoured with a dinner in Paris by the Aero Club de France. She insisted on flying the final leg of her journey back home, from Lympne to Croydon on 20 February 1931. Five Bluebirds escorted her back to Britain, including one flown by Winifred Spooner. Amy Johnson also joined the fun in a Puss Moth. Mary's Bluebird was then exhibited in a London underground station.

Flight (now Flight International) magazine said her journey was: "one of the most meritorious that has been made by a woman" (Issue 182). In her own account of the voyage: "The Bluebird's Flight," published in 1931, she made light of the difficulties she had faced, glossing over the dangers.

Her attempt on the world endurance record in August 1932 was less publicised. She flew a Saro Windhover flying boat, with an accompanying aircrew and remained airborne for 55 hours. She was well short of the world record, but created a British record. In November 1934 she tried to fly to the Cape in an autogiro. The plan was to cross the Sahara, and to fly by night as well as by day. She abandoned the project when the autogiro was damaged in strong winds.

Three years later in 1937, she founded Air Dispatch, a small freight and passenger-carrying airline in Croydon using two De Havilland Rapide aircraft, and an Avro 642. Her planes were the first to carry air hostesses, and made the fastest flights between London and Paris. During the war the company moved to Cardiff and concentrated on aircraft repair, operating up to 32 aircraft in co-operation with the military. The company flourished and she became a millionaire.

In 1941 Mary divorced her husband. She almost stood for parliament as an independent in 1945, but withdrew before the election. She died at her home in London, on 21 May 1990. Not only was Mary Bruce an excellent pilot, but she was also one of the few women of her day to pursue a successful career in aviation.

1930

AMY JOHNSON (UK) 1903 - 1941

The typist from Hull who changed aviation forever

O n Saturday May 24th, 1930, Amy Johnson's battered biplane touched down on Fannie Bay racecourse in Darwin Australia, instantly opening doors to women that had never existed before. She had taken off from Croydon, UK, with only 85 hours of solo flight under her belt and flown alone in an open-cockpit De Havilland Gypsy Moth for almost 20 days, covering 11,000 miles and enduring severe hardship en route. She later wrote in her book 'Flying Alone to Australia': "Although I have since made many other flights, nothing can ever quite equal the elation of my very first flight to Australia, nothing can compare with doing the job yourself, sinking or swimming by your own efforts."

Amy was born into a middle-class family on 1st July 1903. An accident in her schooldays where she lost her front teeth caused her great distress, despite the fact that her false set looked real. For the rest of her life she felt that she was disfigured, which led to bouts of depression. However, she was a determined character and unusually for a woman at the time, went to university, where she earned a degree in economics as well as learning shorthand and typing.

At this point there was no hint of the heroics to come. She was in the midst of an eight-year relationship with an older man of whom her parents disapproved. She wrote: "I couldn't take any serious interest in a career because I imagined at that time that my career was to be a home and children. I was taking this affair so seriously that I went to cookery classes in the evening."

The affair ended and she headed to London, where she led a sporadic life living in hostels and bedsits and drifting in and out of jobs, until something happened that altered the course of history. She wrote: "One fine Saturday afternoon...I climbed on top of a bus going in the direction of Stag Lane. I jumped off...and ran up Stag Lane to find at the end the notice 'London Aeroplane Club. Private.' Disregarding the notice I walked on ...I had to learn to fly."

She took up flying lessons in September 1928, scraping enough money together to gain her pilot's licence. She also became the only woman in the world to hold a ground engineer's licence. Then she decided to attempt the world speed record to Australia. She wrote many letters asking for sponsorship, but less than two months before the flight she still had no aeroplane. Lord Wakefield, head of the Wakefield-Castrol oil company eventually agreed to share the £600 cost of an aircraft with her father. This was a huge level of financial and emotional commitment for William Johnson, since he was by no means wealthy. Amy christened her Moth "Jason", after the family trademark.

Jason was a small, single seat open cockpit aircraft with a top cruising speed of eighty-five miles per hour. During her epic journey Amy encountered major tests, such as almost hitting the edges of the Taurus mountain range in Turkey during turbulence at 8,000 feet where she had minimal visibility. An unexpected gale caused her to land in the desert near Baghdad, where she waited for two hours until the storm passed. She also made two emergency landings and her aircraft suffered wing and propeller damage in Rangoon. Friendly strangers helped her fix the wing, but she then had to contend with constant rain and poor visibility and suffered mechanical problems over Indonesia. She was shattered. Flying ten to twelve hours was hard going and she got lost, finally reaching Atambua on May 24, the launching point for the most dangerous phase of her amazing quest. She flew 500 miles over the shark-infested Sea of Timor, landing in Australia to media uproar. King George V, the Lindberghs, and Louis

She married the playboy aviator Jim Mollison in 1932 and they made the first direct flight from the UK to the USA together. They were greeted with a frenzied ticker-tape welcome along Broadway in 1933. They attempted several records and races together. However, Amy found her fame difficult to handle. The flamboyant Mollison did little to help. They parted after only three years because of his heavy drinking and womanising and were divorced by 1938. For a year Amy ran her own air cruise company until her marriage broke up. She was shocked by Amelia Earhart's disappearance in 1937 and stopped flying until 1939. Many aviation companies refused to hire her, dismissing her as a 'stunt pilot.' This was a low point in her life and she suffered from depression and financial difficulties.

Things changed at the outbreak of the Second World War when the Air Transport Auxiliary (ATA) was formed to ferry aircraft from factories and ports to airfields. Amy signed up in 1940 and was paid six pounds a week – a fortune at the time. She was totally dedicated to her job, despite further bouts of depression, where she was heard to say she would "finish up in the drink."

On 4 January 1941 Amy set off from Prestwick to deliver an Airspeed Oxford to Kidlington near Oxford. She landed near Blackpool and spent the night with her sister Molly. The next day she was advised not to take off because the weather was so bad, but she insisted that she would "smell her way" to her destination.

Several hours later sailors in the HMS Haslemere in the Thames Estuary saw a parachutist drop from the thick cloud, followed by an aeroplane in a slow spiral dive. The parachutist fell into the water and witnesses heard a woman's voice shout: "Hurry, please hurry," before disappearing under the stern of the ship. Amy was never seen again. The Haslemere's captain dived into the sea to rescue what he thought to be another airman, but was probably Amy's bag. He subsequently died of exposure.

Because she was 150 miles south of her intended destination several lurid rumours circulated, ranging from suggestions she was on a secret flight to Europe with a mystery passenger to hints that she tried to fake her own death. The UK's Ministry of Defence website dismisses these, pointing out that Amy was likely lost above thick clouds and running low on fuel. She would have seen a barrage balloon floating beneath her, presumed she was flying over land near the coast and assumed it was safe to bail out and leave the aircraft in "trim" to fly out to sea where it could crash safely away from civilians.

On the Johnson family website Molly Jones wrote about the last time she saw her sister: "She picked up her zip holdall and smiled as she went out of the door. That is my last picture of her, a neat trim figure in her smart navy blue uniform, her fair hair falling softly round her face, the understanding blue eyes and reassuring smile…. she waved and was gone."

Blériot were among the illustrious people to send congratulatory telegrams. She later wrote: "It remains forever a mystery to me why I wanted to fly to Australia and an equal mystery why the flight caught the public's imagination. I can only explain both things as being typical of their time."

A million people lined up to see her when she got back to England. She was awarded the Commander of the Order of the British Empire and the Daily Mail newspaper made her a gift of £10,000.

Her background set her apart from the wealthy women who had previously gained fame as fliers. Her humble roots led to public adulation, which continued as Amy went on to complete five further record-breaking flights to India, Japan and across the Sahara, and alone to the Cape twice. Fashion houses were desperate to be associated with her. Chanel sent her clothes, as did Elsa Schiaparelli, who created a navy blue suit to contrast with the duck-egg blue of the plane Amy flew in her second record-breaking trip to South Africa in 1936.

Events in 1930

- The Zip fastener and Nylon are born
- TWA begins the first regular passenger flights between New York and Los Angeles.
- Elm Farm Ollie becomes the first cow to fly in an airplane and also the first cow to be milked in an airplane.

An inspiration to many pilots Amy died tragically young. There are several books about her, including the excellent "Amy Johnson, Enigma in the Sky" by David Luff. In 1941 the Amy Johnson Memorial Trust was established to fund a scholarship to help women attain professional standards in aviation. Contact address; The Amy Johnson Memorial Trust, 12 Church Lane, Merton Park, London, SW19 3PD

Mary du Caurroy – Duchess of Bedford (UK) 1865 - 1937

"My only apprehension, was that we should land in the bison enclosure, which from the air looked particularly attractive, instead of in safer but less open parts of the park."

Duchess of Bedford writing about landing at her country seat after her first flight

he jaunt was a typical adventure for Mary du Caurroy Tribe Russell, wife of the 11th Duke of Bedford, who would eventually become known as the "Flying Duchess." She led a colourful life. Born Mary du Caurroy Tribe on 26th September 1865 in Hampshire, as a young woman she lived in Simla in India, where her father had been made Archdeacon of Lahore. At 21 she met Herbrand Russell, second son of the ninth Duke of Bedford. They married in 1888. A year later, they had a son, Hastings.

In 1891, the ninth Duke died, followed shortly afterwards by his son and Herbrand's elder brother, the tenth Duke. Unexpectedly, the couple became Duke and Duchess of Bedford. Mary was not content to be a decorative figurehead and opened a small cottage hospital at Woburn, the Bedfords' ancestral home. This endeavour ultimately earned her a Dame Commander, Order of the British Empire (DBE) in 1928 for her work in radiography and radiology.

Always a fan of winged things, her chief hobby had been bird watching. This was soon ousted by the chance to become airborne herself. The new adventure sport of "Flying," was all the rage after World War I. Mary suffered from hearing problems after having had typhoid in India. She had discovered that background noise gave her some relief, for example she could hear voices far better in a car, for instance. A friend suggested she try flying.

Although she had a good few decades on most of her contemporaries in June 1926, at the age of 61, she made her first flight as a passenger - in an open cockpit two-seater De Havilland Moth. The London Aeroplane Club's chief instructor flew her from Croydon to Woburn at the sedate pace of 70mph. Happily her fears of landing among the bovines were not met. What did happen is that she fell in love with this new way of travelling and started to charter Moths regularly for her social visits, eventually buying her own aircraft, an emerald-green Cirrus Moth for GBP 750. She also hired a former military commander and test pilot, Charles Barnard, to take her around.

On one occasion they decided to pop off to the Continent. She wrote: "My luggage consisted of two small suitcases, a small attaché case carried on my knees, a hat in a bag and a little leather handbag," En route to Biarritz, they started to run out of fuel, so Charles climbed to 5,000ft, in case they needed to glide back to earth when the engine cut out. Mary found it curious that the engine had stopped. Charles asked whether she minded a fast descent.

She wrote: "We came down quickly by some amazing corkscrew turns, landing neatly at the bottom." He also asked her wither she would like to try "a little spin and some nose dives." Of course she agreed, but did not find the experiences as much fun as he had promised. They returned to Britain, to be greeted by the press. They had broken a record, having flown more than 4,500 miles.

Realising her chances of seeing the much-vaunted eclipse were slight, she persuaded Charles to take her to Harrogate, where the prospects of seeing the sun go down were best.

It was a wise decision. She was one of the few people to witness the last solar eclipse visible in Britain on June 29, 1927. Climbing to 10,000ft one summer morning to make sure they did not miss a thing, Mary and her pilot had set off at 5.30am to witness this total eclipse of the sun. She wrote afterwards in her diary: "As far as the eye could see there was a wondrous panorama of piled masses of clouds."

Although the entire spectacle lasted little more than a few seconds, the Duchess and her companion would have seen the complete corona and a flare of light before normal daylight returned. She was entranced and noted: "I had just time to note a beautiful rose and pale yellow tinting of the southern sky, where a few small cirrus clouds were lit up by it."

Several hundred thousand people made their way to the line of totality to witness the spectacle, which ran from North Wales to Hartlepool, Co Durham. Some intrepid watchers climbed to the top of Mount Snowdon, the highest mountain in Wales. Londoners flocked to Hampstead Heath, the capital's tallest point. Sadly, it was a bit of a washout. 1927 saw the worst British summer in almost 50 years and thick cloud hid the line of totality from view. On top of Snowdon visibility was down to 30 yards.

However, Mary and her pilot did get to see the eclipse, as did Prime Minister Ramsay McDonald, who was holed up in Gilggleswick in North Yorkshire.

Itching for more adventure, Mary's next plan was a return trip to India in a larger Fokker aircraft. In another record-breaking trip, she sat next to the pilot in a comfortable chair, wrapped in a rug. This time she took the controls for a short time, flying the aircraft herself. She built on this and by the end of 1929 she had logged 496 hours in the air.

She made two more important historical flights, both record breakers. One to India again in 1929 and one to South Africa in 1930. She set off again and experienced more amazing adventures. She endured forced landings, an attack by Moroccan tribesmen and carbon monoxide poisoning, which forced Mary and her two co-pilots to put their heads alternately out of the cabin windows to keep awake.

It seemed crazy not to learn how to fly for herself. At 64, she was the oldest female student pilot around. Barnard agreed to instruct her. Because of her deafness and the difficulty the pair had communicating, he insisted that she performed ten perfect takeoffs and landings before allowing her to solo in April 1930. That year, he left her employ to set up Barnard Air Tours, Britain's first air circus. So Mary hired an ex military aviator, Flight Lieutenant Bernard Allen. She finally got her own wings in 1933.

She enjoyed many jaunts with Charles until he crashed his plane and died only three miles from Woburn. Mary was supposed to have been with him that day and was devastated by the news. 'I have lost not only a skilled pilot but also a loyal and trusted friend,'" she wrote.

In spring of 1937, aged 71 Mary had flown solo for 199 hours and five minutes, which she planned to bring up to 200 with another flight. She took off from Woburn in her Moth at 3.30pm on March 22. She had planned a triangular route that would have taken her to Buntingford, then on to Cambridge and finally back to Woburn. She never returned.

The Duke called the Chief Constable of Bedfordshire and ten RAF stations set out to look for her. She was never found. On March 31, the family arranged a memorial service for her in Woburn parish church. Two days later, a strut washed up at Yarmouth. Later, the remaining three struts were washed up further down the coast.

Mary's body was never discovered. However, her larger than life spirit lives on in the numerous books and articles written about her, notably Lettice Curtis' splendid biography *Winged Odyssey*. Mary proved that age is not a barrier to living a dream and lived life to the full right up to her last drop of breath.

More events in 1930

- British Airship R101 crashed in France en-route to India on its maiden voyage.

- Astronomers discover Pluto, the ninth planet.

1931
ELLY BEINHORN-ROSEMEYER (GERMANY) 1907 – 2007

Elly Beinhorn flew solo around the world and created several records in the 1930s. She lived to be 100.

Unlike the Hon. Mrs Bruce and the young Baron Koenig-Warthausen who set off round the world with very few hours, Elly Beinhorn had racked up considerable experience, including a long trip to Africa, and an engine failure that caused a forced landing.

Elly Beinhorn was born in May 1907 in Hanover, Germany, the only child of a merchant family. In 1928 when she was 21, friends took her to a conference where Hauptman Herman Köhl was speaking. Kohl had been one of first pilots to cross the Atlantic, east to west, in a Junker. By the end of his talk Elly knew she had to fly.

She had a small inheritance and moved to Spandau in Berlin. She learned to fly at Berlin-Staaken airport, quickly soloing in a small Klemm KL-20, getting her pilot's licence shortly afterwards. She went on to learn aerobatics, which enabled her to join the barn-storming circuit and earn enough money to keep her airborne.

However, she yearned to make long distance flights. In 1931 she flew to Portuguese Guinea (now Guinea-Bissau), West Africa, as part of a scientific expedition. Her engine failed on the return leg, resulting in a crash-landing in the Sahara. She was forced to abandon the machine and was rescued by locals and taken to Timbuktu after a four-day trek through the desert. She later said: "My emergency landing caused more headlines than my wildest flights."

A few months later, Elly started out for India and Bali, flying another Klemm aircraft. Although this was not her initial intention, this flight took her around the world. This time she made sure that she was better equipped, and carried spare parts, a tropical hat, mosquito net, insect powder, a water filter and a 10 litre water-bag.

She was beset with problems. Her Klemm developed problems near Bushire in Persia (now Iran). Moye Stephens, another pilot helped her to fix the aircraft. According to a website for pilots who have flown solo around the world, she had a forced landing near Bandar-e-Deylam, because of dirt in the fuel, which clogged the carburettor. She had to tie the Klemm down and travel by road to Bushire, some distance further south. No one could understand her and she was unable to send a telegram. She finally received help from the German Consul, and was able to carry out the necessary repairs and continue on towards India.

She also used the flight to see the world, visiting the Taj Mahal and the Himalayas. In Calcutta she could not find Rangoon airport, a common problem for aviators in the day. She eventually landed on a path between rice paddies, and locals pointed the way. Despite the dangers of taking off in a crowd, Elly headed off again, and eventually found the airfield. She met the Thai royal family in Bangkok and reached her initial planned destination, Indonesia, just in time for monsoon season.

Grounded by the weather and unwilling to go back to Germany the way she came, she decided to fly to Australia. She met a Dutch pilot, Captain Pattist, who had made the same perilous flight the year before in a Fokker Trimotor. He was anxious about the Klemm's ability to cross the shark-infested Timor Sea, a distance of 490 nautical miles, but gave Elly all the help he could. The toughest moment of her flight was taking off from the waterlogged Kupand Airfield. She arrived in Port Darwin fatigued but happy during a tropical storm. This made her the second woman to fly solo from Europe to Australia, after Amy Johnson. Her next stop was Sydney where her aircraft was dismantled and shipped to New Zealand. There it was reassembled and shipped to Panama.

Elly resumed her flight and tracked the western coast of South America. She was presented with a medal in Peru and pushed the tired aircraft over the Andes. She shipped the Klemm from Brazil to Germany, where it was put together again to fly to Berlin on June 26 1932.

Elly was famous. She had flown around the world solo. However, she was more than 15,000 marks in debt. She had a reprieve when she was awarded with the Hindenburg Cup and the 10,000 marks that accompany it. The German aeronautical industry also took her under its wing and she wrote articles and sold photographs of her travels to raise funds and became solvent again.

Any money she had went towards flying. She next embarked on an African tour in a single seater Heinkel. She flew down the east coast all the way to Cape Town, then back along the west coast via Casablanca. The following year she sailed to Panama with her Klemm, and flew through Mexico to California and across the United States to Miami, where the aircraft was shipped back to Europe. While in the US she got to know Amelia Earhart, whom she warmed to enormously.

She arrived in Europe on January 13, 1935. The same year she met racing driver Bernd Rosemeyer and they were married on July 13th 1936. They were a true celebrity couple, and the toast of Nazi Germany. Heinrich Himmler commanded a reluctant Bernd to become a member of the SS.

Elly's next ambition was to fly solo between two continents in a single day. She chose the latest in aviation technology a super fast Messerschmitt Bf 08, with retractable landing gear. She achieved her goal by taking off from Gleiwitz, the most easterly German airport and landing in Istanbul. From there she took a short hop to the other side of the Bosphorus, in the Asian part Turkey, and returned to Berlin. Elly christened the Bf 108: "Typhoon," and the manufacturer retained the name. She bettered her record in 1936 and flew over three continents in one day.

Germany now was in the grip of the Nazis. Both Elly and Bernd were critical of the regime and deposited prize money Bernd had won in America in a US account in case they were forced to leave Germany. Elly had a son, Bernd, in November 1937. Ten weeks later her husband was killed attempting a speed record in January 1938. As a national hero, he was mourned publicly. Elly received condolences from prominent Nazis, including Hitler, but requested a simple funeral ceremony. Her wishes were ignored and several Nazis gave speeches at the graveside. Some accounts suggest that Elly walked off in protest. She wrote his biography as a tribute: "Mein Mann, der Rennenfahrer (My husband the car racer)." The book was a best seller and more than 300,000 copies were published.

Spring 1939 saw her start another long flight in the "Typhoon". This time her destination was to be Japan. However, she had to turn back in Bangkok when she discovered China and Japan were at war, and Europe was on the brink of war.

Elly remarried in 1941 to a Dr. Wittman, and they had a daughter, Stephanie. After World War II, as Germany was not allowed to have powered aircraft, she took up gliding. Like many German pilots, Elly headed to Switzerland to fly and bought a Piper Cub. She reapplied for and received her pilot licenses in Switzerland in 1951. In 1952, she made another flight to Africa from Switzerland, and flew all the way to Benghazi in Libya, via Rome, Tunis and Tripoli. Once the flying ban was lifted in Germany, she successfully participated in numerous competitions. She also worked as a journalist, flying her Piper Cub throughout Europe.

In 1959 she took part in the Powder Puff Derby in the USA. She learned that the Ninety-Nines wanted to produce an Amelia Earhart stamp, but the project had stalled because of insufficient funding. Elly remembered the money that she and Bernd had deposited more than twenty years before. She discovered the amount had become a fairly large sum and happily contributed this towards the stamp.

In 1979, aged 72 and after 5,000 mostly solo flight hours, she turned in her pilot licenses. In her later years she lived in Bavaria, near Munich. She died on 28 November 2007, at the age of 100.

Events in 1931

- Wiley Post and Harold Gatty fly round the world in a Lockheed Vega.

- Empire State Building is completed.

1932

GIDSKEN NILSINE JAKOBSEN (NORWAY) 1908 – 1990

Pioneering adventuress who conquered Norway's icy plains

At 900 meters above Norway's deep dark Sognefjord, the propeller started to vibrate, and suddenly fell off the plane. It landed with a huge splash far below. Without the weight of the engine to balance it out, the aircraft tipped backwards, and was set to plunge tail first into the icy waters. Gidsken Jakobsen and co pilot Birger Johnsen scrambled into action. To rebalance the craft they crawled to the front. Gidsken forcibly stopped their young passenger from jumping to his death. The aircraft regained balance and the two pilots were able to glide it down safely onto the fjord. The miracle was that no one was hurt.

One of the aircraft's saviours, Gidsken Nilsine Jakobsen was born on August 1 1908 in Hemnesberget a tiny village near the Arctic Circle. She grew up in Narvik, where her father was in the lumber trade. At the age of 15 she dreamed of going to Hollywood to become a movie star. However, her father needed help in his office, so Gidsken was despatched to Oslo to learn business studies. She was seemingly destined for a more humdrum existence.

She was slightly compensated by the gift of a Chevrolet. Aged 18 she participated in a motor race, but was stymied by an accident, so missed a winner's place. She was also an enthusiastic motorcyclist. In 1931 she and a girlfriend took a road trip from Narvik, touring through Norway, Sweden and Europe all the way to Naples.

In 1928 airship pilot Umberto Nobile went missing en route from the North Pole. A huge international rescue operation was launched from Spitsbergen, north of Norway. During the mission a Swedish Junker G34 three-engine seaplane landed in Narvik. Gidsken saw it and was convinced that flying was for her. That year she started flying lessons at the Aero-Materiels civila flygskola, a civilian school in Stockholm, Sweden. At that time Norwegian flight schools were all military, and closed to women.

She was the only female out of 18 students. She flew a De Havilland Moth with wheels and skis. She soloed after seven hours and graduated top of her class. On March 15 1929, she earned "Certifikat nr. 28" in Sweden. Thirteen days later on March 28 she received an international flying licence from the Royal Swedish Aero Club. Gidsken was now authorised to fly without passengers. She was the second Norwegian woman to get a flying licence. (Dagny Berger was first on September 27, 1927.)

In summer 1929 Gidsken headed to Helsinki, Finland to learn to fly seaplanes at the Sääski ("Mosquito") Aircraft Company. The Fins were known to be expert seaplane pilots and Gidsken would have to fly a seaplane, since there were no civilian airfields in Norway. In August 1929, backed by her father, she bought a double-winged open seaplane with two seats from Sääski. The aircraft was a Finnish variant of the de Havilland Moth.

Gidsken named her aircraft "Måsen" (Seagull). With her instructor Georg Jäderholm, she flew from Helsinki, through Finland and Sweden and back home to Narvik. The journey was illegal, because she had not got permission from the Swedish authorities to cross the border. Jäderholm tried to stop her, but she was determined, and said to him: "This is my plane, and I make all the decisions on board."

On 23 August they landed near Narvik harbour, where huge crowds awaited them. That evening Norwegian radio broadcast the news

summer Gidsken and a hired pilot flew around the north offering tourist flights.

They were grounded by the weather for the winter. The following summer Gidsken took her seaplane to the famous tourist magnet, the Vestlandet fjords. Along with her new pilot, Birger Johnsen, she sold sightseeing trips to wealthy travellers eager to see the beautiful landscape from the air. Gidsken and Birger became an item. He was 15 years older than she was and had lived in the US for many years, making a living out of barnstorming.

The couple returned to Balestrand in the summer of 1934. On June 27, they had their terrible Songefjord accident when Birger was testing a new propeller. Gidsken sold the wreckage and bought two small Junkers K16 aeroplanes from Germany.

In August 1934 she fronted a new airline, Bergens Aero. Norwegian politicians were debating the future of aviation. It seemed likely that one company would become the national airline with privileges from the state authorities. Gidsken's plan was to get a licence for post and passenger airlines along the coast. She also had plans for routes to the UK. Unfortunately, the authorities decided to appoint Det Norske Luftfartselskap (Norwegian Airlines). Although disappointed, Gidsken continued to fly tourists over the fjords.

In 1936 she founded her third airline, Norsk Aero (Norwegian Aero). She went with Birger to Akron, Ohio, to buy a new aircraft, having borrowed money from two local businessmen. She bought a Loening amphibian air yacht, nicknamed "Narvik."

She split with Birger in the US and hired another pilot for the 1936 summer season. On July 2 she and some friends were in a crash at sea, their aircraft flipped over, submerging the cockpit underwater. Luckily, one of the passengers was incredibly strong and punched a hole the window and hauled himself out on to the wing. From there he helped the others to get out. Nobody was seriously hurt, but the accident terminated Gidsken's flying career.

She had lost a great deal of money in aviation, and her father needed help with his business. He became ill in 1939 and Gidsken took over as company manager. She signed a huge export contract with Germany and the company prospered until war broke out in 1940. She was jailed, suspected of trading illegally and spying for the Germans. She was released and continued to trade with her German customers. After the war she was put into custody again, but was never proven guilty.

She started up in business again after the war and again was successful. She retired in the 1970s. Gidsken lived out her life with her two younger sisters in a little village near Lillehammer. She died on June 13, 1990 and is buried in Mosjøen near her birthplace. She is considered an important pioneer in Norwegian aeronautical history. She was awarded "Æres-Svarta Bjørn" of Narvik in 1982 and Norwegian Air Shuttles sports her picture on the tail of one of its aircraft. Historian Olav Gynnild has written a compelling biography about her entitled: "Seilas i storm. Et portrett av flypioneren Gidsken Jakobsen," loosely translated as "Sailing in the storm. A portrait of pioneering aviatrix Gidsken Jakobsen." The Norwegian Aviation Museum has a replica of Gidsken's first plane the "Måsen" on display.

Events in 1932

■ Amelia Earhart, flying a Lockheed Vega, becomes the first woman to make a solo flight across the North Atlantic.

that Gidsken had flown home. She was the first woman in the country to own and fly an aircraft.

On December 18, 1929 Gidsken and a Finnish aviator, Ville Leppänen, set off from Narvik, for the naval base in Horten ostensibly to licence the seaplane. It was another illegal flight. The aircraft was unlicensed, Ville was not permitted to work in Norway, and Gidsken's licence did not allow her to carry passengers.

Conditions above the Arctic Circle in midwinter are grim, with no sun for more than a month. On December 18 there would have been a maximum of three or four hours of daylight. The weather is freezing cold with gale force winds. Norway is mountainous, which makes flying overland extremely hazardous.

Gidsken and Ville flew south in an open cockpit aircraft along the coast to Trondheim, then down to Vestlandet on the west coast, finally crossing the Filefjell Mountains. Their flight took them over the frozen inland region to Oslo, where they landed on January 20, 1930. Their trip had lasted for 35 days, gripping the entire nation. Due to bad weather and problems with leaking pontoons, the two pilots had spent the most of the time on the ground. They had also fallen in love.

Most people applauded them. Nobody had ever flown the distance from north to south in winter before, and nobody had ever crossed the Filefjell Mountain in an open cockpit aircraft. Her detractors thought the journey had been much too risky. After a few weeks in Oslo, Gidsken flew back to Narvik. In August 1931 she was forced to sell Måsen in Helsinki since she could not pay the entire purchase price.

In 1932 she co founded Nord-Norges Aero (North Norwegian Airlines) with her father and a third investor. They bought a ten-year-old Junkers F13W seaplane, and christened it "Norge". That

AMELIA EARHART PUTNAM (USA) 1897–1937

"Courage is the price that life exacts for granting peace with yourself."

Amelia Earhart

What happened to Amelia Earhart? The subject of one of the world's most enduring aviation mysteries is also one of the few pilots most people can name. Earhart disappeared in the South Pacific two thirds of the way through an extremely risky attempt at a world record. Her best friend test pilot Jackie Cochran (herself no stranger to danger) was hugely concerned by Earhart's plans for a round the world flight and urged her not to undertake the journey. She might as well have talked to the wind. Earhart once said: "Please know that I am aware of the hazards. I want to do it because I want to do it. Women must try to do things as men have tried. When they fail, their failure must be a challenge to others."

Born on July 24 1897 in Atchison, Kansas, Earhart spent her childhood in various towns, including Kansas City and Des Moines. She had a troubled childhood, and kept herself going by creating a scrapbook of newspaper clippings about women succeeding in a man's world. She began college in Pennsylvania in 1916, but found it stifling and left after just one year.

She headed to her sister in Canada, where she took a Red Cross course in first aid. Earhart then cared for injured soldiers during World War I at Spadina Military Hospital in Toronto. Later she enrolled as a premedical student at New York's Columbia University, but returned to Long Beach, California.

On 28 December 1920, her life changed. She and her father visited an airfield where stunt pilot Frank Hawks gave her a ride.

"By the time I had got two or three hundred feet off the ground," she said, "I knew I had to fly." She worked several jobs, including as a photographer, truck driver and stenographer at the local telephone company and managed to save $1,000 for flying lessons. To put that in context, in 1921 you could buy a new bungalow in Oakland for $2,200.

Her first lesson was on 3 January 1921, at Kinner Field near Long Beach. She had to take a bus, then walk four miles. Her teacher was Anita "Neta" Snook, a pioneer aviator who taught her pupils in a Curtiss JN-4 Canuck. Six months later, Earhart bought her first aircraft, a second-hand bright yellow Kinner Airster. On 22 October 1922, she flew it to an altitude of 14,000 feet, setting a world record for female pilots. On 15 May 1923, she became the 16th woman to be issued a pilot's license by the Fédération Aéronautique Internationale,

Her parents divorced in 1924 and she and her mother relocated to Boston. There Earhart worked first as a teacher, then as a social worker. She maintained her interest in aviation and wrote newspaper columns promoting flying. In 1925 the thrilling young German aviatrix Thea Rasche crashed her aircraft at Dennison airfield. To counteract any negative headlines this might draw about female pilots, Earhart jumped into one of the Waco 10s on site and put on a display for the crowd.

In Boston she met her husband, publisher George Palmer Putnam, who chose her to be the first female passenger on a transatlantic flight. Earhart flew with pilot Wilmer Stultz and mechanic Lou Gordon from Newfoundland to Wales aboard a Trimotor Friendship. Since most of the flight was on instruments, she did not touch the controls. When interviewed after landing, she dismissed her contribution, saying: "Stultz did all the flying - had to. I was just baggage, like a sack of potatoes." She added, "...maybe someday I'll try it alone." However, she received instant fame, which fuelled her desire to earn the accolades in her own right.

She entered the "Powder Puff Derby" in 1929 and came third. The same year, together with several other female fliers, such as Thaden and Ruth Nichols, she founded the Ninety-Nines; the international organisation for women pilots and served as its first president. Earhart championed women's rights, and campaigned hard against discriminatory wage practices. She eventually worked with Purdue University to inspire women to look at aviation and engineering as a career and the school helped sponsor the twin engine Lockheed Electra, used in her final fatal flight.

One of her best friends was Eleanor Roosevelt – the president's wife. Susan Butler's biography "East to the Dawn" documents how Roosevelt was keen to take up flying and Earhart volunteered to teach her. However, the president dissuaded his wife, saying that lessons would be a 'waste of time' since she could not afford to buy a plane.

Earhart's husband was more encouraging and published two books that she wrote about her flying adventures: "The fun of it", and "Last flight." Putnam had already published Charles Lindbergh's writing, and saw his wife's flights as bestsellers. They were married in 1931, but Earhart continued her aviation career under her maiden name. Putman organised Earhart's flights and public appearances, and arranged for her to endorse a line of flight luggage and sports clothes. These endorsements helped finance her flying. She also developed a passenger airline service, along with Lindbergh, the Transcontinental Air Transport (TAT) regional shuttle service between New York and Washington. TAT later became TWA.

She continued to strive for excellence and in 1931 set a world altitude record of 18,415 feet (5,613 m) in a Pitcairn PCA-2 autogiro.

She is perhaps best known for her transatlantic flight. On the morning of 20 May, 1932, Earhart set off from Harbour Grace, Newfoundland, armed with that day's edition of a local newspaper to prove the date she took off. She aimed to fly to Paris in her single engine Lockheed Vega 5b, copying Lindbergh's solo flight. Aviator Bernt Balchen helped her prepare, acting as a decoy for the press, who thought he was chasing an Arctic record. Almost 15 hours later, after battling strong winds, ice and mechanical problems, Earhart landed at Colored, Northern Ireland, the first woman do make the flight alone. She also became the first person to cross the Atlantic twice. She received the Distinguished Flying Cross from congress – the first woman to achieve that accolade. She was also awarded the Cross of Knight of the Legion of Honour from the French Government and the Gold Medal of the National Geographic Society.

She continued breaking records. In January 1935, she became the first person to fly from Honolulu, Hawaii to Oakland, California. This made her the first person to solo anywhere in the Pacific, as well as the first person to solo both the Atlantic and Pacific Oceans. That April she soloed from Los Angeles to Mexico City. Her next record was a non-stop flight from Mexico City to New York. Between 1930–1935, she set seven women's speed and distance aviation records in a variety of aircraft.

In June 1937, Earhart embarked on her fateful final flight. Before she set off to circumnavigate the world she said: "Women must try to do things as men have tried. When they fail, their failure must be but a challenge to others." The venture was dogged with problems from the outset. Her original team had fallen through. Her twin Lockheed Electra 10E developed mechanical problems and she had to abort her first flight plan and fly in the opposite direction. Navigator Fred Noonan was an unreliable heavy drinker. On 2 July 1937 the pair took off from Lae in New Guinea after 22,000 miles of flying. Their intended destination was Howland Island, just 6,500 ft (2,000 metres) long and 2,556 miles (4,113 km) away in the middle of the ocean. The US coast guard ship Itasca was standing by at Howland, ready to help guide them in.

That morning the Itasca received strong and clear voice transmissions from Earhart, however she apparently was unable to hear them. At 7:42 am she said: "We must be on you, but cannot see you – but gas is running low. Have been unable to reach you by radio. We are flying at 1,000 feet." Her last known broadcasts came at 8:43 am. "We are on the line 157 337. We will repeat this message. We will repeat this on 6210 kilocycles. Wait." A few moments later she said: "We are running on line north and south."

They were never heard or seen again.

In 1939, Putnam wrote Earhart's biography, "Soaring Wings", as a tribute to his beloved wife. She was enshrined in the National Aviation Hall of Fame in 1968. There are numerous books about her and her birthplace is now a museum.

She is deservedly one of America's national treasures.

More events in 1932

- Charles Lindbergh's baby boy is kidnapped and later found dead.
- Luftschiffbau Zeppelin begins regular trans-Atlantic services between Germany and Brazil.
- Amy Johnson breaks the UK-Cape Town speed record in a de Havilland Puss Moth.

ANNE MORROW LINDBERGH (USA) 1906 – 2001

A lady who was not averse to flinging herself off mountains in pursuit of knowledge and fun, Anne Morrow Lindbergh's achievements are not as widely known as those of her husband, flamboyant aviator Charles. However, she was a noted writer and aviation pioneer in her own right.

orn on June 22nd 1906 in Englewood, New Jersey, Anne Spencer Morrow came from an affluent background. She was the second of the four children of US Senator Dwight Morrow and poet and women's education advocate Elizabeth Cutter Morrow. The family encouraged achievement and each day 5pm her mother would drop everything and read to her children. As the children grew, they learned to set aside that hour and would use it to read by themselves, or to write poetry and diaries. This stood Anne in good stead in adulthood as she was already accustomed to writing regularly. She eventually published several volumes of her diaries.

Anne finished at the Chapin School in New York in 1924, and went on to Smith College, graduating with a Bachelor of Arts degree in 1928. While she was there, she won two writing prizes; one for an essay she wrote on women of the eighteenth century and another for her fictional piece entitled "Lida Was Beautiful".

She met her husband to be, Charles Lindbergh, in Mexico when her father, who was Charles' financial adviser, invited him over. Anne and Charles were married at her parents' home in Englewood on May 27th, 1929. Their 45-year marriage produced six children and many glittering achievements.

Aviation permeated their life together from the outset. Within a few months of their wedding, Anne flew solo for the first time. The following year she became the first American woman to earn a first class glider pilot's license. This came about through the Lindbergh's helping Charles' enthusiastic friend, engineer W Hawley Bowlus develop his gliders. Bowlus was keen to get people using his prototype sailplanes and gliders, which he believed would make aviation cheaper and more accessible. Anne gamely tested some of them out. Author Anne Lewis Cooper writes in "Stars of the Sky: Legends All" of Anne's initial terror about being winched off a mountain alone in the prototype aircraft that her husband's friend Hawley Bowlus had built to make flying cheaper for young people. Fortunately that fear turned to joy as she soared over the fields. She was pregnant at the time with her first child, the son who was to die in terrible circumstances.

Anne and Charles spent a great deal of their early marriage flying. She acted as co-pilot, navigator and radio operator to her husband and they flew several exploratory missions. They set out to plot potential air routes for commercial airlines. One of their tasks was to survey the continent and the Caribbean to map out Pan American's air mail service. In 1931 they flew a single-engine Lockheed Sirius over uncharted routes from Canada and Alaska to Japan and China. Anne wrote about this journey in her first book," North to the Orient."

Tragedy struck when on March 1, 1932 their 20-month old baby son Charles Augustus Lindbergh III, was kidnapped from their home in New Jersey. After an enormous search, a baby's body was found on May 12, four miles away on top of a hill on the Hopewell-Mt. Rose Highway. The Lindberghs were right at the centre of huge media attention. Bruno Richard Hauptmann was charged, convicted and executed for the crime. The couple eventually had enough and

fled America. They moved first to England, to a house called "Long Barn" owned by Harold Nicholson and Vita Sackville-West, and then to the small island of Iliec, off the coast of France. They had five more children: three sons: Jon, Land and Scott, and two daughters Anne and Reeve.

Shortly after the death of Chares Jr in 1932, perhaps partly to escape the attention and come to terms with their loss, they took off in 1933 on a five and a half month 30,000 mile (48, 280 kilometre) survey of North and South Atlantic air routes. They flew in the same aircraft that they had used two years earlier. Anne's next book, "Listen! the Wind" documents that flight. Charles had made his name internationally with his pioneering New York-to-Paris flight back in 1927 in the "Spirit of St. Louis." However, he said that their 1933 expedition was more difficult and hazardous than his earlier epic journey.

In 1933 Anne was awarded the Cross of Honor of the US Flag Association for her part in the survey of transatlantic air routes. The National Geographic Society honoured her with its Hubbard Gold Medal in 1934 for her accomplishments in 40,000 miles (63,374 kilometres) of exploratory flying over five continents alongside her husband. She was the first woman to achieve that honour. In 1993, sixty years after she had received the Cross of Honor, Women in Aerospace presented her with a special Aerospace Explorer Award in recognition of her achievements and contributions to the aerospace field. In addition, she was inducted into the National Aviation Hall of Fame, the National Women's Hall of Fame, and the Aviation Hall of Fame of New Jersey. She was also a recipient of the Christopher Award for the fifth volume of her diaries, "War Within and Without."

Over the course of their 45-year marriage, Charles and Anne lived in New Jersey, New York, England, France, Maine, Michigan, Connecticut, Switzerland, and Hawaii. Charles died on Maui in 1974. Anne survived him by another twenty-six years and died on February 7th, 2001 aged 94 at home in Vermont. She remained close to her children throughout her lifetime.

Anne wrote thirteen published books. They include "Earth Shine," in which she wrote of being at Cape Kennedy for the first moon-orbiting flight and how moved she was by the beauty of the earth when she looked at the pictures beamed back form the Apollo 8 flight. She talked of having "a new sense of Earth's richness and beauty." Perhaps her best known work was "Gift from the Sea," as well as five volumes of diaries and letters from the years 1922 - 1944.

Events in 1933

- ■ **Hitler becomes German chancellor**
- ■ **Esquire debuts as the first men's magazine**

■ The Lindberghs left a truly great legacy, both in actions and consequences of their actions.

Fifty years after Charles' epic fight, their friends created the Charles A. and Anne Morrow Lindbergh Foundation in 1977. Luminaries such as General James H. Doolittle and astronaut Neil Armstrong were involved in its inception. Their intent was to honour the Lindberghs' pioneering contributions in aviation, exploration, conservation, sciences, and the humanities. The Lindberghs believed it was important to strike a balance between technological advancements and the preservation of the human and natural environments they cherished. The Foundation today seeks to support present and future generations in working toward such a balance. This is entirely in keeping with Anne's statement in her book "Earth Shine" that "power over life must be balanced by reverence for life."

JANET HARMON BRAGG (USA) 1907 – 1993

The bumblebee who was not aware she could not fly

According to recognised aeronautical principles the bumblebee cannot fly. But the bumblebee does not know this. The bumblebee goes ahead and flies anyway. Thus went Janet Bragg's response to critics who told her black women did not have the mental ability to fly. She stood up to racism and sexism to become the first African American woman to earn a full commercial pilot's license.

Janet Bragg was born Janet Harmon in Griffin, Georgia, in 1907, the youngest of seven children. Her parents Cordia Batts Harmon and Samuel Harmon, a brick contractor were determined to give her the best grounding possible and transferred her from a public elementary school to St. Stephens Episcopal School, which was a better learning environment in those days of strict segregation. Janet's grandfather had been a freed slave of Spanish descent, and her grandmother was a Cherokee.

Janet also attended Fort Valley Episcopal High School in Georgia. She went on to major in nursing at the all female, all black Spelman Seminary in Atlanta, Georgia. A testament to the benefit of a loving and supportive background, Janet said: "We were a very happy family. We were not a rich family, only rich in love, which... meant everything."

She did her practical training at MacBicar Hospital, where she was one of only two of the twelve students who entered the course to graduate after her probationary period. Nursing students helped out during operations and performed other procedures usually handled by interns.

This meant they had first class on the job experience. Janet received her registered nurse degree in 1929. She moved to Chicago and nursed at Wilson Hospital. There she met her first husband, Evans Waterford. She divorced him a few years later, but retained his name until her second marriage.

She worked for an insurance company in Chicago during the depression and the owners encouraged her to pursue her education. She had been interested in flying since she was a child. The story

goes that she spotted a billboard in 1933 with a drawing of a nest containing chicks. The caption read: "Birds learn to fly. Why can't you?" This sparked her interest.

She had also dated one of the first African American flight instructors, Johnny Robinson. She was so fired up by the notion of flying that she saved enough money to take flying lessons herself. In 1935 she enrolled at the Curtiss Wright Aeronautical School. The school segregated its black and white students, and Janet was the first black female student in a class of 24 men. They had no tools, so she bought a set from Sears. She learned how to take care of aeroplanes. She was also able to take a few lessons at a private airport, but this proved costly at $15 per hour.

While doing postgraduate work at Loyola University and the University of Chicago, she worked as a registered nurse at several hospitals. She spent $500 on a 2,100 lb, red biplane with a Curtiss OX-S 90-horsepower engine, which she rented to other students to make it earn its keep. Thanks to Janet the others were also able to learn to fly. This group became the foundation of the Challenger Aero Club.

Like her contemporary Willa Brown, she constantly battled discrimination on two fronts: she was African-American and female. She had to deal with the constant gloom of segregation.

In that era black people were banned from airports that served white pilots and passengers. So she suggested the Challenger Aero Club members pool their resources and buy land in the all-black town of Robbins, Illinois.

There they built their own airfield. They carved a runway paved with crushed coal cinders and built a hangar from scrap wood. Members would take- off from this rudimentary airfield and fly around the US, promoting aviation to other African-Americans. They eventually moved to Harlem airfield. As the club grew, it needed more aircraft. Again, Janet funded its growth and bought two more aeroplanes, a Piper J3 Cub and a Piper Cruiser.

The Challenger Air Pilots Association, (CAPA) later evolved into the Coffey School of Aeronautics, run by Willa Brown and Cornelius Coffey. This was the fruition of pioneering barnstorming aviatrix

Programme, that offered advanced flying degrees and certificates for civilians. The interviewer [a female] said to her: "I didn't know there was any colored girls flying." Janet replied: "There are plenty of them flying."

However, since the training was at Sweetwater, Texas, the interviewer concluded that there would be no place for Mrs. Bragg to stay. Janet appealed and that, too, was unsuccessful.

Determined to help with the war effort she applied to fly with the military nurse corps, but was told that the quota for black nurses was filled.

In 1942 she was ready to take her commercial pilot's license test in Tuskegee, Alabama, where African American pilots trained. She passed her written exams and her flight test. However, the Federal Aviation Administration white instructor was not about to award a black woman a pilot's license in Alabama. He said: "She gave me a good flight. I will put her up against any of your flight instructors. But I've never given a colored girl a commercial license, and I don't intend to now."

America was so set on denying black people the opportunity to fly that Eugene Bullard and Bessie Coleman had to go to France to learn. Bullard went on to fly combat missions and was highly decorated in both World Wars.

Janet finally received her commercial license in 1943 at the Pal-Waukee Airport near Chicago, becoming the first black woman to do so. In 1946, she purchased a Super Cruiser, in which she logged many hours of cross-country flying.

She continued to work as a health inspector and decided to go into business for herself. Together with her brother, she bought a health care facility for patients on welfare benefits. Their idea eventually grew into a nursing home, housing sixty residents. In 1951 she married her second husband Sumner Bragg. The Braggs built up a successful nursing home franchise, which they operated until 1972.

During the 1970's, Janet travelled extensively in Africa. She had visited Ethiopia decades earlier at the behest of Emperor Haile Selassie. She was an active participate in the Tucson Arizona Urban League, Habitat for Humanity, and the Adopt-a-Scholar Program at Pima College.

Bessie Coleman's dream of a decade earlier. This school and five other black colleges participated in the Civilian Pilot Training Programme (CPTP) that later fed students into the Army Air Corps training program at Tuskegee, Alabama.

Janet passed her private pilot's license test in the spring of 1934, after thirty-five solo hours. During this period, she wrote a weekly report for the newspaper that had championed Coleman a decade earlier, the Chicago Defender. Her column was called, "Negro Aviation," by-lined "Janet Waterford."

Janet's father had taught her never to let her race or gender stand in the way of realising her dreams. In 1939, she reportedly applied to enter the Women's Auxiliary Service Pilots (WASP). She was rejected because she was black. Along with other African-American aviators, she was denied entrance into the Civilian Pilot Training

Events in 1934

■ **Jean Batten sets a new women's speed record between England and Australia. She flies a de Havilland DH.60 and makes the trip in 14 days 22 hours.**

■ **Mao Zedong begins the Long March north with 100,000 soldiers.**

■ **Clyde Barrow and Bonnie Parker ambushed by lawmen in Louisiana. John Dillinger is shot outside Chicago movie theatre**

Her achievements were finally recognised in the 1980's. She was invited to appear at aviation events around the country and received many awards and honours. She died in Blue Island, Illinois, on April 11, 1993. Her autobiography, *Soaring Above Setbacks*, with Marjorie Kriz, was published in 1996.

Janet Bragg earned her place as one of the greats because she refused to become cowed or embittered. She once wrote: "I hope that my experiences and the experiences of others will serve a twofold purpose:

1) to convey the price that had to be paid to lay the foundation for today; but more importantly:

2) I hope black youth will realise the kind of strength of character, the kind of determination and the importance of setting a goal, and [not] allowing anything to deter one from achieving that goal."-

1934

FREDA MARY THOMPSON (AUSTRALIA) 1906 – 1980

Long distance pioneer who championed women in aviation

reda Thompson believed that nerves of steel were more important than brute strength. By 1980 the globe trotting aviatrix had logged over 3,330 hours of flight time in a variety of airframes, from Gypsy Moths to World War II military aircraft. She had acquired an impressive array of licences, qualifying her to fly in all weathers and at night, by relying on her instruments and wits. For Freda, flying was not a means to greater wealth or celebrity. It was her passion and she indulged it with every winged fibre of her being.

Freda Thompson was born on 5th April 1906 in South Yarra, Melbourne. She hailed from an affluent family. Her father was a successful banker. One day, shuffling home from Toorak College, she was brought out of her reverie by a small aeroplane skimming over the rooftops. The ungainly contraption struck a harmonious chord in the young girl.

Thanks to her wealthy family Freda was a member of the privileged propeller-set few, able to travel by aircraft when commercial air travel was expensive and still in its infancy. In 1926 on a trip with the rest of the family to Europe she wrote in her diary that the plane ride from Paris to London was a "Jolly fine fly. Would go again if I could."

She did indeed go up again, this time in May 1930 when she had her first flying lesson at Essendon, Melbourne. She caught the flying bug. On 16th December that year she gained her private Class A licence. In 1932 she became the fifth woman in Australia to be awarded a commercial Class B qualification. Then just a year later she achieved a first for any woman in the Commonwealth British Empire by qualifying for a flying instructor rating. However, research suggests that she never used the rating to train others.

Her plan to become a world-class yachtswoman had been ditched, as her burgeoning ambition turned towards aviation. The privileged pilot had accumulated close to 290 hours of flying experience, and decided to enter the upcoming 1934 air race from England to Australia. She needed a suitable aircraft for the marathon challenge.

She set sail for England and purchased a factory fresh De Havilland Moth Major, fitted with long-range fuel tanks in preparation for the competition. For the sum of £1,000 she was at the controls of her new biplane, which she christened the "Christopher Robin." While in England she obtained a "Great Britain Air Ministry Private Pilot Certificate," giving her the licence to fly a variety of aircraft types.

Her dreams of race glory were dashed, as she was too late in submitting her entry application, so her place in history was denied. Mitigating her disappointment, Freda decided to undertake a solo flight to Australia, with hopes of beating New Zealander Jean Gardner Batten's record time of 14 days and 22 and half hours.

Freda's epic journey began at Lympne Aerodrome in Kent on 28th September 1934. Her destination would have been La Bourget airport in Paris, but she never arrived. En route, she battled severe weather and had to alight at an airfield in Marignane several miles from her destination. She sought refuge in a local hotel and was blissfully unaware that her absence had sparked a desperate search by the French authorities for the missing aviatrix.

The next day she took off in calmer weather and headed towards Rome, with the intention of making Greece before nightfall. Confusion over time zones between the Italy to Greece leg resulted in her having to fly in complete darkness without night vision aids. She was forced to land in an olive grove in Megara, 30 miles from Athens. The landing caused significant damage to the plane as she clipped telephone wires and broke her undercarriage. In relative isolation the grounded aviatrix dusted herself off and managed to locate the nearest town. The friendly folk of Megara came to her aid. The local mayor intervened personally in arrangements for her aircraft to be repaired in Athens. The delay was costly, close to three weeks, with her aspiration of slashing Jean Batten's record looking slimmer.

The Christopher Robin repaired and its tanks topped up with high-octane fuel, the intrepid Freda finally returned to the skies on 21st October. This leg of the journey took her to Damascus through Nicosia. She made it as far as Baghdad before landing at Bushire, Persia. So far, so good on the voyage, her proficiency and mounting confidence in navigation using basic maps and a compass had seen her through the overland portion of the journey.

Eventually the final perilous challenge stretched before her. Over 500 miles of choppy ocean lay between her and Darwin. The East Timor Sea crossing filled her with dread, as she did not have the luxury of dry land to cushion an emergency landing. She flew almost blind for approximately two hours at a height of 2,000 feet to avoid the ominous cloud layer. Below miles of ocean stretched

before her, and Freda later described herself being "in the blue funk" during the crossing.

Her fears were unfounded as she and her Moth landed safely in Darwin on 6th November. Her entire journey had taken over 39 days, but her actual flying time was 19 days, missing out on beating Jean Batten's record by five days. Homeward bound to Melbourne she became lost and had to set down in the Northern Territories in order to get her bearings in the featureless landscape. Serendipity smiled on Freda as a mounted policemen had pinpointed her location 16 miles south of Darwin.

Word must have reached the local flying clubs from New South Wales to Essendon as Freda received a light plane escort all the way to her destination. The final aircraft to guide her in were from the club where she had learnt to fly, the Royal Victorian Aero Club. For her bravery she was awarded the George VI Coronation Medal in 1937.

At the onset of the Second World War Freda parted with her adored Moth. During the war years, she served as commandant of the Women's Air Training Corps from 1940- 1942. She also attempted to join the Women's Auxiliary Australian Air Force, but was surprisingly unsuccessful in her application. Instead she volunteered with the Australian Women's Army Service in 1942, serving as an ambulance driver. In 1945 Freda also took on the role of ferrying decommissioned Royal Australian Air Force aircraft to Geelong

Following the war, Freda returned to flying and bought a De Havilland Hornet Moth from fellow aviatrix Nancy Lyle. The aeroplane was appropriately named the Christopher Robin II. Freda used her new Moth for further endurance records, taking her as far as Papua, New Guinea. She competed in air races, such as the Adelaide Air Derby, winning a total of 47 trophies in her prized aeroplane. Freda was also an honorary life member of the Royal Victorian Aero Club, becoming its president in 1948.

In 1952 she flew as co-pilot on a Norseman plane operated by Gibbes Sepik Airways, flying to Papua New Guinea. 1953 saw Freda awarded the Elizabeth II Coronation Medal, culminating in an Officer of the British Empire (OBE) appointment in 1972. She was a founder member of the Australian Women Pilots' Association (AWPA). AWPA honoured her in 1973 by establishing the Freda Thompson Aerial Derby, a race for women pilots with its circuit around Port Philip Bay. She was also a member of the American women's pilot organisation, the Ninety Nines.

Freda lost her fight to cancer on 11th December 1980, but not before flying one last jaunt in a Tiger Moth in May of that year. A quote from one of Freda's papers expresses her nostalgia and affection for the early days of pioneering aviation: "In those days we just landed in paddocks, or on dirt roads wherever we wanted to go…The planes were like kites—you could fly them anywhere and they were graceful little craft to travel in."

Freda did not covet fame. Her awards and recognition came by virtue of her selfless deeds in promoting flying to women. Perhaps this is why her country remembers her so fondly. Even today the National Library of Australia has an extensive collection of her logbooks, diaries, licences and flying gear on display.

More events in 1934

- Benjamin and Joseph Adamowicz brothers, amateur pilots, flew across the Atlantic
- Imperial Airways extends its airmail service to Australia.
- Hitler becomes Führer when chancellorship and presidency are united.

1935

JACQUELINE COCHRAN (USA) 1906 – 1980

Jacqueline 'Jackie' Cochran's exact birth date isn't clear; research cites anything between 1906 and 1910. But what is unequivocal is the extent to which she rose like a fiery phoenix to reduce her ragged past to ashes. By founding a cosmetics empire and holding more speed, altitude, and distance records than any other male or female pilot ever, she had discovered the alchemist's formula of turning lead to gold.

Jackie Cochran's destitute beginnings were certainly at the start of the 1900s. She found a home with a poor foster family in Pensacola, Florida. Growing up fast in the sawdust roads, cotton fields and textile mills of the sweltering panhandle, it was alleged that she had never known her biological parents. Toiling in the cotton mills by aged eight, she only started to wear shoes by the age of nine. No bed to sleep in, she resorted to curling up on a hard wooden pallet, or just an even harder floor. Unsubstantiated folklore has it that she chose her name 'Jacqueline Cochran' from a phone book. The harsh existence deprived her of an education. She left after two years of schooling and would always have difficulties with reading and writing. Later in life taking an exam to earn a pilot's licence would necessitate the concession of an oral test as opposed to anything written.

During her early teens Jackie left her foster family and ebbed out a meagre existence as a nomadic nanny living in to care for new arrivals. Menial work at a beauty parlour in Montgomery Alabama was the turning point for Jackie. From sweeping floors she became an accomplished hairdresser, adept with a wave-inducing machine. Jackie demonstrated a flair for styling to become a firm favourite among regular patrons.

Relocating to New York in 1920, she started weaving her hair magic at the swanky Antoine salons in Saks Fifth Avenue, New York and outlets in Miami. Such was the demand of her hairdressing skills that she would visit clientele residing in Miami Beach. A chance encounter in 1932 with dashing millionaire businessman and her future husband, Floyd Bostwick Odlum inspired her to reach for her lofty goals by learning to fly. She spent a three-week summer vacation in 1932 at the Roosevelt Flying School in Long Island, New York. In that short time she defied convention by gaining a pilot's licence. She then embarked upon establishing a string of aviation records throughout the thirties.

In that same decade Jackie's entrepreneurial spirit helped her establish her own cosmetics company with a factory in New Jersey and offices in New York. Her successful enterprise, whose motto

was "Wings to Beauty," funded her passion for flying and competing in air races.

In 1934 she flew and tested the first turbo-supercharger ever installed on an aircraft engine and gained her commercial transport licence. By 1935 she became the first woman to compete in the Bendix Transcontinental Air Race from Los Angeles to Cleveland Ohio. Mechanical problems forced her to abandon the race. In 1936 her whirlwind romance with Floyd Bostwick Odlum bloomed into marriage. His business interests in pioneering aviation companies and political clout would eventually leverage Jackie into the cockpit of jet fighters during the post war years.

Pushy, abrasive, disliked by many, and at times manipulative, Jackie was not one to take "no" for an answer, or be denied the chance to achieve what was perceived by many as impossible. In 1937 she attained first place in the women's division of the Bendix race and third overall. During that year Jackie flew from New York to Miami in a record-breaking 4 hours and 12 minutes and made the first blind instrument landing for a woman.

Flying an experimental Republic P-35 Seversky fighter allowed her to slide into first place and finally capture the elusive Bendix Trophy in 1938. For her aviation accomplishments thus far, she received the General Willie E. Mitchell Memorial Award. In addition to this she was awarded the Clifford Burke Harmon Trophy as the "most outstanding woman pilot" successively from 1938 to 1940. It would be a trophy she would win fourteen times thereafter. Her air racing exploits introduced her to Amelia Earhart and the two became firm friends. She served as president of Amelia's Ninety Nines organisation for US women pilots from 1941 until 1943.

The onset of war in 1939 prompted Jackie to approach General 'Hap' Arnold to suggest the use of women pilots for the war effort. He promptly rejected her plans, saying the loss of women pilots in air combat would not be acceptable. The general's dismissal caused her consternation, but Jackie went on to set further altitude and speed records during the early 40's, winning a succession of awards in the process.

Another first for Jackie was the piloting of a US bomber across to England in 1941 at the behest of General 'Hap' Arnold. Sensing a severe pilot shortage, he had recruited her to investigate the British women's Air Transport Auxiliary operation (ATA), with a view to creating a similar organisation in the US. Jackie did so and eventually returned to England with a select group of 25 American women to fly for the British ATA. Their ostentatious, hard partying and cavalier approach was often frowned upon by many of the more reserved members of the ATA.

Jackie continued her crusade for the inclusion of women in the air force, ruffling more than a few feathers in the upper echelons of the US government and the Air Corps. Her vocal lobbying was the complete antithesis to Nancy Harkness Love and her more amenable approach for the establishment of a women's air force unit. In anticipation of the pilot shortage Jackie was made head of the Women's Flying Training Detachment (WFTD), tasked with training civilian women pilots in

Events in 1935

■ Nazis enact Nuremberg Laws against Jews to prevent "racial pollution." Heinrich Himmler starts breeding programme to produce "Aryan super race.

■ Howard Hughes, flying the Hughes H-1 Racer, set the airspeed record of 352 mph.

November 1942. In August 1943 it was merged with Nancy H Love's Women's Auxiliary Ferry Squadron (WAFS) to establish the Women Air Force Service Pilots (WASP). Jackie was made overall commander of the WASP with Nancy serving as director for the aircraft ferrying operations. From 1943 to 1944, 1,074 women trained and flew over 60 million miles (96,561,000 km), ferrying aircraft, towing targets, and performing other logistical flying duties.

Much to Jackie's dismay the WASP was disbanded in December 1944, despite their exemplary and often better performance than the lesser-qualified male pilots. The Distinguished Service Medal awarded to her failed to assuage her disappointment.

The ending of the WASP marked a new chapter for Jackie's adventures in aviation. She competed again for the Bendix trophy in 1946, finishing a respectable second. The dawning of the jet era brought with it new challenges. In 1953 Jackie became the first woman to simultaneously establish a new speed record of 652 mph (1,049 km/h) and break the sound barrier in an F-86 Sabre Jet fighter. Legendary test pilot Chuck Yeager assisted Jackie throughout her jet flying exploits from Edwards Air Force base. In 1959 she became the first woman president of the venerable Federation Aeronautique International.

In 1961 Jackie set eight speed records in the new T-38 trainer adopted by the USAF. In the Talon she would establish a new altitude record of over 55,000 feet (16,764 metres). Later that year she flew in the F-104G Starfighter to claim a third speed record of over 1,429 mph (2,300 km/h) beating the existing women's record of 1,266 mph (2,037 km/h) held by the well-known French aviatrix Jacqueline Auriol. Cochran and Auriol would tussle with one another from afar, each trying to overturn the other's speed and altitude records. Her obsessive record-breaking initiatives in jet airframes would continue from 1962 until 1964.

But ill health would ground her during the seventies. A living legend, in 1971, Jacqueline Cochran became enshrined in the Aviation Hall of Fame in Dayton, Ohio, the first woman to have the honour bestowed upon her.

On August 9, 1980 Jacqueline Cochran died at her home in Indio, California. Memorial services were held at the US Air Force Academy, Colorado Springs, Colorado. Jackie's ascension was nothing short of meteoric. A rags to riches story from barefoot forsaken child working in a textile mill to presiding over a women's militarised air force, and finally her unrivalled success in establishing many speed records in jet fighters. Much has been written about Jackie through the ages with some of it being subject to conjecture, or even embellishment. Her name may not be spoken as much as that of Amelia Earhart, but her contribution to aviation and creation of opportunities for women is undeniable.

Jackie Cochran's birth date may not be known exactly, but when she entered the world the concussive force from the sonic booms of her pioneering achievements made everyone sit up and take note of this remarkable and fearless aviatrix.

LOUISE MCPHETRIDGE THADEN (USA) 1905 – 1979

Won first "Powder Puff Derby," and took home first prize competing against men in the Bendix Transcontinental Air Race

wonder what we've done wrong now!" Louise Thaden proclaimed in exasperation to her co-pilot Blanche Noyes in the Beechcraft Staggerwing at the end of the 1936 Bendix air race. The large group of men rushing towards them was intimidating. Both nervous of the impending confrontation there was little expectation of a warm reception let alone a place in history...

Louise McPhetridge Thaden was born on November 12th 1905. She was quite possibly dreaming about flying from the moment she opened her eyes for the first time. Raised in Bentonville, Arkansas, her father was a travelling Mentholatum salesman. He encouraged Louise's tomboy pursuits, such as hunting, fishing and fixing cars. A $5 joyride in 1919 with a barnstormer was her first experience with powered flight. She attended the University of Arkansas from 1921 to 1925 but left without completing her degree in journalism.

Relocating to Wichita Kansas she found employment as a sales clerk with a coal and building materials company, JHJ Turner Coal. The proprietor, Jack Turner was intrigued by the amount of time the young woman spent visiting a local aircraft manufacturer, the Travel Air Company. He introduced a starry eyed Louise to his friend and owner of Travel Air, one Walter Beech. Impressed by her enthusiasm and spirit for airplanes he offered her a job as a saleswoman at a Travel Air distributor dealership in Oakland California. Part of her remuneration was flying lessons and she soloed by February 1928 earning an official pilot's licence on May 16th.

Amid her flying lessons romance would bloom for Louise when she met Herbert von Thaden, a former United States Army pilot and engineer at Oakland Airport. He was developing one of America's first all-metal aircraft. Louise and Herbert Thaden were eventually married on July 21, 1928.

Orville Wright's signature gracing her licence gave Louise the permission to take the aviation world by storm. She became the first and only pilot to claim altitude, solo endurance and speed records in straight rapid-fire succession. Five months after tying the knot, in December 1928 she established the women's altitude record of 20,260 feet flying a company owned Travel Air. This was followed by a solo endurance

record in March 1929. Louise stayed airborne for an uninterrupted 22 hours. She then throttled towards a speed record of 156 mph in April. Barely pausing for breath in 1929, Louise became the fourth aviatrix in the United States to qualify for her commercial transport licence.

With the ink hardly dry on her commercial licence, Louise caused quite a stir at the first 'Powder Puff Derby' in August 1929. She tore through the 2,500-mile Transcontinental Women's Air Derby stretching from Santa Monica to Cleveland, Ohio to win the race. Brushed aside were equally capable flyers such as Amelia Earhart and Blanche Noyes in a race featuring several mishaps and one fatality. Gladys O'Donnell finished second to Louise and Amelia Earhart came third. Louise recalled her privileged moment of observing other competitor planes roar across the finish line until "a glistening row of wings shimmered in the sun, lined up in front of the longer centre grandstand."

Later that year, Louise along with Amelia and others founded the Ninety-Nines, an organisation dedicated to the needs of licensed women US pilots. Louise would serve a stint as vice-president and treasurer for the organisation, which would one day expand to encompass women pilots beyond the shores of the United States.

The 1930's sparked an interest for setting endurance records, with a few tenacious and pioneering women vying to establish unbreakable records. In 1932 Louise, along with Frances Marsalis, demonstrated real staying power by flying 196 hours straight from 14th to 22nd August to set a new refuelling endurance record over Long Island, New York. The endeavour required their aircraft, a Curtiss Thrush, to be refuelled a staggering seventy-eight times by an overhead supply plane. Food, water, oil, and fuel were passed down to the two by means of a rope from the designated lifeline plane. The press were intrigued by the marathon undertaking describing the event as "the Flying Boudoir". Both Louise and Frances also managed to deliver a series of live radio broadcasts from their noisy open cockpit biplane.

Louise then immersed herself into the commercial world of aviation by taking on the role of demonstration pilot for the Beech Aircraft Corporation. In this capacity she shared a similar career path to another pioneer, Nancy Harkness Love, who was also

Events in 1936

- ■ The first flight by the Irish airline Aer Lingus takes place.

- ■ 1936 Summer Olympics open in Berlin, Germany, and marks the first live TV coverage of a sports event.

employed by Beech Aircraft. Like Nancy, Louise would be recruited by Phoebe Omlie in 1934 to work for the Bureau of Air Commerce as part of the air-marking project. The endeavour involved identifying prominent landmarks visible from the air to serve as additional navigation aids for pilots. Louise was assigned to the western part of the country having an eagle eye's view for instructing the painting of compass points upon water towers, barn roofs and hillsides.

The year 1936 was the defining moment for Louise when she managed to scoop the Bendix Transcontinental Air Race trophy. This was the first race where the ban imposed upon women pilots had been lifted allowing them to compete equally with male participants.

Louise didn't achieve this milestone alone. Blanche Noyes was in the co-pilot seat of her Beech Staggerwing C17R. It was Olive Beech who convinced her husband Walter Beech to loan the bi-wing plane to Louise for the New York to Los Angeles run. She believed that a victory would whip the media into frenzy if the pilot were a woman.

The bright blue Staggerwing with its intrepid occupants battled severe weather and an inoperative radio. They finally crossed the finishing line a little red faced. Fearing that they had come in last and landed on the wrong side of the finishing line, Louise and Blanche tried to taxi inconspicuously away from the throng of spectators in the grandstands. Ducking down in the light blue plane was futile; the large group of animated men looking like a lynch mob gave chase to sheepish crew of the trundling Staggerwing.

An article by Irene Stuber described the commotion on the ground and cockpit conversation when it transpired, much to their astonishment, that after fourteen hours and fifty-five minutes since leaving Brooklyn that theirs was the first plane across the finish line. The lynch mob was in fact race officials trying to catch their attention and inform them of their victorious standing. It was not long before the triumphant pairing faced a stroboscopic display of popping flashguns. The reed thin Louise and Blanche stood

smile, both pocketing the top prize of $5000 in addition to the $2000, the agreed consolation award set aside for women competitors. The token gesture was the decided compensation payable to the first woman to finish. The predominantly male officials believed that none of the women would actually complete the course. For Louise and Blanche it made for a sweeter victory by having successfully fended off the entire racing contingent of men to capture the coveted trophy. Furthermore their achievement laid waste to the claim that women were perceived not as accomplished and skilled as their male counterparts in the art of flying.

For her achievements in 1936, Louise won aviation's highest honour given to a female pilot, the Harmon Trophy, in April 1937. She also took charge at one time the Penn School of Aviation in Pittsburgh, where both men and women alike trained to fly. During her tenure she demonstrated that women took no more time or resources in learning to fly than male students.

Louise did return briefly to the Beechcraft Company before hanging up her flying jacket for good and retiring from the competition circuit in 1938. That same year she penned her memoirs entitled High, Wide, and Frightened. In 1938 the Bendix trophy would be won by another woman, Jacqueline Cochran, flying an experimental P-35 Seversky fighter to claim the trophy.

Louise turned her energies towards raising a family during the thirties. She did a stint with the Civil Air Patrol during the war years, rising to the rank of colonel, following a battle with alcoholism.

In addition to her memoirs, she wrote numerous newspaper and magazine articles dealing with various aviation issues, and continued to be active in several aviation organizations. She flew everything from jets to gliders.

Louise McPhetridge Thaden passed away on November 9th 1979 at High Point, North Carolina aged 74. The Bentonville airport was named after her in 1951 and a national Staggerwing Museum was also dedicated in her name. In 1980 she was enshrined in the Arkansas Aviation Hall of

1936
JEAN GARDNER BATTEN (NEW ZEALAND) 1909 – 1982

The Greta Garbo of the skies

ose to nose in the traditional Maori greeting; Jean Gardner Batten was welcomed home by the chief of a local tribe, following her magnificent flight. The indigenous Maori, tough warriors and explorers themselves, honoured her return to Rotura, New Zealand by bestowing her with the title "Hine-o-te-Rangi," "daughter of the skies." For the intensely private aviatrix, the ceremony was the culmination of a long and difficult journey.

The enigmatic flyer eventually swapped celebrity for anonymity, much to the bemusement of many who felt she had the world at her feet. Her striking beauty, along with her eccentricities, coined her the nickname used as the title of Ian Mackersey's excellent biography: *Jean Batten: The Garbo of the Skies.*

Jean Gardner Batten was a ruthless and ambitious aviatrix who broke a few hearts as well as records en route to her place in history. New Zealand's answer to Amy Johnson offered much hope and diversion to those ensnared by the talons of the Great Depression.

Her journey began in Rotura, New Zealand. She was born on September 15th 1909, the youngest of three children. Her mother, Ellen, may have had a flash of inspiration when she pinned a photograph of pioneering pilot Louis Bleriot on the wall next to her daughter's cot. Her father went to fight in World War I, and by the time he returned from the trenches the relationship between Jean's parents deteriorated enough to a force a separation. The family was split along gender lines, and Jean took up residence with her mother.

Gifted academically, Jean excelled in most subjects and toyed with the idea of becoming a concert pianist. However, in 1927 she was intrigued by the exploits of Charles Lindbergh and his epic transatlantic flight. The following year Australian bomber pilot

Charles Kingsford Smith crossed the Pacific in his Fokker Tri-motor named Southern Cross.

Both gutsy endeavours fomented new passions within the starry-eyed teenager and she sought out the intrepid Kingsford Smith. Jean declared her desire to fly to the pioneer. The indomitable Ellen shared her daughter's enthusiasm, later travelling with her daughter to Sydney and convincing Smith to give the ebullient teenager a joyride in his famous Southern Cross.

In early 1930, Jean and her mother sailed to England where she took flying lessons at the Stag Lane Aerodrome in London. She became the first woman from New Zealand to be granted a Class A licence in December 1930.

Her aspirations to best Amy Johnson's marathon flight from England to Australia were often dismissed by those familiar with her flying skills. Many had remarked that she was a slow learner and terrible at landings. Unfazed by her detractors, she set about getting sponsorship. Acquiring corporate sponsorship in such harsh economic times proved difficult. She decided to get a commercial B licence to make herself more of a viable prospect. However, at a cost of £500, the B licence was not cheap, so she resorted to mercenary tactics to raise the cash.

Her first saviour was Fred Truman a New Zealander flying for the Royal Air Force (RAF). Seduced by her charms and beauty, he handed over his entire life savings in return for promised matrimonial bliss. She used the money to get her licence in December 1932, and promptly ditched the love-struck pilot without paying him back.

Her next suitor was Victor Doree, who bought her a Gypsy Moth DH-60 by borrowing £400 from his wealthy family. In April 1933 Jean set off on her perilous voyage. Valiantly battling several sandstorms her beleaguered plane succumbed to engine failure, and crash-landed in India. Jean was unhurt, but stranded. She was rescued by Lord Wakefield of the Castor Oil Company, who arranged her passage back to England. Undeterred, she tried to winkle another plane from a stony faced Victor, who refused, causing an end to the relationship.

Engaged now to Edward Walter, a London stockbroker, Jean had made quite an impression on Lord Wakefield, who gave her a gift of a new Gypsy Moth, registration G-AARB. The plane was airborne in April 1934, only to suffer another mishap by running out of fuel over Rome. The resultant forced landing caused minor damage. Returning home she borrowed the lower wings from her fiancé's DH-60 and made a third attempt on May 8th 1934. Fighting extremes of inclement weather, on this occasion she successfully alighted in Darwin, Australia after 14 days and 22 and half hours. She had slashed Amy Johnson's record by five days. In the wake of this accomplishment she was lauded as a hero and showered with grants and lucrative lecturing opportunities.

While in Sydney she met and fell in love with airline pilot Beverly Shepherd, which spelled the end of her engagement to Walter in London. Jilted and bitter, he sent her a bill for the borrowed wings from his neglected Gypsy Moth.

Later in 1935 Jean flew back to England in her trusty G-AARB, becoming the first woman to complete a return trip. Now the darling of the aviation world, the RAF sought her as its glamorous poster

More events in 1936

- Beryl Markham makes first east-to-west solo crossing of the Atlantic by a woman in a Percival Vega Gull.
- King George V dies; succeeded by son, Edward VIII, who soon abdicates to marry an American divorcée.
- The British Broadcasting Corporation (BBC) debuts world's first TV service.

girl for recruitment films. Parting with a princely sum of £1,750, she traded in her Gypsy Moth for a Percival Vega Gull monoplane. Incorporating the latest technology, the plane sported a metal propeller, enclosed cockpit, reserve fuel tank, landing flaps and a 200 horsepower engine. In this cutting edge machine she established the first record flight from England to South America in November 1935. The first leg of her marathon flight took her to Senegal in West Africa. Jean then embarked upon the most hazardous part of the flight, crossing the South Atlantic, and arriving at Port Natal in Brazil using only a compass and watch as navigation aids. She had beaten the previous record to set a new duration of 61 hours and 15 minutes for the entire 5,000-mile journey. Following a rapturous welcome, she was awarded the Order of the Southern Cross in Brazil, a first for a British subject not of royal stock. Jean was also made an honorary member of three air forces.

Vanishing from public scrutiny for a year, she returned to better her previous England to Australia flight en-route to her final destination of Auckland in October 1936. The Percival Gull purred through the long voyage to deposit Jean in Sydney six days later, slicing her previous time in half. Again the adulation was unprecedented. Despite the epic journeys, she always adjusted her makeup and ensured she had a good stock of evening wear before disembarking from the cockpit, garbed in her trademark white flying suit.

Her final hop to Auckland involved crossing the Tasman Sea, which was challenging due to the severe weather. She arrived safely ten hours later, establishing a new record of 11 days and 45 minutes for the entire 14,229 miles, a benchmark that remained uncontested for 44 years. Touching down at Mangere Airport in Auckland her arrival attracted enough well-wishers to cause traffic jams to stretch for 13 miles.

Tragedy struck when her fiancé died in a plane crash. He was the only man she ever loved. Her resolve crumbled, but despite her grief, she made one last flight back to England in 1937 to set her final record. She published her autobiography: "My life" the same year.

In the intervening war years, Jean gradually withdrew from public life, although she participated in fundraising activities on behalf of the armed services. Her Percival Gull was requisitioned and pressed into service with the RAF. Jean never joined the ATA. She received many honours including the Commander of the British Empire CBE later in 1936, and the Harmon Trophy from 1935 to 1937. In 1938 she became the first woman to be awarded the Gold Medal of the Federation Aeronautique Internationale, regarded as the highest honour in aviation.

Fading to obscurity Jean and her mother settled quietly in Spain. Ellen passed away in 1965 leaving Jean devastated and further cementing her desire for isolation. She eventually died, alone on 22nd November 1982, due to an infection from an untreated dog bite. Her passing remained undiscovered for several years. She is buried in an unmarked pauper's grave in Majorca.

New Zealand's favourite and most reclusive aviatrix has never been forgotten. Her legendary achievements are honoured by naming a terminal at Auckland International airport after her. Jean's Percival Gull survived, and is now immortalised by being suspended from the roof of the same terminal building.

1936

BERYL MARKHAM (KENYA) 1902 – 1986

Sheer instinct drove the young child to engender the respect of the fiercest of African warriors. The untamed bush was Beryl Markham's nursery, playground and school shaping her into a fearless and independent woman to triumph in intensely male pursuits.

Accomplished horse trainer, courageous pilot and celebrated author, Beryl Markham threw caution to the winds but always landed with her undercarriage intact. The six-foot power-house blossomed into a beautiful rose in a romantic colonial setting. But beneath the feminine veneer flexed the sinew and beating heart of the raw, invincible soul of a liberated Africa…

Hailing from Ashwell, Leicestershire, England, Beryl Markham was born on 26th October 1902. Her parents, Charles and Clara Clutterbuck, although not wealthy were from aristocratic stock typical of the gentrified countryside. They bred horses and indulged in blood sports such as fox hunting. Beryl's childhood in England was a forgotten glimmer when the entire Clutterbuck clan moved to Njoro, Kenya when she was just three. It was a time when the British had laid a protectorate claim over the peoples of East Africa, with Kenya becoming a colony of the burgeoning British Empire.

Charles had equestrian interests but his aim was to prosper from the vast arable lands by establishing a farm in Njoro. Although riches as enjoyed by many other white farmers were in the offing, the Clutterbucks began humbly in an African mud hut some 70 miles from Nairobi. Clara attempted to settle into the austere existence but the comforts of Edwardian England enticed her to return along with her eldest son, Richard. Beryl remained with her father to tough it out in the wilds of Nairobi.

Away from the heirs and graces of upper class British society, Beryl literally went native in her adoptive home. Her father otherwise occupied with his expansive farming activities left Beryl to her own devices. She was to embrace the African

way of life with great gusto. In the care of local farm workers the Lakweit (little girl) as she was called soon engaged with the customs and languages of numerous tribes people. Swahili became her first language, with English second. She struck up a friendship with a local boy named Kibii and the two of became inseparable. As an honorary member of Kibii's tribe she hunted and played hard, learning how to survive and thrive in the wilds. The strict discipline of boarding school failed to tame Beryl, who no doubt felt caged in the stuffy surroundings. Her preference for hurling spears to sharpening pencil contributed to her expulsion and eventual return to the bush she pined for.

Charles discovered his true calling was breeding race-winning horses as opposed to toiling a fruitless land. Training thoroughbred horses for the Nairobi races sparked a new challenge for Beryl, who became an accomplished equestrian herself. Hitting on hard times her father abandoned Kenya for the greener pastures of Peru to breed horses in Latin America. Beryl, just seventeen and well versed with the survival techniques of the Masai herdsman, was left to fend for herself.

Obtaining a horse trainer's licence from the English Jockey Club, she was the first ever woman to do so in the British Empire. Beryl continued her father's winning streak and produced a string of thoroughbred winners that garnered grudging respect from her male counterparts. Her tribe now renamed her "Lady of the Horses".

A romantic liaison with a rugby player, Jock Purvis, led to marriage and then an even swifter divorce. In 1927 she married Mansfield Markham, an English aristocrat on safari with whom she would have a son two years later. It was a clash of cultures; Beryl rejected her husband and abandoned her son despite the trappings of wealth. The call of the wild was proving difficult to ignore. There was scandal that rocked

More events in 1936

- Imperial Airways begins scheduled flights between Hong Kong and Malaysia.
- Japan and Germany sign anti-Comintern pact; joined by Italy in 1937.
- Electric guitars debut

the upper echelons and destroyed the marriage when it was claimed she was having an illicit affair with a member of the Royal family. It was a done deal that her return to Kenya was inevitable.

On her return to Africa she fell for the charms of pilot and hunter Denys Finch Hatton, who introduced her to flying. Tragedy struck as Hatton died in a plane crash, which cemented Beryl's desire to fly. Trading in horse breeding for flight lessons, Beryl received instruction from a friend Tom Campbell Black in a Gypsy Moth in April 1930. Following eight hours of instruction, she soloed and a month later Beryl was granted her class 'A' licence becoming the first in Kenya to achieve the qualification. She then bought her own plane, an Avro Avion IV, which the fledgling aviatrix maintained with the same grooming care she afforded her horses.

In April 1931 she undertook a daring solo flight from Nairobi to England, braving bad weather and a spate of mechanical problems. She even wore an inner tube around her neck in the instance she was forced to ditch at sea. However 23 days later Beryl landed at Heston Aerodrome in England, having accomplished the flight without the aid of a radio or compass.

On returning to Kenya she acquired a commercial 'B' licence and then embarked upon offering her services as an African bush pilot. Her name was becoming known in the colonies, many comparing her to the legendary Jean Batten. She used her plane in a variety of missions from scouting for game on behalf of wealthy hunting parties to serving as an air taxi and airmail pilot. Ferrying the sick and injured she also served as relief airline pilot.

Tiring of the dearth of new adventures, Beryl embarked upon an aviation feat that only a courageous few dared to try. She took up the challenge from wealthy businessman, John Carberry to fly solo across the Atlantic from England to New York. Amelia Earhart had managed the west to east flight but in the same direction as the prevailing winds. However Beryl would have to contend with the powerful oncoming jetstream headwinds over the North Atlantic. Carberry pledged his brand new Percival Vega Gull monoplane to Beryl for the record breaking transatlantic flight. The Vega Gull was also Jean Batten's preferred airplane, which she used to establish many records.

On September 4th 1936, an intrepid Beryl Markham took off in her Vega Gull she nicknamed 'The Messenger' from the west coast of England into a vortex of stormy weather. Anticipated head-winds buffeted and hammered The Messenger sucking more fuel from its tanks. Stuck at a low altitude to prevent the wings from icing over she battled against the punching gusts, spinning and drifting throughout the harrowing flight. The remaining tank sloshed its meagre supply, but a frozen fuel line cut the engine forcing The Messenger to crash landing near Cape Breton, Nova Scotia. After twenty-two hours of turbulent flying the Vega Gull had nosed into a peat bog. Emerging unscathed but crestfallen, Beryl perceived the entire venture as a failure. Whisked away to New York she discovered much to her surprise the thousands cheering and hailing her the hero. Although blown off course, Beryl had by all accounts achieved the impossible by conquering the Atlantic from the east.

Following her epic flight, Beryl settled in the United States to marry her third husband, writer and journalist Raoul Schumacher. Hollywood got interested in making a film about her flying exploits, but it never came to fruition. During the war years Beryl continued to fly, this time joining the Civil Air Patrol.

In 1942 she published her memoirs in a book entitled 'West With The Night.' Although well received the book failed to make the best-seller lists of the day. Rediscovering her roots in 1952 she went back to Kenya returning to her first love of training thoroughbred horses. From 1958 until 1972 her stables delivered a steady supply of race winning horses ensuring a legendary status.

Then a Californian restaurateur came upon Ernest Hemingway's papers to discover the lavish acclaim he showered upon Beryl's autobiography of 1942. This lead to a reprinting in 1983 of 'West With The Night' and on this occasion it became a bestseller. The book plucked Beryl from relative obscurity during her final years with television documentary makers visiting her in Kenya to chart her life and experiences.

Beryl Markham passed away in her native Kenya on 3rd August 1986. The 50th anniversary of her famous flight across the Atlantic happened to be on 4th September 1986. A Thanksgiving service for Beryl's life was held at St Clement Dane's Church in London on that day with many of her friends and acquaintances in attendance.

Beryl Markham may have mixed with the establishment but she set the tone of the association, never lingering longer than necessary, escaping when the next challenge ensnared her insatiable appetite for adventure. She was a tribal warrior and she lived by the code that only the strongest understand the laws of the jungle. Even if some of those laws masquerade under the banner of a civilised society.

1937

WILLA BROWN (USA) 1906 – 1992

Champion of African American aviators

One ordinary day in 1936 a stunning young woman in white jodhpurs, jacket and boots, strode into the newsroom of the *Chicago Defender*. The typewriters sputtered to a halt and she had all the male attention in the room. The city editor assumed she was a model representing a new product and was preparing for some gentle flirting. "I'm Willa Brown," she said, and announced that she was an aviatrix, and wanted some publicity for a black air show at Harlem Airport. She got it.

Willa Beatrice Brown was born on January 22, 1906 in Glasgow, Kentucky. She received her Bachelor of Science degree in business from Indiana State Teachers College in 1927. She taught public school in Gary, Indiana, and Chicago, Illinois, where she developed an interest in aviation. At 21 years old, she was the youngest high school teacher in the Gary school system. However, teaching did not satisfy her penchant for adventure and challenge. She went to Chicago to take up social work, but was thwarted by the lack of opportunity for African Americans at that time. Her next choice of career eared her censure from all quarters.

In Chicago she met Colonel John C. Robinson and Cornelius R. Coffey, both pioneer pilots and mechanics. Both men had also been influential in steering Willa's contemporary Janet Bragg's career. Under their tutelage Willa was able to follow her hero Bessie Coleman into the air. She later organised the annual memorial fly-over of Bessie Coleman's grave.

Willa enrolled in the Aeronautical University in Chicago, earning a master mechanic's certificate. She naturally gravitated towards flying. In 1934 she started studying with Coffey at one of Chicago's racially segregated airports. Three years after her mechanic's ticket she added her private pilot's license on June 22, 1938, with a test score of 96 per cent.

In 1939, she received her commercial ticket. She was the first black woman to make a career of aviation and, according to biographer Betty K. Gumbert, was the person most responsible for preparing black pilots for World War II. When she added her mechanic's license in 1943, she became the first American woman to have both a mechanic's license and a commercial pilot's license.

She also earned a masters' in business administration (MBA) from Northwestern University and a Civil Aeronautics Administration (CAA) ground school instructor's rating. She married Coffey. The pair established the Coffey School of Aeronautics at Harlem Airport to train African-American pilots and mechanics, thus fulfilling Coleman's cherished dream of a black-owned private flight school.

Willa fought hard for recognition for black aviators. The press was full of the exploits of her white contemporaries, such as Amelia Earhart and Louise Thaden. The Defender newsroom incident came about because she was seeking advance publicity for a black air show. The newspaper was a highly influential African-American and operated newspaper. Enoch Waters, the city editor, wrote about her visit and the air show in subsequent editions.

"In a businesslike manner she explained that she was an aviatrix and wanted some publicity for a Negro air show at Harlem Airport on the city's southwest side. Except for the colorful 'Colonel' Hubert Fauntleroy Julian, who called himself the 'Black Eagle' and who had gained lots of publicity for his exploits, and 'Colonel' John Robinson, a Chicago flyer who was in Ethiopia heading up Haile Selassie's air force, I was unaware of any other Negro aviators, particularly in Chicago.

"'There are about thirty of us,' she informed

Events in 1937

- Amelia Earhart and navigator Fred Noonan disappear on a flight from Lae, New Guinea to Howland Island, and are never seen again.

- Pan Am and Imperial Airways flying boats conduct joint survey flights over the Atlantic in preparation for the commencement of regular services

- Walt Disney's first full-length animated feature, "Snow White and the Seven Dwarfs," hits theatres

- The Golden Gate Bridge is completed.

me, 'both men and women.' Most were students, she added, but several had obtained their licenses and one, Cornelius Coffey, was an expert aviation and engine mechanic who also held a commercial pilot's license and was a certified flight instructor. He was the leader of the group. She informed me that she held a limited commercial pilot's license.

"Fascinated by both her and the idea of Negro aviators, I decided to follow up the story myself. Accompanied by a photographer, I covered the air show. About 200 or 300 other spectators attended, attracted by the story in the Defender. So happy was Willa over our appearance that she offered to take me up for a free ride. She was piloting a Piper Cub, which seemed to me, accustomed as I was to commercial planes, to be a rather frail craft. It was a thrilling experience, and the maneuvers—figure eights, flip-overs and stalls—were exhilarating, though momentarily frightening. I wasn't convinced of her competence until we landed smoothly."

This incident persuaded Waters to join with Mr and Mrs Coffey and help to form the National Airman's Association of America (NAAA) in 1939. The NAAA's main purpose was to get black aviation cadets into the United States military. Willa was the organisation's national secretary and the president of the Chicago branch. She led a successful campaign to integrate African Americans into the US army Air Corps. She continually lobbied the government to allow black pilots into the segregated army Air Corps and the federal Civilian Pilot Training Program (CPTP). This later led the United States Congress to vote to allow separate-but-equal participation of African-Americans in civilian flight training programmes.

The US army subsequently chose the Coffey school to provide black trainees for the Air Corps pilot training program at Tuskegee Institute (now Tuskegee University). In 1941, because of her flying service and aviation credentials, the government named Willa as the federal coordinator of the Chicago unit of the Civil Air Patrol (CAP) civilian pilot training programme. It was the culmination of a difficult struggle. She wrote in a telling letter to Eleanor Roosevelt, December 6, 1941 "During the past three years I have devoted full time to aviation, and for the most part marked progress has been made. I have, however, encountered several difficulties—several of them I have handled very well, and some have been far too great for me to master."

Willa became the first African-American officer in this first integrated unit. Approximately 1,500 pilots came through the Coffey school over the next seven years. Some of those pilots later became part of the 99th Pursuit Squadron at Tuskegee Institute—also known as the legendary "Tuskegee Airmen." Willa's efforts were directly responsible for the squadron's creation, which led to the integration of the military in 1948.

At the time very few women were training men. However, there were so few places where African-American men could get official training that the men had to put up with being trained by a woman, whether they liked it or not.

Willa became the coordinator of war-training service for the Civil Aeronautics Authority. She added another first to her prestigious career when in 1946 she became the first African American woman to run for Congress. In 1955, she married Rev JH Chappell and became active in the West Side Community Church in Chicago. She was appointed to the Federal Aviation Administration Women's Advisory Board in 1972 in recognition of her contributions to aviation in the United States as a pilot, an instructor, and an activist. She died on July 18, 1992 at the age of 86.

SABIHA GOKCEN (TURKEY) 1913 – 2001

First Turkish female fighter pilot and symbol of women's rights in her country

The official republican line on women is written on a wall inside Mustafa Kemal Ataturk's memorial at Anit Kabir, Turkey. "The ancient Turk considered men and women to have equal rights...Ataturk was determined that men and women should have equal rights." He put his beliefs into practice when he adopted and promoted Turkey's first female fighter pilot.

Sabiha Gokcen was born in the provincial Turkish city of Bursa on March 21, 1913. Orphaned at an early age, she got lucky at around 12 years old when the national founder, Mustafa Kemal Ataturk, visited her city. She asked him to get her to school. She told him about her story and the conditions in which she was living, so Ataturk did better than sending her to school. He adopted her as his daughter in 1925. He took her to live with him in Cankaya Presidential Residence in the Turkish capital, Ankara. She lived with three of his other adopted daughters, Zehra, Afet and Rukiye, attending Uskudar Girls College in Istanbul.

Ataturk had come to power in 1923 and was determined to shake off the worst excesses of the Ottoman Empire. He worked hard to create a secular, Western-oriented republic. He introduced reformist laws. In 1934 he instigated the surnames law, requiring citizens to adopt surnames. He christened Sabiha "Gokcen," which means "belonging to the sky." Sabiha said that he never used her Christian name again.

Six months after her she received her new name she took to the skies. "I had never thought about flying before," she said in an interview. Ataturk saw the importance of aviation to the country and established the Turkish Aeronautical Association in 1925. He took her along with him to the opening of the Turkkusu (Turkish bird) civil aviation flight training school on May 5 1935. She watched the parachutes and gliders perform at the inaugural air show and became excited. Ataturk noticed her interest. Sabiha told a reporter once that he asked: "Gokcen, can you fly?" he asked. I said yes, so he enrolled me the next day."

He instructed Fuat Bulca the head of the school to induct her as the first female skydiving student. This was revolutionary in an Islamic society of that era and Sabiha was the only woman in her class. Although she was supposed to train as a skydiver, she was far more attracted to the aircraft. After initial glider training, she was chosen to attend advanced training in Russia with seven male students. While she was in Moscow she found out that her sister Zehra had died, so returned home with a heavy heart.

In 1936, Ataturk suggested she go to the Air Force Academy. That meant she would be Turkey's first female military pilot. This was a huge victory for the leader in terms of promoting women's rights. Since she was the first, the school had to create a special uniform for her. She earned her licence there. Describing her first solo flight in 1936, Sabiha said: "When I landed, Ataturk came up to the plane. He was so happy, happier even than I was. He kissed my forehead and congratulated me. But it wasn't really me he was congratulating, it was all Turkish women. He wanted Turkish women to be successful in all walks of life. Turkey was one of the first European countries to give women the vote.

His sponsorship and guidance inspired Sabiha. She was determined to honour the trust she had been given. In 1937 she underwent rigorous training to become a fighter pilot. This was a steep challenge in the male-dominated society of her day. Her success was a beacon for both Turkish independence and women's rights in the new republic. She honed her skills by flying bomber and fighter aircraft at the 1st Aircraft Regiment in Eskisehir air base and participated in the Aegean and Thrace exercises in 1937. The same year she flew in the military push against the Dersim riot and became the world's first female air force combat pilot. According to Turkish aviation authorities, this made her the world's first female combat pilot..

In 1938 she flew around the Balkans for six days on a peace mission. She flew solo through Greece, Bulgaria, Yugoslavia and Romania as part of a publicity campaign to promote the new Turkish republic. She flew alone and carried out her own maintenance as Ataturk did not want her to take a mechanic with her. The tour was a great success. In 1938 Ataturk died, which deeply saddened Sabiha. She loved him dearly and wrote poetry about him.

She joined the Turkkusu Flight School, and was in post there as chief trainer until 1955. She married a colleague, an officer who died in 1943. She became a member of the Turkish Aeronautical Association executive board. She flew internationally for the next 28 years until 1964, including two publicity tours to the US in 1953 and 1959 to promote her country and culture. She flew 22 different types over more than 8,000 hours, 32 of which were active combat and bombing missions. She published her auto-biography, Ataturk'un izinde bir omur ("A Life in the Footsteps of Ataturk") in 1981 to commemorate her hero's 100th birthday.

Sabiha herself was selected as the only female pilot on a poster of "The 20 Greatest Aviators in History" published by the USAF in 1996. She died in Ankara on 22 March 2001 in the Gulhane Military Medical Academy in Ankara. Turkey named Istanbul's second international airport after her.

1937

More events in 1937

- ■ Luftwaffe bombers of Legion Condor attack Guernica
- ■ Japan invades China, conquers most of coastal area.
- ■ The Glenn Miller Band debuts in New York.

1937

LORES BONNEY (AUSTRALIA) 1897 – 1994

The first woman pilot to fly solo from Australia to Cape Town

Forced as low as 300 feet above ground flying over India, Lores Bonney was battling against ferocious headwinds and flocks of birds. It was so hot that she had to wrap her hand in cloth so she could wrestle with the superheated metal throttle. She was not phased, it was only another chapter in the adventure that was her remarkable life.

Lores Bonney was born Maude Rose Rubens in Pretoria, South Africa on November 20th, 1897. She was educated in Melbourne and finally at finishing school in Frankfurt. Uncomfortable with her name, she changed it to Dolores, shortened to Lores. She went back to Australia and married Harry Bonney, a leather goods manufacturer.

In 1928 her husband's cousin, Bert Hinkler, a Queensland pilot who had set a solo England-Australia record, took her flying in his Avro Avian biplane. This inspired Lores to take secret flying lessons at the weekend, when her husband was on the golf links. She got her licence in 1931 and Harry proved to be supportive. He bought her a de Havilland DH-60G Gipsy Moth biplane for £800 and presented her with a pair of custom-made leather flying suits. She named the Moth "My Little Ship." To celebrate, she set an Australian long-distance record, flying 947 miles in one day on her first solo cross-country flight.

She then became the first Australian woman to gain a commercial pilot's license and shortly afterward decided to circumnavigate Australia, the first woman to do so. She completed the flight in 95 hours of flying time spread over six weeks. She had overcome a landing gear collapse, a wing spar that fractured in turbulence, and a forced landing caused by a piston's disintegration.

Lores' aim with her next marathon journey was to beat Amy Johnson's record of travelling between England and Australia in 19½ days, which had been set flying the same route but in the opposite direction three years previously. With 350 flying hours to her credit, she felt ready to tackle her trip to England. She had no radio and sketchy maps, and performed her own maintenance enroute. In preparation she had spent months working as an unofficial apprentice in the Qantas maintenance hangar, learning how to overhaul her Moth and its engine.

She set off from Brisbane on April 10th, and she hit a snag in Singapore. She became ill with food poisoning after visiting the famous Raffles Hotel. She had to stay on to recover, but by then the weather had changed. She had been flying for ten hours and was almost at her destination when she ran into monsoon clouds. She told Gwnn-Jones: "For the previous half hour, building clouds had forced me down below 1,000 feet. I had been warned to stay away from these tropical storms. But I was so close to Victoria Point I was sure I could get through. The nearest alternate airfield was six hours away, and I didn't have the fuel."

She had to fly in zero visibility. She said: "The rain seemed to fall in a solid mass. It lashed my goggles, and I couldn't even see my instruments. I was forced to raise them to see anything at all. My small glass windscreen provided no real protection, and the rain stung my eyes and face like driving sand. My Little Ship bucked and rolled, then a sudden downdraft flung us toward the water. Even with full power I couldn't check the descent. I regained control about 50 feet above the water. "I was really terrified and knew it was time to get out of there."

She turned back to a small island she had noticed. The tide was out, so she headed for the strip of sand. Unfortunately a buffalo grazing nearby got into her landing path and she had to swerve. She turned into the water and the aircraft smashed up in the sea. She told her biographer Terry Gwynn-Jones: "I remember a shower of spray and a sharp pain as the Moth flipped over and my head hit the cockpit coaming. Next I was underwater and hanging upside down in my harness. I recall thinking: "What an inglorious end — drowning upside down in the cockpit." I was struggling to undo the harness pin when the water dropped away. I was only submerged when each wave came in." she released herself and encountered a group of villagers, who befriended her and helped get her aircraft out of the water. Only the fuselage and engine appeared undamaged. The villagers helped her remove the wings, and she used the contents of the petrol tank to wash the salt and sand from the engine. To prevent corrosion, she plastered it with oil drained from the sump.

Six days later a ship rescued her. She ferried her Moth to Calcutta, where repairs took a month. Taking off again on May 25, 1933, she carried on with her knowing she had no hope of establishing any record. She landed at London's Croydon Airport on June 21st, 1933, having completed the 12,300 miles in 157 hours' flight time. According to the Times in March 1994 her first words to reporters were: "There have been two bright days in my adventure from Australia to here the first and the last." Both her father and her husband refused to let her make the return flight to Australia, though she was convinced she could beat Amy Johnson's record at the second attempt. King George V made her an MBE, but Australian's remained apathetic, finally awarding her the Member of the Order of Australia (AM) in 1991.

Four years later she became the first person to fly the 18,200 miles from Australia to South Africa via Cairo. She arrived in Cape Town nearly 19 weeks after she had set off. She flew a newly acquired German Klemm L32 monoplane, which she had christened My Little Ship II. The epic trip took her across Asia, the Middle East and Africa. Even today, few pilots would undertake the journey in a single-engine machine. In a repeat of her 1933 flight to London, Lores was lashed by storms and fried by the heat. She was delayed for a week by monsoon rain in Bangkok and advised by a British airline pilot to go home. Lores told Gwynn-Jones: "That did it. Next day I got through to Tavoy. It was only a short two-hour stepping-stone, but it enabled me to break through the bad weather."

She flew through sandstorms in the Middle East, and was advised to sleep with her pistol under her pillow. She was grounded in Khartoum for a few weeks and decided to wait on an extra few days, hoping to meet the famous Amelia Earhart, who was due to arrive there too. She left Khartoum on July 10th, 1937, missing Amelia and Fred Noonan by two days.

One of the hairiest moments came approaching Nairobi, when Lores was flying blind through clouds crossing the mountains. She was convinced she was 2,000ft over the top and suddenly saw she

More events in 1937

- ■ **Sir Frank Whittle ground-tests the first jet engine designed to power an aircraft at the British Thomson-Houston factory in Rugby, England**
- ■ **A prototype "antihistamine" produced to treat allergies.**

was 30 seconds away from certain death and a crash into the mountain face. She missed the cliff by less than 100 feet. An engineer checked her altimeter (instrument for measuring height) and discovered it was over-reading by almost 2,500 feet.

She was grounded by the Second World War and stopped flying shortly afterwards. She also separated from her husband. She continued to have adventures. In 1963 she visited South America, and, accompanied by a guide and Indian bearers, she canoed up the headwaters of the Amazon to study the primitive Yagua Indians. She lived in Japan for several years, learning the art of bonsai, which she brought back to Australia and taught to students at the University of Queensland.

She died on February 24, 1994. It is sad that she is almost forgotten today. Her life was so full of challenge and achievement. She is recognised here and there. Her name is carved into the wall of the Flyer's Chapel at California's St. Francis Atrio Mission, alongside those of Charles Lindbergh, Charles Kingsford Smith and Amelia Earhart. Since 1933, British aviation has regularly awarded the Bonney Trophy to a deserving woman pilot.

HANNA REITSCH (GERMANY) 1912 – 1979

The woman who refused to give up - even when she lost her nose in a crash.

Piloting her bullet riddled spotter plane through a hail of anti-aircraft tracer fire, Hanna Reitsch escaped a ravaged Berlin as the Third Reich heaved its dying breath. With her wounded lover General Robert Ritter Von Greim by her side she left behind a defeated Hitler ensconced in his bunker and contemplating suicide. Hitler had given both Reitsch and Ritter vials of cyanide in case their desperate last-ditch mission resulted in capture by the advancing Red Army.

The dramatic events of 25th April 1945 were a far cry from her early days as a natural-born glider pilot. Born in 1912, Hanna reluctantly followed in the footsteps of her ophthalmologist father to train as a medical doctor. But her overwhelming passion for flying drew her to the world of gliding, and in 1932 she joined a soaring club. A fresh-faced Hanna unfurled her wings, demonstrating her innate prowess by becoming a gliding instructor at the Horngerb in Swabia. At the time Germany was restricted by the post First World War Treaty of Versailles preventing it from manufacturing, let alone flying, powered aircraft. Hanna was one of thousands of enthusiastic young Germans who would later ditch their gliders for more formidable airframes marked with a sinister twisted cross.

Against a backdrop of a Germany boldly re-equipping its Luftwaffe air force, Hanna established many gliding endurance world records. She accrued a number of trophies, notably the Silver Soaring Medal for a long distance flight in Argentina. She also became the first woman to soar across the Swiss Alps in 1937. Her remarkable feats and talents attracted much recognition, and she was eventually recruited by the Luftwaffe as a test pilot.

She was unique at the time, being the only woman allowed to strap herself into unknown and dangerous airframes. She achieved this in a suppressive atmosphere characterised by an ideology where women were subjugated and secondary to men. Hanna became the

poster girl for the Nazi regime. Appointed by General Ernst Udet at the Luftwaffe test centre in Rechlin, her early duties in 1937 involved speed dive testing of the newly developed Junker Ju-87 Stuka dive-bomber and the Dornier Do-17 twin-engine medium bomber.

Hanna achieved another world first by flying the first helicopter, the Focke-Achgelis Fa-61. Such was her skill that she flew the ungainly machine within the confines of the crowded Deutschlandhalle auditorium at the 1938 Berlin Motor Show. In recognition of this successful showcase of Nazi engineering she was awarded the Military Flying Medal. This also made her "Whirly Girl" number one.

Courage and fearless determination drove Hanna on. She bathed in the adulation and limelight showered upon her by her Nazi sponsors. Hitler himself kept a close eye on the steely aviatrix, regarded as the precious darling of the Reich, and restricted her exposure to actual combat missions. But test flying was fraught with its own perils, as Hanna would soon discover whilst at the helm of some truly dangerous aircraft.

One particularly hazardous flight involved flying a Do-17, equipped with wingtip blades to slice through barrage balloon cables. In a demonstration before Hitler and General Udet she flew the modified bomber into a test cable and almost severed a wing. She nursed the stricken plane back to the runway, and was awarded the Iron Cross, Second Class for her heroism.

Perhaps the most telling insight into her character comes from the story of her testing the unpredictable and highly dangerous Me-163 Komet.

The aircraft was essentially a small, swept winged rocket-powered glider.

This pocket rocket had claimed the lives of three male pilots before Hanna wrestled with it. She crash-landed it on her fifth flight thanks to a landing gear release failure that compromised its aerodynamics. She was trapped in the cockpit of the shattered Komet, but insisted on jotting down the details of the accident and flight handling.

Her injuries were horrific. Bleeding profusely from a cut and crushed face, Hanna discovered her severed

More events in 1937

- Giant German airship Hindenburg exploded over New Jersey. 30 people died.

- Amelia Earhart and Fred Noonan disappear at sea and are never seen again.

- The Duke of Windsor married Mrs Wallis Simpson (a divorced woman)

...ose in her lap, but continued with the mission write-up, battling to remain ...onscious.

It took five months of surgery and facial reconstruction before Hitler's ...avourite pilot could fly again. For her gallantry he awarded her the Iron ...ross First Class and prohibited her from any further risky ventures. She ...vas allowed to test safer designs including stability trials of the V-1 flying ...manned "Buzz-bomb" in 1944. The unmanned bomb was lethal, however ...vhen flown by a pilot it proved unstable – yet Hanna managed it success-...ully. Her exploits were unintentionally glamorised by Hollywood in the film ..."Operation Crossbow" during the sixties.

Hanna was a staunch supporter of the Nazi party and refused to believe ...n the existence of concentration camps. In the last days of the war she flew ...vith her lover through intense ground fire to visit Hitler at his bunker in ...Berlin. Denying her request to die with him, Hitler ordered them both to ...eave and arrest Himmler for his treason. Hanna did as she was told; flying ...again through enemy fire. Inevitably captured, she was interrogated by the ...American military for 18 months prior to being freed. Von Greim chose to ...ake his own life, leaving her rather alone after the war.

Reitsch remained unrepentant and was proud of her accomplishments. ...he called the Luftwaffe the "Guardians of the Portals of Peace". In her ...memoirs "Flying is My Life" she made no apologies and justified her loyalty ...o both Hitler and Nazi ideologies. She proudly wore her Iron Cross ...medals, despite the fact that her parents chose suicide in the face of defeat. ...he attempted to rationalise her involvement with the Hitler's Nazi

...ished an ardent love of her country and had done her duty to the las... Legends formed about my last flight into Berlin. Might I not perhaps hav... hidden Hitler away somewhere?"

Flying restrictions were re-imposed upon Germans, but eventually glidin... was permitted. Hanna returned to her first love, achieving third place in th... 1954 World Gliding Championships in Spain. By 1955 she was the Germa... champion, setting a string of altitude records for women.

In 1959 Hanna was invited by Prime Minister Jawaharlal Nehru t... establish a gliding school in India.

During this visit Flying Officer Kailash Rampal, an Indian Air Forc... fighter pilot (and father to one of the co-authors) had a chance meeting wit... her. Hearing the accounts from her Luftwaffe days, he gleaned that she wa... proud of her contribution to the war effort and that she had actually partic... ipated in a number of combat missions. These included balloon cable-cuttin... sorties in addition to "other" undocumented active combat missions.

Hanna was invited to the White House by President John F Kennedy i... 1961. Perhaps as a gesture of silent atonement, she busied herself fron... 1962 to 1965 by establishing the first gliding school in Ghana. Sh... continued to establish gliding records. Her final accomplishment was th... women's "Out and Return" record across the Appalachian Mountains in th... US. She died in 1979 following a massive heart attack.

Many would argue that Hanna Reitsch was a true legend in the field c... aviation, breaking the barriers for women entering the profession. Howeve... her achievements will always be overshadowed by her misguided allegianc...

VALENTINA STEPANOVNA GRIZODUBOVA (USSR) 1909–1993

Mothers in arms dominating the Russian skies

christmas Crackers! A man's not safe in any job now. But gosh, I'd like to meet them (the Russian female pilots)." Time Magazine, 1942

Thus spoke a World War II British Royal Air Force pilot, who had just read an interview with Major Valentina Grizodubova. She had said that the squadrons of Russian female bomber and fighter pilots were flying in active combat. Some even flew night time raids. Valentina had said: "One friend of mine, Vera Lomako, who has shot down one Nazi plane, was flying a month before the birth of her daughter and soon afterward she shot down another plane." Valentina, herself, was a pretty 31-year old with a five-year old son, nicknamed "Little Falcon," and one of the most feared pilots in the Red Air Force.

Her date of birth is listed differently according to different sources. She was born on April 27th in 1909 in Kharkov in the Ukraine. (According to VE Vlasko, director of the Kharkov museum, her birth date is sometimes also listed as January 31 1910 because of the change in the Russian calendar that took place after her birth). Her father was the renowned aircraft designer and inventor Stepan Vasilevicha Grizodubova. Some reports suggest he strapped her to his waist as a toddler and took her flying. By 1929 she was a member of the Penza aero club and flying gliders. She also worked as a flying instructor at the Tula aviation school. She also married an army pilot captain, Viktor Sokoloff, and they had a son, Valerik.

In the early 1930s pilots were as popular as film stars are today. Young people were passionate about aviation. Valentina would have

been a star. She joined the Red Army in 1936 and by 1937, had set five world records for height, speed and range in Yakovlev UT-1, -2 and Antonov AN-12 aircraft. One came in October, 1937, when she flew non-stop with Marina Raskova on an YAK-12 for a record women's long distance non-stop flight.

However, her most notable flight came between September 24 – 25, 1938, when she flew 4,000 miles (5,900 km as the crow flies, 6,450 km actual) non-stop from Moscow to the Siberian Soviet east coast near Japan in the "Rodina" ("Motherland"), an ANT-37. Her fellow crewmembers were Marina Raskova and Paulina Osipenko. They flew for 26 hours and 29 minutes.

The flight was fraught with difficulty. The weather was appalling. They were forced to climb to a high altitude to get over the heavy clouds en route. This meant that the night was particularly difficult, when the cabin temperature fell to minus 35 degrees centigrade. This knocked their radio out, so they had no contact with the outside world. Despite this, Marina managed to keep them on course. However, they realised they were running low on fuel when they reached the Sea of Okhotsk in the southestern tip of Siberia.

Valentina decided to chance a landing in the dense forests along the coast. This meant that the aircraft might be nose heavy and imbalanced, and would possibly kill them all. So Marina parachuted out from 6,562 feet (2,000 meters). The other two managed to wrestle the aeroplane down in a marsh.

Polina Osipenko later said: "We found ourselves on a large marshy ground with no signs of any human dwelling nearby. The first thought after we touched down was about Marina. To give her a signal as to our whereabouts we began shooting but there was no response. After two

POLINA OSIPENKO

Polina Osipenko came from an entirely different background from her illustrious co-pilots. As a young woman she worked at a collective farm. A small sports aeroplane landed one day, which was a huge event in the rural village. Polina was particularly struck by the fact the pilot was a woman. This pivotal event set her on course. In the years before the Second World War Polina set five international records. She was killed in an accident during a routine flight when her aircraft got into a spin and crashed.

Amelia Earhart's 1932 record flight from Newfoundland to Ireland. They were an inspiration around the world, and even today remain models of determination and courage. Russia honoured them with the country's highest award, the Gold Star of Hero of the Soviet Union. Marina Raskova went on to form the all-female combat regiments, whose members served as bomber and fighter pilots in World War II. Both Polina and Marina died in crashes within a few years.

Valentina, however, lived a long life and went on to contribute much more to Russian aviation. From March 1942 onwards she fought in World War II. She was the commander of the 101st Long-Range Air Regiment, a 300-man squadron of four-engine heavy bombers that maintained contact with partisan regiments. She personally made more than 200 sorties, including 132 at night. She also served as chairman of the Women's Anti-Fascist Committee. In the 1940s she was the sole female member of the Extraordinary State Commission, appointed to investigate Nazi war crimes.

From 1946 onwards, she was deputy chief of the Science Research Centre for Flight Test. She flew test flights towards the development of radar-tracking equipment. She was promoted to chief in 1963 and remained in post until 1972.

According to Women in Aviation International, in her capacity as chief, Valentina helped another great Russian aviatrix, who went on to win many awards. Galina Korchuganova had graduated with the highest honours of her high school and been accepted at Moscow Aviation Institute (MAI), where she majored in Aviation technology. After graduating in 1959, she worked as an engineer at Ramensk Avionics Construction Bureau and competed in aviation sports. In 1965 she set her first world record on a 100km closed circuit, flying a Yak-32 jet. She went on to become the first female world aerobatic champion, winning gold and silver medals at the World Championship in Moscow in 1966.

At this point, with 1,000 hours under her belt, she received a response from the Ministry of Aviation to her request to attend test pilot school. The powers that be reckoned that she could, but on the condition: "If you can find a brave man who is willing to take you as a test pilot, we won't object, as an exception to the rules." No such man existed, however Valentina gave Galina her chance. Galina graduated went on to set 42 world records in Yak-32, Yak-40, and AN-24 aircraft.

Valentina was a firm advocate for women pilots. In 1942 she said: "In my experience, girls make just as good pilots as men. You cannot judge by appearance. I know girls so quiet and apparently timid that they blush when spoken to, yet they pilot bombers over Germany without qualm. No country at war today can afford to ignore the tremendous reservoir of woman power."

She lived to the ripe old age of 83 and died on April 28 1993 in Moscow. According to the Itar-Tass news agency, her death was the result of stomach ulcer complications. A legend in her lifetime, she was awarded the Soviet Hero star, Soviet Red Star, the Order of the Red Banner, the Order of Lenin, and wore the medal of a member of the Supreme Soviet. She is still celebrated today on a postage stamp. She is one of the true greats of female aviation history and has inspired many women to take to the skies.

sunny days the weather changed for the worse. The bad weather told on our spirits. Yet, we were sure people would find us."

Marina spent ten days on her own wandering in the forest in her heavy military gear, with no food, save two bars of chocolate. Valentina and Paulina had to wait for three days before help came. They are reputed to have chased off bears and even fought off a lynx that got into the cockpit. Finally they were all rescued and returned to a heroes' welcome in Moscow, having opened up a route through the seemingly impassable region.

The flight set a female distance record for women, adding one-third on to the range of

Events in 1938

- Lufthansa Fw 200 makes the airline's first flight to Japan. The 8,841 mile (14,228 km) flight breaks distance records, taking 46h 18min.

- Nazis destroy Jewish shops, homes, synagogues in Kristallnacht riots; 20,000–30,000 sent to concentration camps.

1938

MARINA MIKHAILOVNA RASKOVA (USSR) 1912–1943

Russia's "Amelia Earhart," who set up all female fighting squadrons

In the US the Women's Air Service Pilots (WASP) could thank Jacqueline Cochran and Nancy Love for its inception. Pauline Gower performed the same service for the Women's Air Transport Auxiliary in the UK. Soviet women pilots can name Marina Raskova as their heroine. Unlike the units in Britain and America, the Russian girls actually saw active combat.

Born in 1912, Marina Raskova was said to be friendly with a wide range of interests. She was an accomplished pianist who had attended the Pushkin School of Music. She was also fluent in French and Italian and studied chemistry and warfare. At 19 she was hired by the Zhukovsky Aviation Engineering Academy as a laboratory technician.

Her first brush with fame came in 1933. She was the first woman to become a navigator in the Soviet Air Force. Within a year she had her pilot's license and became the first woman to teach at the prestigious Zhukovskiy Air Academy. Aviation in the early 20th century was risky and glamorous. Pilots made headlines the way movie stars do today. Marina was no exception. She entered the public eye when she broke world records with long-distance flights in Soviet aeroplanes. Most of these flights happened in 1937 and 1938, while she was teaching at the academy.

On 24 October 1937 Marina and Valentina Grizodubova, flew a Yakovlev Yak-12 into history when they scored the female world record in a long distance non-stop flight of 898 miles (1,445 km). The following year Marina took part in three record flights: on 24 May and 2 July in an MP-1 flying boat, covering 1,087 miles (1,749 km) and 1,392 miles (2,241 km) respectively. Then on 24-25 September with Valentina and Paulina Osipenko in an ANT-37 she flew just over 4,000 miles (6,450 km) in a pioneering non-stop flight from Moscow to the Pacific. Their aim was to set an international women's record for a straight-line distance flight. They flew a twin-engine plane, the Rodina (the Homeland) Ant-37, a converted DB-2 long-range bomber across the vast stretch of Russia from Moscow to Komsomolsk-on-Amur in the Far East.

Their flight was hazardous. There are different accounts of what happened, but the most often quoted story is that the aircraft iced up over the vast Siberian wilderness and lost altitude. They threw all of the moveable cargo out to lose weight and climb, but to no avail. Marina realised that they would crash, so jumped out. After marking the aircraft's compass heading on a map, she plummeted into the wastelands below. The two remaining pilots flew to safety Marina was found and reunited with her colleagues. The three "Winged Sisters" returned victoriously to Moscow. They had travelled 3,672 miles (almost 6,000 kilometres), across eleven time zones, in 26 hours and 29 minutes and had (again) broken the world record. The trio was awarded the Soviet Gold Star of the Hero for this accomplishment. They were the first women ever to receive the accolade and the only ones before World War II.

Grizodubova went on to command a regiment consisting of all men, the only instance of this ever happening, Osipenko died in an aeroplane crash before the war.

After the German-Soviet war broke out on 22 June 1941, Marina used her personal influence with Joseph Stalin, and her position on the People's Defence Committee, to form all-female fighting units. There were already a few female pilots, who had been trained in aviation clubs by the Osoaviakhim (Society for Assistance to Defence, Aviation and the Chemical Industry). She had the blessing of Stavka (Shtab Glavnogo Verkhovnogo Komandovaniya, or Supreme High Command Headquarters) The Komsomol (Young Communist League) helped her to select suitable candidates. She started to form three all-female aviation regiments in October 1941.

The future aviatrixes trained in the small city of Engels on the Volga River. Their intensive courses took six, rather than the more usual 18 months to complete. The women were issued men's uniforms, which were so big that they

More events in 1938

- Howard Hughes flies a Lockheed 14N around the world in 3 days 19 hours, halving the time Wiley Post took to make the trip.

- Hitler marches into Austria.

- Britain, France, and Italy agree to let Germany partition Czechoslovakia.

were forced to stuff newspaper in their boots and to tie belts around their waists. Marina taught over a thousand women how to perform in the pressure of frontline combat. Most of these women were barely in their twenties.

The three squadrons had different duties. The 586th Fighter Aviation Regiment was the first to take part in active combat on April 16, 1942. The unit participated in 4,419 missions (125 air battles and 38 kills) under Tamara Kazarinova and Aleksandr Gridnev.

The most famous of Marina's regiments was the 46th Taman Guards Night Bomber Aviation Regiment: This unit became known as the infamous "Nachthexen" or "Night Witches," by the German troops it fought. Commanded by Yevdokia Bershanskaya, it originally began service as the 588th Night Bomber Regiment, but was redesignated in February 1943 as recognition for service which would tally 24,000 plus combat missions by the end of the war. They flew the Polikarpov Po-2, an outdated biplane. They remained solely female throughout the war, a distinction they went to some lengths to maintain.

Marina commanded the 125th Guards Bomber Aviation Regiment. The unit flew the most modern of Soviet bombers, the Petlyakov Pe-2, while many male units used obsolete aircraft, which led to much resentment. On 22 November 1942 the regiment was ordered to move to the Stalingrad Front. They fought several battles including at: Orel, Kursk, Smolensk, Vitebsk, Borisov (which it helped liberate) and Mazurian Lakes. It finished operations in May 1943, near Elblag, Poland.

Marina died in an aeroplane crash en route to Stalingrad. Leading a formation of three aircraft on 4 January 1943 in a blinding snowstorm, she crashed her aircraft into the high west bank wall of the Volga River. The entire crew was killed. Since this was a military mission, supplying aircraft to the front, Marina was considered as being killed in Action. She received the first state funeral of the war, and her body was buried in Red Square. The Americans named a ship after her, the SS Marina Raskova, in June 1943.

Her memory lives on long after her death and there are several books and websites devoted to the work she performed for the Soviets during the war.

1939

PAULINE MARY DE PEAULY GOWER (UK) 1910 –1947

Original ATA girl whose joyriding background proved invaluable in wartime

'I have heard all this talk about the futility of training women to fly and I think that the critics are wrong.... Women flyers will be very useful in an emergency. They could ferry planes. They could also act as assistant instructors, thus relieving men instructors for more combat flying." These stirring words are Pauline's, quoted in "A Harvest of Memories," her son Michael Fahie's tribute to his mother. They downplay the enormous contribution she and her colleagues made to the British Second World War effort.

Pauline Mary de Peauly was born on 22 July 1910 at Tunbridge Wells, Kent. She was the younger of Sir Robert Vaughan Gower's two daughters with his first wife. They were wealthy and she enjoyed an affluent lifestyle when she was growing up.

She left school at 18, was a debutante for a season and opted for an unladylike career - flying. Her interest in aviation had been sparked by a joyride during her last year at school. At 19, despite her father's disapproval, she arranged for flying lessons. Her parents would not pay for these, so she taught violin to fund them. After only seven hours instruction she made her first solo flight. On 4 August 1930, with fifteen hours and fifteen minutes flying time under her belt, she was awarded an A (private pilot's) licence. She was the first woman to obtain a flying certificate and first woman to fly solo after such a short period at her school.

She then enrolled at the famous London Aero Club at Stag Lane, where she met Amy Johnson, who had recently come back from her record-breaking solo trip to Australia. She also met Dorothy Spicer, who was to become her partner in several schemes. On 13 July, she won her commercial "B" licence, after completing a night flight. This made her the third woman in the world with a professional flying qualification.

Pauline and Dorothy decided to set up a joyriding business. Pauline would fly and Dorothy would act as engineer. They hired a de Havilland Gipsy Moth and later a second hand Simmonds Spartan two-seater, a twenty-first birthday gift from Pauline's father. He became supportive when he realised she was serious. They made Wallingford in Berkshire their headquarters and flew all over the country, offering joyrides and air-taxi trips.

This was all great fun and they enjoyed the lark of it, until Pauline took off one day without bolting the aircraft's folding wings in position. They then took a step back and applied themselves to their work. Pauline eventually obtained every flying certificate possible and Dorothy every qualification in aeronautical engineering.

In 1932 the pair signed up to the Modern Airways Crimson Fleet air circus and, later, the British Hospitals Air Pageant. Britain had gone 'air mad,' and several flying circuses were operating around the country. Rather like touring big tops, these air displays would trundle from town to town. The pair tired of this after a while and set up Air Trips, an aerial-taxi and joyriding business operating from Hunstanton, Norfolk. This was the first aviation company to be owned and staffed by women. In 1936 they were on the road again with Tom Campbell Black's British Empire Air Display. Pauline was chief pilot and Dorothy senior engineer.

During this tour, Pauline's mother died suddenly. Feeling that she needed to support her father, she gave up the business. Her final project with Dorothy was to write a book, "Women with Wings," which was published in 1938. Amy Johnson wrote the foreword, Pauline the body of the text, and Dorothy the prologue and epilogue.

Pauline earned several honours in the second half of 1938. She was elected as a fellow of the Royal Meteorological Society. She became sought after as a speaker and served on several committees, including the Gorrell committee, which investigated air safety. She was its youngest member and only woman.

War was about to break out. The British Royal Air Force was short on pilots. In order for the RAF aircrew to focus on combat duties, the Air Transport Auxiliary (ATA) was set up. This outfit dealt with tasks such as ferrying new aircraft from factories to the squadrons and bringing back damaged planes for repair.

Pauline was appointed as the second woman Commissioner for Civil Air Defence for London and the Southeast of England, based upon her considerable flying experience. She had 2,000 hours flying

time and 33,000 passengers under her belt, so felt she had a great deal to contribute to the war effort. She flew a variety of aircraft types to various civilian flying clubs and landing fields. In July of 1939 all civilian flying was stopped.

She used her connections and approached Lt. Colonel Sir Francis Shemerdine, the director-general of civil aviation with the idea of using women to ferry planes, alongside the newly formed all-male ATA. There was some resistance, but her persistence paid off. In November 1939 she was asked to head up this effort. She was initially tasked with recruiting eight female pilots to deliver light training aeroplanes, such as Gypsy Moths, from the de Havilland factory at Hatfield to RAF training bases in Northern England and Scotland.

On December 1 1939, she was appointed as a second officer. Two weeks later she took a ten-minute flight-test in a Gypsy Moth, and was immediately promoted to first officer. Her salary of 400 pounds per year was 20% lower than that of her male colleagues – in accordance with treasury rules. However, a milestone had been established. The women's section of the ATA was born.

On December 16, 1939, she assembled her first group of twelve women pilots at Whitchurch, and flight-tested them in a Gypsy Moth. Eight passed muster and were appointed as second officers at a salary of 26 pounds per annum (including flight pay.)

This major step forward for women in British aviation was controversial throughout the war. People were disturbed to see attractive, young and often tiny women clamber out of the cockpits of huge heavy bombers. As the war progressed, more women signed up. Eventually there were more than 150 female pilots serving in the ATA ranks. They flew all types of aircraft, from light trainers to four-engined behemoths. Their contribution was finally recognized when Pauline obtained the same pay for her women pilots as the men received for doing the same work.

She herself rose to the rank of commandant, and in 1942 was awarded a Member of the British Empire medal. Thanks to her leadership and organisational abilities, she was appointed a director of British Overseas Airways on 26 May 1943, becoming the first woman to obtain such a position in any national airline. This added to her workload enormously, since she was still responsible for the women's section of the ATA.

Easter 1945 saw her engaged to Wing Commander William Cusack Fahie and they were married on 2 June 1945 at the Brompton Oratory, London. She died suddenly on 2 March 1947, at home in Chelsea, of a heart attack. She had just given birth to twin boys, Paul and Michael.

Her life was short, but she left an enormous legacy. Without her determination and persistent dedication to aviation, women may not have flown for the ATA. Neither would they have earned equal pay for equal work. Hers is one of the few names of that era that is still recognised in many circles, despite not being as well known as some of her more celebrated peers, such as Amy Johnson and Amelia Earhart. It took many years, but in 1997 the British government finally acknowledged the contribution that the ATA had made to the war.

Events in 1939

■ **September 1: Germany invades Poland. The Luftwaffe plays a key tactical bombing role in neutralising Polish defences.**

■ **September 3: Britain and France declare war on Germany. World War II breaks out.**

1939

LETTICE CURTIS
(UK)

Pilot, flight test engineer and writer, Lettice Curtis brought her many talents to bear on British aviation. Her name will inevitably be linked with the Air Transport Auxiliary (ATA), thanks to her diligent writing about what the organisation really did.

Lettice Curtis was born near Newton Abbot in Devon. In a fascinating interview she gave to Helen Krasner for Today's Pilot magazine in 2007, she revealed that her father felt strongly that girls as well as boys might need to earn their living and should be given a good education. He sent her to Benenden School. She went to Oxford University in 1933, where she studied mathematics. A keen sportswoman, she was captain of the women's lawn tennis and fencing teams and played lacrosse for the university.

She left Oxford in 1937 and was keen to get a job. She told Krasner: "I had become very conscious of the amount of money my parents had spent on my education, and was restless for the day when I would no longer be the burden I felt myself to be on their finances."

Unsure what to do with herself, she stopped at Haldon Airfield in Devon on day and got talking to a pilot there. She discovered that she, too, could earn her living that way and decided to get her licence. She insisted that her motivation was financial rather than passion for the skies.

However, she earned her licence in 1938 and within a month was working for an outfit that performed aerial survey work for the Ordnance Survey. By the time the Second World War broke out she had a fair amount of hours in her logbook, rendering her eligible to fly for the ATA.

Headquartered at White Waltham airfield, the ATA was established in the summer of 1939 for communications work, and performing duties such as ferrying government ministers. Its remit grew and the pilots were required to deliver new aircraft from factories to military bases, thus freeing RAF pilots for operational duties by using civilian pilots. British women flew fighter planes for the first time. The ATA also recruited disabled First World War veterans, as well as pilots who were too old to serve in the RAF.

There were 1,300 pilots based at 14 'ferry pools' scattered all over the country. They would be flown from these airfields to factories where they would pick up factory fresh aeroplanes and fly them, generally solo and without navigational aids, to RAF bases as far north as Lossiemouth in Scotland.

In July 1940, Lettice became one of the second group of 17 women to be recruited. She was first based at Hatfield, where she flew Tiger Moths, before being moved to Hamble and finally White Waltham. She wrote: "People forget how serious the war was in 1941. Ships were being sunk and towns were being bombed. They were building more and more aircraft and it was important they were got away from the factories, because they were liable to be bombed."

ATA pilots worked ceaselessly to move incredible thousands of aircraft, including 57,000 Spitfires. Lettice's logbook soon filled up with various types. According to her autobiography, one day's entry alone featured the following: air taxi White Waltham to Brooklands; Wellington - Brooklands to Little Rissington; Spitfire - Little Rissington to LLandow; Mosquito - St Athan to Ford; Mustang - Ford to Lichfield;

More events in 1939

- **Spanish Civil War ended as Franco took Madrid.**
- **September 3rd: War declared on Germany by Britain and France.**

taxi Puss Moth Lichfield to Castle Bromwich; Wellington - Castle Bromwich to White Waltham. Her total flying time was 4 hours 5 minutes that day.

A skilled pilot, she was the first woman to fly a four-engined heavy bomber. After the war she worked with the Ministry of Civil Aviation for a short time, before becoming a technician and flight test observer at A&AEE, Boscombe Down. This entailed flying aircraft overseas to test the airframes and systems in hot weather. Lettice also took up air racing, and achieved a British women's National Record in 1949. In April 1950, she bought her own aircraft, a two-seater Wicko.

In 1953 Lettice took a position as a flight development engineer with Fairey Aviation at White Waltham. She worked there for seven years, eventually moving on to the Ministry of Aviation. Her role there was to help develop the joint civil/RAF Air Traffic Control Centre at West Drayton. She retired from the CAA in 1976, and took a job with a human resources firm.

Outside of her work, she remained dedicated to aviation. She continued to fly light aircraft and earned her instrument rating in 1974. When she retired a few years later on, she decided she would like to learn to fly a helicopter. This came about thanks to her many networking activities. An active member of the British Women Pilots' Association, Lettice took part in a day BWPA had arranged whereby members could have trial helicopter lessons. She was instantly hooked and decided to carry on to earn her licence. She trained at White Waltham.

Lettice told Krasner, who is a helicopter instructor and author of "The Helicopter Pilot's Companion," that she had found rotary wing flying "hard work". However, she earned her PPL (H) in 1992, and flew several cross-country flights. Within a few years Lettice hung up her wings for good, staying in touch with aviation through the many societies of which she is a member.

The Yorkshire Air Museum at Elvington holds her logbooks and uniform and she has published two books; "Lettice Curtis, Her Autobiography" (2004) and "The Forgotten Pilots," her own account of the ATA (1971). One of the most respected names in British Aviation, Lettice lives in Berkshire and makes occasional welcome appearances at formal aviation events.

> **The ATA moved over 57,000 Supermarine Spitfires - one of the classic fighter aircraft of all time. In the United Kingdom it has become a part of cultural legend, the aeroplane that won the Battle of Britain.**
>
> Because of its success, - in all, an estimated 22 579 Spitfires served in all spheres of the Second World War and afterwards – there are several still available. This means that they tend to get used in films and television shows and the like when depicting events of World War Two. In the 1930s, the Spitfire was cutting edge technology. It remained in service almost until 1950, with several upgraded variants. For many people the sleek Spitfire is synonymous with the most famous aero engine of the War, the Rolls-Royce Merlin.

1939

KATARINA MATANOVIC KULENOVIC (CROATIA) 1913 – 2003

"If I ever earn enough money in my life to buy a decent aircraft, I will fly to the ends of the earth."
Katarina Matanovic Kulenovic, first Croatian female pilot and parachutist

 adly, Katarina Matanovic Kulenovic never realised her dream. Instead, she travelled the hard road from celebrity to poverty; was accused as a traitor and banned from doing what she loved.

Katarina Matanovic was born on 18th March 1913 in the village of Vuka near Osijek. She finished at the local primary school in 1924 and moved to Zagreb in 1927 to continue her studies. By 1930 she was finished at high school and started working at Svab, a construction company in 1931.

She had decided to learn to fly when she saw a newspaper advert offering lessons at the Zagreb Flying School. Since the course was open to women, Katarina decided to give it a go. She was the only female there. She went up for the first time in 1935. She signed up for lessons in 1936 and was taught by Ivan Marko. She earned her wings that same year, garnering Brevet number 139. She graduated after a flight test and written exam in 1936, earning herself a diploma as a sport pilot. This made her the first female licensed pilot in Croatia. She then participated in many different airshows and competitions.

In 1938 she added another first at the inaugural international aeroplane exhibition in Zemun, near Belgrade. The organisers added a big international airshow to the event. There was a rich programme on offer, featuring different types of aircraft and gliders demonstrating their aerial prowess. The famous Italian aerobatic team, "The Squadron of Death" were present, as well as many representatives from all over Europe.

The programme also included the first Croatian group parachute jump, featuring ten parachutists. Katarina added her name to the team roster. In an interview in 1998 she said: "I had insisted that the organiser of the airshow allow me to jump. He did not want to let me at first. I had the impression that they thought that I was joking. But, when they saw

More events in 1939

■ Amelia Earhart is officially declared dead after her disappearance.

■ The United States declares its neutrality in the war.

that I was determined, they suggested that I practice jumping from the parachute tower the day before the real event." The English company, Aluminium Union had built a huge tower of almost 100 meters high on the fair ground. Katarina jumped from it twice. She continued: "They thought that would help me to break my fear of heights. But, I did not have any fear; I was already used to heights as a pilot. I had not had regular parachute jump training, though. However, jumping with the parachute was simply like flying a plane." The jump took place on 5th of June 1938 from a height of 1,500m above the field.

During the seven days of the exhibition Katarina stayed with the mother of a pilot, because all the hotels were full. The woman refused to believe her when she told her she intended to make the jump. Katarina said: "She didn't believe me, like everyone else. They all thought that I must be crazy. This lady did not want to talk to me any more. Only after I had jumped, and all the newspapers had written about that, then everyone believed me."

She arrived at the airfield early in the morning of the day of the meeting. The first thing she did was to ask the air force military commander whether there would be any parachute jumping. His replied that there would be and asked her: "Do you really want to do this? I thought you were joking." Several of the other pilots tried to dissuade us, but she refused to listen. The parachute manufacturers Knebl and Dietrich were on hand to help the jumpers into their life-saving "Irvins." They wrestled her into her parachute, but because she was dwarfed by it, they had to tighten the safety straps with a handkerchief to prevent it from sliding off her shoulders.

She described what happened next: "I could not get into my aeroplane seat straight away; it was hard for me to get climb in with two parachutes. The reserve one was tightened around my waist, and the main one was firmly on my shoulders. Knebl and Dietrich were scratching their heads and saying: Damn! How are you going to come out when you can't even get in? I answered: I'll get out very easily, I will just fall out"

She became the first woman in both Croatia and the Balkan States to jump out of an aircraft. A big media star, she was extremely popular on the airshow circuit. She jumped ten times in total, injuring herself slightly only once and not enough to bother her. 1938 saw two her star in another big aero meet. The following year, she was the star turn at a female aero meeting in Zagreb, where she both flew and jumped. Such was her popularity that a popular Croatian author wrote a novel about her exploits, called "The case of Miss Katarina" in 1939.

Around the same time, she beefed up her flying skills, attending further training in Pancevo, where she flew several different types of aircraft. In summer 1939 she flight-tested a new, strong glider, called the "Komar". There was a great deal of glider manufacturing in Zagreb in that era and 16 new gliders had come on to the market.

In 1941 she joined the Independent State of Croatia (NDH) Croatian air force and was promoted to Lieutenant. She flew for the 19th Air Force unit. Her duties included mail runs, and ferrying war materials and people around the region. She sometimes even flew ministers. She then became a personal pilot to the Minister of the Military Forces, Ante Vukic.

1942 was a busy year for her. She married journalist, Namik Kulenovic, who wrote for the daily newspaper "Novosti". She also undertook more training and became a parachute instructor. She fell pregnant in 1944, but suffered a huge loss when her husband was killed when his aircraft was shot down by the alliance forces on the way to Bihach, She was wounded herself in 1944 when Borongaj airport was bombed. In 1945 she gave birth to her son Namik.

After the war, Katarina was accused of spying for the Germans. Like the majority of NDH military personnel, she was persecuted and thrown out of her flat. She was banned from flying. This was a complete contrast to her pre war existence. Before the Second World War she was a big celebrity. She drifted into obscurity and by 1990 she was completely forgotten and unknown to the public. It is difficult today to find many of the documents and information relating to her flying and post war existence.

However, she was redeemed somewhat in 1998 when the president of the Republic of Croatia, Franjo Tudgman, honoured her for her contribution to Croatian aviation and light aviation. She was bestowed with the Order of Dania Croatia Medal. At this point aviation historian Boris Pulaski picked up on her story and wrote her biography, named, wrote a book about her, "Katarina on wings."

On 26th December 2001 she was given honorary lifetime membership of the Zagreb Aero Club, which took good care of their former star. After 56 years she had finally returned to aviation. She left them her papers and photographs to the club, including the one on this page. She also toured schools and clubs promoting aviation to young people. She died impoverished two years later on 24 April 2003. Zagreb Aero Club paid for the funeral.

Katarina achieved a great deal in her short flying career. She was a pilot at the time when aviators were setting records crossing oceans, with many dying in the process. Long haul flying had not taken off. Certainly it was highly unusual for a woman to be flying aircraft. She paid a higher price than most to earn her wings, but kept the faith and spent the final part of her life back with the society she loved. She may have been forgotten in her lifetime, but her memory lives on.

HILDA YAN YAQING (CHINA) 1906 – 1970

Barnstorming daredevil who flew to save her country

Who knows what the beautiful young aviatrix from China was thinking as she lay in the wreckage of her aircraft, dazed but conscious, and thousands of miles away from her homeland? Her daring mission looked doomed and she was dependent on the kindness of strangers to get her to safety. It was all a far cry from her childhood.

Hilda Yan Yaqing was born on or around 17 January 1906 in Shanghai, the daughter of an eminent well-travelled doctor. In 1922 her father went to Harvard, taking his family with him. Hilda sat the entrance exam for Smith College in Massachusetts without telling her parents. She was accepted, becoming the youngest-ever Chinese student accorded that honour. She had to leave in 1924 without completing her degree when her family returned to China.

In 1925 Hilda attended the Yale in China Institute in Shanghai. There was a great deal of anti foreign feeling at the time and the student union voted that the American president of the school, Dr Edward Hume, must die. Hilda got wind of the plan and told him he was to be shot at dawn. Her intervention saved his life.

Although Hilda's father had a modern outlook, he still picked out a husband for his daughter. He chose Chen Bingzhang, an ambitious young man who aimed to work in government. Yan felt he would be a good match for his headstrong daughter. They were married in 1927 and had a son William, born in July 1928. Hilda was also actively involved in local politics. Her daughter Doreen was born in 1932.

Meanwhile Hilda's uncle, Yan Huiqing, had been appointed ambassador to the Soviet Union. He tried to resign, citing ill-health, but was not allowed to do so. His wife was unsupportive and refused to accompany him to the USSR, and Yan urgently needed help organising the heavy round of formal functions he was obliged to hold. He proposed that Hilda went instead. So in 1935 she abandoned her husband and two children and did exactly that.

She moved into a new world and was in her element. She lived in Russia and Geneva, and addressed the League of Nations in 1935, speaking up for women's rights. She decided to leave her husband in 1936 and signed divorce papers in London, so that she could follow her wishes.

She returned to Shanghai and an event happened that shaped her destiny. Generalissimo Chiang kai-shek was about to celebrate his fiftieth birthday and the good citizens of China dug deep to buy him ten Curtiss Hawk III type aircraft as a contribution towards his defence against the Japanese attack they knew was coming. A huge crowd gathered at Longhua airfield in Shanghai for the presentation.

The most exciting part of the event was an aerobatic display by China's foremost aviatrix Li Xiaqing. Hilda watched and knew she wanted to fly too. The pair met up and discovered they had a great deal in common. They had both lived in Geneva. They also each had two small children and had divorced their spouses, which was highly unusual for the day. They decided to set up a group to encourage women to fly.

Hilda returned to Geneva. She fought against the trafficking of women and children, but her motions were overshadowed by the outbreak of war between China and Japan. On July 7 1937 the Sino-Japanese war broke out and lasted for eight years. China desperately needed a strong air force. Emperor Hirohito and Benito Mussolini signed an anti communist pact and the Japanese invaded Shanghai on August 9 while Hilda was in Europe.

She sailed for New York in 1937. Her family was safe in Hong Kong and she announced that she would fly back to China to fight against Japan. She started to learn in January 1938 at Safair Flying Services in Long Island, paying $700 for her lessons in Fleet Trainers and Curtiss Wright Sedans. She also spent a great deal of her time actively promoting the Chinese cause in Washington.

On November 15 1938 she earned her flying licence. In 1939 her friend Li Xiaqing flew to New York to meet her and the pair planned to barnstorm America to raise funds and awareness for their suffering people back home. They wanted to urge the US to stop supplying Japan with steel and fuel, which it was turning into weapons against China. They also

More events in 1939

- Britain's Women's Auxiliary Air Force is formed.

- The big-screen adaptation of Gone with the Wind premieres and grosses $192 million, making it one of the most profitable films of all time.

...ried to warn the Americans that Japan would surely turn on the Pacific Rim nations. They got two aircraft on loan, with help from star aviatrix Jackie Cochran.

They planned their trip meticulously. The more experienced Xiaqing was to fly longer legs, but Hilda was to take in more cities. Xiaqing would finish in June, whereas Hilda would bring her tour to an end in July. They booked halls and attracted sponsorship from prominent individuals including the Roosevelts, Jackie Cochran and Helen Keller. They refused to accept personal donations, but sent any monies they raised to Washington in support of Relief for China movement.

Walter Beech and the Porterfield Aircraft Corporation each donated an aircraft. On March 23 1939, Hilda and Li took off from Floyd Bennett Airfield in a chirpy red Stinson Reliant SR-9B monoplane, named the "Spirit of New China." Bishop Yubin greeted them at their first stop in Washington.

They were enormously popular. However, they never forgot why they were doing their tour. There were 30 million suffering refugees back home in China and they wanted to alert the world.

On April 1939, the famous aviator Roscoe Turner flew a Porterfield 35-W two-passenger high wing monoplane to Washington. The aircraft was painted dark red and sported identical lettering to its companion. It was also called "The Spirit of New China." Hilda set off, spending two or three days in each city she visited. She lost faith in her aircraft as it kept running out of fuel, so she had to make several forced landings.

Her tour stopped abruptly on May 1 in a cornfield near Mobile. After an uneventful touchdown on April 27, she took off again for Birmingham intending to speak at a presentation that afternoon. She was running low on fuel, so decided to head for Montgomery and fill up. Unfortunately she overshot the city. She spotted a large field and elected to land. She underestimated the height of the crops at the end of the field she had chosen as a runway and aborted her first takeoff. She made the fatal decision to attempt a daring aerobatic manoeuvre. She had noticed a gap at the opposite end between some orange trees flanking the field. She opted to take off and bank steeply at the last minute to clear the trees.

Seconds later she and her aircraft were lying broken in the field next door. Local farm boys pulled her to safety and took her to be patched up.

She lost her flying nerve, but continued her fundraising tour by road. She hooked up with Xiaqing in June and continued to promote the cause as best she could. In 1941, she joined her family in Hong Kong. On December 8 that year, the Japanese bombed HK, the day after they had decimated Pearl Harbor. After eight months of exile, she escaped and flew back to the US via India. In 1943 she attended a concert in Washington to lend support to the black contralto Marian Anderson, who sold out her concert and directed the proceeds to the China Relief Fund.

Hilda also became deeply involved with the Baha'i faith and toured giving lectures on the movement. She met John Male a liaison officer in the UN department of public information and married him in 1948. They were divorced a decade later, but not before they had brought Hilda's children to the US to escape the clutches of Mao Zedong. Unfortunately Li Fuqing had fallen foul of the Gang of Four.

Hilda had a few other relationships and settled peacefully in the US. She died on March 18 1970. Despite all the glory her brave venture brought her in 1939 for a selfless cause, her name is hardly known today. Pat Gully has written an excellent book, telling her story as well as that of two other largely forgotten Chinese aviatrixes. "Sisters of Heaven" is well worth a read as their achievements were every bit as important as those of the more celebrated names featured in this book.

LI XIAQING
(CHINA) 1912 - 1998

"As far as the average person is concerned flying is a man's business – as if women should be excluded – but I want to do something women usually don't have an opportunity of doing," Li Xiaqing

Li Xiaqing was born into a revolutionary family. Her grandmother Xu Mulan operated an embroidery shop, which was a front for a bomb-making factory. Her nickname "Dandan" means "bomb," because her parents used her pram to transport explosives. She had an unconventional upbringing. Her mother contracted TB and died when she was only four. She was reared by her father and his concubines and became a tomboy who knew how to flirt.

She left school at fourteen to become a movie star. She enjoyed a string of film successes, but her father withdrew her from the film industry in 1928 and sent her to Europe to finish school.

In 1929 he brokered a marriage for her with Zheng Baifeng, who was 11 years her senior.

They went to Geneva where her husband worked at the League of Nations. They had two children. Three days after their son Pax was born in 1931 Japan invaded Manchuria.

In 1933 Xiaqing attended an air show in Paris and fell in love with aerobatics. In October 1933, she enrolled for flying lessons. She earned her brevet from the Swiss Aeroclub on 6th August 1934, becoming the first woman to earn a license in Geneva.

She applied to the Boeing School of Aeronautics as she had heard it was supposed to be the best in world. The school was reluctant to take her, but eventually admitted its first female student in January 1935. The instructors were 18 ex-combat pilots and top of their field. The school had Boeing Stinson and Stearman trainers and a Ford Trimotor, which the students were allowed to try out.

Her family saw her off in California, but then went to live in China. Her American teachers were tough and insisted on treating her as they did her male peers. She had to sit on a cushion and have blocks on the foot pedals to control the aircraft and they cut her no slack. She also learned to dismantle and reassemble an engine and how to fly on instruments. Believing that as a pilot she could help her country's war effort, she requested extra aerobatic training from LeRoy B Gregg.

In the middle of her first lesson, during a barrel roll 2,200 feet over San Francisco Bay, she inadvertently achieved a world record. Gregg discovered that his pupil's safety belt had snapped and she was plummeting into the black waters below. He also discovered that she had remembered her lessons well and watched as she floated down to relative safety – the first Chinese woman to be saved by deploying a parachute. However, she was now bobbing in the sea in a heavy leather-flying suit. A Navy reserve amphibian flew out to pick her up, but could not release its pontoons, so flew back to base. She had to wait a full 20 minutes before another arrived to haul her to safety. She was tested for exposure, but coolly told the flocks of reporters converging on the hospital that the whole adventure had been "thrilling." Like Fay Gillis Wells before her, she became a member of the Caterpillar Club, whose ranks are only open to people who have floated to safety after an emergency parachute jump from an aircraft.

She next became the first woman to graduate from the Boeing School in 1935. She moved back to Shanghai in 1936 and threw herself into aviation circles. Xiaqing flew from the Shanghai flying club, which had a Junkers Junior A50 (two-seat monoplane) and an Avro Avian biplane.

Initially the Chinese government did not wish to grant her a license, but she took a test flight with a Chinese air force examiner. She performed so well that Generalissimo Chiang Kai-Shek presented her with the license himself. She was given the use of a government plane and assigned to inspect the airfields throughout China. She was dismayed to discover that the instruments in her aircraft did not work, and the airfields that existed were rudimentary. Her maps were inaccurate, weather reports unreliable and there were no guidance systems in place.

However, she achieved a 30,000-mile long distance flight and worked hard to improve conditions. She organised a new flying school in Shanghai and became the only female flying instructor

there. She divorced her husband, who refused her access to their children. She only got to see them when she bribed his servants.

In 1936 at a fundraising benefit, Xiaqing stunned the crowds with a stupendous aerobatic display, seducing Hilda Yan, who was in the crowd, into the world of flying. This was the first aerobatic display by a Chinese woman and involved a power dive directly over the VIP podium, rearing up inches from the dignitaries' heads before safely climbing into the sky.

She and Hilda had a great deal in common and set up a group to promote aviation to women. This came to naught as the Japanese invaded China in 1937. She marched into the aviation commission and requested that she put in command of a combat squadron and engage in operational flying. She was refused and grounded. She then worked in hospitals with the Red Cross, broadcasting anti-Japanese messages from a radio station. This earned her a spot on the Japanese black list and she had to flee to Hong Kong.

She wanted to contribute to the war effort and hatched a plan to fly round the US raising funds and China's profile. She flew the famous China Clipper to the US and grabbed headlines saying she would fly on behalf of the Red Cross throughout America. Supported by the ex-pat Chinese community in San Francisco, she earned her American private licence and met up with Hilda. Jackie Cochran supported the pair, who were flying two separate aeroplanes around the country on behalf of the China civilian relief committee to support Paul Yubin, the exiled Bishop of Nanking. Xiaqing toured with her 1939 Stinson Reliant SR 9B called "the Spirit of New China," which had an identical paint scheme to Hilda's aircraft.

The tour was highly successful and raised a great deal of money. Xiaqing was given free food and lodging wherever she went, so everything she raised went towards the war effort. Beautiful and dainty, journalists loved her tiny frame and huge spirit. The slogan

Events in 1940

- ■ Winston Churchill becomes Britain's Prime Minister.
- ■ Trotsky is assassinated in Mexico.
- ■ The first McDonald's hamburger stand opens in Pasadena, California.

went "Saving the nation by aviation." She was upset by Hilda's crash and once she knew her friend was all right, she continued with her flight. (Although she switched her aircraft for a Stinson Racer SR 5E, since she was running into mechanical trouble in Chicago.) On June 15, she arrived back at Newark, having been on tour for three months, earning more than $10,000 over 10,000 miles for civilian refuges in her homeland.

Her next venture was to fly round South America. She planned her route meticulously. She took off in her Aeronca heading for Havana. Her plan was to make her way to the Andes, then fly to Buenos Aeries and Rio, then back to Miami in a three months excursion. This caused a sensation. During her journey she took in nine out of fourteen South American countries and covered 18,000 miles. She also took time out to perform a one-hour demonstration of military aircraft over Peru and raised $40,000 in relief aid.

In 1940 she helped Ruth Nichols raise funds for her relief wings venture. Xiaqing was then hired by the United China Relief fund and stayed until the end of the war. In 1940, she flew the Aeronca on a goodwill tour covering 45,000 miles. After the 1941 Peal Harbor bombings, her sponsors were too nervous to let her try risky flying tours.

In 1946 she returned to China and was devastated to see the corruption and poverty in her former hometown. She settled in Hong Kong and lived with her father. She got an HK private pilot's license and flew for pleasure around the region in the 1950s. She met George Yixiang Li, eventually marrying him in 1971. In 1997 she was stood in the Hong Kong convention centre, thrilled at the Handover back from the British. She died on January 24 1998.

Xiaqing's story is the stuff of legends and largely forgotten today. Patti Gully's excellent biography: "Sisters of Heaven" documents the amazing tale and is well worth reading.

1942
NANCY HARKNESS LOVE (USA) 1914 – 1976

Methodical test pilot who commanded the WASP

Nancy was one of that rare breed of flyer, who leads by example. Her strength of character persuaded the US Army Air Force to entrust her and the remarkable women she commanded to fly the most sophisticated warplanes of that era. The giant had reluctantly lent an ear to the steely aviatrix, but it was time for him to reassert his authority.

Nancy Harkness Love was born February 14th 1914 in Houghton, Michigan. Her father was a wealthy physician. Like so many of the contemporary women pioneers, Nancy was drawn to aviation from an early age. She witnessed Charles Lindbergh alighting at Le Bourget, after his historic transatlantic solo flight in 1927. Then a joyride in a barnstormer's biplane sealed it for a teenage Nancy during the summer break of 1930.

She made her first solo aged 16 after just four and a half hours of instruction on a creaking, Fleet biplane. Five weeks later Nancy gained her pilot's licence. However, she erred on the side of caution as the prestigious Milton Academy high school she attended had a strict "no flying" rule code of conduct. Rules did not stop the budding aviatrix from buzzing the campus of a neighbouring university during her freshman year at college.

Enrolling at Vassar College in 1931, Nancy paid more attention to flying than she did to her professors. She was eventually called the "Flying Freshman," and her avid enthusiasm lead her to establish the first student flying clubs in a number of US colleges. She also shored up her allowance by giving joyrides from Poughkeepsie Airport. The amassed flying hours eventually translated into a commercial transport rating in 1933. Now a member of a select few licensed women pilots, Nancy became a charter member of Ninety Nines founded by Amelia Earhart.

The great depression had taken its toll on the family's finances and she was forced to drop out of college in January 1934. She found work in Boston selling aeroplanes on behalf of Beechcraft and Waco airframe manufacturers. She had made such an impression on one notable customer, Joseph Kennedy Sr, that he offered his son's hand in holy matrimony. The proposition was no doubt politely refused as she then went to work and fly for a new start up company called Inter-City Aviation.

This charter flight and aircraft sales enterprise was the brainchild of Princeton graduate and MIT alumni Robert Love. Nancy's feminine charms were not enough to lift the depressing the sales figures at Inter-City Aviation. However, they did have a marked affect on the proprietor of the company, who asked her to marry him.

Recognition of her flying skills brought Nancy to the attention of one Phoebe Omlie of the Bureau of Air Commerce in 1935. She accepted Phoebe's offer to fly for the Bureau and participate in its National Air Marking Program. The endeavour involved identifying prominent landmarks visible from the air to serve as additional navigation aids for pilots. Nancy flew above the eastern seaboard from Maine to Florida, overseeing the painting of over 290 air markers during October 1935.

In January 1936 she tied the knot with Robert Love and their honeymoon consisted of a flying jaunt to California. On her return she flew as charter pilot for her husband's company, and also found the time to serve as pilot for the Bureau of Air Commerce.

In September 1936, on an excursion back to California, she found herself in the midst of competition flying. She took part in the Amelia Earhart Trophy race in Los Angeles, managing to cross the finishing pylon fifth. At another race in Detroit she bettered her position by achieving second place. Finding the frenetic and very haphazard approach to air racing not to her methodical palate, Nancy hung up racing goggles for good.

Between 1937 and 1938, she flew as test pilot on the on behalf of the Gwinn Aircar Company based in New York. Nancy safety tested various aircraft modifications and innovations. She also tested the firm's new fixed tricycle landing gear system mated to a diminutive airframe resembling a car with wings.

From such innocuous beginnings tail sitting planes would be a thing of the past. The new undercarriage system would eventually proliferate throughout the newer bombers and transports rolling off the war production lines.

By late 1938 the prospect of war loomed and was about to engulf Europe. Nancy assisted the war effort in 1940 by becoming a member of Civil Air Patrol. Her experiences flying for the Bureau of Air Commerce had qualified her to ferry light trainer planes to Canada for onward delivery to the allies in Europe. She was not alone, as many experienced women pilots were also ferrying planes to the Canadian border.

She then wrote a letter to Col Robin Olds who was the commander of the newly formed Ferry Command of the Army Air Corps in May 1940. She apprised him of the existence of 49 highly qualified women pilots capable of flying aeroplanes fresh out of the factories to the frontline bases. Col Robin Olds felt the idea had sufficient merit and presented it to his superior, Chief of Staff General Henry 'Hap' Arnold who dismissed the notion of using women as ferry pilots due to the risks of being engaged by the enemy.

Down but not out, Nancy resolved to strengthen her case. In 1942 her husband would inadvertently come to her rescue as a Reserve Major called to active duty to Washington. Robert

Events in 1942

■ A Messerschmitt Me 262 prototype makes its first flight under jet power, replacing propeller.

■ RCA Victor sprays gold over Glenn Miller's million-seller "Chattanooga Choo Choo," creating first "gold record.

mentioned his wife's daily commute to Baltimore in her own aircraft to the head of domestic wing of the Ferrying Division, one Col William Tunner. This set into motion rapid events leading to the creation of the Women's Auxiliary Ferrying Squadron (WAFS) in September 1942. Nancy, at just 28 was appointed overall commander for the group. The squadron operated from New Castle Army Airfield in Wilmington, Delaware.

Starting with just 29 pilots, by August 1943 Nancy was in command of 225 women. That same month the WAFS were merged with Jackie Cochran's Women's Flying Training Detachment (WFTD) to establish the Women's Air Force Service Pilots (WASP). Nancy became executive director of the ferrying portion of the larger WASP entity, commanding six squadrons in total. She and her pilots flew every type of aircraft in the US Army Air Corps inventory, from high-speed pursuit fighters to bombers. Generally the non-commissioned civilian WASP pilots were of a higher calibre in terms of flying experience and academic qualifications than their commissioned male counterparts.

Nancy was always the first to be checked out on the various aeroplanes, from the P-51 Mustang, to the twin boom P-38 Lightning to the Douglas C-47 transport plane. Her proficiency extended to 14 different types and she became the first to pilot a B-25 Mitchell bomber from coast to coast setting a new record in 1943. Silencing many of her detractors, Nancy along with fellow pilot Betty Gilles, flew the venerable B-17 Flying Fortress bomber later made famous by the exploits of the legendary Memphis Belle.

The WASP was disbanded late in December 1944. By then women pilots had delivered over 12,000 aircraft of 77 different types within the continental United States. The WASP had ferried over half the entire volume of fighter planes used in active service during the war.

Soon after the cessation of the war, Nancy was awarded the Air Medal for "Operational leadership in the successful training and assignment of over 300 qualified women fliers in the flying of advanced military aircraft'."

Settling into civilian life, she raised a family of three daughters with Robert, who went on to establish an airline. She succumbed to cancer in 1976 and passed away aged 62. Following her death, a box was discovered brimming with clippings and photographs of all the women who died under her command. Three years following her death the US military officially recognised the women of the WASP for their actions during World War II.

Nancy was posthumously inducted into the Michigan Women's Hall of Fame in 1997 and the National Aviation Hall of Fame in Dayton, Ohio in 2005.

Nancy Harkness Love possessed wisdom beyond her years. She planted the seeds of equality that germinated into the recognition decades later that the same mission can be accomplished by either gender.

Today men and women serve under the auspices of one air force, sharing the same squadron patch. They strive for the same pilot wings. Nancy climbed that impossibly high beanstalk, and finally the giant listened to her quietly spoken words.

1942

LILYA VLADIMIROVNA LITVAK (RUSSIA) 1921–1943

The White Rose of Stalingrada, a beautiful blonde with a heart of ice as far as combat was concerned.

Lydia Vladimirovna Litvyak, also known as Lydia Litvak or Lily Litvak, was a female fighter pilot in the Soviet Air Force during the Second World War. With 12 victories to her name, she is one of Russia's only two World War II female fighter aces, along with Katya Budanova.

Lidya was born in Moscow in August 18th, 1921. Nicknamed Lilya; in 1940 she completed middle school, and flight training at the Chkalov Aeroclub in Moscow. At the age of fifteen she had completed her first solo flight. She refreshed her flying skills at the Kherson flight academy, and qualified to be a flight instructor. She then trained students at the Moscow Aeroclub. When the war broke out in 1941 she had already trained 45 students and applied to fight at the front. She applied to military aviation units and was turned down a few times, because of her lack of experience.

Major Marina Raskova had established three female air combat squadrons, and recruited top talent to train in Engels. Lilya exaggerated her experience and began military training on October 15, 1941 on the Yakovlev Yak-1 aircraft. She began her military service in the all-female 586th IAP, where she flew mostly defence missions from January to August 1942. The situation at and around Stalingrad became increasingly grave. In August she was posted to a mixed squadron because of her talent. Along with Yekaterina Budanova and several others she was transferred to the 286th IAD, stationed at Kotielnikovo airfield near Stalingrad.

She flew her first combat flights in the summer of 1942 over Saratov. In September, she was assigned, along with seven other women (including Katya Budanova), to the 437th IAP, fighting over Stalingrad. She flew a Lavochkin La-5 fighter. On September 13, she scored her first two victories, becoming the first known woman in the world to shoot down an enemy aircraft. Lilya was wingman to the regimental commander and spotted three Junkers JU-88 flanked by a fighter squadron of Messerschmitt Bf 109s. Her leader attacked and Lilya followed. She attacked with such vigour that the bombers scattered and dropped their bombs. The commander then shot down one Ju 88, while Lilya destroyed a second.

Lilya then noticed her friend, Raya Belyaeva, defenceless with all her ammunition expended, being targeted by a BF-109. So Lilya shot the German fighter down. He was a highly decorated fighter ace. Few novice pilots at the front managed two kills in one day. Later that year she was moved to the 9th Guards Fighter Regiment. She painted a white lily on each side of her YaK-1 cockpit, which was often confused for a rose, giving rise to her nickname. According to her mechanic Inna Pasportnikova she was so fond of flowers that she often picked wildflowers and carried them with her on missions. The white lily became infamous among the Germans, who definitely did not want to get close enough to smell it.

At the end of January 1943, she was transferred to the 296th along with two other skilled female fighter pilots. On February 17th, 1943, she was awarded the Order of the Red Banner. Two days later she was promoted to junior lieutenant and soon after to senior lieutenant.

She was shot down and injured twice. At the beginning of 1943, some reports suggest she married fighter ace Aleksey Solomatin, who was killed in action shortly afterwards. On 22 March, she got into a dogfight with four Messerschmitt Bf 109s over Khakov. She had shot down a Ju 88 that was flying with them. She managed to shoot down two of the German fighters, and drove off the rest. This engagement coincided exactly with the only two German Bf 109s lost in the same area on this date.

The two German fighter pilots shot down were lieutenant Franz Müller and Unteroffizier Karl-Otto Harloffof the 9th squadron, fighter wing 3. German records say that these men, who both survived, reported being shot down by Russian fighters. After the intense 15 minute dogfight, Lilya-wounded from the deadly engagement, limped back to base in her bullet riddled and stricken Yak fighter. She went to hospital and was ordered to rest for a month. But she discharged herself early and went back to the front.

On her return, the 296th IAP had been renamed the 73 Guards IAP. On 5 May 1943 Lilya, still unwell, took part in dogfights, and notched up another kill. Two days later she shot down another Bf-109. She was wounded again in combat on July 16. She was shot

More events in 1942

- A Messerschmitt Me 262 prototype makes its first flight under jet power, test-piloted by Fritz Wendel. Previous flights had been driven by a propeller.

- US government establishes Manhattan Project to coordinate efforts to design and build atomic bomb.

down in German-occupied territory, but managed to escape on foot. Three days later she took off again. On July 19, she lost her friend Katya who was shot down in a duel with three Messerschmitts.

On 21st July she flew as wingman to her unit's commander. Seven Bf 109s attacked them. Lilya managed to shoot down one of the 'Messers', but her Yak was heavily hit and she belly-landed. Within a few short months she had been involved in intense fights, had been wounded and had experienced the death of close friends, such as Katya and Alieksiey Solomatin. She was physically and mentally exhausted.

Lilya was shot down on August 1st 1943, during one of the most horrendous air battles of the war. Her mission that day was on the front line, looking for enemy bombers. Ten miles from the front they found some. Ivan Borisenko, her commander that day wrote later to Vera Tilomerva, the commissar of the women's fighter regiment: "Lilya just didn't see the Messerschmitt 109's flying cover for the German bombers. A pair of them dived on her and when she did see them she turned to meet them. Then they all disappeared behind a cloud." Lilya's luck had run out, but no one saw her aircraft crash.

She went missing behind enemy lines. The Air Force command announced that her body must be found before she would be awarded the Hero of the Soviet Union. In the summer of 1979 high school students in the Ukraine, reportedly learned that she had been buried in a common grave.

The authorities agreed that her aircraft had come down near Dmitrovka, a village in Shakhterski and that she had been killed in action. In March 1986 the Ministry of Defence acknowledged that the remains were hers. Four years later in May 1990, President Mikhail Gorbachev posthumously awarded her Hero of the Soviet Union. This was added to the Order of the Red Banner, Order of the Red Star, and Order of the Patriotic War that she had been given.

There are so many conflicting reports around this great World War II ace, that it is hard to separate the facts from the fiction. She was blonde, pretty and young and the predominantly male reporters of the day were given to flights of fancy in describing her prowess. She was given the hyperbolic nickname "White Rose of Stalingrad," by the press.

There are also conflicting records of her kills and no official records to verify the facts. The numbers most often quoted are 11 individual kills and three team kills. She also shot down an observation balloon on May 31st, 1943. However, Yekaterina Polunina, former senior mechanic and historian and archivist of the 586th Fighter Regiment in which Litvyak initially served, maintains that Lilya had only five independent kills, and shot down an enemy observation balloon as well as an Me-109 in group combat. She also says that Katya shot down six enemy aircraft independently and four in group combat. Thus Budanova should be considered the top Second World War woman ace.

A major stumbling block in researching Litvyak is the variables in her 'published' name. So far discovered are: Lidiya, Lidiia, Lidya or Lilya, Lili, Lilli, Lily and family names Litviak, Litvak, Litvyak, Litvjak. What is certain that, although her body and aircraft were not found during the war, her countrymen have now honoured her. A marble monument, with 12 gold stars—one for each enemy aeroplane that she is supposed to have shot down—is erected in her memory in Krasy Luch, in the Donetsk region.

1942

JESSIE HANYING ZHENG (CHINA) 1915 – 1942

China's first female air force pilot

essie Hanying Zheng caused quite a stir when she arrived in Vancouver in the spring of 1941. The only woman officer in the Chinese air force, Jessie was one step ahead of the female pilots she befriended in Canada, who were not allowed to fly for their country at all. Jessie's trip to Canada achieved many firsts and the people of Vancouver took her to their hearts. She had been the first woman to learn to fly in Hong Kong. She was the first Chinese woman sent to Canada in any official capacity and became the first woman in Canada to possess an international flying license issued by the Royal Aero Club in London, UK. She was one of a handful of female diplomats, proficient in five languages and an authority on flood relief and Red Cross work. And she was still only 26 years old.

She was born on January 17 1915 in Guangdong province. Her father had been an active revolutionary in 1911 and her aunt Zheng Yuxiu was incredibly powerful, second only to Mrs Chiang Kai-shek at the time. In the early 1930s Jessie graduated from Hong Kong High School and went to the famous Paris Sorbonne to study law.

She was in Paris at a time when the city was liberal and free thinking, but flanked by fascism. Hitler had risen to power in Germany in 1933, and Mussolini was ruling Italy. Occasionally, fascist sympathisers disrupted university lessons. Back home Mao Zedong was threatening Chiang kai shek. Jessie meanwhile had learned French, Italian, German and English and was comfortable in high society thanks to her aunts' regular parties in Shanghai and her world travel. Aviators Hilda Yan and Li Xiaqing were both regular guests at her aunt's parties.

Over in Paris Maryse Hilsz had flown from Paris to Saigon and back in 1931, then extended her feat in 1936 by flying to Tokyo. Jessie's

brother had also caught the flying bug and took her for a spin. In 196 she watched the great Li Xiaqing perform at Chiang kai shek's birthday celebrations and knew she wanted to become a pilot.

She enrolled at the Far East flying training school in Hong Kong in 1937. Her brother was also a student there and it was reputed to be the best flying academy in Asia at the time. Lessons took place from the Kai Tak airport in Kowloon and were conducted in two Avro 626 trainers and two Avro 631 cadets. There was also a Fairey Fox and a de Havilland DH.87 Hornet Moth. It was a British Royal Air Force approved training school, and one of the Avros was kitted out with military training equipment. This allowed Jessie and her peers to learn bombing, gunnery, aerial photography and instrument flying. There was also a forced landing field nearby as the students had to learn how to cope with them as an almost inevitable part of their flying life.

Jessie was the first Chinese woman to sign up for flying lessons there and the South China Morning Post turned up to interview her the first morning she arrived, which embarrassed her enormously. Two months into her training Xiaqing paid a visit, giving her an enormous psychological boost.

On August 13 1937 the Japanese invaded Shanghai. Hong Kong airspace was strictly controlled, and students were not allowed to fly beyond a three-mile radius of the aerodrome. Jessie eventually won her wings and earned international flying licences from the FAI, allowing her to fly anywhere in the world.

She was invited north to help fight the enemy and offered an appointment onto the national commission on aeronautical affairs. She helped promote the "Saving the nation through aviation" programme and toured China. In 1938 Chiang kai shek gave her a commission to the Chinese air force. She was the only woman allowed to sign up. Xiaqing and Hilda had been refused, as had Chinese American Hazel Li. However, Jessie had RAF training in operational flying and had trained

More events in 1942

- James Doolittle leads the first US attack on the Japanese mainland. A force of 16 B-25 Mitchells flew from the USS Hornet against Tokyo in what is known as the "Doolittle Raid"

- Nazi leaders attend the Wannsee Conference to coordinate the "final solution to the Jewish question," the systematic genocide of Jews known as the Holocaust.

- Casablanca premieres in the cinema

for the Foreign Service, so was likely more qualified than many of the male applicants to the forces.

She was given a specially designed dress uniform in the Chinese flag colours with a red stand-up collar in gold and a slit skirt that fell just below the knee.

She also became an expert on flood relief. The Yellow river was flooded in 1938 and inundated a huge area. Jessie moved to Chongqing to help with the war effort. Air raid shelters were carved into the walls. The Chinese air force was ramshackle and unlike the Japanese, whose mission was to hit their target and die, the Chinese pilots had to return their scarce aircraft. There were stories of badly injured fliers limping back to base, bullet riddled but determined to bring their planes back.

In 1938 she was transferred to Hong Kong and lived a hedonistic life after the deprivations of Chongqing. Bright young things were dancing at the Peninsula Hotel and the Lido in Repulse Bay. There she met Wilfred Bien-tang Seto, a Canadian and fell in love with him. Their affair resulted in her pregnancy. He did the ungallant thing and fled back to Canada. However, he reckoned without a determined Jessie who was not about to throw away her hard fought career.

She arrived in Vancouver and camped on his doorstep. The scandal was an open secret in Vancouver's Chinatown and Jessie was never popular in the Chinese community there because she embarrassed such a prominent family.

The foreign office sent her to Canada in 1940 to support the Chinese consulate general in Ottawa. Like the US, Canada was not taking the Japanese occupation of China seriously. One of Jessie's roles was to educate Canadians as to what was happening. Her daughter Beverley Anne Seto was born and deposited with Wilfred and his parents and Jessie kept her a secret.

Although Vancouver at the time was tainted with racism against the Chinese, Jessie never appeared to experience prejudice. She befriended local female pilots and flew regularly with seven women. This seven opened a ground school in Vancouver guessing armed forces would soon need extra training. They wrongly assumed the government would let them fly in conflict. However, the Aeroclub enlisted and trained provisional pilot officers, saving the Canadian government $750,000 in training costs.

Jessie toured tirelessly in 1942 promoting her country's cause. She continued to tour in 1943 and test flew an Anson Avro II. She wore herself out, but refused to concede defeat and contracted TB. She died on September 7 aged 28. She dictated her will to a lawyer, leaving her possessions to a children's home. She requested that her private papers be burned, apart from her flying licence. Her coffin was carried through Vancouver by a Royal Canadian Air Force honour guard.

Like Hilda Yan and Li Xiaqing, Jessie's story has been largely forgotten. Patti Gully's excellent: "Sisters of Heaven" documents her rise through the ranks and is a fitting tribute to this brave aviatrix.

EKATERINA VASYLIEVNA BUDANOVA (RUSSIA) 1916 – 1943

Katya Budanova was one of the elite female fighter pilots in the Soviet Air Force crack squads during the Second World War. With 11 victories, she was one of Russia's two female aces along with Lylia Litvyak.

he villagers in Antracit in Russia's Oblast region who witnessed a vicious aerial dogfight between their own country's Yak 1 fighters and lethal German Messerschmitt Me109 fighters reported seeing one of their own aircraft make a precise controlled landing, even though it had obviously been badly damaged. When they reached the aircraft to tend to the pilot, they discovered that she was already dead.

That pilot was Ekaterina (Katya) Vasylievna Budanova.

Katya was born on December 7, 1916 into a peasant family in Konoplanka village in Smolensk Oblast. She moved to Moscow, where she landed a job at an aircraft factory. She became fascinated by aviation and joined an aero club, where she received her pilot training. During the first two decades of the Soviet era, there were a number of military flying clubs known as Osoaviakhim. Girls were welcome to join these clubs along with boys.

They learned at a young age how to parachute and fly gliders. Consequently, many 17-year-old flying club students had more flying experience than the Soviet Air Force pilots at the front when war broke out. Katya studied hard and gained her instructor's certificate, and worked as a flight instructor from 1937 onwards. She was also known to have taken part in several air parades, flying the single-seater Yakolev UT-1.

In 1939, the Soviet Union signed a non-aggression pact with Nazi Germany. The Soviets allowed the Germans to invade Poland and were given a piece of the land as a reward. The Soviets upheld their pact with Germany for the next two years. However, on June 22, 1941, after some 500 violations of Soviet airspace by Nazi reconnaissance aircraft, the Germans attacked Russia from the west and south. The Nazi attack and attempt to conquer Russia is known as Operation Barbarossa,

When the Germans attacked, Katya enlisted in the military. Because of her flying skills, she was assigned to the all-female 586th Fighter Regiment (586 IAP), formed by Marina Raskova. She flew her first combat missions in April 1942 over Saratov.

In September that year, she was assigned, along with other women, including her friend Lylia Litvyak, to the 437th IAP, which was engaged in the fighting over Stalingrad. This elite squadron flew Yak 1 fighter aircraft. Katya was an aggressive and skilful pilot. On October 6, 1942 she is reported to have attacked 13 Junkers Ju 88 bombers by herself, shooting down her first aircraft. That November, she also downed two Messerschmitt Bf 109 fighters and another Ju 88. She was credited with taking down several more aircraft over the following months.

In January 1943, she, and Lilya were moved to the 296 IAP, later renamed 73 IAP (Guards IAP), the fighter regiment of the 8th air army. On February 23, she was awarded with the Order of the Red Star.

According to her mechanic, she was killed in active combat on July 18, 1943, when she was involved in a solo dogfight with three Bf 109s while escorting a group of Soviet dive-bombers. Katya dispensed with one, but the second managed to shoot her down and escape the battle with a damaged aircraft.

More events in 1942

- A Messerschmitt Me 262 prototype makes its first flight under jet power, replacing propeller.
- RCA Victor sprays gold over Glenn Miller's million-seller "Chattanooga Choo Choo," creating first "gold record.

Like the reports of Lilya Litvak's quota, there are different tallies for Katya's scores. The most commonly reported figure is 11 kills (six individual and five team kills). However, the 586 IAP archivist, Yekaterina Polunina, said that Lilya "downed over 20 aircraft". She was awarded the Order of the Red Star and the Order of the Patriotic War. Although it was proposed, she was not awarded the title of Hero of the Soviet Union during the war. That came after a long wait on October 1, 1993, when she was posthumously awarded with a "Hero of the Russian Federation title."

Katya and Lilya were not alone in fighting for Russia during World War II. Thousands of Russian women and girls courageously fought for their Rodina (Motherland), serving with the Voyenno-Vozdushniye Sily (Air Forces). In 1942, three air regiments were formed entirely from female volunteers.

Each regiment had three squadrons of 10 aircraft each and included some 400 women. The pilots the mechanics and the other ground support personnel were all female. The regiments comprised the 586th Women's Fighter Regiment, the first regiment to go to the front. The 586th's primary mission was to force back enemy bombers. The 587th Women's Day Bomber Regiment also stepped up to the plate. This regiment initially flew Petlyakov Pe-2 2-engined bombers with a 3-person crew including a pilot, navigator, and radio operator/gunner.

Finally, there was the infamous 588th Women's Night Bomber Regiment, the vicious "Night Witches," who flew Polikarpov Po-2 biplanes and fought the Germans with such ferocity that they acquired their dark nickname. Several of the members of the 588th became "Heroes of the Soviet Union." This unit remained totally female throughout the war. Fighter aces, Lilya Litvyak and Ekaterina Budanova, both members of the 586th, joined the all male 73rd Fighter Regiment and fought in the battles over Stalingrad.

Many other women also served alongside men with other aviation units. In 1944, 1,749 women served with the Zabaikalsky Front. A further 3,000 women and girls are believed to have served with the Far East 10th Air Army. There were also 437 women in the 4th Air Army of the Second Belorussian Front, which comprised the crack 46th Guards Women Air Regiment. This included 237 female officers, 862 sergeants, 1,125 enlisted women and 2,117 auxiliaries. Women also flew and fought as gunners in the famous Il-2 and Il-2M3 Shturmovik tank busters, also known as the "Flying Bathtub."

Katya Budanova was one of those brave women. She died young. However, she died doing what she believed was right for her country – and, by all accounts – doing the job she loved. The memory of her courage lives on long after her death.

YAK-1

At the beginning of the war there were 425 Yak-1 built, or in production.

Since most air combat took place below 13,000 feet, (4,000 metres), the new Soviet fighters, designed for high-altitude performance, were at a disadvantage. The aircraft's major problem was fuel leaks caused by failure of spot-welded fuel tanks from vibration. Also, the canopy could not be opened at high speeds, potentially trapping the pilot in a falling aircraft. However, the aircraft was well loved by the fighters and twenty-four of them were sent to the elite all-female 586 IAP.

1942

Betty Huyler Gillies (USA) 1908 – 1998

The '100-pound dynamo' who flew 54,000 lb heavy bombers, was president of the 99s and served as chairman of the All Women Transcontinental Air Race from 1953 - 1961

n March 1943 Betty Huyler Gillies became the first woman to fly the Republic P-47 Thunderbolt, also known as the "Jug," the largest single-engined fighter of its day. She was checked out to fly it at Wilmington Air Force Base. Her "check out" consisted of an explanation of the aircraft's systems, handling characteristics and emergency procedures. Since the P-47 had but one seat, she had to solo on her checkride. All in a day's work for squadron leader Gilles.

A highly competent individual, Betty began flying in 1928 while she was a student nurse at the Presbyterian Hospital in New York City. She earned her licence on May 6, 1929, after 23 hours flying, including instruction. She immediately began building hours. She also joined the US women pilots' organisation the Ninety-Nines, an international club of female flyers formed that year by Amelia Earhart and Fay Gillis Wells. Betty went on to enjoy a long association with the institution.

By June 1930, she had acquired more than the required 200 solo hours necessary to be awarded a transport license. With her skills, she became a marketable entity in aviation circles. Curtiss Wright Flying Service on Long Island took her on as a sales woman. She sold aircraft and flight training courses. She had to contact prospective buyers, and then demonstrate the aircrafts' performance and handling characteristics. She would also promote aviation, touring round the area and speaking about flying to different groups. Her colleague Helen Weber headed up the company speakers' bureau, and Betty frequently had to fly her to distant cities for speaking engagements. She also worked in a similar capacity for other companies, ferrying aircraft from the factories to different bases, charter flying, and some instructing.

In 1939 Betty became president of the 99s and served a two year term. During her stint as leader, the organisation set up the Amelia Earhart Memorial Scholarships Fund (AEMSF), which helps licensed pilot members to fund advanced training and education in aviation and aerospace. The training can include additional pilot certificates and ratings, college degrees, and technical training. There is also capacity for research grants, plus provision for new pilots.

Betty was president of the 99s while America was preparing for war. Jackie Cochran took over in 1941 and served as the organisation's wartime leader. In July 1941, just before the Japanese bombed Pearl Harbor, the Ninety-Nines held their annual meeting in Albuquerque, New Mexico. The group that met felt strongly that its members could contribute to the war effort. They drew up a resolution publicly deploring the exclusion of women in the Advanced Civil Pilot Training Program. They sent a letter to the president stating that: "loyal American Ninety-Nines pilots offered to serve individually and collectively" in whatever crisis lay ahead.

The women flew back home and the Civil Air Patrol was organised and welcomed women pilots. They took on many roles including: link training, ground school, and flight instruction. They manned air warning posts. In 1942 the Women's Auxiliary Ferrying Squadron (WAFS) began operation at Wilmington, Delaware, spearheaded by Nancy Love. Jacqueline Cochran had been over to England to assist with the war effort there. When she returned in November the same year, she started the first Women's Flying Training Detachment class. Both services drew heavily on the Ninety-Nines membership.

The women ferried the fastest aircraft and flew the giant bombers. They towed targets for anti-aircraft work and flew searchlights at night. They simulated strafing missions, laid smoke screens, and flew photographic and radio controlled missions. Some flew engineering test flights. Many Ninety-Nines taught army and navy cadets, steering them through primary, advanced, instrument and cross country courses, building a vast pool of pilots. According to the 99s' website, in the first year of activity the women set a new safety record in military aviation, flying the equivalent of 3,000,000 miles for each fatal accident. That rate was .02 less than that of the overall fatality rate in the United States Air Force.

Betty was flying for Grumman Aircraft Engineering Corporation when the war broke out in America. At the time she had around 1,400 flying hours. By September 1942, she was in the intake of the first 25 WAFS, alongside Nancy Love. When Nancy transferred to Dallas to start a new WAFS unit, Betty was promoted to squadron leader of the WAFS 2nd Ferrying Group, New Castle Army Air Base in Wilmington, Delaware.

One of her most famous missions was in April 1943. Her squadron delivered four Fairchild PT-26s from Hagerstown, Maryland, to Alberta in Canada, a flight of over 2,500 miles (4,023 kilometres). Betty led the contingent. With a cruise speed of around 100 mph (161 km/h), they had to break the journey into stages. The four pilots set off from Hagarstown on April 18, and spent the night at Joliet, Ill, 697 miles (1,122 kilometres). They flew a further 585 miles (942 kilometres) to North Platte, Nebraska, and then took off for a long leg of 846 miles (1,362 kilometres) to Great Falls, Montana. On April 21 they flew the final 275 miles (443 kilometres) to DeWinton, Alberta. All four women were back at the 2nd Group by Friday evening, April 23, and were commended by Colonel Baker for their efficient and prompt delivery.

In 1943 the WAFS `was merged with the WFTD to become the Women Air force Service Pilots

More events in 1942

- Harvard University chemist Louis F. Fieser invents napalm, a jelly-like mixture of gasoline and palm oils that sticks to its target until it burns out.

- Radar comes into operational use.

(WASP). Betty is quoted as saying: "Just as well I was in on the ground floor...I was too short for WASP entry requirements." On August 15, that year, Nancy and Betty qualified as the first female commanders on the Boeing B-17 Flying Fortress heavy bombers, and made three deliveries together the same month. They were actually on the runway at Goose Bay in Labrador en route to England from Cincinnati on September 2, 1943, to deliver a B-17F, the "Queen Bee," to England when the message came through to abort the mission. General Hap Arnold reportedly did not believe they could manage the task.

Betty remained as squadron leader of the WASP stationed at the 2nd Ferrying Group at New Castle Army Air Base until it was disbanded on December 20, 1944.

She got married after the war. Aviation was truly in her blood. Her husband "Bud" was a naval aviator and vice president of Grumman Aircraft. They had three children, two of whom became commercial pilots. Sadly their daughter Barbara died of leukaemia when she was only four years old. Four of Betty's grandchildren also became pilots.

According to the 99s, Betty was a firm advocate of drawing more women into aviation. She was particularly proud of her tenure as chairman of the All Women Transcontinental Air Race. She held the position from 1953 - 1961. Betty felt that the role was one of her key achievements since it was inclusive and entertained all women inclined towards sport aviation. Under her supervision the race almost doubled in size, growing from 49 aircraft (90 pilots) in 1953 to 101 aircraft and 201 pilots in the 1961.

She continued her involvement with the 99s and worked with co founder Fay Gillis Wells in 1963 to persuade the US Post Office to issue an Amelia Earhart airmail stamp on July 24, Amelia's birthday. They finally got the project off the ground and several 99s gathered at Amelia's place of birth in Kansas, to stamp several thousand envelopes. In the first of the organisation's "once in a decade" flyaways from AE airport in Atchison, the covers were flown to all four corners of the US. They were then sold to raise funds for the AEMSF. The 99s have subsequently issued several other commemorative covers, including the 50th anniversary of Amelia's solo Atlantic flight and the 60th anniversary of Harriet Quimby's flight over the English Channel. Usually 100 covers are issued each year and they are numbered 1 to 100. The number 99 is always sent to 99s' Headquarters in Oklahoma City.

In 1964, President Johnson appointed Betty to the first FAA Women's Advisory Committee. She also received a Paul Tissandier Diploma from the Federation Aeronautique Internationale in 1977 and the National Aeronautic Association Elder Statesman of Aviation Award in 1982.

After 50 years flying, Betty hung up her wings in 1986 due to vision problems. She continued to attend the annual 99s Forest of Friendship celebrations in Atchison, Kansas. She died on October 14 1998 leaving a strong legacy of service to aviation in her wake.

1944

EVELYN BRYAN JOHNSON, AKA 'MAMA BIRD' (USA) 1909 -

Love at first flight

Evelyn Bryan Johnson learned to fly in 1944 and logged 57,635.4 flying hours before she hung up her wings. That is equivalent to almost seven years in the air. She was the oldest flight instructor in the world when she retired. Her achievements are impressive. She has trained more pilots and given more FAA exams than any other pilot, which has earned her a place in the Guinness Book of World Records. She is an inductee of six halls of fame and has been awarded a bronze Carnegie Medal.

Evelyn Bryan Johnson was born on November 4th, 1909 in Corbin, Kentucky. She is also known as "Mama Bird" and is the female pilot with the most number of flying hours in the world. Mama Bird showed an aptitude for learning from an early age and earned a scholarship to Tennessee Wesleyan School, graduating in 1929. She taught for a few years, then enrolled at the University of Tennessee, where she met her husband, W.J. Bryan. They married in 1931, and in 1933 borrowed $250 from his father to start a dry cleaning business, where they worked 18 hours a day.

Her flying career took off on October 1st 1944, during World War II. She had been working solidly and needed a break. She says: "My husband was doing military service and I was working at our laundry and dry cleaning plant. I was working long hours, and it was getting tiresome and boring. I thought 'I have to get a hobby for an hour or two a week.'" One Sunday she spotted a three-inch advert in the paper, exhorting locals to learn to fly. So she telephoned the air school. She continues: "The next week after church I took the train to Jefferson City terminal. I took the bus to the end of line near the Island Airport. I had to walked down to the river for about one block and then had to get a ride across river, as there was no bridge in those days." There she took her first flying lesson in a Piper J3 Cub. She says: "It was love at first flight. 63 years later I still feel the same way."

Evelyn soloed after just eight hours on November 8, 1944. The instructor jumped out, leaving her to fly the aircraft alone: "You required eight hours dual in those days before you could solo. I'm glad nothing happened, I did not know so much then. I went round a couple more times, and I was real pleased I'd done it in the minimum amount of time."

She gained her private pilot licence in June 1945, her commercial ticket a year later and became a flight instructor (FI) in 1947. She took her first student up the day she got her FI. She says: "The day I got it I had 15 students on my books straight away. Times were different then." However, she did not have time to go off on charter trips and joy rides, as she was so busy with her business when her husband returned. She was named designated FAA examiner in 1952. Since that time she administered over 9,000 check rides – ie flight-tests to assess a student's proficiency.

She is philosophical about the testing process and unfazed by a student's status outside the cockpit. "If you are not correct you don't pass. You have to do more training. If you miss two months you have to do the whole thing again." She recommends that instructors who liked to instruct stay within the field, rather than just heading off to the airlines. "If you like to teach instructing is a great thing to do."

Her past students have included high profile individuals, including airline executives. She gave Tennessee Senator Howard Baker his PPL check ride in a Beech Debonair. When it came to test

stalling, the senator said the plane was not built for stalls. Evelyn says: "I told him the airplane doesn't know it is not made for stalls. If you have not learned how to do the stalls, you don't get your pilot's license." He was persuaded and passed.

According to Evelyn, improvements to aircraft and busier airspace have changed teaching and learning exponentially. She says: "Flight instruction was easier in the early years, as there was not as much to do. There were no radios or lights, so it is very different now. There is lots of equipment and operational aspects to the course. I used to teach all levels, improvers and starters. There is so much more to learn than there used to be. You had to learn to take off and land and get that down first."

A passionate pilot herself, between 1951 and 1954, and in 1960, she entered "Powder Puff Derbies." She also flew in an international women's air race from Washington to Havana, Cuba, but had to stop competing, as she was too busy at work. She says: "Gasoline got really expensive. It is $5 now, but we thought it was too expensive at $1. There was just not time for racing. I was involved in all sorts of occupations, so had to choose one."

She continues: "We bought half of the Morristown FBO, Morristown Flying Service, in 1949. In 1960 the city decided to build the airport. We were already there since May 23 1953. We had to move all of our six aircraft over to the new site. I became airport manager."

A few years later she was on the airfield alone apart from two young children. A helicopter pilot had landed for fuel. As he was ready to leave, he turned into the wind. The helicopter lurched violently to the side and fell to the right. Evelyn says: "I saw what was going to happen. I called for an ambulance, grabbed the fire extinguisher and ran over." The tail rotor was still spinning, so Evelyn crawled underneath the wreckage and stopped it. She saw that the transmission was beginning to burn, so she put the fire out. She takes up the story. "I saw that the passenger was dead. He had three drops of blood coming out of his nose. The pilot was unconscious and moaning. I tried to pull him out, but had learned on a first aid that you don't pull on someone with a broken back because you could kill them. I rubbed his hands until help came. It took five of us to get him out." The Carnegie Foundation gave her a bronze medal for her actions.

Evelyn's contributions to general aviation go beyond flying and flight instruction. A Cessna dealer for 19 years, she flew their whole range of aircraft. She owned several aeroplanes, including an Aeronca Champ. Alas, she says, she was often too busy with her flight school to fly her own machines. Her awards bear this out. She was FAA Flight Instructor of the Year in 1979 and has been inducted into the women in aviation pioneers hall of fame, the national flight instructor's hall of fame and the Kentucky and Tennessee aviation hall of fame. She also became one of the first female helicopter pilots and was involved in the Civil Air Patrol. She also served on the Tennessee Aeronautics Commission for 18 years and was chairman for four of them, helping to allocate state funds for airport improvement projects throughout the state.

A car crash on September 10, 2006, forced doctors to amputate her leg. Although this curtailed her flying, at 99 years old she remains in post at her job, which she has held for 55 years. In 2003 the city of Morristown celebrated her 50th anniversary. When asked if there will be a 55th celebration she laughs: "I guess they'll do the next one in 2053 when I've been here a hundred years."

Events in 1944

- ■ Howard Hughes sets a new transcontinental speed record, in Lockheed Constellation

- ■ June 6: Allies invade Normandy on D-Day

1948

BETTY SKELTON FRANKMAN (USA) 1926 –

First lady of firsts who still has more combined aviation and automotive records than anyone in history

Betty Skelton Frankman is known as "the First Lady of Firsts." She has set 17 aviation and racecar records. Nearly 35 years after her retirement, Betty still holds more combined aircraft and automotive records than anyone in history. She won the International Feminine Aerobatic Championship three times: 1948, 1949 and 1950. She was the first woman to perform an inverted ribbon cut at only ten feet above the ground. She set several light plane altitude records: in 1949 she soared to 25,763 feet in a Piper Cub. She beat this in 1951, when she recorded 29,050 feet in the same type. She also holds the world speed record for a piston engine aircraft – hitting 421.6mph in a P-51 racing plane over a three-kilometre course.

Betty Skelton was born in Pensacola, Florida on June 28, 1926 to teenaged parents. David and Myrtle Skelton encouraged her to indulge in active pursuits and in her formative years, she played with model aeroplanes, rather than dolls. From the age of eight onwards she bombarded her parents with the message she wanted to fly. So her mother and father regularly drove her out to the local municipal airport, where she would snatch rides whenever she could. Kenneth Wright, a young naval ensign taught the whole family how to fly.

Her mother learned first, and her father acquired a flight school. When Betty was 12 she dedicated herself to practice, carefully rehearsing each manoeuvre over and over until it was perfect. Her perfectionism kept her from ever having a serious accident. She was only twelve years old when she made her first solo - Wright let her take the controls of his Taylorcraft. She made that legal on her 16th birthday, rapidly followed by her private license. By 17, she had acquired the necessary hours to join the WASPs, but they disbanded before she reached the required entry age of 18 and a half.

However, she knew she wanted an aeronautical career, so took a job as a clerk for Eastern Airlines at night, enabling her to fly during the daytime. She earned her commercial ticket at 18, with her flight instructor and multi-engine ratings a few months later.

At 19, she joined the Civil Air Patrol, and began instructing at the Pete O' Knight Airport in Tampa. She felt stymied by the lack of employment opportunities for women in either the military or the airlines and knew she wanted to do something with her talent. She took lessons from aerobatic pilot Clem Whittenback, easily picking up a loop and a roll and gave her first public display a fortnight later in a Fairchild PT-19. In 1946 she bought her own aircraft, a 1929 Great Lakes 2T1A biplane. Thus began her professional aerobatic career at the Southeastern Air Exposition in Jacksonville, Florida, along with a new US Navy exhibition team, the Blue Angels.

Betty became a regular on the famous southeastern air show circuit, earning her place in the legendary group of post-war performers. She took her first International Feminine Aerobatic Championship on January 1, 1948 in her Great Lakes. When she was there she fell in love. Phil Quigley, had brought his tiny Pitts Special S-1C – at the time the world's smallest aircraft. She pestered the owner until he sold it to her in August 1948 for $3,000. It was an experimental single-seat open-cockpit biplane, and the tiniest aerobatic aircraft around. Because the registration number NX86401 was so long and the Pitts so small, she asked the Civil Aeronautics Administration for a smaller registration number to match. The CAA gave her the shortest number available, N22E. She won the next 1949 Feminine International Aerobatic Championship held at the Miami All American Air Manoeuvres, with The Little Stinker. She travelled to a several major air shows to perform, including the International Air Pageant in London, and the Royal Air Force Pageant in Belfast, Northern Ireland. She said later: "I didn't just sit in that little airplane, I wore it. If I sneezed, it sneezed with me." She named the plane "Little

Events in 1948

■ Gandhi assassinated in New Delhi by a Hindu militant.

■ Orville Wright dies in Dayton, Ohio aged 76.

■ Berlin Airlift begins; ends May 12, 1949.

■ Truman ends racial segregation in US military.

Stinker" and had it painted in scarlet and white. In it she became the first woman to perform an inverted ribbon cut at ten feet above the ground. In 1949, the Pitts was repainted with a unique red and white scheme and a skunk decoration. She won her third and final Feminine International Aerobatic Championship in 1950. She also had a small Chihuahua, Little Tinker, who flew with her in her lap.

Betty went on to win two more consecutive International Feminine Aerobatic Championships in 1949 and 1950. At the end of 1950, she had earned the highest scores in aerobatics but was again disheartened by the lack of opportunities for women. She had had enough and in 1951 retired from competition aerobatics and sold The Little Stinker to Bob Davis. George Young, Paul Lehman, and Drexell Scott owned the aircraft until Skelton repurchased it in 1967.

Betty decamped to North Carolina, and flew charter flights out of Raleigh. She struck up a friendship with Bill France, the founder of NASCAR, who suggested she drive at Daytona Beach during Speed Week. She drove the pace car and set a new stock car record in the process. She suddenly had a new career. As the car industry's first female test driver, she guided "L'il Miss Dodge," a jump boat, over a 1955 Custom Royal Lancer on a ramp at Florida's Cypress Gardens. A super achiever, she went on to have a high flying executive career. In 1956, Betty became one of the top women advertising executives working with the General Motors Company. Betty earned a total of four Feminine World Land Speed Records and set a transcontinental speed record. She was also the first woman to drive a jet car over 300 mph at the Bonneville Salt Flats.

Betty married TV director/producer and navy veteran Donald A. Frankman in 1965. The pair bought back Little Stinker and donated it to the National Air and Space Museum. It is now displayed in the new Steven F. Udvar-Hazy Center at Dulles Airport – inverted of course.

Don died in 2001. Betty remains active driving her Corvette and has received many honours for her achievements. She has been inducted into the International Aerobatic Hall of Fame, the International Council of Air Shows Hall of Fame, and the Corvette Hall of Fame. Each year the United States National Aerobatic Championships honour the highest placing female pilot with the "Betty Skelton First Lady of Aerobatics" award.

Betty's enviable record is still recognized today by pilots and competitors, and she is frequently referred to as "The First Lady of Firsts." In 1959 Betty underwent the same physical and psychological tests given to the original Mercury 7 astronauts. Although she made the cover of Look magazine in 1960, she knew fine well that her gender precluded her from selection for the Mercury programme. However, the other astronauts were smitten by her skills and personality and dubbed her "7 1/2." She received honorary wings from the United States Navy and held the rank of Major in the Civil Air Patrol.

In recognition of her achievements, Betty Skelton was inducted into the National Aviation Hall of Fame in 2005. She may be older now, but is obviously as feisty as ever. In 1991 she wrote to Patty Wagstaff and said, "Receiving my first Medicare card a few months ago was not much of a thrill ...I wanted to burn it immediately and go out and buy a Pitts!"

Nancy Bird Walton (Australia) 1915 –

My God it's a woman! Australia's first lady of aviation never let her gender stop her. She pioneered air ambulance services in the 1930s, and founded the Australian Women Pilots' Association in 1950.

Nancy Bird was born in a tiny country town, Kew, New South Wales in 1915, one of six children. The town was so remote that it had no doctors and she was delivered by the midwife, a local woman who waded through flooded rivers and creeks to help her neighbours deliver their children. At 13 Nancy visited an air pageant at neighbouring Wingham and knew she wanted to fly. She took a ten-shilling flight then gave the pilot her entire week's wages to do some aerobatics with her. She bought a book on flying and studied it assiduously. She left school at 14 to help her father with his business.

In an interview she gave to Film Australia's Australian Biography series in 1992, Nancy described how when her father realised she was serious about flying, he became concerned and told her that he: "couldn't afford to keep a crippled daughter." She got round him by telling him she had saved up 200 pounds for lessons with Charles Kingsford-Smith. The legendary aviator had flown the Pacific, circumnavigated the world and crossed the Tasman. He was a hero in Australia and had been barnstorming around the country. He opened a flying school in August 1933 at Mascot. Nancy became one of his first pupils. She started training on 11 August 1933 in a de Havilland Gypsy Moth.

She had her 'A' license by 28 September and spent as much time as possible in the air. There was no syllabus or formal training – or runway. Nancy said she learned: "by talking with people, by looking at maps asking them how you plotted a course and so on." For the 'A' license test students had to climb to 1,500 feet, cut the engine and come down in a series of gliding turns. She took her higher licence before she set off, becoming the youngest commercial ticket holder in the Commonwealth in 1934.

Aviation was in its infancy, and many people were afraid to fly. Nancy described the passion of the aviation community and the love-hate relationship it had with the press: "When the press wanted to take pictures of crashed support of the press when they wanted to do any long distance flying, like Charles Kingsford-Smith or Jean Batten." The oil companies were also prescient early supporters. Nancy she was smitten by the German aviatrix, Ellie Beinhorn when she went to hear her speak after her record braking flight to Australia in 1932. The pair became close friends until Ellie's death in 2007.

Nancy bought an aircraft with the help of her family. To recoup her investment, she went barnstorming with co-pilot Peggy McKillop, Peggy was wealthy and refused to take money from Nancy. The pair became the first two women ever to fly by night. In 1935 Nancy logged the fastest time between Melbourne and Adelaide.

She learned navigation from the famous PG Taylor. He had twice navigated Charles Kingsford-Smith across the Tasman to New Zealand. During the flights he had to climb out on the wing strut and take oil from one dead engine and transfer it to the other, saving the lives of the entire crew. Nancy said: "He did that six times behind the slip-stream of that great motor that Smithy held it in the air with, because he had to cut back the other motor. It was the most courageous thing that had ever been done."

While she was barnstorming she met Reverend Stanley Drummond of the Far West Children's Health Scheme who asked her to go to Bourke to fly his baby clinics service out to isolated areas, bringing medical treatment to remote communities within one hour rather than six. She ferried nurses to the outback and patients to town if they needed more urgent hospital treatment. She could do this because she had upgraded to a de Havilland Leopard Moth, which could take two passengers in the back and, one in front. It cost her ,800 pounds, so she had to fly it to pay it off. She flew with Far West for nine months, becoming known as the "Angel of the Outback."

She then moved into Queensland and worked in a voluntary capacity for the Queensland Bush Children's Health Scheme. She tried to get the Queensland Government to establish the same sort of thing in Charleville, but they were not interested. In 1937, the Royal Flying Doctor Service was established at Broken Hill, but that was still 300 miles away from where Nancy was stationed.

She got a fright one day when she landed at the remote town of Gadooga. She picked up a man and flew him to Sydney. Returning west, the clouds came down on the mountains. Nancy said: "I thought, 'I can't get through'...everything in me revolted about going back. It was like being on a rearing horse - that aeroplane just didn't want to go back. I turned back to Sydney, landed, and burst into tears and I never wanted to fly again." Although her fellow pilots tried to comfort her, she had a crisis of confidence.

Dutch airline KLM then offered her the chance to go with them to Europe. She sold her aircraft, recouping her initial investment. She toured Europe, meeting with airlines all over the region. She brought a collection of her findings back to Australia. During the tour she flew to Russia with Scandinavian Airlines, becoming the first person to fly from Moscow to London in a day via Sweden as a passenger. She regularly wrote back to Australia and Connie Robinson, editor of the women's section of the Sydney Morning Herald printed her letters.

She took in the Paris Air Show. She visited the UK and saw the first

Events in 1950

- Communist Chinese forces invade Tibet.
- Korean War begins when North Korean Communist forces invade South Korea.
- P-51 Mustangs of No. 77 Squadron RAAF are sent to Korea as part of Australia's contribution to the war.

Spitfires. She spent time in Germany and saw the first Heinkels and Messerschmitts. She said: "Of course I didn't know their significance. I didn't know anything about politics. I had wonderful friends in Germany and they obviously didn't think I was any security risk because I was invited to the Junkers factory." Ellie Beinhorn took her round. Nancy was lucky to miss the outbreak of war. She was in Russia in May 1939.

She visited the US to meet all the international women pilots in New York. They had arranged for her to come across America. She met her husband on the ship on the way home. They married and had two children, a daughter in 1945 and son in 1946.

During World War Two, she became Commandant, Women's Air Training Corps. There was no actual flying for female pilots in Australia at the time because there were too few aircraft to make that necessary. The group comprised a number of women who tried to train themselves to be ready to support aviation in the event of a war. They supported the Royal Australian Air Force in other ways, predominantly as clerks and drivers.

Nancy reactivated her license in the 1950s, flying on a student ticket. She had formed the Australian Women Pilots' Association in 1950. She described herself as: "the Penguin President, you know, the non-flying president." In 1958 she decided to fly in the Powder Puff Derby in America. She had an invitation, but could not get a seat as a co-pilot. She said: "If I am going to fly in this race, forget everything else, hire an aircraft get a co-pilot and fly in the race yourself." She did so, flying in a Cessna 172, which was her first experience of flying in an aircraft with a radio and a tricycle undercarriage.

She received an Officer of the Order of the British Empire medal (OBE) in 1966 and in 1977 became a Dame of St John (Knights of Malta). She has published two books: "Born to Fly" and "My God! It's a Woman." Qantas Airlines has also honoured her by naming its first Airbus A380 after her.

Nancy is still going strong. She attributes her success to: "Enthusiasm self-discipline, being prepared to do anything - not saying, 'It's not my job' You'll never reach your greatest potential if you walk past the dishwasher without emptying it or leave your costume on the bathroom floor."

1950

ADA ROGATO (BRAZIL) 1920 - 1986

First woman in South America to obtain a glider pilot's licence in 1935, first to parachute at night and first to fly a Cessna across the Andes

There was nothing alcohol induced about Ada Rogato's courage, despite the fact she famously featured on the label of the highly potent "Voadora" rum, distilled in her honour. A symbol of courage in her native Brazil, Ada broke records, disarmed prejudices against women and was nationally celebrated.

Ada Rogato was born in Sao Paulo on December 2, 1920. She achieved a great many aviation 'firsts' in her lifetime. She was the first woman in Brazil to receive a glider pilot licence in 1935 aged 15. She was also the first person to fly a light aircraft across the Andes. A keen parachutist, she was the first to jump at night, and the first to jump in Sao Paulo and in South America. She ultimately became a champion, with 105 jumps under her belt over 5,000 hours of flight. There are those that would contend parachuting is still the toughest sport, because, despite the technological developments in building more robust aircraft, the human body remains its same vulnerable self. In Ada's day, parachuting as a hobby was a novelty. She was mad to learn it and toured all over the country in order to practice.

This early aviatrix had fallen in love with aviation and spent time as a volunteer for the Ministry of Aeronautics. She received the National Merit Comenda Aerospace, for having crossed the Andes twice in a single engine aircraft of Brazilian origin. By the time she crossed the first time, she may have already travelled through the four countries of South America.

She worked at the Institute of Biology (IB) for the Animal Health Surveillance Section. There she flew aircraft and performed aerial crop spraying experiments on coffee beans. She had a crash in Chantebled in

1948. Sao Paolo's Correio Paulistano newspaper published an article on March 10, 1948 about aviation in farming. It said that the only way to stop the decimation of coffee crops by insects was to use an aircraft. It went on to praise "aerial acrobatics," which it said were transformed into "the most terrible weapon against agricultural pests." The newspaper interviewed the intrepid crop duster and Ada explained that her accident had occurred because of a minor technical problem with her aircraft. She spent some time in hospital recuperating.

Once she had recovered, Ada flew the single engine Brazilian-built Neiva CAP-4 Paulistinha for the first time. Henrique da Rocha Lima, the famous pathologist and then director of the Biological Institute, nicknamed the aircraft the "Grasshopper".

In 1950, she was asked by the government to fly a goodwill tour. Aged 31, Ada flew alone in a Cap-4, 65HP, Paulistinha, nicknamed "Brasileirinho" and visited Paraguay, Argentina, Chile and Uruguay during a trip of 6,959 miles (11,200 km) over 116 hours. As a reward, when she returned to Brazil, she was given a Cessna 140, 90HP, nicknamed "Brazil".

On April 5, 1951, flying Brazil she took off from Santos Dumont Airport on another epic journey. Ada flew the small two-person single-engine high wing 90 HP aircraft 25,000 miles (40,234 km) solo across the Andes, to Alaska and across Canada and the United States. Her trip took almost seven months. She beat the record for distance solo flying when she travelled the 31,730 miles (51,064 km) connecting Tierra del Fuego to Alaska, in just 326 hours. Her main aim was to forge closer ties between Brazil and its neighbours. Her flight was a tribute to her courage. Flying such a trip today is routine in modern airliners; however back in the day Ada flew without the advantages of modern navigation equipment. Despite her meagre apparatus by today's standards, Ada made her extraordinary flight unaided. She landed home on November 27, 1951 at 2pm. There was a rapturous welcoming committee awaiting her. The whole town turned out it seemed: civil authorities, soldiers, airmen, journalists, photographers and film-makers, as well as ordinary citizens. After an official reception, she was borne through the streets in a procession flanked by motorcyclists.

It was difficult to cap that feat, but on June 20, 1952 Ada took off from Cochabamba airport in Bolivia in her small Cessna to climb the high wall of the Cordillera Real mountain range towering over La Paz in the Andes. Her route was 202 miles (325 km), at an altitude of between 8,530 to 13,356 feet (2,600 to 4,083 metres) with no possibility of escape in the case of a forced landing. She rose to the challenge and succeeded in a time of two hours and 10 minutes.

In 1956 she travelled on behalf of the government of the State of Sao Paulo to all the capitals of Brazil, via the Amazon forest without a radio and in a small aeroplane.

More events in 1950

- **The first Xerox machine is produced.**

- **Albert Einstein warns that nuclear war could lead to mutual destruction.**

- **The first race in the inaugural FIA Formula One World Championship was held at Silverstone, England.**

Ada received numerous awards throughout her life and was president of the Santos Dumont Foundation and director of the Museum of Aeronautics and Space. She was the first woman to receive Brazil's Comenda National Aeronautical Merit; was also honoured with the Comenda Kites of the Brazilian Air Force and the title of the FAB Pilot Honoris Causa. She was named "Condor of the Andes" in 1952 for her La Paz adventure. The Bolivian Air Force also awarded her a Kite of the Bolivian Air Force trophy.

Ada died on November 17 1986. In 2000, the Brazilian mail service issued a postmark and stamp commemorating the 50 years since Ada had first crossed the Andes in her Brasileirinho.

She was a woman of great courage who rose to great heights in many ways. However, there is no record of whether she was brave enough to try the 47 degrees proof spirit brewed in her honour...

Lucy Lúpia (Brazil)

Ada Rogato's principal biographer is Captain Lucy Lupia. Captain Lucy is the first woman in Brazil to work as a professional pilot and the country's first airline transport pilot and first senior commercial pilot.

A native of Rio de Janeiro, she worked as a pharmacist for a while, until a chance visit to the local airfield in August 1967 with her husband caused her to fall in love with aviation. She earned her private pilot's license three short months later. Within a year she had added her commercial and instructor's licences. Then she began the long process of trying to get work. Her first job fell through because the school went bankrupt. She then had to counter prejudice and heartache as she battled for a job. She flew freelance for several air taxi companies. On July 8th 1970, she finally performed her first commercial flight with Captain Dornelles on a twin engine Beech Twin Bonanza (BE-50). She then instructed at the Nova Iguaçú Air Club in 1973, and then flew for Lider Táxi Aéreo.

In 1975, she started work with Top Táxi Aéreo and completed her ATP (Airline Transport Pilot) license by the following year. She received a lower category senior commercial pilot's license, since the law changed retroactively during her training. She then took aircraft manufacturer Embraer's ground training, in São José dos Campos, becoming the first Bandeirante captain. She married again in 1981, and started training as a lawyer, in order to fight her case to become an airline pilot. She flew in 16 different single-engine and 18 twin-engine airplanes, and a helix-turbo "Bandeirante" (EMB-110). She ferried many Department of Civil Aviation aircraft between São Paulo and Rio de Janeiro and once flew a 13-ton Sabreliner. She continues attending aviation events and has written many books, including several on Brazil's aviation history.

Her website is www.captainlucyl.nom.br

1951
JACQUELINE AURIOL (FRANCE) 1917 – 2000

"I feel so happy when I'm flying. Perhaps it is the feeling of power, the pleasure of dominating a machine as beautiful as a thoroughbred horse. Mingled with these basic joys is another less primitive feeling - that of a mission accomplished. Each time I set foot on an airfield, I sense with fresh excitement that this is where I belong." Jacqueline Auriol

Jacqueline Marie-Thérèse Suzanne Douet was born on 5 November 1917 in Challans, France. Her father was a prosperous ship-builder and timber importer and Jacqueline had a privileged upbringing. A keen skier, in 1936, she met her future husband, Paul Auriol, through a friend who was a ski champion. His father, Vincent, was a prominent leader of the Socialist Party. Both families opposed the relationship, believing that socialists and wealthy industrialists generally do not make good bedfellows. She was sent to Sweden, and he to Italy.

She returned to her studies and graduated from the University of Nantes and went on to study art at the Ecole du Louvre in Paris. On weekends, she would ski in the French Alps and two years after they met, she married Paul in 1938 at a small mountain chapel. They divorced in 1967, but remarried twenty years later. She outlived him.

When World War II broke out, she refused to leave France because her husband was in the resistance movement. She lived under a false identity and had two young children. She told the Washington Post in 1970: "I began to realize that I loved danger." Jacqueline managed to evade the Gestapo. When the war ended, Vincent Auriol became President of France. Jacqueline's husband served as his father's press secretary and she was thrown into the social whirl of the Palais Elysee. She was considered an elegant hostess. However, a court wife's life was not for her. She and Paul took up flying in 1946 after a conversation with a French pilot, who told them the sensation of flight, "gave a feeling of freedom."

She earned her private license in 1948 and started stunt flying. She was critically injured in July 1949 when a seaplane, in which she was a passenger, crashed into the Seine. She proved to be a true warrior. She did not see her two sons, Jean-Claude and Jean-Paul, until her face was healed. Despite having 22 operations to rebuild her face over the following two years, she resolved to apply herself to flying. She said: "It was very difficult politically for my father-in-law because so few women flew at this time. I was pretty and I knew I was pretty. There was publicity and I began to be heavily criticized for my flying."

Her husband gave up flying, and she dropped out of the political world. When the accident happened she told the Post: "I was broken into a million pieces. I had no face, no nose, nothing. I had the chance of my life to really become a good pilot. Now that my beauty was gone I would have to derive a reason for being from the plane which had taken it away."

Aerobatics were no longer enough. Her goal was to break the sound barrier. She watched the Vampire fighter being built in 1951 and volunteered to be one of the first to fly it. To occupy her mind during recuperation, she studied algebra, trigonometry, aerodynamics and the other subjects necessary to attain her goal. Between her final two reconstructive operations she earned her commercial license in 1950. The following year she went to the United States and picked up her helicopter rating in just four weeks at the Bell Aircraft factory in New York. Lawrence Bell, the president of Bell Aircraft, allowed her to take the flying lessons and later called her "the most extraordinary woman in the world. She has met fear head-on and conquered it."

Her ambition grew. In 1950, she joined the almost exclusively preserve of men and earned her military licence at the Flight Test Centre at Bretigny. She became France's first female test pilot. Only Hanna Reitsch of Germany, a test pilot for the Third Reich had performed such a role before. Test pilots must have an excellent knowledge of aeronautical engineering, in order to understand how aircraft are tested and why. They must also possess both excellent analytical skills and the ability to fly accurately, whilst following a flight plan.

Jacqueline had all of those attributes. She set a new women's speed record on 11 May 1951, flying a British Vampire jet at 508.8 mph (818.9 km/h). This bested American aviatrix Jacqueline Cochran's previous record, set in a P-51 Mustang. For this exploit the French aviatrix earned her first Harmon Trophy in 1951. The record also kicked off a friendly rivalry between the two pilots. They traded the women's world speed record for over a decade. Jacqueline Auriol beat her own record on 21 December 1952 in the Mistral with 531.3 mph (855 km/h) on the clock. The American took it next, flying a Canadian built Canadair F-86 Sabrejet, she set

Events in 1951

- ■ Bill Bridgeman sets a new airspeed record in the Douglas Skyrocket of Mach 1.88 (1,245 mph, 1,992 km/h).

- ■ Libya gains independence from Italy (Dec. 24).

- ■ Yul Brynner makes his first appearance as the king of Siam in The King and I.

- ■ Colour television introduced in the U.S.

a new speed record of 652.337 mph (1,049.8 km/h) at Edwards Air Force Base, California on May 18th, 1953. The same day she became the first woman to break the sound barrier, with famed aviator Chuck Yeager as her wingman.

On 3 August 1953, Jacqueline Auriol became the second woman to break the sound barrier flying a Dassault Mystere IV. Jacqueline won the Harmon trophy again that year, which was presented to her by President Eisenhower. Jacqueline also reclaimed the speed title from Jackie Cochran on 31 May 1955, flying the Mystere IVN. Jackie C throttled back and snatched the record in 1961, the year she took eight records. She lost again to the Frenchwoman on 22 June 1962, when Jacqueline set her fifth world speed record at Istres, France. She had trained for weeks and took off in a Dassault Mirage IIIC, determined to break Jackie Cochran's record. She failed first time round because she passed inside one of the turn points. Officials redesigned the course and added six points. She took off again that same afternoon. Flying at 37,000 feet for 63 miles, she took the record in 3 minutes and 23 seconds, at a speed of 1,149.65 mph (1,850.2 km/h).

She had bested Jackie Cochran's record by 367 mph (590.6 km/h), breaking the men's record set in 1959 for good measure. Jacqueline enjoyed victory again on 14 June 1963 in the Mirage IIIR. However, Jackie C had the last word with a speed of 1,303 mph (2,097 km/h) clocked on the Lockheed F-104 Starfighter. Despite, or perhaps because of this intense rivalry, the two women became good friends.

In addition to three Harmon trophies in 1952, 1953, and 1955, Jacqueline won the Paul Tissander Diploma in 1953, and the 1963 Gold Air Medal, La Grande Medaille de L'Aero Club de France in 1963. She was also awarded he Legion d'Honneur for her record-setting achievements.

As a test pilot, Jacqueline tested around one hundred aircraft types, including the prestigious Mistrals 2, Mystere IV and Mystere 20. She had a narrow brush with death in October 1956 when her Mystere IV plane went into spin and she managed to bring it back under control just feet from the ground. She was also one of the first to try out the supersonic Concorde.

After leaving the Flight Test Centre, she worked with the Ministere de la Cooperation, using remote sensing techniques to gather information for agricultural development. The United Nations Food and Agriculture Organization presented her with the Ceres Medal for her significant contributions in that field, too. She wrote her story in her 1970 autobiography "I Live to Fly," published in both French and English.

Jacqueline Auriol died on February 11, 2000 aged 82. On her death, President Jacques Chirac called her "the incarnation of courage and modernity for the French people."

But had her struggle been worth the pain? In an interview she gave to Colliers Magazine, she spoke of the rows of flowers on the grounds of Elysee Palace. "Poor creatures," she said, "guardians and ornaments of the Elysee. Once my life was like theirs." She then smiled broadly. "Perhaps I should teach them to fly," she said.

1955

JEAN ROSS HOWARD PHELAN (USA) 1916 - 2004

Jean Ross Howard in 1955 made the world a smaller place for women helicopter pilots spanning the five continents. She established the Whirly Girls, an organisation or haven for women accredited to fly the helicopter. From its original six pioneering charter members, the Whirly Girls has grown to encompass thousands of women from many countries and a variety of backgrounds.

ean Ross Howard was born on September 5th, 1916, her fifth generation roots in Washington stemming from an influential family. Her grandfather, John W. Ross, was a commissioner in the capital of America.

Always fascinated by flying, she once sacrificed a day of school and pocket money for her first ever aeroplane ride. On another occasion, the arrival in town of aviation legend Charles Lindbergh was like a visiting movie star for an awestruck Jean. Furtively gaining entry to the Mayflower Hotel balcony overlooking the ballroom, she listening intently as Lindbergh addressed the breakfast gathering held in his honour.

A brief stint at Connecticut College saw her transition over to George Washington University, graduating in 1939 with a degree in history. The summer months were spent broadening her horizons by vacationing across Europe in the company of her mother. Following graduation she seized the opportunity to fly by taking advantage of the government-sponsored Civilian Pilot Program. The free flying lessons sans personal liability insurance was offered during the war years on condition that an agreement be signed binding the student pilot to serve in the armed forces in the event of conscription.

Her passion for flying was such that Jean readily declined a $1,800 per annum government job to pursue a career in aviation. This was met with much disbelief and dismay from her family members. Gaining her pilot's licence in 1941 she briefly worked as a reservations clerk for Eastern Airlines. She then stumbled into a position selling Piper, Taylorcraft and Aeronca light observation aircraft to the army air corps.

With America on the brink of war she was galvanised by a recruitment speech delivered by Jackie Cochran, head of the newly formed Women's Air Force Service Pilots (WASP). Jean volunteered to serve with the WASP, but failed to complete her pilot training. However, at Jackie's behest she stayed on in an administrative capacity.

A year later she returned to Washington and joined the Civil Air Patrol. This was followed by a stint as programme manager for the Red Cross on the Italian island of Capri. In 1945 she joined the Aviation Industries Association later renamed Aerospace Industries Association (AIA) in a tenure that would almost last an entire lifetime. She started as a humble administrative assistant, and eventually retired from the body in 1986 as director of the helicopter division. Jean continued to invest much of her personal time in flying. She competed in the 1951-52 Transcontinental Air Races, affectionately dubbed the "Powder Puff Derbies."

She transferred into the AIA's helicopter division in the early 1950s. This serendipitous position gave her the opportunity to communicate her desire to learn to fly helicopters by lobbying several senior helicopter company executives. She cited the need to enhance her on-the-job performance as the reason for acquiring a licence to fly the unconventional aircraft.

Seven years of perseverance finally paid off. Larry Bell of Bell Helicopters relented to a tenacious Jean. He arranged for her to take helicopter lessons in Fort Worth, Texas. Just eighteen days later Jean soloed and proficiently learned to fly the helicopter. Her on-the-job performance was likely to go from strength-to-strength from then on.

One time when Jean executed a landing, the Bell instructor by her side remarked: "Well Jean, you're a real whirly girl now." She was quite taken by the name. There and then, the title of Jean's pioneering organisation had just been created. She was the eighth woman in the Americas, and thirteenth overall in the world to achieve a licence to fly helicopters.

Intrigued by the existence of other of female

Events in 1955

■ **George F. Smith becomes the first person to survive a supersonic ejection, from a North American F-100 Super Sabre travelling at Mach 1.05.**

■ **Churchill resigns.**

helicopter pilots, Jean set about canvassing civil aviation authorities around the world to learn of twelve other licensed women helicopter pilots. She wrote to all twelve, and six of them responded eventually to gather around a table in person on April 28th 1955 at the historic Mayflower Hotel.

The three Americans, two French and one German pilot swapped stories and ruminated about their passion for flying helicopters. They decided they needed an informal organisation dedicated to the support of women helicopter pilots. So on that fateful day the Whirly Girls came into being. So scattered were the finite number of women who had achieved the difficult task of controlling a helicopter that the women perceived the organisation as a lifeline. To be granted the official government nod to continue to fly the challenging beast also needed to be celebrated. In an interview with American Helicopter Jean described the flying characteristic of the aircraft as "patting your head and rubbing your stomach at the same time."

At the very outset the Whirly Girls always had a sense of fun attached to them, and being informal they did not have meetings, but annual "hoverings." Without officers, dues, or formal records, the intrepid twelve realised that maintaining contact between the swelling numbers of charter members would be difficult. Administrative efforts would be vital for its survival. Jean was the mother hen of the group and assumed that responsibility. Under her auspices the international organisation thrived. Jean served as executive director of the Whirly Girls until 1988.

Membership of the Whirly Girls is a simple affair. Each lifetime Whirly Girl is provided a number according to when she received her official helicopter rating. Whirly Girl #1 was Hanna Reitsch, the famous test pilot who flew for the Luftwaffe during World War Two. She not only accomplished a world first by flying the first practical helicopter, she achieved the feat by flying indoors. The legendary pilot, regarded by many as the best in the world, skilfully manoeuvred the unwieldy Focke-Achgelis Fa-61 rotary machine in an enclosed auditorium during the 1938 Berlin Motor Show, much to the delight of an overawed crowd.

Whirly Girl # 2 was Ann Shaw Carter, the first American woman to be certified to fly helicopters. She also has the distinction of being the first commercial helicopter pilot. Another luminary is Jacqueline Auriol, Whirly Girl # 8. The striking and courageous French aviatrix flew both helicopters and jet fighters. She fortunately survived a horrific accident as a passenger in a seaplane. The founding mother hen herself, Jean Ross Howard, had the honour of being Whirly Girl # 13.

By 1961 the Whirly Girls had 41 members. By December 2007, Whirly Girl membership had achieved a milestone 1,500 in its ranks, representing over 45 countries. Today, membership includes corporate and commercial pilots, flight instructors, military pilots, heliport designers, flight surgeons, attorneys, paralegals, cattle ranchers and students.

Throughout her lifetime Jean Ross Howard tirelessly promoted rotorcraft aviation. She travelled across America advocating the use of heliports to assist in emergency medical evacuation. Recognised for her contributions, in 1988 she was awarded the Whirly Girl's Livingston Award and made an honorary fellow of the American Helicopter Society. She was also a member of the Ninety Nines and in 2003 was voted by Women in Aviation as one of the "100 Women Who Made A Difference."

After her retirement from the AIA, she married in 1986 James Phelan, a Second World War aviator and veteran helicopter pilot. James served as the president of the Whirly Girls Men's Auxiliary. This latter group was established in 1971 to help support the scholarship fund to support women in the acquisition of a helicopter rating. Another scholarship fund was added in 1991 in memory of Major Marie Rossi, an army helicopter pilot killed during Desert Storm.

On January 29th 2004, Jean Ross Howard, Whirly Girl #13 passed away in her native Washington, aged 87. Her legacy of laying the foundations of an altruistic organisation is firmer than ever. From its humble beginnings with initial financial support from aviation pioneer Howard Hughes, Jean brought together a multitude of women who shared a common skill and ability to fly the most challenging of aircraft.

Hoverings over the years continued. There was a grand hovering in April 2005 when the Whirly Girls celebrated their 50th anniversary in the appropriate ambience of the Mayflower Hotel. The gathering of the 160 Whirly Girls from across the globe was a fitting tribute to the selfless efforts of their founding mother, one inimitable Jean Ross Howard Phelan.

1956

YAEL FINKELSTEIN ROM (ISRAEL) 1932 – 2006

First Israeli Air Force pilot, who fought for women's rights her entire life

On June 29, 2001, Israeli Air Force (IAF) veteran pilot Lt. (Reserves) Yael Rom-Finkelstein watched as the IAF graduated its first female fighter pilot in its 53 years of existence. Lt. Roni Zuckerman had just become the fourth woman to complete the IAF's pilot course and was the first to become a fighter pilot to much media fanfare. "I was angered a bit," Yael told the Jerusalem Post. "Things needed to be put into some kind of order here. [Zuckerman] may be newest, but we were the first." The Air Force subsequently invited her to fly down to the Hatzerim air base to attend the passing out parade.

Remarkable though Roni's achievement is, she was not the first woman in the IAF. That accolade went to Yael Finkelstein Rom, who earned her wings in 1951, aged 29, and went on to fly Douglas Dakota DC-3 transport aircraft. She was one of only two females in her class commissioned as officers, and the first of five women to fly in the IAF in its early years.

Two of her colleagues flew light aircraft as sergeants and the final woman became an airborne wireless operator. At that time all IAF cadets graduated from a general flight course and went on to specialise once they were assigned to a specific aircraft.

Yael flew as a reservist during 1956, the year Egypt took control of the Suez Canal. Israel launched an attack on Egypt's Sinai Peninsula to drive toward the canal. In Yael's most famous flight on October 29, she headed up a formation of 16 Dakotas that flew in formation to drop a full battalion of paratroopers into the heart of Sinai. The objective was to block the eastern entrance to the Mitla Pass. This would cut off the major route of possible Egyptian reinforcement in central Sinai.

Yael flew low, at about 1,200 feet over the drop zone. She later described a young paratrooper in the back of the aircraft shouting the "Paratroopers' Prayer" over the roar of the engines. Two dozen soldiers listened and then

yelled "Amen." The formation maintained radio silence and varied its altitude down to 100 feet in order to avoid detection. The slow moving transports would have made easy targets for Egyptian Mig-15s, based only a few minutes away.

The Dakotas spent five days shuttling supplies to the ground forces at the drop zone, and returning to pick up the wounded in a barren desert valley, which sucked the wheels down into its greedy clutches.

The IAF was experimental and she once had to fly a Dakota with a jeep strapped to its belly to be dropped by parachute. She said: "stupid me, I flew with it." One aircraft was known to be particularly jinxed and Yale and another pilot with just eight hours of flight time experience between them had trouble with its landing gear. The green light that showed whether the gear had locked into position had broken, so the crew did not know if the undercarriage was up or down. To find out they circled over the air base, performing aerobatics so that the commanders on the ground would see and signal them. The entire base came out to watch the spectacle. Witnessing the display was commander of the IAF and eventual seventh Israeli president Ezer Weizman. He had just returned from a year-long course in England. Yael remembered what he said: "I go away for a year and you let a woman fly? You've all gone crazy."

She described the differences between fighter and transport pilots in her time. "The fighter pilots were into glamour The Dakota pilots have a different character: We're friendly. The Dakota is a friendly airplane. Fighter pilots are egoists. They train and train and train for that one mission. We transport pilots, we're giving a service."

She went on to work as a first officer for Arkia Airlines, which had been established in 1949 to provide a direct airline service between Eilat and the centre of the country. Arkia leased Dakotas from the IAF. By the end of the decade the airline was carrying over 70,000 passengers a year. She resigned from the IAF in 1963.

She then joined the prestigious Technion Israel Institute of Technology in Haifa in 1960. There she developed academic programmes to

Events in 1956

- Autherine Lucy, the first black student at the University of Alabama, is suspended after riots.

- A B-52 Stratofortress drops US's first air-dropped hydrogen bomb on Bikini Atoll.

- With many hit singles, including "Heartbreak Hotel", Elvis Presley emerges as one of the world's first rock stars.

boost achievement among minority groups, veterans and the physically disabled. She continued to work for gender equality until her old age. She also acted as an unofficial advisor to the air force on women's issues. In September 1987, she headed up the Na'aleh project, which steered young women toward careers in engineering and technology.

Speaking to the Jerusalem Post in 2001, Yael said that she did not think that the flying course had changed significantly since 1951, when she trained. "It was as hard then as it is now," she said. She did say, however, that she felt less pressure because of her relatively low public profile. Four other women took the flying course in 1976, but did not complete it. Alice Miller fought a highly public media battle and took the IAF to the Supreme Court in order to join the air force. Justice Eliyahu Mazza ordered the army to invite her for tests, and if she passed, to accept her to the course.

Yael had got in decades earlier because of her flying talents. She was one of 30 people training to be flight instructors for Gadna (the high school pre-army programme). Only three students survived the course. She was one of them. They were all advised to join the air force and all three accepted. Yael explained to the Post: "I was not an emblem, I wasn't a breakthrough for the army. The social pressure, being alone, being a female whom everyone is interested in - it's damaging." She subsequently advised the army to keep all its women out of the media spotlight.

However, Yael was convinced that the problem of so few women in the air force then and today is one of numbers. Around ten percent of the men entering the IAF pilots' course graduate. Therefore 10 percent of seven women entering the course would not give even one female pilot. Yael said: "When the air force takes a group of 1,000 men, a handful become pilots. If you only take in several girls, it is statistically impossible that they will succeed." She advocated changing the drafting process to attract more women. She continued: "The army has to select women for the course the same way it selects men - by going into the schools to find the appropriate candidates and inviting them to the course."

Speaking to the Post in 2001, Yael said that Roni Zuckerman's graduation was a vindication to her and the four other early women fliers who had trained when she had. She said: "Being a pilot requires the highest quality of people. You have to be technically adept, and able to set and meet challenges and have coordination and mental aptitude," she said. "I am very happy today that there is finally a new female pilot. It took a long time. And now they have to change the method to bring in more women."

She added: "It is the first in 50 years and that is a great achievement. But you must also remember us. When we flew, they told us we were crazy and that it wasn't a profession for women. And now we see that women have finally followed us. It's a great celebration. I wouldn't give up on this. I have to be there, and it is very moving for me."

She died on May 24 2006 in Haifa at 74, having challenged the status quo and smoothed the path to success for countless disenfranchised people of both genders.

In November 2007, the Haaretz newspaper reported that the IAF would appoint a female deputy freight transport squadron commander, Captain Yifat. She began her career in the IAF as an assistant controller in the force's control unit. She later volunteered to take part in the IAF's prestigious flight course, which she completed with honours in 2002. She was stationed with the "Karnaf" squadron, and oversaw the flight course at the Hatzerim air force base's flight school.

1959

GERALDYN M. 'JERRIE' COBB (USA) 1931 –

**The expansiveness of the night sky had a marked impression
on a young Jerrie Cobb. She dreamed of being amongst the stars,
knowing all along that she had the 'Right Stuff'.**

Born on 5th March 1931 in Norman Oklahoma, Jerrie spent her high school years in Classen, Oklahoma City. Her father, Lt Col William H Cobb served as a pilot with the United States Army Air Corps. It was he who first introduced his wide-eyed daughter to the wonders of aviation.

Jerrie's first exposure to actual flying came about when she was 12 years old. Her father gingerly placed her in the backseat of his 1936 Waco open cockpit biplane. From then on an aviation legend was in the making. While still at high school Jerrie soloed her first aeroplane and by the age of 16 she was barnstorming above the Great Plains in a Piper J-3 Cub. Joyrides and dropping leaflets announcing the arrival of an elephant circus troupe provided the enterprising Jerrie with the necessary funds to keep the little Cub flying. It gave her the opportunity to hone her flying skills; her dedication was such that she slept under the wing of the precious Cub, never far from her winged soul mate.

The tenacious Jerrie obtained an official pilot's licence at 17 and by 18 she triumphed with a commercial rating. In concert with her flying, she moved from high school to a stint at Oklahoma City College and also played semi-professional women's football for Oklahoma City Queens. Dropping out of college, much to the disapproval of her parents, and abandoning her professional sporting career, Jerrie decided to focus on her first true love-flying

Firing on all cylinders, she threw herself into finding a job. But the deluge of returning male pilots from World War Two during the early 1950's made it nigh impossible for employment as a pilot. Furthermore it was apparent that her gender lessened the opportunities. Jerrie's enthusiasm hardly dampened when she took up the less attractive jobs such as crop dusting and patrolling oil pipelines. She went on to earn her multi-engine, instrument, flight instructor and ground instructor ratings in addition to an airline transport pilot's licence. By the age of 19 she was comfortably teaching men to fly planes.

A job at Miami airport led to a chance encounter with a former Second World War pilot who helmed a business ferrying surplus warplanes to customers worldwide. She was just 21 and suddenly at the controls of almost brand new fighters such as the P-51 Mustang, P-47 Thunderbolt and huge bombers like the B-17 Flying Fortress. The arduous task of ferrying such aircraft around the world was fraught with danger. Flying with minimum fuel, over treacherous jungle terrain and shark infested waters, Jerrie successfully delivered many planes to the Peruvian Air Force. In one instance she had fallen foul of the Ecuadorian authorities, who arrested her on suspicion of espionage whilst on a refuelling stop. Also during her ferrying tenure a three-year romance with another pilot ended in tragedy when his airplane exploded over the Pacific.

From 1957 onwards Jerrie immersed herself in setting aviation records. She established three-world altitude, speed and distance records in a twin engine Aero Commander. In 1957 she was awarded the Amelia Earhart Gold Medal of Achievement. The manufacturer, Oklahoma's Aero Design and Engineering Company swiftly appointed her as test pilot and promotion manager for the Commander. Becoming the first woman to fly in the world's largest air exposition, the Salon International de l'Aeronautique in Paris – ie the Paris Air Show, fellow airmen named her "Pilot of the Year" in 1959. Still in her twenties Life Magazine bestowed upon her the honour of being one of nine women celebrated in the "100 most important young people in the United States."

In 1961 Jerrie soloed in the Bell 47G-2A helicopter after only 83 minutes of dual flight instruction. Upon gaining her helicopter rating she became a member of the Whirly Girls, an international women's organisation established by Jean Ross Howard Phelan in 1955. Jerrie became Whirly Girl # 53, denoting that she was the fifty third female in the world to accomplish a helicopter rating.

The American space programme was still in a relatively fledgling state during late fifties. The first astronauts making the grade were the celebrated all male 'Mercury 7' team.

By now Jerrie was recognised and ranked as one of the best pilots of the era, having amassed thousands hours in the cockpit of many different types of aircraft. In 1959 she was selected by Dr W Randolph Lovelace to undergo the same gruelling fitness-testing regime that he devised to procure the 'Mercury 7 astronauts'. She was the first American woman to endure the demanding three-phased tests, passing them with flying colours. Buoyed by their success, Jerrie and Dr Loveless recruited a further 25 eligible women pilots to experience the same tests. The entire initiative was funded by another legendary aviatrix, one Jackie Cochran, cosmetics entrepreneur and former commander of the WASP group of women pilots during World War Two. Twelve of the intake made the cut and along with Jerrie they were dubbed the 'Mercury 13' of women astronauts in the making.

Jerrie was appointed by the National Aeronautics and Space Administration (NASA) as consultant to the space programme in 1961, with the prospect in the offing of being the first woman to fly into space. However, at the time NASA required its astronauts to be drawn from a pool of experienced military test pilots. With women denied access to military jet hardware this by default excluded the 'Mercury 13' from the possibility of being granted a spacecraft mission. The convening of a Congressional hearing to debate the matter in 1963 ruled in favour of excluding women from the space programme. In that same year Jerrie's burning ambition of being the first women in space was dashed when Soviet cosmonaut Valentina Tereshkova became the first to get there.

Crestfallen, Jerrie resigned from NASA, mitigating her disappointment by dedicating herself to the new frontier of humanitarian causes. Flying in a faithful Aero Commander plane, nicknamed as the 'The Bird' she would spend the next 35 years serving the indigenous people residing in the Amazon.

Her missionary activities centred on flying medicines and delivering supplies to the scattered Indian villages inhabiting the vast Amazonian Forest. The Jerrie Cobb Foundation was established by her fellow Oklahomans to fund her selfless humanitarian effort. Jerrie financed the 'The Bird' and maintained its airworthiness through separate consultancy work and government sponsored aerial survey assignments. In addition to being honoured by many of the Latin American countries she was nominated in 1978 for the Nobel Peace Prize for her tireless humanitarian work.

Flying and good causes ran hand in hand for Jerrie, who in 1973 was awarded the Harmon Trophy by President Nixon as 'the top woman pilot in the world'. Jerrie has the distinction of being recognised the world over for her contributions to aviation and her relief efforts. The governments of Peru, Columbia and Brazil honoured her for her 'humanitarian flying in the service of primitive tribes.' In 1990 she was inducted into the Oklahoma Aviation and Space Hall of Fame. Then in 2000 she gained recognition of the Women in Aviation International Pioneer Hall of Fame. In 2007 Jerrie, along with seven other surviving members of the 'Mercury 13,' were conferred honorary doctorates by the University of Wisconsin.

The awards and honours are bountiful, but the milestone of experiencing spaceflight eluded Jerrie. In 1998 Senator John Glenn, one of the legendary 'Mercury 7' astronauts returned to space aged 76, flying aboard the Space Shuttle to examine effects of weightlessness on age.

This sparked a resurgence of interest in 67-year-old Jerrie, still considered fit and healthy, to be afforded the chance of her own space shot denied to her during the sixties. Assisted by friends and influential supporters a campaign was launched to convince NASA of her viability as an astronaut.

Many years later Jerrie remains positive that one day her dream of flying into space will be fulfilled.

Geraldyn M. "Jerrie" Cobb was destined to be an extraordinary pilot, shunning fame and fortune she simply indulged her passion for flying. Along her journey she discovered a way to help the forgotten and forsaken, risking her life for the benefit of others. Perhaps one day she will be given the opportunity of orbiting the earth. For this living legend deserves to look down from a weightless vantage to see her home of Oklahoma and maybe the Amazonian rainforests and inspire the next generation looking up at the stars.

Events in 1959

- Tibet's Dalai Lama escapes to India.

- Explorer 6 sends the first picture of Earth from space.

- Luna 2 crashes onto the Moon as the first man-made object on the moon.

1963

Valentina Vladimirovna Tereshkova (USSR) 1937 –

Textile worker who won the space race

Flying high above the world in a gleaming MiG-15 jet fighter, Valentina Tereshkova contemplated the darker upper regions of the atmosphere, a universe away from her former existence as peasant girl toiling in a textile mill. She had truly travelled far. She was the first woman in the world to fly into space on 16th June 1963. This was a far cry from her humble beginnings.

Born on 6th March 1937 in Bolshoye Maslennikovo, Valentina grew up in a small town in the Yaroslavl Oblast region. Her tractor driver father was drafted into the Finno-Russian conflict of 1939. He was eventually listed as "missing in action," never to return. This left her textile worker mother to struggle alone to raise Valentina and her siblings.

To shore up the family finances, Valentina left school in 1953 to work in the textile mills, but continued her education through correspondence courses. From an early age she was interested in parachuting, and joined the local DOSAAF (Freewill Society for Army, Aviation and Navy Support) Aviation Club in Yaroslavl. She made her first jump aged 22 on 21 May 1959. Her passion for parachuting would eventually lead Valentina into the cosmonaut programme. In 1961 she became secretary of the local Komsomol (Young Communist League).

A month after her 24th birthday in April 1961, the USSR made history by launching fighter pilot Yuri Gagarin in Vostok 1 to become the first man in space. This was a proud and pivotal moment for the Soviets, who were now ahead of the lagging Americans in the space race.

To maintain their advantage over the US, cosmonaut chief Kamanin broached the idea of the first female spaceflight to the Soviet Air Force chief designer Korolev. Driven by patriotism, he believed it was imperative that they superseded the Americans by being the first to blast a woman way beyond the stratosphere. The idea gained momentum, and with final approval from Premier Nikita Khrushchev, the search was on for the first female cosmonaut.

In October 1961 space was made for five women amongst the intake of 50 new cosmonauts. Flying experience was not necessary as the Vostok space-craft were pre-programmed for automatic flight. Early cosmonauts were just there for the ride. But parachute experience was essential, as the cosmonaut would have to eject on re-entry and descend using a personal parachute. Furthermore, at that time, female Russian pilots were rare, but there were many women parachutists to bolster the candidate selection pool.

Valentina fulfilled the entry qualifications of being under 30 years of age, an accomplished parachutist, under 170 cm tall and below 70 kg in weight. However, the fact that her father was "missing in action," as opposed to being "killed in action," raised speculation over his possible desertion. However, her loyalist activities as leader of the Komsomol allowed her to become one of the 40 women to enter the rigorous selection process in Moscow in January 1962.

By 16th February 1962 five women were awarded the opportunity to become cosmonauts. These included Valentina, along with Tatiana Kuznetsova, Irina Solovyova, Zhanna Yerkina and Valentina Ponomaryova. The other four were more qualified than Valentina, being test pilots, engineers and champion parachutists.

The five were then subjected to an intensive and secretive training regime involving weightless flights, 120 parachute jumps, and isolation and centrifuge tests. All were trained as pilots on the diminutive MiG-15 UTI trainer jet fighter. Valentina struggled with the engineering and academic subjects compared to the others, but excelled in the physical tests. All were commissioned as junior lieutenants in the Soviet Air Force. Valentina was interned as a loyal member of the Communist Party of the Soviet Union.

In 1962 the first American in space John Glenn met cosmonaut chief Kamanin during a visit to Washington. Glenn had imparted to an alarmed Kamanin that an American female astronaut from the selected "Mercury 13" would make a three-orbit flight in a Mercury capsule by the end of 1962. This accelerated the Soviet programme.

The two Valentinas – Ponomaryova and Tereshkova - were short listed on November 16th 1962. Tereshkova was nominated over the academically superior and more experienced Ponomaryova due to her undisputed loyalty to the Communist precepts and ideals. Ponomaryova valiantly subjected herself to interviews but was relegated to back-up pilot to Tereshkova who had the answers on the day.

Premier Khrushchev gave Valentina Tereshkova his final seal of approval, impressed by her attributes of being the "New Soviet Woman." From peasant origins to glamorous cosmonaut, Khrushchev felt Valentina possessed the right look and background to enter the world of state-controlled celebrity. She would later earn the title of "Gagarin in a skirt."

Valentina watched Vostok 5 launch on June 14th 1963, carrying male cosmonaut Valery Fyodorovich Bykovsky. Donning a bulky spacesuit two days later she was strapped into Vostok 6. On 16th June 1963 with call-sign "Chaika" (Seagull) she blasted off without incident to become the first women in space.

It was only in 2007 that the actual events of the difficult Vostok 6 mission were revealed. Valentina suffered nausea throughout the three-day flight, vomiting several times. She also endured debilitating cramps from being strapped into her seat, which restricted both movement and circulation. Her helmet ring cut into her shoulder, and a rash had developed beneath a sensor pad.

Events in 1963

- Kenya's independence.
- President Kennedy shot and killed in Dallas
- Beatlemania hits the UK

Vostok 6 made 48 orbits around the earth and came within five km of its sister ship, Vostok 5, with brief communications initiated via radio between the two vessels. Although on automatic, Valentina spotted a potential problem with the attitude of her craft, which could have resulted in her untimely demise on re-entry. The ground support teams initially did not believe her assertions, but eventually verified her reports and corrected the craft's orientation remotely.

Jostled by re-entry, Valentina ejected herself from the capsule to parachute to safety. In the process she had logged more spaceflight time than any US male astronaut of that era.

Publicly paraded and lauded, reports suggest that behind closed doors there were many in the Soviet ranks who attempted to discredit Valentina. This was largely due to the embarrassment caused to senior managers because of the incident of the misaligned orientation of Vostok 6. Many of the festering generals believed she should have accepted death than report the problem. But cosmonaut chief Kamanin proved to be her strongest ally deflecting all accusations and unfounded impropriety away from Valentina. Her detractors were silenced and swiftly re-assigned.

Valentina later married fellow cosmonaut Andrian Nikolayev, with whom she would have a less than happy relationship. Premier Nikita Khrushchev seized upon this union as another propaganda coup.

Their wedding was almost a state occasion held at the Moscow Palace of Weddings on 3rd November 1963. They had a daughter Elena Andrianovna, who became a doctor.

No other Russian woman flew into space for several years...it would be 19 years before Svetlana Savitskaya became the second in 1992. Valentina subsequently obtained an engineering degree from the Zhukovskiy Military Air Academy and, following graduation; the female cosmonauts were disbanded in 1969. Valentina took up several leading positions within the Communist party and represented the Kremlin at a number of international women's' events.

She later divorced Nikolayev and married physician Yuliy Shaposhnikov following a failed attempt at returning to the cosmonaut ranks during the late seventies. There had been resurgence in female cosmonaut training because of the looming prospect of American women about to fly into space on the space shuttle.

Surviving her second husband who died in 1999, Valentina long ago retired from party politics and the air force. Regarded as a living legend, she holds many awards and international medals, one of which is "the hero of the Soviet Union," the highest honour from the Soviet era. She has lost none of her passion for spaceflight. On her 70th birthday she told former President Vladimir Putin of her desire to fly to Mars – even if it was a one-way flight.

Valentina towed the party line, but asserted enough of her own personality to shape her own destiny. From textile worker to celebrated cosmonaut, she survived the machinations of her political opponents and the dangers of primitive spaceflight with courage and grace. In 2008 she was honoured again by being named as one of the bearers of the Olympic torch for the 2008 Beijing games.

1963

DIANA BARNATO WALKER (UK) 1918 – 2008

Atagirl who loved glamour and speed

There are likely to be a few Spitfire pilots who became temporarily stuck upside down, playing forbidden aerobatics with their machines. There is likely only to have been one whose vision was obscured by face powder billowing through the cockpit as she wrestled to right herself. Diana Barnato found herself in this tricky position. She wrote in her 1994 biography 'Spreading my Wings: "While I was wondering what to do next, from out of my top overall pocket fell my beautifully engraved silver powder compact. It wheeled round and round the bubble canopy like a drunken sailor on a wall of death, then sent all the face powder over everything."

She landed to be greeted by an RAF flight lieutenant. She said: "One glance was enough. His mouth dropped open. 'I was told,' he gasped, 'that a very very pretty girl was bringing us a new aircraft. All I can see is some ghastly clown."

The episode typifies the spirit of Diana Barnato Walker. She was born on January 15 1918 into a highly talented Jewish family. Her grandfather was a former London comedian, who made his way to Johannesburg, where he co-founded the De Beers mining group. Her father, Woolf, won the Le Mans 24-hour race in three consecutive years from 1928 to 1930. Diana and her sister Virginia were totally cosseted. Diana was given a Bentley as a gift by her indulgent father for her 21st birthday. In 1936 she came out as a debutante. She felt hemmed in by that world and decided to escape the constrictions of high society by learning to fly.

Off she went to Brooklands in 1938 and spent her pocket money on a few lessons in a Tiger Moth, soloing after six hours. The lessons were pricey - £3 per hour. She wrote: "In those days I was far too much of a snob to learn to fly with what I thought would be the hoi polloi [in the Civil Air Guard], even though it cost only 7/6d per hour". She ran out of money and stopped.

When the Second World War broke out, she worked with the Red Cross. She applied to the Auxiliary Air Transport Corps (ATA), despite having only 10 flight hours to her name. The ATA eventually set up a training programme and, Diana became an "Atagirl" in December 1941. The organisation existed to ferry aircraft to frontline bases. Its pilots were trained to fly aeroplanes from trainers to bombers. Diana wrote that she "strapped an extraordinary assortment of aeroplanes to her backside." Speaking at a British Women Pilots' Association Christmas dinner in 2003, fellow Atagirl Jackie Moggridge spoke of having had spiral bound checklists thrust at her at unfamiliar airfields and being told to climb into whichever aircraft she was ferrying and learnt as she flew. The list of aircraft Diana flew was impressive. It included the Spitfire, Hurricane, Defiant, Mustang, Avenger, Wildcat, Vengeance, Firefly, Barracuda and Tempest. She also flew the Oxford, Anson, Wellington, Warwick, Mosquito, Hudson and Mitchell. The Spitfire was her favourite.

She detested the Supermarine Walrus air-sea-rescue amphibian pusher biplane. She wrote: "I would not have liked to have been killed in one, a most unglamorous end." On 19 September 1944 she was flying a Walrus from Cosford to Eastleigh when the engine sprang a leak and oil cascaded over her windscreen. At 1,500ft and approaching the Southampton balloon barrage with no power, all she could do was to push the nose down and make a swift descent. Fortunately she missed the cables, coming down a few feet above the aerodrome.

She attributed her survival to her "guardian angel" and a man who had stopped her, as she was about to take off on her first solo flight at Brooklands. His hands and face were horribly burned. He looked at her and said, 'Don't fly, Miss Barnato. Look what it's done to me.'" The sober warning ensured she flew carefully. She also refused to fly unless she was well turned-out, always combing her hair and putting on make-up when she landed.

In 1942, she became engaged to Wing Commander Humphrey Gilbert. Some accounts say that when she was forced to land at his base during foul weather, he removed her aircraft's spark plugs and suggested she stay to dinner. They were engaged within three weeks. Two days after he proposed he was killed.

She continued with her work, and in 2005 told the Times about one memorable incident. One morning in January 1943, aged 25 she was flying a Spitfire towards Worcester when the clear sky clouded over. She climbed, levelled off and turned to fly back the way it had come. Losing height, Diana looked out for an airfield. She said; "I couldn't bale out! My skirt would have ridden up with the parachute straps and anyone who happened to be below would have seen my knickers!"

She emerged from the cloud just a few hundred feet above the ground, banking sharply to avoid nearby trees and made a perfect landing in heavy rain on the grass airstrip of what turned out to be RAF Windrush. The minute she climbed, out, her knees buckled. An RAF pilot was heading her way with a cape to shield her from the rain. She did not want him to think anything was wrong. She said: "I knelt on the

wing and scrabbled in the cockpit for my maps." The pilot replied: "I say, Miss, you must be good on instruments."

However, Diana never used instruments. The ATA did not train its pilots to fly blind. It also expected its pilots to fly in all weathers without navigational aids. As a result of this, and the fact that they flew unarmed and without radios, service in the ATA was one of the most dangerous activities in the whole war. Out of the 108 female pilots recruited, 16 were killed - including Amy Johnson, the first woman to fly solo from England to Australia, who died ferrying an Oxford aircraft in 1941.

In 1944 Diana married Derek Walker, another decorated pilot. They flew together in a pair of Mk IX Spitfires on a honeymoon trip to Brussels - officially classed as reconnaissance, although actually unauthorised. She was docked three months' pay as punishment. Four months after the end of the war he was killed, flying to a job interview in a Mustang.

Unlike many of her contemporaries, Diana found a job flying after the War. She earned her commercial licence and was appointed Corps Pilot for the Women's Junior Air Corps, giving cadets training and air-experience flights at weekends and amassing many flying hours in Fairchild Argus and Auster aircraft. She continued flying for a few more years. In 1963 she was awarded the Jean Lennox Bird Trophy, presented annually to a British woman pilot, for her work there.

The same year Wing Commander John Severgne, suggested that Diana might like to fly one of the RAF's new supersonic English Electric Lightning jets. She jumped at the chance and attained 1,262mph (Mach 1.65) in a two-seat T.4 trainer, becoming the first British woman to exceed the speed of sound.

Shortly after her record-breaking flight, she was diagnosed with cancer and she had to undergo three operations. Once she had the all clear she devoted an increased amount of time to the Girls Venture Corps Air Cadets (as the WJAC had become known), becoming its vice-chairman. She was also Commodore of the Air Transport Auxiliary Association, helping to keep together its members from 29 nations. She was appointed MBE for her services to aviation in 1965. She last took the controls of a rare, twin-seat Spitfire trainer when she was 88 - "impolite not to," she grinned. She published her memoir Spreading My Wings in 1994.

When she died many of her obituaries mentioned that she had a 30-year relationship with American racing driver and Hurricane pilot Whitney Straight, who went on to be chairman of British Overseas Aircraft Corporation. They had a son Barney Barnato in 1947. Diana never asked Straight to leave his wife. "I was perfectly content," she explained. "I had my own identity." Whitney Straight died in 1979. She lived for another twenty years and died on April 28 2008 aged 90.

More events in 1963

- Joe Walker flies a North American X-15 to a record altitude of 106,010 metres (347,800 feet). This flight qualifies as a human spaceflight.

- "March on Washington," civil rights rally; Martin Luther King delivers "I have a dream" speech

- Lee Harvey Oswald, accused Kennedy assassin, is shot and killed

1964

JERRIE MOCK
(USA) 1925 –

She swapped knitting for the controls of an aeroplane and became the first woman to fly solo around the world in a light aircraft

n 1964 a tiny aviatrix from Columbus Ohio smashed world records because she "wanted to see the world." That year two female pilots raced to take the title of first round the world: Geraldine Mock and Joan Merriam Smith. Although the Hon. Mrs Victor Bruce had flown around the world in 1930, she had not flown across oceans because of the technical limitations of her aircraft, which had to be ferried by boat. Like several others, Amelia Earhart had died in her 1937 circumnavigation attempt.

Geraldine "Jerrie" Fredritz Mock was born on November 22, 1925 in Newark, Ohio. According to a website set up by her granddaughter Rita Juanita Mock, as a little girl, Jerrie played with boys because all the girls lived across the street, and her mother would not allow her to cross the road. Consequently, she preferred the games the boys played. Aged twelve, Jerrie visited her father's workplace. There she observed a woman stopping work and knitting for half an hour to fulfil Ohio's Women's Protective Laws, which said that a woman could only work for five hours, then must take a thirty-minute break. Rita writes that Jerrie resents these laws even now as a retired grandmother.

Jerrie was working as manager of the Columbus Airport in Ohio when she started flying lessons in 1958. She told the Columbus Dispatch in 1994: "Women were often laughed at around the airports. In today's lifestyle, you might say they were harassed, but we didn't dare say that then. They would have made it worse. I'd hear them, and I'd ignore it." Married to Russell Mock, she had three children, one of whom was a toddler. In 1962 Jerrie complained to her husband that she was bored. His response was to reply: "Why don't you fly around the world?" Discovering that no woman had managed the feat, she set out to become the first woman to attain the record. With 750 flying hours, including an Instrument Rating to enable her to fly in all weather conditions, she declared herself ready.

Like Polly Vacher decades later, Jerrie had been meticulous and thorough in her pre flight preparations. She took eighteen months to prepare, poring over charts and working out all

her calculations. She studied the route she was going to take, and checked out the aircraft and all the equipment she would need. This was a far cry from the scant preparations made by Mrs. Bruce, who set off on her world flight only eight weeks after obtaining her pilot's licence, with luggage more suitable for a weekend away.

Jerrie owned a 1953 high-wing Cessna 180 tail dragger, christened "The Spirit of Columbus," but nicknamed "Charlie." She had two extra ferry tanks fitted in the cabin, bringing the total fuel on board to 178 gallons. This gave her an endurance of 25 hours and a range of 2,400 nautical miles. She added an HF radio for long-range radio communications. Engine manufacturer Continental donated a custom-built powerplant.

At the same time Joan Merriam Smith was also planning a solo flight around the world. However, Jerrie was first to register her intentions with the National Aeronautic Association, which represents the Federation Aeronautique Internationale (FAI) in the US. FAI rules stipulate that only one pilot at a time can apply to make an attempt to set the same record.

The two pilots insisted they were not racing against one another, however Russell pushed his wife to fly faster throughout her journey. The newspaper her husband worked for, the Columbus Dispatch, sponsored Jerrie. To satisfy the rules to set a record she was supposed to file logs for publication throughout her journey. The FAI requires pilots setting world records to keep a log of their flights, which are stored in its archives in Lausanne, Switzerland.

Jerrie took off from Columbus on March 19, 1964, nervous but determined. She experienced several terrors during her epic adventure. She accidentally overheated the long-range antenna to her HF radio. Smoke filled the cabin and she was scared she might have set her aircraft on fire. Grounded in Bermuda, she had the radio repaired. Russell told her that Joan was also struggling - stuck in Suriname with a leak in one of her ferry tanks. He harried his wife to get going again. The planned flight logs went awry, too. Jerrie told the Dispatch in 1994: "In the Azores, the only telephone lines went to Lisbon.

Events in 1964

- US Congress authorises war against N Vietnam

- Cassius Clay Beats Sonny Liston for World Heavyweight championship

- Nelson Mandela sentenced to life imprisonment in South Africa

There was no way I could telephone back anything. In some countries the communications office was open only certain hours, but not hours I could conveniently get there," she said.

En route to Casablanca in Morocco, she had to fight severe icing. Tired when she landed, she stopped to visit some friends. Russell urged her to keep moving as Joan had left the Americas and was on her way to Africa. At this point Jerrie's aircraft developed problems with the brakes and the tail wheel. She landed in Bône, Algeria on the 30th March. Her husband pushed her to go even faster. She made it to Tripoli in Libya on the 31st. Unfortunately, she had landed at a Soviet missile base at Inchas, mistaking it for Cairo. After two hours of interrogation, she was allowed to fly on.

She took time out the next day to visit the pyramids and ride a camel, despite her husband's protestations. She was in Karachi in Pakistan by the 4th April. Joan was making good ground, too. On the 5th, Jerrie reached India, and ignored Russell's instructions to fly on to Calcutta. She elected instead to stop in Delhi.

Author Ann Lewis Cooper writes about the worst moment of the flight in her book "Stars of the Sky: Legends All." Jerrie was flying over the shark-infested South China Sea en route to the Philippines from Thailand. Her engine ran rough. The fix was to fly with carburettor heat on, which guzzled more fuel than she had allowed for. Flying over the middle of the ocean she had to transfer fuel from the ferry tanks in the cabin to the wing tanks and allow the engine to stop completely. She then had to switch off the pumps until the engine restarted. She kept calm and made it to Manila on the 8th of April.

She continued to Guam and the 13th saw her take off for Hawaii. Then came the last haul – the long leg from Hawaii to California. She finally landed at Oakland after flying more than 2,400 miles over 18 hours. Her husband was there to greet her, along with journalists, television cameras and a huge crowd. Joan had reached Singapore.

Jerrie finally arrived home on April 17th having covered 22,858 miles in 30 days, and flown 158 flying hours. President Johnson awarded her the FAA's Gold Medal, and she was honoured in many other countries. The FAI presented her with the Louis Blériot Silver Medal. She set two official FAI records: Feminine record, and speed around the world, Class C1-c. She also set five unofficial records, including the one she is best known for: first woman to fly solo entirely around the world. Joan Merriam Smith completed her flight and landed in Oakland on May 12th. Sadly she was killed in an aircraft accident the following year.

Cessna gave Jerrie a new aircraft in exchange for the Spirit of Columbus, which was displayed in their Wichita factory. It eventually went to the Smithsonian Museum in Washington.

It now hangs from the ceiling at the Udvar-Hazy Center at Dulles Airport. Jerrie continued to fly her new Cessna, a C P206, in which she set five more speed and endurance records. She stopped flying in the 1970s, citing the expense. She wrote her autobiography "Three Eight Charlie" in 1970. She now lives in Tallahassee, Florida.

Jerrie has set world records and lived through the Great Depression, World War II and the Cold War. Rita writes. "When I asked her what she considered her greatest accomplishment, I thought she would respond that it was her record-breaking flight around the world. Instead, she answered that her greatest accomplishment was the fact that out of three childhood dreams, which were to fly around the world, ride a camel across the Sahara Desert and ride an elephant in the jungle. She accomplished the first two, despite being "just a woman."

SHEILA SCOTT (UK)
1922 - 1988

The obsessive beauty who broke more than 100 world records

heila Scott stormed her way into aviation history with more than 100 flying records. She made three solo flights around the world and set records for single-handed London-Cape Town and Cape Town-London flights. She started flying when she was almost 40.

She was born Sheila Christine Hopkins on 27 April 1922 in Worcester, UK. The only child of a baker, her solid middle class background was shattered when her mother Edyth ran away with an actor in 1925. Sheila was sent off to her grandparents and two aunts. According to former British Women Pilots' Association (BWPA) archivist Enid DeBois, the whole family felt the shock of the defection and ultimate divorce, which were a terrible disgrace at the time. Edyth was effectively eliminated from the Hopkins family and Sheila never knew anything of her mother.

Her father remarried Aileen Harper when Sheila was ten. Sheila clashed terribly with her mild-mannered stepmother. She became obsessed with finding her mother, and frequently played truant from the Alice Ottley School for Girls in Worcester. She failed her school certificate, and only managed to pass on her second attempt because Aileen locked her in her room to study.

As a young woman she trained as a nurse at Haslar Royal Naval Hospital in Portsmouth and loved the social life at the wartime naval base. In 1943 she was posted to London, where she decided on an acting career and took the name Sheila Scott. She married Rupert Leaman Bellamy in 1945, a lieutenant colonel in the Royal Electrical and Mechanical Engineers (REME). The union lasted five years. Whilst Rupert was away on duty Sheila took private drama tuition and enrolled on a Lucie Clayton modelling course. She went on to appear in small roles for theatre, film, and television and worked as a model between 1945 and 1959. After her divorce in 1950 she became chaotic. She was beautiful and intelligent with a penchant for parties – perhaps too much of a penchant. DeBois wrote that Sheila experienced periods of drug and alcohol dependence necessitating psychiatric treatment.

With a string of half-started careers behind her, in 1958 Sheila took herself to Elstree airfield to learn to fly. She was anxious, a heavy smoker and nervous student. She had failed her driving test four times and found learning to fly just as challenging. She transferred to Thruxton airfield, but it was nine months before she flew solo. However, she was persistent, and finally achieved her private pilot's licence (PPL) in 1960. She cultivated a strong social life in the flying community and joined as many clubs as possible, including the Royal Aero Club (RAeC), the Tiger Club, and the British Women Pilots' Association.

Sheila bought an old Thruxton Jackaroo biplane, which was actually a converted Tiger Moth from the Royal Air Force (RAF). She had it painted blue with silver wings and christened it "Myth," the feminine of "Moth." She also had her secret logo painted on it. She got braver and tried non-radio flights to the Channel Islands and won her first trophy at the Jersey air rally. Although she had a bare six months to learn how to fly fast over a set course, she entered the 1960 national air races. She earned enough points to become air racing champion of her class and won the De Havilland national air racing trophy. She was awarded the BWPA's Jean Lennox Bird trophy for her success. This sparked an obsession in her soul and she entered as many races and rallies as possible, immersing herself in aviation.

During the next decade she shone. Cessna and Piper paid her to be a demonstrator and let her use an aircraft for her air races. Cessna invited her to the US for Cessna sales week. There she discovered that flying was a good deal cheaper than in the UK, so she earned her commercial licence and instrument rating. She then upgraded her aircraft to a borrowed Piper Comanche 250 for her racing. She returned to the US in 1964 and picked up her commercial seaplane and helicopter ratings in just three weeks. This bagged her the Amelia Earhart trophy and membership of the Whirly Girls Club. She then discovered that there were fifteen European light-aircraft records that had lain dormant for several years, so borrowed a single-engine Piper Comanche 400 and broke them all in thirty-six hours. This meant flying for 2,300 miles over ten and half hours.

Sheila became obsessed with a round-the-world flight and threw all the cash she had into a Piper Comanche she named "Myth Too." She left London on 18 May 1966, and flew around 31,000 miles in 189 flying hours over 33 days. She arrived back at Heathrow thirty-three days and three minutes later. This won her the US Harmon trophy for the year's most outstanding

Events in 1966

■ The unmanned Soviet Luna 9 spacecraft makes the first controlled rocket-assisted landing on the Moon.

woman pilot. She also became the first female winner of the Guild of Air Pilots and Navigators (GAPAN)'s silver award of merit. She received an invitation to meet the Queen at Buckingham Palace, and also met King Hussein, an avid pilot. Italy bestowed the "Isabella d'Este" title upon her.

Sheila next took Amy Johnson's London to Cape Town record in July 1967, followed by the north and south Atlantic records in 1967 and 1969 respectively. According to soloflights.org, a website dedicated to pilots who fly around the world, the weather during this flight was dreadful, with thunder and snowstorms. She also suffered technical problems. Taking off from Singapore she lost all radio contact, leaving her with no means of communication. Then her navigation instruments died. Sheila continued her flight, navigating by "'dead reckoning." – ie manual plotting using known speed, elapsed time and course.

However, she got lost. She said that for several hours she imagined she could hear voices on her dead radios and later believed she was hallucinating. She finally landed on a military airfield in the Celebes, miles off track. She went on to circumnavigate the globe and was awarded an Officer of the Order of the British Empire (OBE) in 1968. She wrote the first of her two books: "I Must Fly" the same year.

1971 saw her most difficult solo flight - equator to equator over the North Pole then resume a third round the world flight. For this she earned her 100th world record. When she flew over the Pole, she dropped a British flag out of her aircraft, yelling happily into the radio: "I am at the top of the world." Flying a specially modified twin-engine Piper Aztec christened "Mythre," she worked with America's National Aeronautics and Space Administration. NASA was conducting environmental and biomedical experiments together with the British Royal Air Force's Institute of Aviation Medicine. The idea was to explore sleep patterns and problems of long-distance pilots. Sheila came back from this flight with debts of £20,000 (In 1971 an average British house cost £5,631). Any further plans for long distance flights foundered when Mythre was wrecked by cyclone Agnes in Pennsylvania in 1972. The aircraft was at the Piper factory to be over-hauled. Sheila was devastated.

Her active flying life stopped. During ten years she had taken 107 international records, won the Brabazon cup three times, and taken the RAeC Britannia trophy in 1967. In 1971 she had been presented with the RAeC's Gold Medal and BWPA's Jean Lennox Bird trophy.

She fell on hard financial times and throughout the 1970s and early 1980s tried to commit suicide and was committed to psychiatric clinics. In 1973 her friends helped her write a book about her flying, published as "On Top of the World," in the UK, but titled "Barefoot in the Sky" in the USA. She also started to work with troubled teenagers. She continued to support aviation associations worldwide and was a founder and first governor of the British section of the American Ninety Nines.

She became president of the European Women Pilots' Association in 1984 and as European vice-president of the World Aerospace Education Organisation; she attended a conference in Delhi inaugurated by Rajiv Gandhi. She was diagnosed with terminal lung cancer in 1987 and died on 20 October 1988 aged 61. She was cremated and her ashes scattered over Thruxton airfield.

1967
FIORENZA DE BERNARDI
(ITALY) 1928 –

Passionate pioneer who has eased the way for many who have followed her

Professional female pilots have a great deal to thank Fiorenza de Bernardi for. With five decades of aeronautical achievements under her belt, she is a tireless campaigner for better conditions for women in aviation. She is a pioneering record setter, who, throughout her career, has shown a willingness to be adaptable and to change in order to do the job she loves. She is licensed to fly numerous aircraft including: the Twin Otter, the Queen Airf, the Yak -40, and the DC-8. Her career has taken her all over the world. Writing in her book, "Pink Line" Fiorenza says: "Perhaps I caught little by little the 'disease' from which there is no cure – a passion for flying."

Fiorenza was born on May 22, 1928, in Florence, Italy. Her father was Colonel Mario de Bernardi, a world champion seaplane racer and aerobatics champion. He was also a test pilot and pioneering fighter pilot in World War I with the Baracca squadron. She learned to fly in 1951 and used her license to enter air races both in her home country and throughout European countries during 1953. In 1959 her father was killed during a demonstration flight of his "Aeroscooter" plane. He managed to land the aircraft, but sadly died before he could cut off the engine. He obviously had a huge impact on his daughter's life and Fiorenza says she has dedicated her success to him.

She writes that her father would have been "pleased with her career" and "amused" at her early efforts as she found her wings. She writes: "I played hide and seek amongst aeroplanes as a child." However, she never imagined she would become a pilot herself. She continues: "I began to fly in small tourist planes. I flew as a hobby and entered competitions." At this stage she would team up with friend and fellow pioneer Grazia Serena Sartori, or co pilot for Robert Goemans, a Piper rep in Europe, who was a friend of her father's. She eventually took an instrument flight course on offer at the military flight training school in Algerho. She also had theory lessons from Alitalia instructors and learned the fundamentals of meteorology.

She eventually passed her commercial licence in 1967 and went on to notch up numerous "firsts." She became the first women airline pilot in Italy and one of the first woman airline pilots in Europe when Aeralpi hired her in 1967 to fly the Twin Otter. She says: "I was one of

the first four women pilots in Europe." (The other three were Jacqueline Camus in France, Elizabeth Overbury in the UK, and Turi Wideroe in Norway. Only Maria Atanassova of Bulgaria preceded them). She went on to become the first woman airline captain in Italy in 1969.

At the start of her commercial career Fiorenza flew mountain flights for Aeralpi, which was a tough run in more ways than one. She says: "at first the male pilots resented me. They thought a woman would complicate things." However, she proved her worth and the harassment stopped. Eventually her colleagues started to encourage her, and they became good friends.

Unfortunately the airline went bankrupt. Alitalia hired her male colleagues, but were loath to take Fiorenza onto their books. She says: "Neither Alitalia nor ATI wanted to be the first. Italian men were still too prejudiced." Even though she had flown Alitalia flights at Aeralpi, the airline was too conservative. According to Fiorenza some of these sector passengers had been pleased to see a woman flying the aircraft and several even requested to be on her flight.

Her next job was with Aertirrena, a Russian outfit, for whom she flew the Yak 40 trijet. She says she enjoyed this job because of the varied routes she flew. After a month's training, she also took the aircraft on a demonstration trip around the world. She says: "I went to Australia with stopovers in many places. It was a fascinating tour from both the technical and traveller's point of view'." She also did a brief stint with Olympic Airways in Athens, flying tourists to Greek islands, such as Mykonos and Skiathos. The Yak 40 can land on short runways and carry up to 27 passengers, so is ideal for the task. She then flew scheduled flights between Florence, Alenga and Bologna.

Aertirrena was absorbed into Avioligure. Fiorenza was flying the same sectors as a regular airline, shuttling between Florence, Milan and Rome. At this point she was allowed to take courses at Alitatila's training center in order to get rated on the DC8. She said: "I studied hard on the simulator and on the aircraft." She then joined Aeral, a cargo and charter company in Fiumicino, flying long haul to New York and Nigeria. Alas, it was a private company, and it, too, went bankrupt. Undaunted, Fiorenza did charter work in a Yak 40 throughout Europe

Events in 1967

■ **The first Boeing 737 (a 100 series) takes maiden flight.**

■ **U.S. astronauts Gus Grissom, Edward Higgins White, and Roger Chaffee are killed when fire breaks out in their Apollo 1 spacecraft during a launch pad test.**

and Italy, flying for an aerial photography company.

During the 1960s she also took up gliding and qualified as a glider pilot. She was the first woman in Italy to earn a glacier pilot certificate. She said: It was spectacular landing on mountains. Once a few of us got stuck on the Adamello glacier and had to build an igloo where we sheltered for the night." This was in February at temperatures of 20 degrees below zero. She continued to work as a professional pilot for 18 years, and retired after suffering severe injuries in a car accident in 1985.

Even since retirement, Fiorenza has championed women's prospects in aviation and joined several networking associations to that end. She has always promoted the female cause. In 1956 she joined the international US group the 99s. She founded, and is vice president, of API- Associazione Italiana Donne Pilota, the Italian Woman Pilots' Association. This association has expanded its remit to include skydivers and is now named ADA- Associazione Donne Aria. She says: "We unite efforts of all the women who have obtained licences in Italy. We also campaign for greater understanding toward newcomers on the part of the authorities and all connected with the industry."

She is also heavily involved with the Federation of European Women Pilots – FEWP. In 1984 she published a book, *Pink Line*, which is a compendium of pioneering European women pilots. Many of the women featured in her book are also on her website.

In 1985, Fiorenza signed up to the International Society of Women Airline Pilots (ISA+21), adding more contacts and networking to her already impressive portfolio. ISA+21 named an annual scholarship in her honour. This award goes to a commercial pilot applicant wanting to develop her career.

This is entirely in keeping with Fiorenza's ethos. She wrote: "It is okay when women keep to flying as a sport. We are cordially accepted every-where. This is not surprising as people who practise sport have a sporting spirit. In flying as a profession the old barriers are hard to knock down. We experience the same old taboos, professional resentment and even the envy of those who have nothing to do with aviation." Despite the considerable barriers she had, she has managed to cut out a path that today's young pilots may find easier to follow.

1968
Turi Wideroe
(Norway)

First female airline pilot in the Western world

Turi Wideroe came of good aviation stock. Her father Viggo Wideroe was one of Norway's pioneering pilots, who lived and breathed flying. He founded an airline in 1934, which also flew air taxi and ambulance flights, flight training, aerial photography and aerial advertisements.

Turi remembers her father fondly and said: "Flying was my father's occupation and greatest hobby. He started his interest early in life and built model aeroplanes as a small child. My father was born in 1904, which is the year after the Wright brothers first flew." He lived until he was almost 98 years old and died in 2002. He obviously had a profound effect on his daughter. He was concerned, however, that she would realistically not be able to make a living as a pilot.

She got round that by earning her own money and took lessons with the airline pilots at the base when they had spare time. According to Turi, they were allowed to teach her "when they had nothing better to do."

Turi learned in a tail wheel Piper Cub, Luscombe and at the local aero club's Piper Colt. She took her glider pilot's license and earned her private pilot's licence (PPL) in 1962.

She flew as a PPL for several years and also checked out on seaplanes. In 1965 she was accepted to fly for the Wideroe company in North Norway. She flew 10-seat de Havilland Canada DHC-3 single Otter seaplanes. This built up her logbook hours and experience. She flew for two seasons as co-pilot, simultaneously studying for her commercial and instrument ratings.

She said: "It was fascinating. It was tough flying, but the scenery was so beautiful. It was the best part of my flying career." In her third year she was promoted to captain, flying on the seaplane routes. She also flew mercy missions. She found this a profoundly moving experience initially. She said: "It was this great feeling that you were out there to save someone's life."

She had a memorable early flight. They were delayed because of fog and finally made it out to an isolated island on the North Coast of Norway to pick up a small child who had sustained a head injury. Rather than complaining, the parents were grateful and said how lucky they were that the aircraft had come so quickly.

However, she soon became acclimatised to such events and was able to concentrate on her job. She is proud of that part of her career. The rural communities accepted her. Gender was a non-issue. She explained: "It was different in the North then. It was a tough life for everyone, men and women. They accepted me fairly well."

After a while it became difficult to be both the only woman in the airline, but mainly the boss's daughter. On both counts she felt permanently on show and that she had to live up to extremely high standards. She also wanted to stretch her skills, so wrote off to the then three airlines in Norway.

Scandinavian Airlines System (SAS) was the only one to write back. They also invited her to interview and tests. In 1968 they hired her. The following year she was certified as co-pilot on a Convair 440 Metropolitan, becoming the first female pilot in an international airline in the western world. She said: "SAS told me that. It was not in my mind to become the first; I just wanted to be a pilot. Russia and Bulgaria had women airline pilots, but they were not in ICAO. I have a great respect for these women and for the many pioneers in the earlier generation.

As soon as she started, so did the media circus. SAS made a great deal of the fact they had hired a woman and Turi was wheeled out at every opportunity to speak or act as an ambassador.

She said: "I did not like the media pressure at all. I did it initially because I was grateful to SAS for hiring me as a pilot. I did a great marketing job and I never charged them a penny. But the whole thing got out of balance and I had to ask them to stop." The intense scrutiny affected both her private and professional life. Fortunately her colleagues were helpful for the most part and shielded her from journalists when they could.

She went on to fly SAS' first jet aircraft, the Caravelle, and the DC-9 before she ended her flying career. Turi was a pioneer, so everything she did was a first.

Having children posed a difficulty. She had to take months of unpaid leave when she had her children. There was no such thing as maternity leave or privileges at that time.

Finding herself single with two small children was a struggle and she took a long leave of absence. Eventually she came to a point where the airline asked her to make a choice. Turi said: "They asked me to come back into a full time position. It was the hardest decision of my life. I chose to concentrate on my children."

After 13 years of commercial flying, she never flew again. She would have happily worked, as a pilot part time when the children were small, but felt that there was little point to doing PPL flying just for the sake of it.

Turi feels there was a huge discrepancy between her treatment and that of her male colleagues, who were required to take time out to fly for the air force.

She said: "Having children seemed to be regarded as a private pleasure at that time. The male pilots on military service were paid full salary no questions asked."

She took a job in a broadcasting company and worked there for seven years.

She trained as a journalist and said: "It was good for me because I could come home at night and was on the right side of the microphone for a change." She went on to take a masters degree in history, for which she wrote about her father's great adventure mapping out Antarctica from the air.

Turi Wideroe took the first painful steps into the airlines, breaking the barrier to entry for other women.

Her first uniform is displayed in the National Air & Space Museum in Washington DC. She was awarded the Harmon Aviator Trophy in 1969 and the FAI Paul Tissandier's Diploma in Paris in 2005.

She lives in Norway and has her own communications consultancy.

Events in 1968

- ◼ Martin Luther King, Jr., civil rights leader, is slain in Memphis

- ◼ Russian space pioneer Yuri Gagarin is killed in a training flight crash.

- ◼ NASA launches Apollo 7, the first manned Apollo mission (Wally Schirra, Donn Eisele, Walter Cunningham). Mission goals include the first live television broadcast from orbit.

1973

ROSELLA BJORNSON
(CANADA) 1947 –

The first woman in North America to fly a jet for a commercial airline, Rosella Bjornson has spent countless hours supporting the aviation community she loves.

osella Marie Bjornson was born on July 13, 1947, in Lethbridge, Alberta in Canada. Her parents owned a farm and she attended the local high school in nearby Vulcan. Her father, Ken learned to fly in 1946 and regularly took his daughter flying in his Aeronca Champ from the time she was a young child. She said: "I decided when I was quite young that I wanted to be a pilot when I grew up. I remember thinking flying was more fun than driving."

Her parents were highly supportive of her interests. Rosella's 17th birthday present was a first formal flying lesson at the Lethbridge Flying Club. She completed her Private Pilot's Licence (PPL) in two months and became a popular classmate, as she would take her friends flying in her father's Cessna C170B during final year at high school. She said: "I recently attended a reunion and some of them remembered that."

She headed to the University of Calgary, mainly because she felt she would find it easier to get a job as a pilot if she had a university education. She majored in geography and geology, but believes she would have done better had she spent more time on campus and less time at Calgary Airport during term time. On the plus side, she spent her summers accumulating flying hours and obtaining her Commercial Licence in 1967. In the same year, she competed in the Alberta Centennial Air Race. She and her female co-pilot came first by completing the race with the exact estimate of their flight time and within one tenth of a gallon of their fuel consumption estimate.

She was inducted as a member of Canada's Aviation Hall of Fame in 1997 at a ceremony in Calgary, Alberta. In March 2004, she was recognised in the Women in Aviation Pioneers Hall of Fame at the Women in Aviation Conference in Reno, Nevada.

In 1969, Rosella received her Instructor's Rating and moved to Winnipeg in 1970, where she instructed at the Flying Club. A year later she had a Class II Instructor's Rating. On May 25, 1972, the Royal Canadian Flying Clubs Association awarded her the 89th Gold Seal of Proficiency. She also took time out to organise the Manitoba Chapter of the Ninety-Nines, the International Women Pilots' organisation.

By 1973, Rosella had 3,500 hours flying time, an Air Transport Rating and a Class I Multi-engine Instrument Rating, and applied to fly with the all the airlines in Canada. She said: "In 1973, Transair of Winnipeg was willing to take a chance and hired me to be a First Officer on the F-28. This is my claim to fame – I was the first woman in North America to fly a jet aircraft for a commercial airline as a first officer."

This also made here the first woman to be hired by a commercial airline in Canada and the first female member of the Canadian Air Line Pilots Association. There was some initial confusion as the airline wondered how to cope with its new recruit. Should she wear a different uniform to the men? Rosella was adamant that she would not. At six feet with a slim figure, the male uniform was entirely suitable for her and she did not want to stand out as being different.

She loved her time there. She said: "It sounds really glamorous. I was flying into exciting places like Thompson, Lyne Lake, Flin Flon, Las Pas, Churchill, and all the hot spots of Northern Manitoba in good and bad weather. My personal life was pretty good too – I was quite popular with the guys and had lots of fun. There was one fellow I could always depend on – Bill Pratt – he was a corporate pilot and flew a Lear Jet out of Winnipeg. By 1977, we decided to get married."

She said her peers accepted her and one of the greatest compliments she had was when a colleague had a friend in the jump seat of the cockpit. The friend asked her captain what it was like to fly with a woman. He replied: "I don't think of her as a woman," and promptly apologised. Rosella knew what he meant and was delighted to be judged on her skills alone.

In 1979 her first pregnancy with her son Ken was another pioneering act. There was no precedent set for a pregnant pilot. She took a leave of absence and returned to work in 1980 as first officer on the Boeing 737 with Pacific Western Airlines (PWA), which had purchased Transair.

Bill's company had sold its corporate jet, so he also took a job with PWA flying the Hercules. The family moved to Edmonton. After a second pregnancy in 1984, she was involved in discussions with Transport Canada about how to deal with pregnant pilots. Subsequently, the regulations were changed to allow a pilot who is pregnant to fly "while under her doctor's supervision". Rosella returned to PWA, which had now become Canadian Airlines, as first officer on the Boeing 737.

In 1988 she received several awards. In June, she was inducted into the International Forest of Friendship in Atchison, Kansas. The international organisation of Ninety Nines gave her a certificate of appreciation in recognition of the leadership roles she had undertaken. She also received a Pioneering Award from the Western Canada Aviation Museum in Winnipeg.

In the winter of 1990, Rosella and Bill bought a house and a hangar in an airpark and had to deal with the challenges of being young parents with their own elderly parents becoming frailer. That year Rose became the first female captain with Canadian Airlines International and the first woman to be promoted to captain with a major Canadian air carrier. Around the same time she was featured in a poster campaign by the Alberta Government, "Dream/Dare/Do", encouraging young people to set goals and strive towards them.

In 1991, she was honoured again and received the National Award of Achievement at the National Transportation Day kick-off celebrations in Halifax in May. She also was the recipient of the Manitoba Award of Achievement at the NTW Conference in Winnipeg on June 6. The Award of Achievement is presented for innovation and initiative in bringing positive and measurable improvements of significant and enduring benefit to transport in Canada.

The year 2000 was a milestone year for the family. Air Canada bought out Canadian Airlines. Four years later Air Canada decided to close the Edmonton pilot base and stop operating the B737. Bill decided to go to the Toronto base to fly the Airbus 320 and Rosella chose early retirement.

She said: "It was quite a let down for me to stop flying – I still miss it but have filled my time with a full-time volunteer job as the administrator of Canada's Aviation Hall of Fame." She is actively involved in family life, her son is an air maintenance engineer, but her daughter definitely does not want to follow the family career path.

Rosella has tracked down her father's old Cessna 170B and it sits outside her house in the airpark. She flies it regularly, though not as often as she would like. She was inducted as a Member of Canada's Aviation Hall of Fame in 1997. Her message to young people, especially young women, is that they too can fly if they commit to it. It is tough and expensive, but commitment and dedication will see them through to a rewarding and worthwhile career.

Events in 1973

■ A ceasefire is signed, ending involvement of American ground troops in Vietnam.

1976
CHANDA BUDHABHATTI (INDIA)

Chanda Budhabhatti, non-conformist champion of female pilots in India, who picked up a couple of world firsts along the way

When most pilots meet the legendary Chuck Yeager they are deferential, bowing to his aeronautical prowess. However, when he told Chanda Budhabhatti that he had trained Pakistani fighter pilots for the India/Pakistan wars of 1971 she sniffed: "That's why they lost then." She had no idea who he was. The great aviator roared with laughter and the pair were firm friends from that moment on.

Chanda Budhabhatti was born in Kutch, south of Karachi. Her father was progressive and brought her up to play the same sports as her brothers. She loved to ride horses, swim and play tennis. As she grew up, she realised she did not want to head towards the same professions as her friends, who were opting for careers as doctors and lawyers. Instead she chose aviation.

Chanda lost her father when she was twelve years old and her mother, who was a deeply religious and conservative woman did not agree or approve of Chanda's thinking. When she was 16 she went on two days' hunger strike to convince her mother to let her fly. After that she joined Bombay Flying Club, which was not an easy task. She described what happened when she first turned up in 1957.

"It was different. Very bad. I felt as if I did not belong there. The boys did not like me being there as they could not swear or run around with their shirts off. They would keep me waiting from 7am to 7pm for 12 hours a day and still not take me flying. Finally one of the instructors said he would take me up. He took a Chipmunk and went and did all he could with acrobatics for half an hour. I was thinking "God help me." After 30 minutes we came down and I had an upset stomach. I did not want to be sick. He ran to the bathroom and chucked up. I slowly got out and tried to walk straight with all the boys watching me." It was traumatic, but at 17 she was determined she did not want to give them any reason not to respect her. She passed that test and the boys started teaching her. After nine hours she was ready to solo in the club's Tiger Moth, but had to wait until she had 13 hours and was of age. She eventually became a club star, coming first in the spot landing competitions.

Once she had earned her PPL she decided to opt for anther career. However, when she started earning her own money she returned to flying for pleasure and earned her commercial licence in 1964 flying a Piper PA-18 Super Cub.

In 1965, Isabelle McCrae, a US Ninety-Nine member, came to India and visited Bombay Flying Club. She was shocked to see a woman flying in her sari. Isabelle took down the names of the women who were at the school and by mistake she wrote to Chanda, inviting all five to join the 99s. Chanda was equally shocked to discover there were more women flying at her school, and also took their names down. She said: "It took an American woman to give me the names of five other female pilots in India. We were not even talking to each other. It was a real eye opener."

She soon remedied that and called up the other girls. They founded the India section of the 99s. By 1976 she was its charter governor and set up the Indian Women Pilots' Association (IWPA) the same year. From those humble beginnings with just five members, there are now over 200 pilots. These include commercial pilots, military pilots and commanders. One of Chanda's real strengths is that she has leveraged this group of strong women to bring pressure to bear on the powers that be. When the group started there were no professional flying jobs for woman in India. The situation is totally different today thanks to the proliferation of the aviation industry. It is fair to say that Chanda has been a constant pressure point. She has regularly visited Indian Airlines and the Indian Air Force (IAF) to drink tea and point out that women can do a great job in the cockpit. There are now female pilots in the IAF piloting helicopters and transport planes and the IWPA is pursuing with the IAF how to get women into fighter planes.

The 99s went on to fund one of its early Indian members, Saudamini Deshmukh, to get her commercial licence in the US. Today she is deputy general manager of Indian, formerly Indian Airlines. Chanda and her colleagues have systematically campaigned for more recognition and employment opportunities for women. Chanda describes how she visited on airline bigwig when Saudamini got her licence.

He said: "We don't want girls crying in the cockpit." Chanda explained that a female pilot was likely to be highly capable if she was able to carry 300 passengers. She added: "Give a woman a chance." Saudamini was hired when she passed her tests, pipping 400 other candidates to the post.

British record breaker Sheila Scott was also a great pal who came to India regularly to speak at IWPA conferences. Chanda paid tribute to the woman who circumnavigated the globe three times in a single engine aircraft. She said: "She guided me a lot. I was so fortunate to have been her friend."

Chanda's own flying was enhanced when she got a scholarship from Ingram Flying School to get a commercial pilot's licence in 1967. She became the first woman in India to obtain an FAA commercial licence, obtaining 97% in her written exams. In 1982, Madine Carpenter, a US 99, invited her to participate as co-pilot in the Baja-California International All Women Race. They came third and Chanda received a co-pilot's trophy.

This inspired her to take her flying to the next level. She has subsequently broken two speed records. The first was in 1998 from Tucson to Guaymas in Mexico, flying a Piper PA-28. The second was from Tucson to Bullhead in 2004. She said: "I loved it. When my friends realised I was the first Indian woman, they kept challenging me 'girl you can do it'." Chanda said: "It was just regular cross country flying, except I checked for a faster tailwind to earn the best time. I was in constant touch with the weather man." Today she flies a seaplane, and was the first Indian woman to earn a commercial seaplane certificate. She said: "Taking off on water is much more thrilling to me."

For many years her day job was as a construction company PR. She travelled the world and has tirelessly championed women pilots and aerospace. She also chaired the Women in Flight conference in Tucson for several years. She organised the first international aerospace education and safety world congress in Delhi in 1986. She followed this with a further three successful congresses in Bombay in 1994, in Kathmandu in 2000 and at an international conference for women in aviation in Bombay in 2002. Another of Chanda's key initiatives was the foundation of an aviation and space artefacts exhibit at the Aerospace Hall at Nehru Science Centre museum in Bombay, the first museum of its kind in India. It attracts almost 2,000 visitors, mainly young people, daily. She also promotes aviation to young people in America and divides her time between Bombay and Tucson.

Chanda has won several awards for her outstanding leadership and dedication to aerospace education including prizes from: the World Aerospace Education Organisation in Washington, the Ninety Nines, the Lions Club, the Zonta Club, the Rotary Club and the Kutch Industrial Group. She was also the first Asian woman to win the Chuck Yeager Aerospace Education award. She has also been honoured with the Dadabhai Nevroli International award for excellence and lifetime achievement in India.

Perhaps, though, her greatest achievement is the acceptance of women in professional flying roles in her mother country. Chanda would like to make sure they remember the legacy donated by the pioneering female pilots. She is pleased, however, that they do not have to suffer the same hardships as the first comers. "Young girls and boys today share the same platform. Men and women are developing hand in hand, not below or above - but equal."

Events in 1976

- Khmer Rouge leader Pol Pot becomes prime minister (and virtual dictator) of Cambodia after Prince Sihanouk steps down.

- The first commercial Concorde flight takes off.

1979

Major Ana Gan (Singapore)

Wearing a captain's stripes in Singapore with pride

Most Singaporean female airline staff milling around Changhi Airport are clad in cabin crew uniforms. Not Major (Retired) Ana Gan. She wears her captain's stripes with pride. The first female flight instructor in the Republic of Singapore Air Force (RSAF), her illustrious career has spanned twenty-four years. She now flies for Jetstar Asia, a Singapore-based low cost carrier. She has been with them from the start.

So what attracted this dynamic pilot to flying in the first place? Born into a society where women were not encouraged to fly Ana Gan never expected to find herself teaching aspiring fighter pilots how to fly. That changed when she saw a recruitment advertisement for the RSAF, which was actively recruiting women for the first time.

She said: "I never thought it would be something I could do. You never dream of this. There were no female pilots in the air force. I never had a chance to learn to fly commercially. It was beyond my means. I love to try different things and thought it would be an exciting and outrageous career."

She was the third female to be taken on by the military and the first of the intake to come in from a flying club. The tests were gruelling and she spent two hard years of intensive training. She had earned her wings after the two years, which was quite an achievement considering she had no past flying experience.

Women were not allowed to fly fighters in those days, so she flew the Shorts Skyvan and later the Fokker-50 transport aircraft as part of an operational squadron. She went on to become an instructor and was so good at it that she spent most of her air force career training young cadets. She said it was easy to spot who would be good in terms of natural aptitude. "Some have it, some don't. After basic training we screen those who will go on to receive advanced training. Pilots are graded. We can pick up those who are excellent and those who have two left feet, or who can't taxi or fly straight. Those in between are the hardest to choose. Some learn very fast."

According to Ana she experienced little chauvinism in the air force. However, there were so few women pilots that the first three always felt that they had to succeed. She said: "There is always pressure to do really well. You have to demonstrate that you can do everything a guy can do." On the plus side her male colleagues were generally supportive. However, the RSAF is still fairly light on female pilots.

After 24 years, she left the air force. She then went to work for Singapore Airlines subsidiary SilkAir.

They wanted to hire the first female commercial pilot in the country. The director of training approached Ana since he wanted someone with a great deal of experience. Once again the first woman had to be seen to do well.

Ana said: "This was the opportunity of a lifetime."

She flew for SilkAir for three years; before Jetstar Asia made her another offer she could not refuse in 2004. She also flew charter for Pacific Airlines in Vietnam and remembers vividly Chinese New Year 2005 when passengers were carrying chicken on board as they travelled between Ho Chi Minh City and Danang. She said to Jetstar Asia's magazine: "It brought me back to Singapore during the 1950s when people did carry chickens going back home for the new year. It is quite amusing. You see people carrying so many different presents for the New Year."

This is the first start-up airline she has worked for. She said: "It is good to be part of a start up and the decision making team. To be one of the first in a company you feel pride in the company growing and becoming established. The airline is growing in a good direction in an orderly procedure. We have a fantastic female chief executive who has turned the company round, so that it is doing well."

Her journeys today take her over some of the most spectacular scenery in Southeast Asia. She still loves the view and said: "This is the greatest job on earth where the scenery changes every day". She added: "Hong Kong is very pretty, which is why every time we take off and the weather is good we turn right and Disneyland is below you. Everyone looks so nice. Coming in you see the giant bridge at Lantau Island. All the kids get excited."

Once again, she finds herself in the training hot seat. Jetstar Asia is training local women, but Ana says there are few applicants for the cadetships. Often female pilots flying for local Singaporean airlines come from abroad. She attributes this partly to culture. When she was in the air force she worked hard at recruiting females and the

Events in 1979

■ **First human-powered aircraft flies across the English Channel: Bryan Allen pilots Gossamer Albatross from Folkestone, England, to Cap Gris-Nez, France.**

RSAF invested heavily in promoting aviation as a career for women. Ana said: "I am not sure what happens. We promote flying aggressively around schools and we get many girls interested. However, they experience parental pressure. In our society you cannot do anything without your parents permission until you are over 21. The girls start to study, become more career-minded and lose interest or do not have the drive to see it through."

Today she sits in the left hand (captain's) seat of Jetstar Asia's fleet of Airbus A320-200 aircraft. She flies domestic short haul routes to destinations including Jakarta, Hong Kong and Phnom Penh and would like to see more local female pilots join her. She concedes that her country would need to see "a population explosion," before that could realistically happen. She is also content with her career achievements and attributes her excellent training skills to a secret key characteristic. She said: "I nag everyone to death."

Jetstar Asia and its sister airline Valuair have one of the world's few female airline chief executive officers. Chong Phit Lian, has over 28 years of management experience in the lifestyle, leisure, tourism, manufacturing and engineering industries. She holds engineering and business administration qualifications. Her impressive CV includes leading Singapore Precision Industries and the Singapore Mint as president and chief executive for 16 years. In February 2006, she took the helm of Jetstar Asia and has turned it from a loss making subsidiary to a profitable and growing airline.

1980

ANN WELCH
(UK) 1917 – 2002

Ann Welch spent over half a century successfully promoting sporting aviation throughout Britain and the rest of the world. She was the wind beneath the wings of gliders, paragliders and microlights, and with her influential assistance they collectively soared to heights beyond expectations.

Ann was born on 20th May 1917 and like many early pioneers was both overjoyed and inspired by the sight of an aeroplane. She studiously maintained a diary list of all planes that happened to float over the family home. Her first opportunity to experience a plane ride came when she was just 13, flying from Wadebridge, Cornwall in an early Fairey aircraft. The seeds of an emerging pioneer were thus sown.

Ann dropped out of school at the age of sixteen, acquired a motorbike and learnt to fly at Barnstaple aerodrome. In 1934 on her seventeenth birthday she gained her Royal Aero Club Aviator's certificate and a month later was awarded a private 'A' licence.

Her passion for gliding began in 1937 when she attended a gliding camp under the auspices of the Anglo-German Fellowship at the London Gliding Club based in Dunstable. Ann was the only female on the course out of the complement of 25 students. It was at the camp that she met the experts Wolf Hirth and Hanna Reitsch, celebrated as the paragon of German gliding. Attractive and just one of the guys, Ann was liked by all of the students. In 1938 Ann with the rest of her British classmates visited Germany whereupon they were treated to dose of emerging Third Reich propaganda.

She returned to England and established the Surrey Gliding Club at Buckland, attracting many members, which swelled the ranks to beyond 100 pilots and students. In 1939 she married Graham Douglas, whose family owned Redhill Aerodrome. He loaned Ann, the necessary £300 to purchase the glider fleet and one towing winch for the club.

The onset of World War Two brought Ann into powered military flight as she joined the Air Transport Auxiliary (ATA). As a member of the ATA she ferried a variety of aircraft fresh from the factories to front line airfields. Ann had the amazing experience of piloting fighters pivotal to the Battle of Britain, such as the Spitfire and Hurricane, as well as bombers like the Wellington and robust Blenheim. At the end of her tenure with the ATA she had flown almost 150 different aircraft.

Almost as soon as the Merlin engine of her very last ferried Spitfire had shut down in 1942 she gave birth to her first daughter. Graham had also become a fighter pilot and was awarded the Distinguished Flying Cross and served an operational detachment in the United States.

Not only did Ann excel as a pilot, she was a talented artist and had an intense affinity for outdoor pursuits. A prolific painter, Ann also authored a number of books, which are still in much demand. She had developed a fondness for sailing and her interest in navigation culminated in her appointment as Honorary Fellow of the Royal Institution of Navigation in 1997.

The war ended with Ann returning to gliding and training a new intake of pilots and potential gliding instructors. She was the natural candidate to be selected as chairman of the British Gliding Association's examining panel, a position she would hold for over 20 years.

With the assistance of Lorne Welch and Walter Morison two former RAF pilots and prisoners of the infamous German Colditz Castle, Ann resurrected the Surrey Gliding Club. She moved the club to Redhill Aerodrome in 1947 before moving again to Lasham Airfield in 1951.

Her marriage to Graham Douglas had ended in 1948 and she tied the knot again with Lorne Welch in 1953. Lorne was part of the British contingent of prisoners who had hatched the original 'Great Escape' plan. His attempt at stealing a German plane failed and he was interned in Colditz. It was there that he was involved in some of the stress calculations of the 'Colditz Cock glider'. Although the escape glider was never used, its airworthiness was demonstrated when a replica was successfully flown in February 2000.

Under Ann's astute management the Surrey Gliding Club flourished. She juggled her duties as full time mother and gliding instructor with great precision. It was not uncharacteristic of Ann

Events in 1980

■ **US breaks diplomatic ties with Iran.**

■ **After weeks of strikes at the Lenin Shipyard in Gdansk, Poland, the nationwide independent trade union Solidarity is established.**

to be shouting orders from her open two seat glider cockpit to her children playing on the airfield below at the same time as instructing a student.

In 1948 she entered the world of competitive gliding by being appointed as manager of the British team. The position came about as a result of the British team competing in the first post war championships held in Samedan, Switzerland. Under her direction the British team triumphed at the 1952 meet in Spain and then again in 1956, this time in France.

In 1954 Ann and Lorne took part in the World Championships staged at Camphill in Derbyshire, flying the British built Slingsby Eagle two-seat glider. Ann then organised the hugely successful World Contest held in South Cerney in Gloucestershire. She would also oversee the annual championships at the Lasham Gliding Centre.

Ann shone as a glider pilot, achieving her international silver badge in 1946 and her gold in 1969. At the 1961 contest in Lezno, Poland she set the new British women's distance record of 528 kilometres, landing just shy of the border between Poland and Russia. The British Women Pilots' Association lauded her twice with the Jean Lennox-Bird pendant for lifetime service to aviation. Her impressive problem solving and organisational skills qualified her to assume the position as delegate to the Federation Aeronautique International (FAI) Gliding Commission.

In 1969 she achieved the FAI bronze medal, the FAI Lilienthal Medal (1973) and the prestigious FAI Gold Air Medal (1980) in recognition of her dedication to the training and encouragement of young pilots. The gold medal ranked her along with other legends such as Charles Lindbergh, Alan Cobham, Jean Batten and Frank Whittle.

Administering the affairs of the British Gliding Association with another gliding pioneer, Philip Wills, Ann felt that a change of direction was necessary to ensure survival of the sport. The rising cost of gliding and the need to attract younger people prompted her involvement in hang gliding and paragliding. She was instrumental in the development of both sports and became founding president of the FAI's Hang Gliding Commission and Paragliding Commission. In 1991 both hang gliders and paragliders merged leading to Ann's appointment as overall president of the British Hang Gliding and Paragliding Association. Then microlight pilots sought her expertise to champion their cause and in 1978 she was elected President of the British Microlight Aircraft Association.

Ann was appointed as Most Excellent Order of the British Empire (MBE) in 1953 and advanced to Officer of the Order of the British Empire (OBE) in 1966. Vivacious and energetic to her very last days, Ann passed away on 5th December 2002, aged 85. Lorne Welch her second husband died in 1988 and both parents were survived by their three daughters. In 2005 the Ann Welch Memorial Award was instituted for outstanding contributions to instruction in air sports. It was first presented in 2006 at the Royal Aero Club's Awards Ceremony.

Anne Welch was the embodiment of a fortunate person who discovered a hobby, which eventually transformed the lives of many around her. She was an excellent pilot and loved gliding and she wanted others to experience the same joys that she did. Her fervent belief in the promotion of flying sports made her the candidate of choice to lead the various organisations she helped to establish and sustain. Ann was a highly respected and very influential member of the aviation community - a pioneer who managed to instil a sense of fun in everything she touched.

1980
SAUDAMINI DESHMUKH
(INDIA)

As their country moves into the busiest time in its aviation life, Indian women have found their wings and are soaring high in search of new horizons. This is made possible by pioneering females who kept the faith and are still living their dreams. One such woman is Captain Saudamini Deshmukh, the first woman in the world to lead an all-female crew.

t did not start out that way. The Science and General Law graduate had a comfortable bank job before she threw caution to the winds and took to the skies. She told the Hindu newspaper in 2003 that flying was her "childhood dream. I always wanted to be among the clouds," she said. She continued, "Since my father could not afford it at that point, I temporarily gave up my dream. And took up a bank job. When I could afford it, I started taking flying lessons at a private club. After paying 25 rupees per hour and completing 250 hours of mandatory flying, I got my commercial pilot's licence. And my dream came true."

That was partly thanks to doing some training with the Ninety-Nines, the American international organisation of women pilots dedicated to furthering female aviators. She went to the US under one of their scholarship schemes. She said: "I had a great time during that period. I got to live with these women and train under them. It was a liberating experience. It taught me much more than just the nitty-gritty of controlling an aircraft" The Ninety-Nines gave her its `Achievement Award.'

She landed a job with Indian Airlines in 1980 as a commercial pilot. She is adamant that she was not singled out for any negative treatment because of her gender. She said: "I was never treated differently because I was a woman. I think it's in the minds of people... this discrimination thing."

The discrimination thing has obviously not been in Saudamini's mind. She has notched up an impressive selection of firsts under her wings. She was the first woman in 1985 to become a check-pilot on a Fokker-27. She was also the captain on the first all-women crew flight on the Fokker Friendship with Nivedita Bhasin flying as her co-pilot in November 1985 on the Calcutta-Silchar route. They also made the first Boeing 737-200 all-women crew flight in September 1989 on the Mumbai-Goa sector. Then, in 1994, she became the first woman to captain an Airbus A320, and in 1995 captained the Airbus with an all-woman crew.

Her first record was purely a coincidence. She happened to find herself flying the Fokker with Nivedita Bhasin, then the youngest pilot in civil aviation in the world. However, the Boeing flight was planned to the last detail in order to promote the airline. The cabin crew were reportedly thrilled with the arrangement and Saudamini said: "It was an exhilarating experience."

She rose through the ranks and is now the deputy general manager of Indian, formerly Indian Airlines. She said she is pleased that India has opened up its skies and that today there is more competition for passengers. She told the Hindu: "I think it's a good move. Our service has improved a lot. Competition has made a difference in the way we operate." Indian has a good track record of hiring women. The airline hired the first female pilot in 1966 and today has several women flying its aircraft across various sectors.

They are flying different machines, but that is not an issue according to Saudamini. She said: "Once you are behind the controls, size does not matter. What does matter is an alert and scientific mind, the power of analysis and judgment, and above all, passion for the job."

As a highly experienced working pilot, Saudamini has to deal with irregular situations all the time. She obviously does not let that faze her. An article in the Tribune in April 2008 describes her smooth handling of a difficult incident. Air India had just introduced a non-stop Kochi-Delhi flight. The aircraft took off as planned at 7.30 am.

Unfortunately, it suffered engine problems and returned to base. The passengers had to wait for a new aircraft to Delhi. This took a further two hours to sort out. When the new aircraft finally reached its destination, it was forced to circle, as the runway was busy. Saudamini was in charge that day and announced that the flight had arrived "without much delay," evoking a laugh from the passengers who were by now hours late.

She realised what she had said and explained that the flight was "only three hours late". As the plane taxied to a full stop she then came back on the public address system and told passengers: "I do not know whether I should tell you or not — a dog crossed our path just as we crossed all hurdles to reach our destination."

When she started out, Saudamini was one of very few women to earn a licence. Today the situation has changed. Some employers are even actively seeking women pilots. Business magnate, Mukesh Ambani has said he plans to employ only women pilots to fly most of his cargo planes. Statistics show that there are around 250 women commercial pilots in the country. Parents have become more open minded, attracting more females into the profession. The figures add up to around 15 per cent of the total numbers of pilots in the country.

Captain Mamatha K, the first woman pilot from Andhra Pradesh is also the first woman to set up a flight training academy. With the aviation industry booming in India, the future looks good for girls.

Some of the world's most attractive flying jobs are available in India today, as the industry gallops alongside the booming economy. Ex pats are even arriving to fly India's aircraft. Even the Indian Air Force now hires women, although not to fly its fighter planes – yet.

Saudamini Deshmukh was one of the pioneering few who helped opened the doors so that her younger sisters can follow suit. Still actively flying today, she is one of the most respected names in Indian aviation. The good news is that she still loves her job. When asked by her interviewer what was the one overpowering emotion that she experienced when she enters the cockpit and takes control of the aircraft? She replied with an emphatic. "Joy. Absolute Joy."

More events in 1980

- Former Beatle John Lennon dies in hospital after being shot outside his New York City apartment by Mark David Chapman

- Global Positioning System time epoch begins.

- The Voyager 1 probe confirms the existence of Janus, a moon of Saturn.

DEANNA (DEE) BRASSEUR (CANADA) 1953 –

I remember my first solo [in the CF-18 Hornet]. There I was taxiing out to the end of the runway thinking to myself, 'Can you imagine this, look at me driving this $35 million jet!'"
Deanna Brasseur, Canadian 99s website profile

Dee Brasseur has a powerful arsenal of 'firsts' under her belt. One of the first two women in the world to fly Canada's most powerful jet fighter aircraft, the CF-18 Hornet, she was also one of the first women to earn her wings in the Canadian Air Force.

It was not a path she had expected to take. Deanna Brasseur was born in Pembroke, Ontario on September 9, 1953. Her father was Lieutenant Colonel Lyn Brasseur. She followed him into the military and in 1972, aged 19; she took a job typing in a dental office. It took her two weeks to realise she could do more with her life.

By September 1973 she had applied for a commission and moved on to the Officer Candidate Training Program. She worked as an air weapons controller, which she said stood her in good stead in later years. She served tours with 22nd NORAD Region HQ at North Bay, Ontario and 23rd NORAD Region HQ at Duluth, Minnesota. A key event took place during her tenure. She had the opportunity to take a ride in the back seat of a T-33 Utility Jet Aircraft following some high altitude training. She loved the experience and it stayed with her.

She enjoyed being airborne so much that she began working on her private flying license at a school in Duluth. She stopped when in 1979 the Canadian Air Force opened its doors to female pilots. She was advised not to pick up any habits that might interfere with her military training. Fortunately her instructor was an ex F4 pilot who had flown in Vietnam, so she had a good initial training. Dee was one of four women accepted on to the basic pilot training as part of a trial programme called the "Study of Women in Non-Traditional Environments and Roles (SWINTER)." Three of them graduated with their wings in February 1981, making Canadian military history.

It was tough on many levels. Not just the intensity of the training, but the huge media circus that ensued once they had gained their wings. Dee said: "Nothing prepared any of us for what followed. From the moment we arrived, TV, newspaper, radios were all there with questions like 'how are the men treating you?' It added additional pressure."

Some of the men were not treating them well and Dee suffered harassment and abuse. However, she kept going, even when the going got really rough. She pointed out: "There was always at least one 'port in the storm' a friend who would help you to keep the faith." She added another first to her CV in June 1981 when she became the first female flight Instructor with 2 Canadian Forces Flying Training School in Moose Jaw, Saskatchewan. This also saw a turning point in her career in terms of her colleagues' acceptance. She was flying a night sortie with a student when a bird flew into the only engine on her aircraft, stopping it dead. She had two choices, either eject or attempt a forced landing to get the plane to the ground. She opted for the latter course and made it safely to the airfield. She had never practised forced landings at night since it was deemed to be too dangerous. Following a thorough debriefing, the Base Flight Safety Officer told Dee that he felt very few of the pilots he knew would have held their nerve and tried to land the crippled aircraft. For her efforts, Dee received a "Good Show" the highest Flight Safety honour awarded for demonstrating outstanding flying skills during a critical in flight emergency.

This action earned her immense respect from her peers. Another incident occurred shortly afterwards when she found herself on the verge of defending the fact she was a woman in a 'man's world'. She told her interrogator that it was his problem not hers if he did not like her presence in the military. This is a philosophy she has adhered to ever since. During the same period she attended Air Command Flight Safety Officer and Canadian Forces Staff School courses and served as Unit Flight Safety Officer, Senior Course Director and Deputy Flight Commander.

In March 1986, Dee was assigned to be the Air Force representative on the National Defence Headquarters' Charter Task Force on Human Rights. She was tasked to investigate expanding women's roles in the air force. Effectively she got to write her own ticket to fly fighters. After the report was completed, Dee was posted to Base Flight Cold Lake, Alberta as

Events in 1981

- ■ Pope John Paul II wounded by gunman.

- ■ Lady Diana Spencer marries Charles, Prince of Wales.

- ■ Ronald Reagan appoints the first female U.S. Supreme Court Justice, Sandra Day O'Connor.

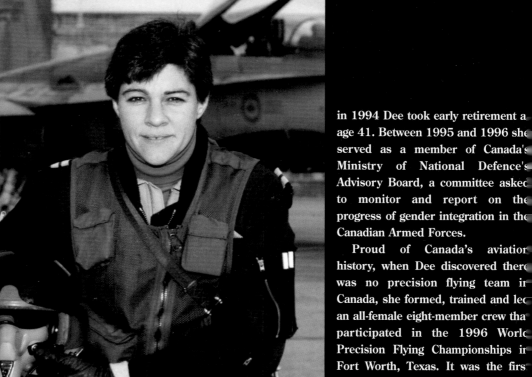

he first female Flight Commander. She flew and was responsible for managing a fleet of 12 T-33 Utility Jet Aircraft, and supervising eight junior pilots. Remembering her own early pleasure in jumping in as a passenger, she naturally often carried a mechanic when they travelled to their various destinations.

In 1987 she became an Instrument Check Pilot, essentially a military pilot licence examiner. Shortly thereafter, in June 1988, she was chosen as one of the first two women in Canada to commence fighter pilot training on the CF5 aircraft. In June 1989, along with Captain Jane Foster, Dee graduated as one of the first two female CF-18 Hornet jet fighter pilots in the world. She went on to fly the CF-18 in Canada and Europe. She described her first flight: "I landed, taxied in, shut down and was halfway back to the hangar when I stopped, turned to look back at the aircraft and thought 'I just flew that thing.' I looked up and I saw someone in the circuit overhead and I said, 'I was just doing what he's doing right there.'" It took a while for reality to sink in. Only the top ten per cent of all pilots make it as CF-18 pilots. They are also in the top ten per cent in terms of physical fitness. The aircraft is capable of a speed of Mach 1.8, which is almost twice the speed of sound, and can go from take-off position into an 89 degree vertical climb travelling to 35,000 feet in one minute.

She served as plans officer with 416 Squadron until an unfortunate chronic elbow injury forced her into a ground job with the Directorate of Flight Safety. Following successful completion of the Aircraft Accident Investigator's Course at the Cranfield Aviation Institute of Technology in England and the Canadian Forces Flight Safety Officers' Course at the Transport Canada Training Institute in Cornwall, Ontario Dee commenced work at National Defence Headquarters in Ottawa in August 1990, achieving yet another first, becoming the first female aircraft accident investigator, responsible for monitoring all Canadian Military jet trainer and fighter aircraft accidents and incidents.

After 21 years of distinguished service and 2,500 hours of jet flying time

in 1994 Dee took early retirement at age 41. Between 1995 and 1996 she served as a member of Canada's Ministry of National Defence's Advisory Board, a committee asked to monitor and report on the progress of gender integration in the Canadian Armed Forces.

Proud of Canada's aviation history, when Dee discovered there was no precision flying team in Canada, she formed, trained and led an all-female eight-member crew that participated in the 1996 World Precision Flying Championships in Fort Worth, Texas. It was the first Canadian participation following after a 17-year absence. The Canadian Aircraft Owners and Pilots Association rewarded them with the 1996 Achievement Award for their outstanding contribution to Canadian Aviation.

In June 1998 Dee took her seat among Canada's aviation stars, such as Roberta Bondar, the first Canadian woman in space and John Glenn, the first American to orbit the earth, for her contributions to aviation. She was inducted into the International Organisation of Women Pilots' Forest of Friendship in Atchison, Kansas - the birthplace of Amelia Earhart. There is an engraved plaque and Canadian flag next to a tree, especially flown in from Canada and planted in her honour. On February 3rd, 1999 Dee was named a Member of the Order of Canada. More recently, in February 2007 Major Brasseur was inducted into the Women in Aviation International Pioneer Hall of Fame at a ceremony in Orlando, Florida.

Since retiring from the air force, Dee established Unlimited Horizons where she conducts business as a professional motivational speaker, personal performance coach and trainer of Neuro Linguistic Programming. She shares her personal secrets to success and how she overcame many hurdles to rise through the ranks in the Canadian military. With no regrets, Dee no longer flies and is content to have flying as part of her past. After all she said: "You can't do a roll in a 737." She is still competitive, however the arena has changed somewhat. Dee is now actively involved in showing and coursing her fleet of foot Champion Afghan Hounds.

1982

SVETLANA YEVGENYEVNA SAVITSKAYA (USSR) 1948 –

Having jumped from the stratosphere at an early age, it was small wonder Svetlana Savitskaya was the first woman to walk in space

What was Svetlana Savitskaya thinking as she plummeted through the air from eight and a half miles above the earth? Whatever it was, it had the power to drive her back up into the sky and further than any woman had been before. Unlike the first woman in space Valentina Tereshkova, Svetlana Savitskaya did not hail from a peasant upbringing, far from it. She came from a more privileged background than her predecessor who had travelled to space in 1963. Nineteen years later in 1982 Svetlana would make the same journey.

Svetlana Savitskaya was born in Moscow on August 8th 1948, the same year as the Berlin Blockade and in an atmosphere of heightening tensions with the West. Against the sombre backdrop of the Cold War, her father Yevgeniy Yakovlevich Savitzky was commander of the Soviet Air Defences. A highly decorated World War II fighter ace, he was twice awarded the most prestigious honour of that era, the Hero of the Soviet Union. With such a prominent father, Svetlana's eventual progression into the cosmonaut corps was almost assured.

A product of her father's powerful influence, Svetlana transformed herself into an accomplished aviator, flying everything from turbo-props to jet fighters during her illustrious aviation career. From an early age she loved aeroplanes. Her father's exploits during the war with 22 dogfight victories had left a marked impression on his young daughter.

Svetlana bowed to her parents on the academic front. She took up reading music, learning English, and swimming, in addition to her normal school classes. She was also a keen long distance runner and talented figure skater.

At the age of 16, and without her father's consent, she decided to become a pilot. Her furtive application to a local flying school was rejected on the basis of her being underage. Undeterred, she embraced parachute training instead, which fortu-

nately had no stringent age bar. Her father chanced upon the nature of her excursions following the discovery of a parachutist's knife in her school bag. Svetlana was not practising pirouettes on the ice rink as he thought. Sensing her passion, his consternation soon gave way to active encouragement of her sky diving endeavours.

At 17, and this time with her father's approval, she attempted a record breaking stratospheric sky dive from an altitude of 46,759 feet (14,252 metres). Plummeting a total of eight and a half miles (14 kilometres), she tempted fate by deploying her parachute with only 1,640 feet (500 metres) to spare. By her 17th birthday she had become an expert parachutist with four hundred jumps under her belt. A year later she made her first foray into aviation by taking flying lessons. At the same time she enrolled at the Moscow Aviation Institute (MAI). This prestigious school was part of the larger State University of Aerospace Technology. By the age of 20, Svetlana had soloed in a Yak-18 trainer plane.

Given her lineage, it was hardly surprising that Svetlana soon demonstrated her natural prowess in the air. Her aerobatic skills brushed aside fellow competitors at the 6th FAI World Aerobatic Championships at RAF Hullavington, England in July 1970. Representing the Soviet national aerobatics team, she was crowned as the overall world champion. An awestruck British press covering the competition nicknamed her "Miss Sensation" following her spellbinding and faultless flying displays.

In 1972 Svetlana graduated from the MAI and became a flying instructor at the DOSAAF, (which loosely translates as the "Central technical flying school of the USSR voluntary society for the promotion of the army, air Force, and navy"). Not content with being just another flying instructor, the determined aviatrix had her sights set upon being a test pilot.

Her father's redoubtable stature in the Soviet Air Force no doubt played some part in facilitating Svetlana's entry into test pilot school. However, her innate ability shone through, and she graduated successfully. During her training she took

Events in 1982

- **Pan Am inaugurates longest non-stop flight in the world from Los Angeles to Sydney.**
- **Argentina invades the Falkland Islands.**
- **Princess Grace of Monaco dies when her car plunges off a mountain road.**

the opportunity to set a plethora of world records in a variety of aircraft. In one instance she was the only woman to set a speed record of 1,449 knots per hour (2,683 km/h) in the venerable MiG-21 Jet fighter. Her ratings were such that she was qualified on twenty different types of aircraft, ranging from turboprops to jet fighters.

She joined the communist party in 1975, and a year later was recruited as a test pilot for the Yakovlev design bureau. Having conquered the high adrenaline stakes of flying assorted airframes to the very edge of the flight envelope, luck presented a new opportunity for Svetlana.

It was the late seventies, and the prospect of the first American woman imminently flying on a shuttle mission caused the Russian bear to rise up and take note of the aspirations of its capitalist adversary. Not wishing to be left behind, the cosmonaut programme flung its doors open to women again.

Valentina Tereshkova, the first Russian woman in space, seized upon the chance to re-enter the elite band of cosmonauts. Despite her experience and credentials, her application failed to impress the selection board. This could have been because she had divorced her husband and fellow cosmonaut Andrian Nikolayev. The break-up of Premier Kruschov's fairytale "space family" was not easily forgotten by the Kremlin, which had actively used the marriage to fuel its propaganda machine.

The modern cosmonaut would not be a throwback to the earlier "spam in a can" ride of the Vostok missions. He or she needed to be an accomplished aerospace engineer in addition to possessing extensive flying experience. Svetlana was an ideal candidate, successfully negotiating the selection process to join the ranks of the cosmonaut corps in 1980. Then the gruelling and intensive training began, involving the usual weightless and centrifuge tests, as well as the more in-depth famliarisation of the Soyoz and Salyut spacecraft.

On August 19th 1982 Svetlana was given her space shot. She lifted off in the Soyuz T-7 spacecraft to become the second Russian woman in history to fly into space. It would be a full ten months later before Sally Ride would become the first US woman to reach outer space in the Space Shuttle.

The Soyuz T-7 carrying Svetlana and two other male cosmonauts docked with the orbiting Salyut 7 space station. The voyage was scientific and Svetlana returned after seven days and 21 hours in the Soyuz T-5 ship, docked at the other end of the space station.

Her second mission on July 17th 1984 in Soyuz T-12 docked with the Salyut 7 for an extended 11-day stay at the orbiting platform. This excursion saw her become the first woman in the world to perform a space walk or "Extra Vehicular Activity" (EVA). The EVA lasted for three hours.

A third mission with Svetlana commanding an all female crew was due to be launched on 3rd April 1986. However, the mission, coinciding with International Women's Day, was scrubbed due to problems with the ailing Salyut 7 and an exhaustion of available Soyuz T series launch vehicles.

Svetlana never flew into space again and it would be more than eight years later before a third female cosmonaut Elena Vladimirovna Kondakova would be involved with the space station MIR.

Now a celebrated space veteran, Svetlana worked as a prominent engineer on the heavy lift Energia launch rocket vehicle design for a number of years. In 1989 her influence extended to the Russian parliament, as she became a member of the State Dumas in representation of the Communist party. In 1993 she retired from active flight status to pursue her political interests in a changing Soviet Union.

Svetlana eventually married Viktor Khatkovsky, an engineer and pilot at the Ilyushin aircraft design bureau. Family connections notwithstanding, Svetlana Savitskaya proved she had the "right stuff" by always eyeing the next challenge and never being afraid to try the impossible. A quiet and unassuming pioneer, she has comfortably assured her place amongst fellow aviation greats to become a living legend in her own right.

1983
SALLY KRISTEN RIDE (USA) 1951–

Sally Kristen Ride was convinced she would become a tennis pro. However, the lure of science yanked her from the courts all the way to outer space. As the first American women to fly beyond earth's atmosphere, her achievements and support of young people will no doubt inspire several to become future astronauts. To many this is a straight-sets victory for science.

ally Ride, a native of Los Angeles, California, was born on May 26th 1951, and grew up in the San Fernando Valley. From an early age she had a strong affection for science and excelled academically. She was a gifted athlete and by the age of ten she was a nationally ranked tennis player, attending the prestigious Westlake School after winning a scholarship.

She had always been captivated by space flight and the exploration of outer space. In its early days the US space programme had a reputation for exclusively recruiting astronauts from an elite pool of military test pilots and naval aviators. The swelling ranks of the astronaut corps were predominantly male, servicing the needs of the pioneering Mercury, Gemini and Apollo programmes. The only women considered were the famed "Mercury 13," selected and trained, but never actually assigned to fly on any of the missions.

However, Sally was more concerned about the quality of her forehand shots than the traditionally male preserve of the National Aeronautics and Space Administration (NASA)'s astronaut corps. After graduating from high school she briefly attended Swarthmore University in Pennsylvania, only to drop out to pursue a professional tennis career. She honed her athletic skills, but discovered that the tennis circuit was not for her. Discarding all notions of lifting trophy cups, she enrolled at Stanford University in California. She gained a bachelor double in English and Physics and acquired a PhD in physics. Physically in good shape, Sally had many opportunities open to her. In 1977 she spied a tantalising advertisement in the Stanford University newspaper, which was to change her life forever.

The United States Air Force (USAF) had opened its pilot training to women and NASA followed suit in 1978 by actively encouraging women to apply for the space shuttle programme. The new reusable space glider demanded astronauts from all scientific disciplines to crew future shuttle missions. This meant that the selection of potential astronauts would no longer be confined to military pilots. Aged 27, Sally saw that NASA was calling for all would be astronauts, including women, to apply.

She did just that and out of 8,900 applicants for just 35 potential astronaut slots she was selected. She was one of only six women to enter the space programme in 1978. Another was USAF pilot Lt. Eileen Collins, who would later be the first woman both to pilot a space shuttle, and become a shuttle commander.

Sally embarked on an intensive training period, which lasted almost a year. Astronauts in the making undergo parachute jumps, survival techniques, flight instruction and weightless training. The last is performed in a Boeing 707 known as the "Vomit Comet," which conducts parabolic dives to simulate zero gravity. The experience can

lead the uninitiated to be uncontrollably nauseous during the controlled plummet. Sally prevailed and loved the flying parts of the training. She enjoyed it so much that she would eventually transform flying into an enduring pursuit. She graduated to full active flight status in 1979, joining the elite rank of astronauts awaiting assignment on the new Orbiter. Dogged by initial technical problems the space shuttle Columbia eventually made its maiden voyage on April 12th 1981.

Following the pioneering flight by veteran Apollo era astronauts John Young and Robert Crippen, the shuttle programme entered a new operational phase. Sally was an integral part of the early support teams underpinning the second and third Columbia missions. She acted as communications officer responsible for transmitting radio messages between mission control and the crew of the orbiting shuttle. She was also part of the team tasked with the development of shuttle's robotic manipulator arm, designed for the retrieval and release of satellites.

Amid a blaze of media interest, Sally Ride was officially declared a member of the seventh space shuttle mission designated STS-7. She was to become the first American women in space in the second shuttle, the Challenger, which would be the first to carry five astronauts.

On June 18th 1983, clutching a life support system pack, Sally

boarded the Challenger and blasted off from Kennedy Space Centre into history. Her mission was televised the world over and dominated headlines. She was the third female in the world to fly into space, ten months after Russian cosmonaut Svetlana Savitskaya. The first was Valentina Tereshkova in 1963.

The six-day mission involved using the robotic arm to deploy satellites on behalf of Canada and Indonesia, plus the successful retrieval of another from low earth orbit. The first formation flight with another satellite in orbit also formed part of the mission. Material and pharmaceutical research experiments rounded off the project. The Challenger alighted on the dry lakebed runway at Edwards Air Force Base on June 24th 1983.

Sally flew again on the Challenger designated STS-41-G on October 5th 1984. The flight accommodated the largest crew thus far, a total of seven astronauts. Aboard was another female astronaut, Kathryn Sullivan, who became the first American woman to perform a space walk or EVA (Extra Vehicular Activity) during the mission. Sally was involved in deploying more satellites during the eight-day flight. By the time the Challenger returned to Kennedy Space Centre on October 13th 1984, she had amassed 343 space flight hours.

The seasoned space "veteran" was in training for her third Challenger flight when tragedy struck the overall programme. On 28th January 1986 the Challenger exploded moments after take off with the loss of the entire crew. The catastrophe was especially poignant for Sally as most on board were close friends from her training days. The shuttle fleet and missions were grounded indefinitely and Sally was appointed a member of the Presidential Commission, tasked with investigating the accident. She had to repeat the sombre role following the destruction in 2003 of the shuttle Columbia on re-entry.

Events In 1983

- Dick Smith achieves first solo circumnavigation of the globe in a Bell Jetranger III helicopter.

- The introduction of compact discs puts vinyl records into a steep decline.

After the Challenger investigation, Sally was assigned to NASA's Washington headquarters to participate in strategic planning initiatives and establishing the agency's Office of Exploration.

She retired from NASA in 1987 and was as a science fellow at Stanford University before her appointment as Professor of Physics at the University of California in 1989. She has authored a number of books; written with the express intention of promoting sciences to younger generations, especially encouraging girls to enter science based professions. She also founded "Sally Ride Science," an organisation set up to create entertaining science programmes and publications for schools.

She has won numerous awards and citations. These include the Jefferson Award for Public Service and the Von Braun Award. She has been inducted into both the National Women's Hall of Fame and the Astronaut's Hall of Fame. In 2006 California Governor Arnold Schwarzenegger included her in the California Hall of Fame.

Sally made the fortuitous career change from talented athlete to astrophysicist without dropping the ball. From thousands of hopefuls she became one of the chosen few pioneering women in NASA's elite team of space flyers. Her successful passion for providing opportunities for emerging generations to explore science is surely a grand slam victory for this former tennis ace.

1984

KATHRYN DWYER SULLIVAN (USA) 1951 –

Kathryn Sullivan has profoundly discovered two distinct, but related universes. One is earth's vast oceans, limitless, powerful and largely still unexplored. The other, similarly uncharted, is the endless space beyond the protective layer of the earth's atmosphere, populated with celestial bodies. Captivated by the mystery of both realms, Sullivan embarked upon an intellectual voyage that took her to a unique vantage point in time and space. Floating high above the earth, she had a unique perspective of how both universes happily co-exist.

athryn Dwyer Sullivan was always interested in maps, landscapes and other geological wonders. She had a penchant for exploration and to understand a little more about the world we live in. As the first woman to walk in space, floating high above the earth was the pinnacle of her exploratory journey.

Kathryn was born on October 3, 1951, in Paterson, New Jersey. From early childhood she latched onto science as a way to explain the order of the world. She hungered for a greater knowledge, not caring what her fellow students thought or expressed about her studious nature.

She migrated towards geology, embracing earth sciences. Remarkably she found little resistance to her passage into the profession, despite her gender. She was resolute, adamant, and obstinate. Her intention was to study languages for the sole purpose of travelling across the world without being restricted by being unable to communicate. Her choice of linguistics as a major necessitated adding at least three science subjects to complete her undergraduate training at the University of California, Santa Cruz. She reluctantly selected oceanography and earth science classes to fulfil the burdensome criteria. To her astonishment, she latched on to the subjects with gusto, and reshaped the course of her academic and professional life.

Graduating with honours in 1973, she went on to complete her doctorate at Dalhousie University, Halifax, Nova Scotia in 1978. Eager to enter the world of research, Kathryn was about to explore the first universe, quite literally dipping her toe in the water.

As part of her postgraduate doctoral degree Kathryn participated in a number of oceanographic expeditions. She worked under the guidance of three bodies: the US Geological Survey, Wood's Hole Oceanographic Institute and the Bedford Institute. Her research into the marine world included the Atlantic Ridge, the Newfoundland Basin and the fault zones bordering the Southern California Coast, with its simmering San Andreas Fault. In interviews she recalled many weeks spent at sea during the early seventies, performing seismic surveys and conducting research in the new field of plate tectonics.

Her first foray into the world of aviation saw her acquire licences in both glider and single engine aircraft before her final leap into the next frontier. With her PhD research nearing completion, Kathryn was striving for the next challenge. Like her contemporary Eileen Collins, she noticed that the National Aeronautics and Space Administration (NASA) had opened up the Astronaut Corps to women in 1978. The thought of exploring space struck a chord with her, and she applied, brushing aside 6,000 eligible applicants to win a place. She was one of the first six women in the new thirty-five strong class of astronaut candidates.

Rigorous NASA training, survival courses, and numerous classes followed until in 1979, Kathryn was pronounced an active astronaut

ready for a mission. Most astronauts in waiting undertake a variety of roles, and she performed a number of support assignments.

In 1979 she inadvertently established an altitude record of 63,300 feet, becoming the first women to fly at such a height. She was using sophisticated infrared camera equipment in a modified WB-57F reconnaissance plane flown by NASA for high altitude and meteorological survey work. For nearly four hours Kathryn, garbed in a pressure suit, diligently operated her cameras high above West Texas, blissfully unaware of how close she was to outer space.

Her first mission inevitably credited her as the first American woman to undertake a space walk. She blasted off from Kennedy Space Centre on October 5th 1984 aboard the Challenger designated as flight STS-41G. The crew deployed a satellite and conducted a number of scientific experiments. Kathryn was a mission specialist with Sally Ride, also part of the crew and on her second flight in the Shuttle. On a previous mission Sally had become the first US women to fly into space.

Kathryn's task was to work with fellow astronaut David Leetsma on trials involving the refuelling of satellites running low on fuel. The experiment was to determine the feasibility of such a venture by practicing a pretend space refuelling exercise. Donning a bulky space suit, Kathryn went 'EVA' (Extra Vehicular Activity) into space and helped set up the test for transferring volatile fuel gases from one tank to another.

Tethered by a 50-foot umbilical cord to the Orbiter, she floated above the earth, taking in the panoramic vistas and the still oceans below. Beyond the fuzzy penumbra lay the vast blackness of space and Kathryn was suspended between the two realms. STS-41G completed 132 orbits of the earth in 197.5 hours before landing at Kennedy Space Center, Florida, on October 13, 1984.

On her second shuttle mission aboard the Discovery in April 1990 she served again as mission specialist and became part of another milestone of aerospace history. The primary mission for STS-31 was to deploy the deep space Hubble telescope. This telescope platform opened up a huge portal to unlock the mysteries of the universe. It continues to beam back clear visuals of distant stars that were once invisible even to the largest of earth-bound telescopes.

Events In 1984

- Emily Warner and Barbara Cook direct first all-female commercial airline crew.

- Richard Branson's airline, Virgin Atlantic, begins services to North America.

Kathryn's third and final mission took place in 1992 in the Atlantis, designated flight STS-45. She served as payload commander on the first Spacelab mission dedicated to NASA's "Mission to Planet Earth." Her final flight drew upon all of her experience and skills of oceanography as well as geology.

When she hung up her space boots, Kathryn had logged a total of 532 hours in space. She retired from active flight status and NASA in August 1992. She then took on the role of chief scientist, National Oceanic and Atmospheric Administration (NOAA). She presides as president and chief executive, center of science & industry in Columbus, Ohio.

In between shuttle missions she continued her oceanic research activities by participating in National Oceanic and Atmospheric Administration's National Undersea Research Program, achieving another first by diving a submersible to a record of 6,500 feet.

To maintain her links with oceanography Kathryn also signed up with the US Naval Reserve, holding the rank of captain. Her passion for education was such that she also pioneered the design of the original "Challenger Center" programme now in service with more than 30 Challenger learning centres in the US and Canada.

Dr Kathryn Sullivan was inducted into the US astronaut's Hall of Fame on May 1, 2004. A quirk of fate involving the mandatory selection of science courses during her undergraduate days led her to explore the oceans of both earth and outer space.

In interviews she often advocates the need to monitor and maintain the delicate balance of the various ecosystems now wavering and shuddering from the effects of pollution and climate change. Suspended between the two realms, it is possible that Kathryn had a greater insight into the effects of mankind on the planet than that of just another scientist seated safely somewhere at a desk examining streams of data …

JEANA YEAGER (USA) 1952 –

The daring draughtsman who went round the world on one tank of gas

The shark infested waters off the coast of Mexico loomed large. Both of the Voyager's front and rear engines had failed and refused to restart. Precious altitude ebbed away and the prospect of ditching was imminent. Jeana Yeager had cut off her long flowing locks before the milestone flight, trading its weight for an extra four miles of fuel. She could hear the voice of pilot Dick Rutan calmly rattle off the rapidly depleting altitude. The aircraft pitched nose down towards an ocean teaming with carnivorous, cold blooded man-eaters.

It was all a far cry from her quiet origins. Jeana Yeager was born on May 18th 1952. She hails from the Lone Star state of Texas, Fort Worth. In 1986 the pioneering aviatrix gained international fame for flying with the legendary Dick Rutan on a non-stop round-the-world record attempt in the purpose-built Voyager aircraft. Their epic flight was full of hair-raising incidents. The intrepid pilots were aloft for nine days, three minutes and 44 seconds on a single tank of gas. Circumnavigating the globe, tackling extreme weather conditions and denied access to certain airspaces, the Voyager covered a total distance of approximately 28,000 miles. This more than doubled the distance record previously set by the larger eight-engine behemoth the B-52 Stratofortress in 1962.

In her formative years Jeana studied for a technical draughtsman qualification at high school. Little did she know that later her skills in producing precise technical schematics would prove invaluable to the development lifecycle of Rutan's Voyager aircraft. A keen horseback rider and an avid track runner, Jeana was also captivated by helicopters, secretly harbouring an ambition to fly them one day. Aged 19 she was briefly married to a police officer.

Following her divorce, Jeana moved to Santa Rosa, California and found work as a draughtsman and surveyor. She gained her private pilot's licence by the age of 26. As the fledgling pilot flexed her new wings, she met veteran rocket scientist Bob Truax who gave her the opportunity to work in the aerospace industry. She was employed at his company as a draughtsman working on experimental reusable spacecraft designs.

Fate served up a new twist when she had a chance encounter with the legendary Rutan brothers at an airshow in 1980. Dick Rutan, a highly decorated former Vietnam War fighter pilot, was slotted in to fly an aerobatic routine at the air show in Chino, California. Accompanying him was his gifted younger brother and aircraft designer Burt. Both helmed the specialised Rutan Aircraft Company (RAC), with Dick serving as test pilot for his brother's revolutionary designs. Jeana became romantically involved with Dick, and this inexorably led to her working for RAC.

Folklore has it that Burt broached the idea for the round-the-world non-stop flight at a restaurant table in 1981. Jeana and Dick signed up immediately for the proposed endeavour, deemed impossible by many. Burt then sketched out the initial design of the aircraft, which would be christened "Voyager," on a napkin.

Detailed engineering schematics spawned from this rough drawing. It was imperative that the aircraft be composed of the lightest materials. Eventually a composite of Kevlar and fibreglass was used to create the spindly airframe, with nearly every cavity and space used for fuel storage. The five-year enterprise to build the Voyager took place out of an airport hanger in the Mojave Desert. Jeana handled project funding and promoted their aspirations through the "Voyager Impressive Peoples programme."

Word soon spread of their lofty ambitions. Relying on private donations initially, they were soon joined by volunteer aerospace engineers. Aircraft companies loaned equipment. This indicated the camaraderie of spirit and support within the industry for their pioneering endeavour. During this time Jeana set a number of speed records in other Rutan experimental home-built kit aircraft, such as the Rutan EZ series. She also acquired a commercial pilot's licence, in addition to multi-engine and instrument rating qualifications. In preparation for the Voyager flight she also underwent a water survival-training course with the US Air Force.

Jeana was to serve as co-pilot and flight engineer to the more experienced Dick. The day of reckoning came on the morning of 14th December 1986 when Voyager took to the air from Edwards Air Force Base. Dick Rutan was no stranger to danger, having flown the F-100 Super Sabre in Vietnam. He had survived being shot down behind enemy lines. His flying experience was in excess of 8,000 hours compared to Jeana's admirable 1,000 hours logged, which meant

Events In 1986

- The Space Shuttle Challenger is destroyed at launch

- Haitian President Jean-Claude Duvalier flees to France (Feb. 7th).

- The Oprah Winfrey Show hits US television.

that he tackled most of the handling of the unpredictable airframe. The start of Voyager's epic and hazardous journey was far from auspicious. Laden with fuel (ten times the weight of the empty airframe) the wing tips inadvertently scraped along the runway and sustained damage during the aircraft's lengthy takeoff roll. Clambering into the air the compromised wingtips were broken off by deliberate pitching manoeuvres, preventing further damage to the delicate wings.

The incident-packed journey was fraught with peril and heart-stopping moments. Severe weather fronts jostled them like a leaf in a tornado. Mechanical problems tested their resolve and knowledge of the unwieldy plane. They had to evade sensitive airspace and hostile territories, primarily a few unfriendly African states and certain regions in South East Asia. The cramped and claustrophobic cockpit made their task highly demanding, especially during the numerous in-flight emergencies.

With an eye on the fuel gauge, the Voyager pilots gingerly picked their way through narrow spaces between converging walls of 70,000-foot high thunderclouds, and negotiated 14,000-foot mountain ranges. On several occasions they were at the mercy of extreme turbulence threatening to tear apart the fragile aircraft. All the while precious fuel burned away.

At one point a red warning light announced an imminent engine seizure. This had Jeana scrabbling to add necessary oil to the rough engine, overcoming the need to ditch. Seventy-two hours of continuous flying later Dick gave into exhaustion. Jeana took command of the Voyager and flew for an entire night, giving Dick the opportunity to sleep.

More engine problems occurred off the West Coast of Mexico when their only functioning rear engine spluttered and died. The powerless glider pitched towards the ocean. Their repeated attempts to restart the recalcitrant engines became increasingly desperate. The altimeter needle was a whirling blur until about 5,000 feet. The shifted centre of gravity had pushed much-needed fuel to the starved engines, which coughed back to reassuring life. The guardian angels perched on their shoulders had lifted them from the brink of testing Jeana's ocean survival techniques in shark-infested waters.

Adrenaline kept exhaustion and recent mental traumas at bay on the last leg of the journey. Finally on 23rd December 1986 at 8:06 am, Voyager's considerably lightened airframe kissed the runway back at Edwards to a triumphant, heroic welcome amid a blaze of media interest. Jeana and Dick had completed the milestone non-stop around-the-world flight with just four gallons to spare.

Honoured as a national hero for this astonishing feat, Jeana was presented with the Presidential Medal of Freedom by President Reagan in 1986. She was also awarded the Harmon Trophy, the FAI De L Vaulx Medal and was the first woman to receive the Collier Trophy.

Following their historic flight, Jeana and Dick's shared passion for aviation was not enough to save their relationship. They went their separate ways. Jeana was a pivotal member of the Rutan team in getting the Voyager off the ground. Her dedication and ability to weather hardship and danger are a testament to her strength and belief in achieving the monumental flight into the unknown.

Today their achievement hangs immortalised at the Smithsonian Institute, Washington, which is Voyager's last and peaceful resting place. The spindly, surprisingly resilent airframe has come a long way from its humble origins scrawled on the back of a napkin.

1987

ALLISON HICKEY (USA)

"All social change is forged by those with a pioneering spirit, those who are unafraid to topple barriers, conquer uncharted terrain or lay the groundwork for future generations. While history is full of examples of women's triumphs, each pioneer still has an individual story worth telling. One such pioneer is Brigadier General Allison Hickey, a woman of many firsts." Directorate of Total Force Integration USAF

eneral Allison Hickey certainly has a story worth telling. A 1980 graduate of the US Air Force Academy, she was in the USAF's first class to admit women. She has served in all three of the air force's components. This includes ten years on active duty; one year with the Air Force Reserve and 13 years with the Air National Guard. She also has more than 1,500 hours in the KC-135 Stratotanker and KC-10A aircraft as a commander and pilot.

In an article written by Capt. Michaela Eggers, Staff Sgt. Tonda Sallee, and Julie Brubach, of the Directorate of Total Force Integration, General Allison Hickey is described as "living life purposefully." Her story indicates that she is a woman of great intent.

The daughter of an Army officer, Allison had a peripatetic childhood and was constantly on the move. Obviously from a close family, she fell naturally into the lifestyle she knew from childhood. According to her biographers, she wanted to sign up, but was thwarted by rules in those days that dictated she could not attend a military service academy, since they were all closed to women.

That all changed in October 1975 when the US military service academies were opened up to females. Allison applied to the Merchant Marine Academy, West Point and the Air Force Academy and crammed hard to gain her entry qualifications. She said: "I think I gave up every spare minute of my senior year and my entire Christmas break studying for that test."

She was out for a run one afternoon when her sister came dashing over to let her know there was a phone call for her. Rep. James Howard was on the other end. Allison said: "He told me that he did not have a West Point invitation to give me, but he did have one for the Air Force Academy. The catch was I had to give him my answer right on the spot. That moment sure tested the concept of 'jumping in with everything you've got.'"

She jumped and in June 1976, she along with 156 other women entered the USAF Academy as its first female cadets. To ease things for them, the school had set up a mentor programme for the new cadets, consisting of 15 female lieutenants handpicked to be air-training officers.

Four years later Allison graduated and headed to Columbus Air Force Base (AFB). Her path took her through combat crew training for the KC-135 at Castle AFB, where she graduated with honours. Between October 1984 and October 1985, she was stationed at Grand Forks AFB, flying KC-135A tankers for the 905th Air Refuelling Squadron. This made her initially the first female KC-135 pilot and then commander at Grand Forks.

When she started at Grand Forks, she reported that there were fears female pilots might not have the strength to cope with several different emergency responses, such as the ability to land the aircraft in the event of a combined engine and hydraulic power failure. Before women joined up, a pilot had to prove that he was capable of coping by "standing on the rudder" to accomplish this procedure. This would happen only once in his career. Allison said that: "It got to the point where it became no big deal to me because I was doing it nearly every time I flew with someone new." However, she pointed out she was willing to do whatever it took to alleviate any unfounded fears. She said: "Some people need to see things for themselves to be comfortable with a change. If it was going to help them make the leap, I'd gladly stand on another rudder."

According to the USAF writers, at another point, the Air Force was not sure if hormone or birth control pills would have some type of negative physiological impact on women aviators. Consequently, women who were prescribed these medicines were grounded for several months.

Because of her gender, there were several amusing moments in Allison's early career. She was once on a refuelling mission over Grand Forks. She described the occasion: "When I cleared the F-4

(Phantom) to the refuelling position there was this long, drawn-out pause before the fighter pilot came onto the frequency jokingly saying, 'Holy cow, the next thing you know, they'll be giving them the vote!' These guys had never heard a woman's voice on any military aircraft before. I think during the pause he was 'breathing deeply' through his nose. This was a pretty big change to process."

Allison's career went from strength to strength. Between 1986 and 1990, she was a pilot for the then brand new state-of-the-art KC-10A Extender aircraft for the 32nd Air Refuelling Squadron and 2nd Bomb Wing at Barksdale AFB. She had by then met her future husband. She was asked to choose between two excellent career opportunities: taking an air staff training residency assignment, or flying the KC-10. When she asked her career advisor for his opinion she reported that he said: "It doesn't matter which you choose, getting married will end your career."

Fortunately he was wrong. Allison credits her career successes to two very significant influences: the "Grace of God," and Rob, her husband of 21 years. "My husband has carried a great load as a spouse, advisor and friend."

In 1987, Allison clocked up another "first." She was in Spain on a KC-10 flying mission. Without her regular team around her, she developed symptoms of appendicitis. She was taken to a nearby hospital for treatment. She described the situation to her biographers: "The language barriers melted away when they started pointing at the sonogram screen and saying 'baby.'"

Her timing was impeccable. Just days earlier, the air force had added a new waiver, which allowed pregnant women to fly for up to six months. She was an unusual case. There were few officers, particularly aviators with children. Her colleagues were supportive and the deployment crew stuck a "Baby on Board" sign in the boom pod of the aircraft she was flying. She now has three children.

She continued to climb the ranks and in 2004, while working in the Strategic Planning Directorate of Headquarters Air Force, she was asked to start a new directorate dedicated to integrating the three component of the USAF: regular, Guard and Reserve. Her hands-on experience with all three components provided her with a direct knowledge of the total force capabilities. She is now director of the Total Force Integration Directorate. The staff is composed of regular, Guard, and Reserve Airmen, as well as civilians and contractors.

Working at the highest level, Brigadier General Allison Hickey has proved that it is possible to forge a career in the USAF and enjoy the pleasures of marriage and motherhood. Her career has included working at many levels, and she has travelled a great deal. She is philosophical abut her success and said: "Life is not always about what you first started doing, what you already know how to do, or going where others have already made a path. So when faced with it, breathe deeply and frequently and take the leap. There is more opportunity than you can imagine on the other side of change."

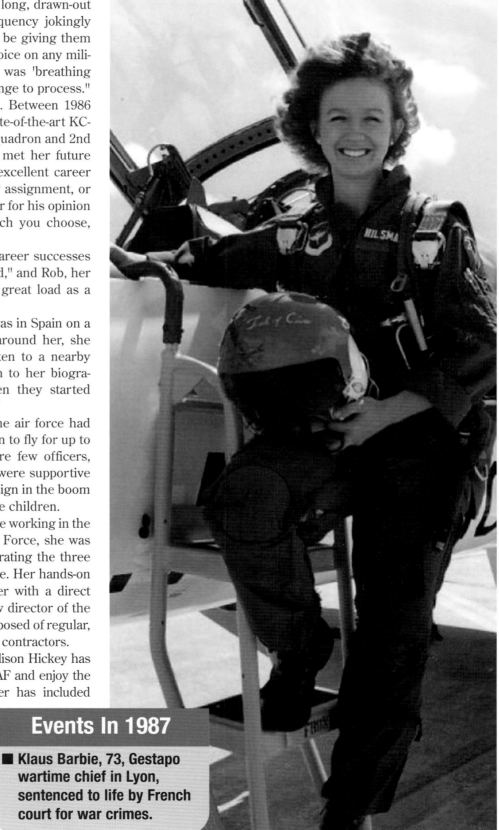

Events In 1987

■ Klaus Barbie, 73, Gestapo wartime chief in Lyon, sentenced to life by French court for war crimes.

1990

NIVEDITA BHASIN (INDIA) 1963 –

Forging a path for Indian women

January 1, 1990, saw a minor argument in the flight deck of flight IC-492 on the Bombay-Aurangabad-Udaipur sector. Congratulatory messages were pouring in for the newly promoted Indian Airlines pilot. First officer Vikram Thosar was graciously accepting the radio calls, thanking his colleagues for their support. Captain Nivedita Bhasin had to put him straight. "They are for me," she told him. Vikram was surprised. "No, they are for me," he said.

They were both correct. At 26, Nivedita was flying into history as the youngest woman to command a commercial jet. Meanwhile Vikram was on his first ever flight in the right hand seat. Nivedita laughs: "We were both on top of the world that day and flew well. Small things like that strengthened my confidence."

Nivedita was born on July 6 1963 in Delhi, one of three children. She says: "As a child I always wanted to do something totally different. To stand out and hold my own I wanted people to look up to me, including me." There were few female pilots in India at the time. Durba Banerjee was the first, who had joined Indian Airlines around the year Nivedita was born.

She days: "It was difficult when I joined. I was not accepted by men or women.

"In India women flying was considered a no-no. A woman's place was at home. People like us stepped out and got into unconventional jobs. However, I had a lot of encouragement from my parents. I got into aviation in a really gradual way." She started by heading to the local gliding club when she was 15 years old, but was discouraged and pointed at the aero modelling society instead. Even there she was unusual, as all the other 200 other members were boys. This fuelled her determination to do well and she went back to the gliding club at 16. She finally won a scholarship to learn to be a pilot.

She went to Patna to learn to fly, which was a tough experience. She says: "The boys hated me. I was not so tactful in that age, which made matters worse. It was not such a happy time of my life. I felt so totally unwanted, so was determined to succeed no matter what they did. It made me stronger. It is good now, because I can cope with any kind of situation. That made me strong and able to sail through many difficult things in my life."

Nivedita joined Indian Airlines in Hyderabad in 1984. There she met her husband, Rohit, with whom she has two children. She says the combination of her marriage and rising through the ranks to sit in the left hand (commander's) seat, earned her the respect she had been lacking in her earlier days. She says: "My life changed and became really beautiful, so much easier, I suddenly had lots of esteem." Although the intensive training was gruelling, she did well.

She attributes part of her success to the excellent tuition she received from her B737 instructor. Twenty years later she is still in touch with him, and regularly asks him for tips as she upgrades her skills in other aircraft. She praises his teaching style: "Sometimes you build a rapport with someone. He gave me so much confidence. He would say: 'Just be yourself. You can do well.'"

Once she started flying regularly she sometimes flew with Saudamini Deshmukh on the Fokker Friendship. "She was my senior and 11 years older than me, but it was good to be together. I had just turned 21 when I joined the airline and not so confident." She laughs, adding: "It is so different today. My 16 year old daughter is more mature now than I was at 21."

Nivedita subsequently notched up several firsts. In November 1985 She was the co-pilot on the first all-women crew flight on the Fokker Friendship F-27 with Captain Deshmukh in command on the Calcutta-Silchar route. The duo also made the first Boeing all-women crew flight in September 1989 on the Mumbai-Goa sector. In January 1990 she became the world's youngest jet aircraft commander at the age of 26 on the Boeing aircraft.

Indian Airlines showed solidarity with International Woman's Day on March 8 1999 by operating three flights with an all-female crew: one on domestic and two on international routes. Two flights were operated from Mumbai and one from Delhi. All check-in staff were also female on that day at both Delhi and Mumbai airports. She says: "We felt total euphoria that day to be part of an all female crew. We were part of history, we were so happy. The first flight was a little subdued, but the second one was so highly publicised that the atmosphere was completely festive on board."

Thirteen percent of Indian Airlines workforce is female. As an extra surprise, all women passengers travelling on Indian Airlines flights leaving Delhi that day were given a silk scarf. Nivedita was captain on flight IC 813 on the international Delhi-Kathmandu-Delhi route, alongside co-pilot captain Indrani Singh. Both women were commanders on Airbus A300 aircraft. In addition to the cockpit crew, there were 11 cabin staff. Nivedita flew Delhi-Kathmandu, whist Indrani took the controls on the way back.

Nivedita went on to become jet training captain on the Airbus A300 aircraft. She is now based at the central training establishment for Indian Airlines, Delhi, and has almost 15,000 hours in her logbook. Check pilots need a minimum of 500 hours' command experience on type, total command experience of 1,000 hours, and total flying experience of 3,000 hours. After proficiency tests and approval by the Directorate General of Civil Aviation, the pilot can carry out route checks for licence renewal, pilot-in-command and performance monitoring of other pilots, as well as training flights for co-pilots.

Both of her children want to follow their parents into the airlines. Her son is already flying for Air India and her daughter has expressed an interest incoming a pilot. Motherhood also turned her into a pioneer. Her female predecessors had not had children, so again Nivedita was cutting the first path. She says: "When my instructor on the 737 found out I was pregnant, he told me to stop flying. I was three and half months gone. At that point there were no such thing as maternity guidelines." She stopped flying and was given six weeks off once the baby was born. There was no paid maternity leave. Today the rules are much better and women have six months leave, and are offered ground jobs during their pregnancies so they do not have to take holiday.

Nivedita recently completed her type rating training on the Airbus A330 with Oxford Aviation Training in the UK and Stockholm. She now flies on international routes from Delhi to Seoul, Hong Kong and London. She was thrilled with the course she took, finding it a totally different experience to the battle she had two decades earlier, even though she was once again the only female in her class. She says she is "delighted" with the Airbus. "I am having a love affair with this aircraft, the glass cockpit is beautiful. It flies so well with the side stick. The instructor calls it a 'ladies' aircaft.' I agree."

India today is totally different from the India of 20 years ago. Airlines are now clamouring for pilots, male and female and women have more opportunities to embrace a flying career. Thanks to Nivedita and other early female pilots, the path to success is already forged. She says: "I hope that I will be an inspiration to young girls and encourage them to take up a career in aviation."

If she achieves her goal of becoming an instructor on the A330, she may well follow in the footsteps of a famous FI of almost a century ago. Hilda Hewlett in the UK taught her son to fly. He went on to have an illustrious aviation career. Both of Nivedita's children are keen pilots. Time will tell…

1991

PATTY WAGSTAFF (USA)

"She was not quite what you would call refined. She was not quite what you would call unrefined. She was the kind of person that keeps a parrot."
Mark Twain

Despite the fact that she has retired from competition aerobatics, Patty Wagstaff continues to fly a heart stopping, hard-core, low-level aerobatic routine for millions of airshow spectators each year. Her thrilling performances have won her legions of fans and shelves full of trophies.

Born Patricia Rosalie Kearns Combs on September 11, 1951 in St. Louis, Missouri. Patty's father was a 747 captain with Japan Airlines. He moved his family to Japan when Patty was nine years old. At ten years old when her father let her take the controls of his DC-6, her lifelong love affair with aviation began. She says: "My career was not something I set out to do, but if somebody had told me what would happen when I was ten years old I would not have been surprised. Racing cars, horses or fast airplanes were right up my alley."

After school in Japan, she travelled extensively throughout Southeast Asia and Europe and eventually took a six-year work-study programme in

Australia and lived and travelled up the west coast in a small boat. In 1979 She moved to Dillingham, a small town in the southwest of Alaska, to work for the Bristol Bay Native Association. Her job entailed travelling to each of the remote villages in the region, areas only accessible by air. However, her first experience with bush flying was not a positive one: the aeroplane she chartered crashed. So Patty learned to fly herself, hiring friend, and later husband, Bob to travel with her in his Cessna 185 floatplane. Her aviation career had taken off.

She rapidly earned her commercial, instrument, seaplane and commercial helicopter ratings. She is a flight and instrument instructor and is rated and qualified to fly many aeroplanes, from World War II warbirds to jets.

A lifelong curiosity drew her to her first airshow in Abbotsford, British Columbia in 1983. She watched the aerobatic pilots perform and knew that was what she wanted to do. She says: "I bought a small plane and constantly worked hard to reach the next level. I set small goals along the way, but I was not sure where I would end up. I was not sure if I would be good enough." However, she was determined and flew in as many airshows and competitions as she could, steadily improving her technique. She laughs when she talks about her first competition and says: "I did not win, but I did not come last." In 1985, just five years after gaining her pilot's license, she bagged a place on the US aerobatic team, where she stayed until 1996. By 1987 she had earned the Rolly Cole memorial award for her contributions to aerobatic sports.

Patty is constantly striving to outclass herself. A six-time member of the US aerobatic team, she has won the gold, silver and bronze medals in what is an Olympic-level international aerobatic competition. She is the first woman to win the US National Aerobatic championships and one of the few people to win it three times: in 1991, 1992 and 1993. She says: "The first thing I felt when I won it in 1991 was 'this is not enough.' I wanted to do

it again. I was thrilled when I did it again - twice." She says that she found competitive flying "nerve wracking." She adds: "I was very nervous before a competition. I am never nervous before airshows, I am just focused. Psychologically competition flying teaches you a lot about yourself. That is part of the beauty of it. You learn so much." She retired from competition flying after the World Aerobatic Contest in 1996, when she was the top scoring US pilot. She explains: "I had achieved my goals, and when you're flying in competitions there is no room for anything else in your life. Everything is focused on that competition."

From 1988 to 1994, she won the Betty Skelton First Lady of Aerobatics award back to back. Her trophy shelf is bursting with awards, including several magazines readers' favourite pilot awards. In 1996, she took home the GAN and Flyers Magazine Reader's Choice awards as favourite female pilot, as well as the inaugural Charlie Hillard trophy for Aerobatic Excellence. She also holds the Sword of Excellence from the International Council of Air Shows.

The National Air & Space Museum (NASM), Smithsonian in Washington has recognised her as a pioneer. In 1994 the museum placed her Extra 260 aeroplane on display between Charles and Anne Morrow Lindbergh's Lockheed 8 Sirius "Tingmissartoq" and Amelia Earhart's Lockheed 5B Vega; and underneath General James "Jimmy" Doolittle's Curtiss R3C-2 Racer. NASM also gave her a Lifetime Achievement award for her outstanding air show performances. "I was really honoured to receive that award. It's strange seeing the plane. I remember every detail about flying it. It is unusual because it is a prototype. The fuel system was unique and there were a lot of management issues to take care of when flying it."

Patty has earned a place in several Halls of Fame, including the Arizona Aviation Hall of Fame, the International Women's Aviation Hall of Fame, the National Aviation Hall of Fame (where she is one of only seven female inductees) and the International Council of Air Shows Foundation Hall of Fame. In 1997, she was the recipient of the NAA Paul Tissandier diploma, and she won the Katherine and Marjorie Stinson award in 2002. Recently she was

awarded a Lifetime Achievement Award from the Air Force Association, was inducted into the EAA/IAC Hall of Fame, and in 2005 received the NAA/99's Katherine Wright Award.

Along with her dedication to competition aerobatics, Patty always flew in airshows as well. She has also trained with the Russian aerobatic team in Russia. She coaches and trains aerobatic competitors when her time permits, and her aircraft, the Cirrus Extra 300S is featured on Microsoft's Flight Sim software.

Patty's specialty is displaying aircraft. Patty performs at between 15 and 20 airshows per years both in the US and internationally in her Cirrus Extra 300S, the Hawker Beechcraft Texan II, the T-6 Texan and a P51 Mustang, in addition to having performed in a number of other aircraft. Her motto is: "Have helmet will fly!" Her company, Patty Wagstaff Airshows, Inc is based in St. Augustine, Florida. In addition to performing in airshows she has worked as a stunt pilot for television and motion picture projects, is a member of the Motion Picture Pilots' Association (MPPA), the Screen Actors Guild (SAG) and the United Stuntwomen's Association (USA). During the off season, she gives bush and recurrency training to the pilots of the Kenya Wildlife Service in Kenya. She is also an Emeritus Board Member of the National Air and Space Museum.

She is the only female member of the MPPA available to double both men and women and fly both men and women's parts. Her movie credits include: Drop Zone; Forever Young; and Up Close & Personal.

Today Patty has "good balance" in her life. Her interests include her Jack Russell terriers, Cassidy and Ripley, her parrots Buddha and Bandit, and her horse Bebo Gigolo. Bandit flies with her to airshows and events. She says: "He misses me when I'm gone. I put him in his cage at the back of the aircraft when we travel to shows and when we get airborne he sits on top of it and looks out the window." She hints where her ambition may take her next: "I enjoy flying different airplanes. I always like something different and am interested in Warbirds." If anyone can show off some of those glorious old machines to their best, this woman can.

Events In 1991

- US-led forces attack Iraq in a massive air assault after a United Nations deadline for the withdrawal of Iraqi troops from occupied Kuwait passes unheeded.

- Europeans end sanctions on South Africa.

- South African Parliament repeals apartheid laws.

1991

MARTA BOHN-MEYER (USA) 1957 – 2005

Marta Bohn-Meyer achieved the distinction on October 3rd 1991 as one of the fastest women on the planet. She was the first female crewmember of the SR-71 Blackbird spy plane, which has the unrivalled capability of flying at three times the speed of sound. Sadly she lost her life while flying an aerobatic plane, denying the aerospace industry of a remarkably gifted engineer and pilot who had still so much to give…

Marta Bohn Meyer was an aerospace engineer at the National Aeronautics and Space Administration (NASA) at Dryden Flight Research Centre, Edwards, California, in the Mojave Desert. Dryden is the traditional home of NASA's many cutting edge aerospace projects, using a variety of military and civilian aircraft in the pursuit of advancing aviation technologies.

Born in 1957, Marta was a native of Long Island, New York. By the age of fourteen she had developed an interest in both aviation and horses. Her father, who worked for Grumman Aerospace as a flight engineer, gently steered the young Marta towards the world of aviation as opposed to equestrian pursuits. Taking up flying lessons she soloed in an airplane aged just sixteen. Her acumen for technical engineering was demonstrated while still at high school. She spent an entire Christmas vacation ensconced in her father's garage rebuilding the engine of her 1967 Ford Falcon.

She embarked upon a degree in aerospace engineering at the Rensselaer Polytechnic Institute in Troy, New York. During her undergraduate years, Marta served an apprenticeship with NASA at the Langley Research Centre in Virginia. As part of the cooperative education program from 1976 to 1979 she participated in helicopter research, as well as wind tunnel and flight safety projects using small civilian aircraft as test platforms.

Graduating with a bachelor of science in 1979, Martha was swiftly appointed as junior operations engineer at NASA's Dryden flight research facility. Her first project was on the F-104 Starfighter equipped with a special pylon slung under the fuselage. The purpose of the pylon was to serve as a high speed flying wind tunnel testing the strength of an adhesive developed for bonding thermal tiles to the Space Shuttle.

Following on from the Starfighter adhesive project, Marta was assigned to work on the Variable Sweep Laminar Flow Flight experiment. The test aircraft this time was an appropriated US Navy F-14 Tomcat fighter aircraft. The initiative entailed the attachment of aerofoil structures over the wing of the Tomcat or 'gloves' to better understand the underlying reasons for a natural laminar or smoother airflow over the wings. This represented a pivotal project for Marta - as one of the assigned flight engineers she would ride in the backseat of the F-14 Tomcat.

Nine years of working as a successful operational engineer led to her first project management role on the General Dynamics F-16XL. This was the Supersonic Laminar Flow Control project. The F-16XL was one of two special prototypes developed for the military and eventually handed over to NASA for further research. Marta was instrumental in identifying extensive runs of laminar flow occurring over the F-16XL's delta wing during supersonic flight.

The premise behind Martha's pioneering activities was to develop technologies to lessen the sonic boom effect of supersonic airliners of the future. New wing and airframe designs that take advantage of the natural laminar smooth airflow are likely not to disturb people who live under flight paths frequented by such high-speed future aeroplanes. Marta indicated that the F-16XL delta wing shape was a glove fit for the project, as its shape would be very similar to supersonic civilian airliners of the future.

In 1991 Marta entered the history books by flying aboard the SR-71 Blackbird former spy plane as the first female crewmember.

> ## More events In 1991
>
> ■ **Lithuania, Estonia, and Latvia win independence from USSR (Aug. 25); US recognizes them**
>
> ■ **Solar Eclipse of record totality occurs.**

However, her mission was not to spy on enemy missile silos or airfields. Acting as navigator, she performed aerodynamic, propulsion, thermal and sonic boom related experiments from the cramped rear seat. Martha would be garbed in the same bulky spacesuit worn by active duty personnel for all high performance missions in the Blackbird. NASA used three SR-71 aircraft to assist with high-speed and high-altitude aeronautical experiments. All three were on temporary loan from the United States Air Force, and following the test deployment the trio were retired and relegated to history.

The SR-71 is a sacred relic of the cold war, designed and manufactured under a shroud of secrecy at Lockheed's Skunk Works facility in Burbank California. The high speed and high operating altitude meant that the plane was invulnerable to missile attack or being intercepted by enemy fighters. In its hey day of active service from 1964 to 1998 a total of 4,000 missiles were launched at Blackbirds without success. The plane was quicker than the human eye. The unique airframe with its flattened fuselage gave a very minimal radar profile or signature and as such it was difficult to detect. However, despite all the stealthy technologies integrated into the airframe, flying at Mach 3.2 would heat up the outer skin of the aircraft due to compression and friction. This would show up on infrared as a flaming comet streaking across the sky. Furthermore the aeroplane was not immune to radar detection. However, such shortcomings were irrelevant, as at the time there existed no weapons systems capable of downing the triple-sonic plane. For this reason it required no guns or defensive missiles of its own to ward off potential threats. Because of the nature of its high-speed flight and exposure to extreme temperatures much of the airframe was composed of titanium. Ironically the metal was imported from the former Soviet Union, the same country over which the Blackbird would cruise and spy with impunity.

When not flying at three times the speed of sound, Marta exercised her aerospace engineering expertise by building flyable aero-batic aircraft. A certified flight instructor, Marta participated in numerous aerobatic competitions over a twenty-year period. Her husband, also an engineer who had worked on the SR-71 project, shared her enthusiasm for home built aircraft.

Marta had been a member of the US Unlimited Aerobatic team and also served as its team manager. She and her husband had built the Giles 300 used in the many Unlimited team displays. Martha was flying the Giles during a practice session in September 2005 in Yukon, Oklahoma in preparation for the US National Aerobatic Championships when tragedy struck. Her aircraft experienced a structural fault, which led to a fatal crash close to the Clarence E Page Municipal Airport. It was suggested that the fault was such that it incapacitated Marta, causing the aeroplane to plummet uncontrollably earthward. She did not survive the ensuing crash. A memorial service was held at NASA's Dryden operations where she had risen to the rank of chief engineer to assume the directorship of many projects.

Prior to her untimely passing aged just 48, Marta received the NASA Exceptional Service Medal in 1996 "for exceptional service in flight operations and project management in support of several national flight research programs." She was also awarded the Aerospace Educator Award in 1998 from Women in Aerospace and in 1992 was awarded the Arthur C. Fleming Award in the Scientific Category.

Marta Bohn-Meyer was an exceptional engineer who strived to uncover the secrets of supersonic flight through the use of many exotic fighter planes and experimental airframes. Her tireless and dedicated efforts yielded many breakthroughs in the field of natural laminar flows. She subscribed to the ethos that the sonic boom of fast jet flying could be eradicated and her vision was to translate that belief into cutting edge technologies.

Not too far in the future the skies will likely be ruled by silent, high flying dart shapes conveying many hundreds of passengers at close to 2,000 mph. The creation of such a peaceful world of hypersonic air travel would represent Marta's enduring legacy.

1992

ROBERTA LYNN BONDAR (CANADA) 1945 –

"The intriguing planet from afar held new wonders of patterns without texture beneath that canopy of blue green. If I had been able to reach outside of the orbiting spacecraft with my hand, surely I would have felt the layers of colours that define our Earth."

Roberta Bondar, *Touching the Earth*, 2004

A trained physician, scientist, astronaut and photographer, Dr Roberta Lynn Bondar's dream of becoming an astronaut became a step closer to reality when she was selected from 4,000 other hopeful Canadians by the National Research Council. The maple leaf flag was stitched on the shoulder of her spacesuit and she was ready to blast off into the unknown.

Roberta Bondar was born on December 4th 1945 in Sault Ste.Marie, Ontario Canada. In 1992 she became Canada's first female astronaut and achieved the mantle of being the first neurologist in space. Spearheading groundbreaking research in the field of space medicine, an illustrious career at NASA was almost assured. An adventurer at heart, Dr Bondar holds a private pilot's licence in addition to being a certified parachutist and scuba diver.

As a child, Roberta was always enchanted by the notion of flying. She was particularly taken by a bird's innate ability to fly, longing to soar skywards herself and view the planet from a much loftier perspective. The wonders of science also captivated the inquisitive and distinctly precocious Roberta. She would spend untold hours in her father's basement conducting her own chemistry experiments.

From science fact to fiction, she delighted in the silver screen adventures of "Flash Gordon" and imagined herself as an astronaut exploring her neighbourhood as if it were a new frontier. The US Mercury and Apollo missions further fuelled her ambition of one day reaching for the stars as a spacewoman.

Before joining the US National Aeronautics and Space Administration (NASA) Roberta travelled the long academic road to amass an incredible array of credentials in the biological sciences. Her scholastic brilliance was to shine early at the Sir James Dunn High School in her native Ontario. She studied zoology and agricul-

ture at the University of Guelph graduating with a BSc in 1968. She went on to complete an MSc in experimental pathology from the University of Ontario in 1971. This was followed by a doctorate in neurobiology from the University of Toronto in 1974, and culminated with a medical degree from McMaster University in 1977.

In 1983 she was amongst a select group of six Canadians earmarked for the Space Shuttle programme. Roberta, along with her fellow countrymen, was in the first group pitched by Canada's National Research Council (NRC) as official astronaut candidates representing the newly created Canadian Space Agency. Roberta, the only women to be selected, joined the ranks of NASA's astronaut corps in 1984.

Like many of her predecessors she was subjected to the time honoured centrifuge and weightlessness tests as well as flight instruction on the T-38 trainer jet.

The Challenger disaster of 1986 delayed her assignment to a shuttle mission. The entire programme was halted indefinitely pending the outcome of a presidential commission investigation. Roberta turned down an offer of a flight and protracted stay on the Russian Mir Space Station to investigate the effects of zero gravity on the physiology of women.

Both patience and foresight rewarded her when in 1990 she was officially designated as payload specialist slotted to fly on the shuttle Discovery. She would be taking part in the first International Microgravity Laboratory Mission (IML-1) using the Spacelab module. The purpose built laboratory habitat module carried in the shuttle's cargo bay was designed to test the effects of gravity on materials and organisms.

Roberta blasted off in the Discovery designated as STS-42 on January 22 1992, embarking on an historical mission that would last over eight days. As a member of the Spacelab team, she was entrusted by no less than 14 countries to perform experiments within the microgravity environment. This was to be her first and

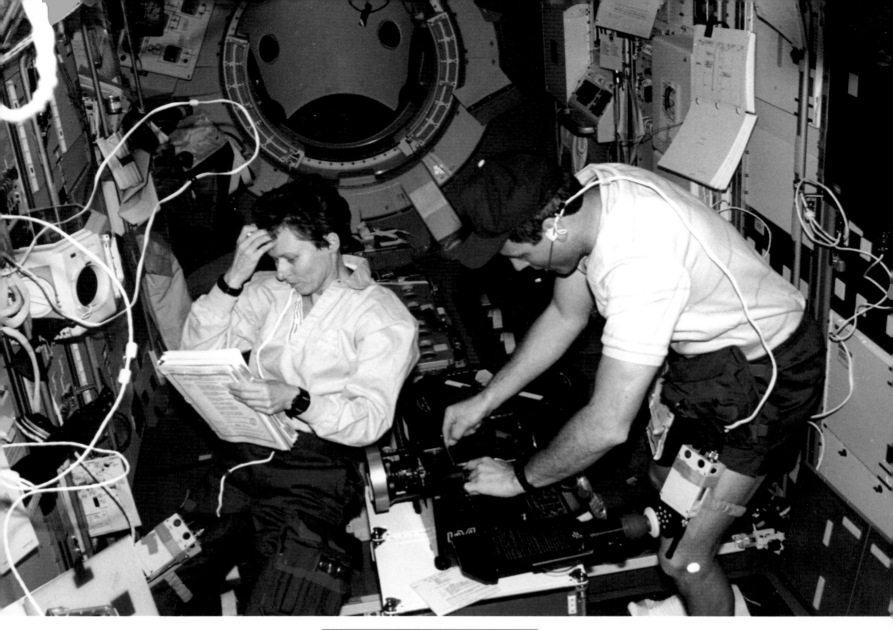

last mission on the shuttle. She the retired from the astronaut corps to focus on her research studies.

Armed with much empirical evidence and data collated from over 24 shuttle missions, Roberta would be instrumental in leading a dedicated team of international researchers for over a decade at NASA in its analysis. Their prime goal was to determine the damaging effects of prolonged exposure to space and microgravity (weightlessness) on human physiology. The aim was to comprehend the underlying mechanisms, which enabled the body to repair itself following such protracted periods in outer space. This would give an indication as to how well the human frame would prevail in the event of future deep space endeavours, such as a mission to Mars or prolonged periods on a space station.

Roberta's zero-g experiments and subsequent research with other internationally renowned medical experts at NASA inevitably contributed much to the field of neurology. The body of evidence led to the examination of earth bound illnesses such as stroke and Parkinson's disease and how to exploit the possible natural mechanisms for recuperation. The techniques she developed at NASA have been used in several clinical studies conducted by research institutions and teaching university hospitals.

Possessing a deep passion for the natural environment, Dr Bondar serves as advisor to both corporations and the Canadian government on environmental concerns. She was also honoured

Events In 1992

- The US FAA approves a helicopter rating for a pilot based solely on flight simulator performance for the first time

- Bush and Yeltsin proclaim a formal end to the Cold War

with the patronage of UNESCOs International Year of Planet Earth, which continues through 2010.

An accomplished photographer, Roberta developed her interest from both her father and uncle. She perfected her photographic skills at university and developed her own colour techniques in photo microscopy. Her flight in the space shuttle permitted her to take many pictures from the orbiting vantage. In 1994 she recounted her astronaut experiences in one of her photographic essay books "Touching the Earth."

For her lifelong dedication to the sciences and unparalleled achievements, Dr Bondar holds a record of 24 honorary doctorates from American and Canadian institutions. She was awarded the NASA Space medal and inducted into the International Women's Forum Hall of Fame and Canadian Medical Hall of Fame. TIME magazine named her as one of "North America's Best Explorers" for 2003. Respected and revered in her native Canada, she was made Officer of the Order of Canada in 1992. She also branched into the field of motivational speaking and television broadcasting.

Her desire for exploration of the new frontier was made possible by both her intellectual prowess and overpowering sense of adventure. Hunched over a microscope would have been satisfying enough for most scientists. But looking at the Earth through the portal of a spaceship represented the ultimate laboratory experience for Dr Roberta Lynn Bondar.

1992

MAE JEMISON (USA) 1956 –

The first African-American woman to fly into space on board the space shuttle Endeavour.

t is a testament to the power of her vision that Dr Mae Carol Jemison watched *Star Trek* as a child and believed she could carve out the Uhura role for herself. She told CNN: "What was really great about *Star Trek* when I was growing up is not only did they have Lt. Uhura played by Nichelle Nichols as a technical officer – she was African." On September 12, 1992, aged 35, Jemison bypassed the final frontier to become the first African-American woman to fly into space on board the space shuttle Endeavour.

Jemison was born in Decatur, Alabama on October 17, 1956, but spent most of her childhood in Chicago. Her father worked for a charity and her mother was an elementary school teacher. Speaking to the Stanford Star in 1996 she explained what powerful role models her parents had been: "My mother always told me to go find out the information myself. She was very directive, in the sense of 'it's your responsibility', sort of like those people who tell you to go look up a word in the dictionary when you don't know how to spell it."

In 1992 she told Ebony magazine about her utter determination to be a scientist, even from an early age. She refused to let anyone dissuade her from pursuing a career in science and said: "In kindergarten, my teacher asked me what I wanted to be when I grew up, and I told her a scientist. She said, 'Don't you mean a nurse?' Now, there's nothing wrong with being a nurse, but that's not what I wanted to be."

Jemison is multi-skilled. She is reported to speak Japanese, Russian and Swahili fluently, and not only is she a doctor and scientist, but she was a good enough dancer to consider taking it up as a profession. She started dancing lessons aged nine and took African dance, ballet, jazz, modern and even Japanese dancing. During her final year in college, she was torn between heading to New York to go to medical school or training to

become a professional dancer. According to the New York Times her mother told her, "You can always dance if you're a doctor, but you can't doctor if you're a dancer."

Jemison was only 16 when she started at Stanford University in 1973. She graduated four years later with a BS in chemical engineering and a BA in African and Afro-American Studies. According to the New York Times she experienced some prejudice there because of her race and gender. "Some professors would just pretend I wasn't there. I would ask a question and a professor would act as if it was just so dumb, the dumbest question he had ever heard. Then, when a white guy would ask the same question, 'That's a very astute observation,' the professor would say."

However, she is quick to point out that she should not be seen as a total pioneer. "When I'm asked about the relevance to Black people of what I do, I take that as an affront. It presupposes that Black people have never been involved in exploring the heavens, but this is not so. Ancient African empires – Mali, Songhai, Egypt – had scientists and astronomers. The fact is that space and its resources belong to all of us, not to any one group."

Jemison earned her medical degree in 1981 from Cornell Medical College, where she continued with her dance lessons at the Alvin Ailey American Dance Company. She later built a dance studio in her home. She has subsequently choreographed and produced several shows of modern jazz and African dance.

When she graduated she joined the Peace Corps from 1983 to 1985 in Liberia and Sierra Leone. She returned to the US in 1985 and worked as a general practitioner in California, where she studied engineering courses. In 1983, inspired by Sally Ride, she applied to the National Aeronautics and Space Administration (NASA) to train as an astronaut. She was one of fifteen candidates accepted from over 2,000 applicants.

More events In 1992

■ **The European Commission approves three new regulations to liberalize air travel within the European Union. EU airlines are gradually given unlimited rights to serve airports in other member states, with the final round of reforms complete by April 1997.**

■ **Flt Lt Nicky Smith becomes the RAF's first female helicopter pilot**

the Scholastic education project. The children were unafraid to ask the questions adults might want to know, but shy away from, such as: "When you are taking off in the space shuttle, what does it feel like?" Jemison replied: "It takes about eight minutes to get from the Kennedy Space Center into orbit. During the last four minutes, you feel a lot of pressure across your chest. You feel like you weigh about three times what you weigh on Earth. We orbit Earth at about 260 miles above the surface."

They also probed her psyche and asked her about the biggest challenge she had faced. She responded that: "The biggest challenge is to overcome the things in yourself that keep you from moving forward. When you do that, then dealing with challenges outside yourself becomes easier." She also gave tips for girls pursuing their goals. "I think people have to stop using the word dream, because it implies something you can't do. I like to say: 'What do you intend to do?' So, the question becomes: 'How will you do what you intend to do?'" She also told them her motto is "Purpose."

Jemison's work with NASA included launch support activities at the Kennedy Space Center in Florida. She was in the first class of astronauts selected after the Challenger accident in 1986 and flew her only space shuttle mission from September 12 to 20, 1992. She was a mission specialist on STS-47, collaboration between the United States and Japan that included 44 scientists. Jemison investigated why bones become weaker during space flight. She logged 190 hours, 30 minutes, 23 seconds in space.

She left NASA in 1993 to start her own company. The Jemison Group develops science and technology for daily life. She founded an offshoot in 1999, the BioSentient Corp, which is an aim to develop a portable device that allows mobile monitoring of the involuntary nervous system. This may allow patients to monitor and control their physiology and become a possible treatment for anxiety and stress.

She is a passionate educator and in 1994 founded the Dorothy Jemison Foundation for Excellence in honour of her mother. One of its projects is The Earth We Share (TEWS), an international science camp where students, ages 12 to 16, work to solve current global problems, like "How Many People Can the Earth Hold?" In 2001 she participated in an online discussion with hundreds of students from

Jemison is a Professor-at-Large at Cornell University, an Inductee of the National Women's Hall of Fame and the National Medical Association Hall of Fame, and a winner of the Kilby Science Award. In 2001 she wrote her autobiography, "Find Where the Wind Goes: Moments From My Life?" On a more light-hearted note she appeared on an episode of Star Trek: The Next Generation in 1993. She is a big fan of the show and the only real astronaut to have appeared on the programme.

She evidently lives by her own philosophy: "Never be limited by other people's limited imaginations...If you adopt their attitudes, then the possibility won't exist because you'll have already shut it out ... You can hear other people's wisdom, but you've got to re-evaluate the world for yourself."

BARBARA HARMER (UK) 1954 –

The Supersonic hairdresser who lived the dream

There aren't too many former hairdressers who can claim to have flown the most iconic supersonic civilian aircraft to rule the skies. Barbara Harmer is quite possibly unique in that respect. On March 25th 1993, the British Airways pilot entered the history books by becoming the first woman to be rated to fly Concorde

At just 39, Senior First Officer Barbara Harmer had achieved what many male pilots could only dream of doing. In 1993 she flew her first scheduled Concorde flight from London Heathrow to New York's John F Kennedy airport. The highlight of her astonishing career was to fly the venerable supersonic passenger aircraft. It was a far cry from her early days of curling tongs and brushing in hair dye.

Her story began in the seaside town of Bognor Regis, West Sussex where she was born in 1954. Barbara left school early at fifteen with the goal of becoming a hairdresser in her home town. However, six years later she found herself huddled over a radar screen at Gatwick Airport serving as an air traffic controller. This was her first introduction to commercial aviation, directing the stacked planes during the intensely demanding shifts.

It was during this time that she felt the need to scratch an academic itch. She embarked on studying for the A-levels that she wished she had accomplished. Getting hold of syllabus material and the recommended text books, she tutored herself in Geography, English Law, Constitutional Law and Politics.

Already directing aeroplanes as an air traffic controller, Barbara wanted to experience what it was like to be directed herself. So she learned to fly. She gained a private pilot's licence and started to accumulate flying hours. She became an adept pilot, and was proficient enough to become a flying instructor. She went on to tutor other fledgling pilots at her local Goodwood Flying School. She then made the jump to aerobatics instructor.

Not content with just being an instructor on light aircraft, Barbara took the next logical step of gaining her commercial pilot's licence. From hairdresser to air traffic controller, and now potentially an airline pilot, Barbara was facing an open sky of opportunities.

Rated now to fly passengers, she landed a job with a commuter airline called Genair. In 1984 she joined British Caledonian, a mainstream airline established during the 1970's. She started flying British Aircraft Corporation BAC-111 aircraft on short haul routes, before transitioning to the larger McDonnell Douglas DC-10 on long haul. British Caledonian ran into financial difficulties during the mid eighties before being taken over by British Airways (BA) in December 1987. The BC crews were absorbed and Barbara donned the uniform of a BA pilot.

She furtively nurtured the ambition of flying the UK national carrier's delta-winged flagship supersonic airliner. At the time BA employed over 3,000 pilots, of whom 60 were women. Given that just over two percent of the serving aircrew was female, Barbara felt her chances of flying Concorde were slim. Gender concerns predominated her thoughts.

Only a select few highly capable pilots were recruited from the pool of aircrew to undergo the rigorous six month training regime that certified them to fly Concorde. In 1992, Barbara could hardly contain her excitement at being selected to undergo the costly training to fly the supersonic airliner.

Barbara's historic flight in 1993 qualified her as the world's first female pilot to fly Concorde. This, and her first excursion to New York, attracted a blaze of publicity, elevating her to celebrity status. The intense public scrutiny on the former hairdresser may have been a little overwhelming. But Barbara took it in her professional stride, flying the Concorde with immaculate precision for a number of years afterwards.

In the challenging times of the post 9/11 tipping point, the writing was on the wall for Concorde. There were several factors. Rising maintenance costs; the loss of an Air France Concorde in July 2000 on take-off from Charles De Gaulle airport, plus the prospect of expensive overhaul requirements, conspired towards the demise of the aircraft. In 2003 the entire Concorde fleet flown by both Air France and BA was formally retired, following a number of celebratory tribute flights.

The last UK flight took place on 26th November 2003. BA Concorde G-BOAF landed at Filton in Bristol, its manufacturing birthplace. All the aircraft were donated to museums, and examples are displayed in Barbados and New York, which were two main destination points for the limited Concorde routes flown.

Events In 1993

■ First humans cloned. Cells taken from defective human embryos that were to be discarded in infertility clinic are grown in vitro and develop up to 32-cell stage and then are destroyed.

Concorde (SST) was a joint venture development between the French airframe manufacturer Aerospatiale and the British Aerospace Corporation.

It was the most successful of supersonic airliners, despite the high investment made by both the British and French governments. The only other comparable aircraft was the Russian Tupolev TU-144, which flew at Mach 2 but a series of unfortunate crashes resulted in its early retirement.

Concorde first flew in 1969, and officially debuted in 1976 flying with national carriers British Airways (BA) and Air France. National prestige prompted both the French and British governments to subsidise the operation of Concorde heavily. A total of 20 Concordes were built, with 14 entering service. BA operated seven of them throughout the aircraft's incredible 27-year reign of the commercial skies. Concorde was powered by four afterburning Rolls Royce Olympus jet fighter engines originally designed for the TSR-2 jet fighter. Given the right temperature conditions, the airliner can reach a top speed of Mach 2 at 60,000 feet. The Mach number would be prominently displayed on an LED counter in order for the passengers to appreciate the speed of the aircraft. The streamlined profile mated to the quartet of high performance jet engines allowed Concorde to traverse the Atlantic to arrive in New York from London or Paris in a little over four hours.

a Harmer retains the poignant title as the only woman to have aircraft as part of scheduled operations. The other notable have commanded Concorde was the French aviatrix Jacqueline owever, her motivation was perhaps just to experience the s part of her record-breaking career in fast jet aviation, and not ir France per se.

or so aircrew in BA were permitted to fly the aircraft to exacting Barbara was lucky enough to belong to that club of elite pilots, her talents as a pilot, plus the high-octane determination that ambition.

flies for British Airways, flying long haul in the rather more ng 777. As guest speaker at the annual Christmas gathering of Women's Pilots' Association in 2005, she remarked on the vast handling characteristics of the 777, when compared to

her cements the uniqueness of the revolutionary jet airliner, technology seen only on jet fighters of that era.

Harmer's story is inspiring and she has gained much public se of her incredible ascent into the upper stratosphere of

favourite for motivational and inspirational presentations. She actively conducts role model talks and after dinner speaking at both formal business events and informal social gatherings.

Like many of the incredible women featured in this book, Barbara shares a penchant for the next challenge. From the skies to the high seas she is also an accomplished qualified RYA Commercial Offshore Yacht Master and commanded the 'Concorde Crew' on several international yachting events.

Flying at 60,000 feet nearing Mach 2 was perhaps the most thrilling time for Barbara. She cites one memorable moment stemming from her time in the cockpit. She had the honour of flying the Manchester United football team in Concorde to Barcelona for the Champions' League final. It was a proud moment of history for her, the thousands of well wishers waving flags and turning out to wish the team luck on the monumental flight.

A former trimmer of hair, Barbara Harmer was destined to be at the cutting edge of aviation. Not bad for a former hairdresser who hails from a seaside resort in West Sussex. Concorde may have departed, but the roar of its engines, sleek sensual lines and raw energy still echoes through the

1994

LIEUTENANT KARA S. HULTGREEN (USA) 1965 - 1994

In 1993 the US Congress had lifted the ban on women serving to fly combat missions in all branches of the armed services. Kara Hultgreen took advantage of this to live her dream.

n 1994 Lieutenant Jeannie Flynn, call sign 'Tally', was the first woman in the United States Air Force qualified to fly the F-15E Strike Eagle. In that same year Lieutenant Kara Spears Hultgreen call sign 'Revlon' trapped the number three arresting wire on the flight deck of the USS Constellation to become the US Navy's first fully qualified F-14 Tomcat pilot. In a few short months her dream was to end in tragedy.

Kara Hultgreen was born on 5th October 1965 in Greenwich Connecticut. She spent most of her early childhood in Chicago. In 1973 her father relocated the entire family to Toronto, Canada. Being the youngest of three siblings, Kara demonstrated a competitive and obstinate streak from a very early age. Her parents separated in 1976 with Kara moving with her mother, Sally, who returned to her hometown of San Antonio in 1981.

Attending the Alamo Heights High School, Kara dreamed about becoming an astronaut. In this manner she was hardly any different from other pioneers such as Eileen Collins who would be the first woman to serve as pilot and then commander on the Space Shuttle programme. No doubt influenced by the early Gemini and Apollo space programmes, Kara surmised the need for a pilot's licence in order to reach the new frontier. She thought the other pathway to the stars would be to acquire a PhD. However, the accomplished basketball and tennis player had a greater affinity for speed than she did with academics. This penchant would later gravitate her towards something she described as a "little pointier and with an after-burner."

Kara flourished academically. Following high school, she secured an appointment at the Naval Academy in Annapolis. However, she was unsuccessful in attaining a numerical spot, which would have facilitated her passage into naval aviation, and the opportunity to fly carrier-based fighters. Her end goal was still to become an astronaut. Undeterred by this setback, Kara opted to study aerospace engineering at the University of Texas.

Graduating in 1987, she enlisted in the US Navy as an aviation officer candidate at Pensacola Naval Air Station (NAS) in Florida. Upon graduating from her class she transferred to Corpus Christi NAS in Texas for the purpose of initial flight training. Kara made the grade and her wings of gold to be selected for jet pilot training. Her ambition was to fly the F-18 Hornet fighter, but she was awarded the opportunity to clamber into the bulbous cockpit of the EA-6A Intruder. She transitioned into the electronic warfare version of the A-6 Intruder bomber at Key West NAS. By now her call sign was 'Hulk.' Lithe, feminine and distinctly athletic, Kara's superhero title was as a consequence of her Hultgreen surname.

The A-6 Intruder has a long history with the US Navy and Marine aviation squadrons stretching back to the 1960's. The aircraft was produced by Grumman Aerospace as an all weather attack bomber and saw much action during the Vietnam War. The A-6 had an impressive bomb carrying capability for a carrier based jet bomber and was last deployed in action during Operation Desert Storm in 1991. The aircraft was finally phased out from the US Navy and Marine units in 1991, replaced by Kara's favourite jet fighter the F-18.

The EA-6A Intruder that Kara had been assigned to fly was one of only 28 aircraft in the US Navy inventory. The aircraft, like its bomber cousin, had no defensive armaments but was purely an electronic counter measures plane packed with technology to confuse enemy radars. The tail fin carried a large bump, which housed much of its electronic warfare capabilities.

Although Kara was a pilot on the Intruder, she still yearned to fly a true jet fighter packing an internal gun and a means to go beyond the subsonic speed of her assigned steed. To this end she continued her requests for transition to the coveted F-18 Hornet, each denial fuelling her persistence to try again.

Kara excelled on the EA-6A mission. In one instance in 1992 she successfully landed an EA-6A with a compromised and inoperative landing gear leg strut. On final approach to Pensacola Naval Air Station she skimmed the runway, alighting the crippled jet without incident to garner much applause and praise for her flying skills.

In 1993 the rules were relaxed and women could compete with equally able men for the fighter cockpit. Kara's persistence paid off and she was finally allocated to a fighter. However it was not the F-18 she craved for. The US Navy cleared her to take the helm of the mighty F-14 Tomcat in 1993.

Twenty-seven tonnes of raw fighting energy, the F-14 Tomcat was a $40 million carrier based jet fighter. Almost 60 feet in length, the Tomcat became the US Navy's mainstay fighter in 1972, gaining international fame through the 1986 movie 'Top Gun' starring Tom Cruise. Flying at almost twice the speed of sound, this legendary gunfighter bristles with an arsenal of defensive missiles and can also serve as a precision laser guided bomber. Manufactured by Grumman Aerospace, the Tomcat hails from the same stable as

Kara's former mount the EA-6A. Variable geometry or 'swing-wings' permit transition from subsonic to supersonic flight, automatically moving during intense high-G combat manoeuvrings. The F-14 was finally replaced in 2006, its mission assumed by the multi-role and much lighter F/A-18 Super Hornet.

Kara embraced her F-14 assignment with great enthusiasm, becoming the first woman to train on the formidable fighter at Miramar NAS in San Diego, also dubbed 'Fighter Town USA'. Her official qualification on the F-14 was achieved on 31st July 1994 when she landed successfully aboard the USS Constellation. She had entered the history books as the first-ever female F-14 pilot cleared for carrier based operations.

Trained and cleared hot, Kara was assigned to the Black Lions F-14 squadron aboard the USS Abraham Lincoln preparing for deployment to the Persian Gulf that year. At five foot ten inches tall, and brash with all the expected bluster of a fighter pilot, Kara's call sign of 'Hulk' was appropriate given that she had to wrestle with a prowling, snarling, and predatory heavy weight such as the Tomcat. The 'Hulk' could bench press over 200 lbs. However, when she arrived one day in the squadron ready room wearing makeup for a TV interview, her fellow fighter jocks adjusted her call sign to 'Revlon'.

On 25th October 1994, 'Revlon' was aligning her Tomcat on final landing approach to the USS Abraham Lincoln, sailing fifty miles from the shores of San Diego. Without warning her port engine failed, with all the burden of keeping the 27 tonne fighter aloft now switched to the still functioning right jet engine. Mere yards from the stern of the carrier deck, Kara valiantly fought to control the stricken Tomcat, but the heavy, unresponsive fighter inevitably stalled. Her radar intercept officer seated behind ejected as the Tomcat plunged into the ocean. He survived the incident with minor injuries. Tragically Kara 'Revlon' Hultgreen ejected a fraction of a second too late and lost her life during the emergency egress.

Her body was recovered and she was buried with full military honours at Arlington National Cemetery. A memorial service was held at the San Antonio Country Club with a flypast of F-14 Tomcats in tribute to her service to the US Navy. Her flight suit, flying helmet, pilot wings and uniform were donated to the Smithsonian Institute.

Landing jet aircraft on carrier decks demands split second reaction times from pilots and support from landing officers guiding the fighters in to snag the arresting wires. Carrier based operations are both exciting and challenging, creating aviators who are the stuff of legends. Being fraught with danger only the most skilled of pilots are entertained to command million dollar jet fighters.

Kara Spears Hultgreen represented the fighter elite, the first woman to tame the formidable F-14 Tomcat from the deck of an aircraft carrier. Indicative of her strength and determination, Kara, call sign 'Revlon,' strived and attained what was once thought impossible. Only fate conspired, preventing her from achieving further firsts beyond the age of 29 and joining the ranks of feted aviatrixes of the future.

Events In 1994

- South Africa holds first interracial national election. Nelson Mandela elected President
- Tom Hanks wins his second consecutive Best Actor Oscar. He won in 1993 for his role in Philadelphia and in 1994 for Forrest Gump.
- Russians attack secessionist Republic of Chechnya.

1994

JUDY LEDEN (UK) 1959 –

At 41,000 feet with eyes frozen shut and face badly frostbitten in temperatures of minus 87 degrees centigrade, there was nowhere to go but down for Judy Leden as she conquered the world hang gliding balloon drop altitude record.

Judy Leden is a super achiever. She is hang gliding and paragliding world champion, six times British women's hang gliding champion, the first woman to hang glide across the English Channel, holder of the world hang gliding balloon drop altitude record, and test pilot for the replica of Leonardo da Vinci's 500-year-old glider.

She was born near London in 1959 and took up hang gliding aged 19, while studying for a nursing degree at the Welsh National School of Medicine in Cardiff. She told Helen Krasner in an interview for Today's Pilot in 2006: "When I started, the only women I saw on the flying sites were with husbands and boyfriends – people had hardly ever seen a woman hang glider." This impeded her learning since the other pilots refused to talk technical with her, as they did not take her seriously.

By 1981 she had left university and bought her own hang glider. That year she entered her first competition. She told Krasner: "I came third and returned with my head full of new ideas, feeling overawed by just how much I had to learn."

Most people would see that as a chance to hit the books and improve their physical skills with a spot of cross-country flying. With few female competitors at the time to benchmark herself against, Judy consistently outperformed herself until in 1983 she gained her first world record – the women's open distance record, for a flight of 145 miles (233 kilometres). Her path was set. She entered more competitions and her passion took her all over the world.

In July 1987 she became women's world hang gliding champion for the first time. She was still holding down a full-time job as well and seeking sponsorship – unlike her male peers. In 1989 she

was dropped from a hot air balloon from 16,000 feet above Dover, so that she could hang glide across the English Channel. This is an incredibly brave thing to do. If she had been forced to land, she would almost certainly have died, as the weight of her equipment would have dragged her underwater.

Her adventures became more extreme. Two years later she conquered fire when she became the first person to hang-glide from the summit of Cotopaxi, Ecuador, an active volcano. In May 1994, she flew a microlight from England to Jordan, an expedition of around 2,250 miles (3,621 kilometres). The adventure, named "Flight for Life," was planned for Judy's friend, Yasmin Saudi, who was dying of lung cancer. Judy and her friend microlight pilot Ben Ashman, worked on a plan to get Yasmin from London-to-Amman, sitting in the back seat of Ben's microlight when she got better. Sadly Yasmin never did recover, but gave her blessing to the project, which eventually raised £70,000 for the Cancer Research Campaign and for the new cancer hospital in Jordan.

Judy and Ben took off from Blenheim Palace without permission to fly over Bulgaria. Unfortunately, they ran out of fuel in Bulgaria and were forced to land at a military airfield, where they were greeted with coffee and fuel. The next time they ran out of gas was in Syria, where they made an emergency landing in a remote field seemingly undetected. However, they had been rumbled and were met at Damascus, by an irate committee who knew the pair had flown over their secret missile silos with cameras. They were allowed to go and directed to follow a flight path of 24,000 feet (7,315 metres) over the desert. Judy and Ben could climb to 6,000 feet (1,829 metres) tops. Speaking to the Sunday Times in 1994, Judy said: "We escaped. We took off and dived down to 30 feet, virtually skimming the tops of the sand dunes. They kept asking us where we were. 'East', we told them,

More events In 1994

- Israel signs accord with Palestinians and peace treaty with Jordan (October 17th).

- 95 million viewers watch O. J. Simpson and Al Cowlings drive along Los Angeles freeways in history's most exciting low-speed chase.

flying due south as fast as the engines would go. It was a risk, they could have shot us down, but we had no option." They made it and were met by an ecstatic welcoming committee in Amman airport.

Incredible heights

Her next major project was her epic balloon drop flight in 1994 climbing to 41,000 feet (12,500 metres) over Jordan hitched to Per Linstrand's hot-air balloon and then making her own way down. "I could see the curvature of the earth," she said afterwards. "I could see the whole of Jordan and Israel, and a large part of Egypt and Saudi Arabia from up there." It took three hours before she reached the ground. Her feet froze and she is likely one of the few people to have suffered frostbite in the desert.

Judy continued to break records, and was women's world champion again in 1991. She went on to win the women's world paragliding championship in 1995. In 2003 she achieved the women's paragliding distance record. That same year a record number of people watched her on television, test-flying a replica of Leonardo da Vinci's 500-year-old design for a glider. She said: "It was a bit scary when they said I shouldn't fly any higher than I was prepared to fall, as the glider would probably break up with my weight, but it proved to be every bit as strong as a modern hang-glider." According to Judy she could control the up-and-down movement well, but found it difficult to steer as she flew it about 300 feet (91 metres) at a maximum height of 30 feet (nine metres).

In 1995 she and her husband Chris Dawes had organised an expedition to Patagonia to fly with Andean condors. She made a similar expedition nine years later, making a film about her experiences. She told GA magazine's Pat Malone: "Hang gliding is the closest you can get to flying like a bird. The ultimate aim is to become a bird, attuning your eyes, ears and nose to sense the rising air that keeps you aloft. After a while you develop a 'bird-brain', where you sense the movements in the air." During the course of

that project, she broke a bone in her foot, as well as chipping a bone in her wrist in the turbulent conditions. However, she did get to fly with the condors. The huge birds circled around dwarfing her little machine. She wrote a book about her experiences: "Flying with Condors."

Judy was awarded an MBE Medal in 1989 for her services to hang gliding. She is also the holder of numerous other awards, including the Hussein Medal for Excellence for her flight to Jordan, and the Jordanian Star of the First Order.

She has flown almost every type of aircraft at some time or another, including hang gliders, paragliders and microlights fairly regularly. She also gained a seaplane rating and has done some gliding. She and Chris run Airways Airsports, a flying school based at Darley Moor airfield, in the Peak District (www.airways-airsports.com). Students can learn hang gliding, paragliding, and microlight flying, as well as more unusual forms of flight such as paramotoring and powered hang gliding. In 2001 Judy devised a new method of teaching hang gliding, based on tandem flying with an instructor, and using a flexwing microlight to tow the hang glider to the cloudbase. This means people can enjoy hang gliding, regardless of strength and fitness without having to lug heavy gear up a hill. Judy has also taught some disabled people to fly using this method, which has enabled wheelchair users to solo more easily. She is a patron of the British Disabled Flying Association and president of Flyability. She and Chris also have an airpark in France and Spain. Their children have been flying from an early age and often fly tandem with their parents.

Although there is likely no other British woman who has floated over a volcano, flown up close and personal with condors and entertained King Hussein of Jordan in her living room. Judy is still relatively unknown outside of aviation circles in her native country. Given her past exploits, that could possibly change…

1994

DR CHIAKI MUKAI (JAPAN) 1952 –

Dr Chiaki Mukai has garnered much affection and respect from her native Japan. She became the nation's first female astronaut to fly on the Space Shuttle programme in 1994. Inspiring many in her country, she is much revered. A proud nation, the Japanese are delighted when a countryman or woman is able to cultivate an honourable impression on a global scale.

The Space Shuttle had been orbiting the earth in the second half of its flight when it was time for the crew to rise. Crew members awoke to the gentle chimes of a Japanese song in honour of payload specialist Dr Chiaki Mukai. In response to the call of "Ohayou Discovery (in Japanese)" from the ground, she called back the greeting 'Ohayougozaimasu'

Chiaki was born in Tatebayashi, Gunma Prefecture on May 6th, 1952. Her family moved to Tokyo where she attended the prestigious Keio High School for girls. Gifted academically, she had a passion for the sciences excelling in all of her subjects. Following high school graduation in 1971 the exemplary student won a place at Keio University to study medicine. She achieved her ambition of becoming a doctor in 1977, whereupon Chiaki rotated between a number of specialities before focusing on general surgery. She completed two residencies in surgery, one at Shizuoka and the other in Kanagawa prior to returning to Keio University Hospital to specialise in cardiovascular surgery.

It was at Keio University that she met her husband, fellow physician Dr Mukai Makio whom she married in 1982. Her career as a doctor leapt forward during the eighties, following her board certification as a cardiovascular surgeon in 1989. She was first promoted to chief resident and then assistant professor in the area of cardiovascular surgery at Keio. Not quite done with academics, Chiaki books again to gain a further degree in physiology.

A glittering a career as a successful medical practitioner gave her much prominence and respect within the profession. However another prominent organisation took note, none other than the National Space Development Agency of Japan (NASDA). The space agency had nominated her to serve as one of three payload specialists for the International Micro Gravity Laboratory missions on the space shuttle.

Established on October 1st 1969, NASDA is responsible for the development of rockets and satellite vehicles as well as astronaut training. Their

nomination had delighted the intrepid doctor. Chiaki was officially selected, making her one of three Japanese payload specialists ripe for training at the USNational Aeronautics and Space Administration (NASA). In 1987 Chiaki was whisked away to the Johnson Space Centre in Texas to join the astronaut corps.

Like many of her fellow astronauts in the making, Chiaki followed the same rigorous training regime. From experiencing the high G flight in the back of a T-38 Talon jet to the weightlessness in the 'Vomit Comet'. The latter is a specially adapted Boeing 707 executing a series of parabolic dives to create a zero g weightless environment. Chiaki would have also been schooled in deep-water survival techniques and familiarisation of working in the Spacelab J module. The module was designed to be accommodated in the payload bay of the shuttle for the purpose of microgravity experiments.

Chiaki was backup payload specialist on the September 1992 Endeavour mission designated as STS-47. This was the 50th Shuttle mission and the first joint venture mission between NASA and the Japanese NASDA using the Spacelab J module. The mission was particularly significant as Chiaki's payload specialist colleague Mamoru "Mark" Mohri was the first Japanese person in space. STS-47 also had the accolade of carrying the first African American woman astronaut and the first married couple on the same mission. The main objective was to conduct microgravity investigations in materials and life sciences in the Spacelab J module. Test subjects included the crew, a Japanese koi fish (carp), cultured animal and plant cells, chicken embryos, fruit flies, fungi and plant seeds, and frogs and frog eggs. About 35 of the experiments were sponsored by the NASDA agency.

Chiaki finally got her chance to fly on the space shuttle in July 1994 to enter the history books as the first Japanese woman to fly into space. Aboard the oldest shuttle in the fleet, the Columbia designated STS-65, she was part of the International Microgravity Laboratory (IML-2) mission. This was the second in a series of Spacelab flights designed to conduct research in a microgravity setting. The first IML flight took place in January

1992 on the Discovery with Dr Roberta Bondar, the first Canadian woman in space, overseeing many of the experiments on that mission. Chiaki performed a number of physiological experiments within the microgravity module associated with her field of cardiac medicine.

Then in April 1998, Chiaki was again to support the Columbia mission designated as STS-90 in the capacity of backup payload specialist. This mission highlight was the deployment of the Neurolab module. The Neurolab is a Spacelab module mission focusing on the effects of microgravity on the nervous system. The aim of Neurolab was to examine the mechanisms responsible for neurological and behavioural changes in space.

In her memorable second and final mission, Chiaki was selected to fly on the Discovery, STS-95 in October 1998. She became the first Japanese national to fly twice into space.

This shuttle excursion carried Senator John Glenn, a former US naval aviator and a member of the legendary Mercury 7 astronauts. He was the first American to orbit the Earth in 1962 in his Friendship 7 Mercury capsule. Establishing himself as the oldest ever astronaut, he referred to Chiaki as the person most likely to win a sumo tournament in outer space. He explained: "Not because of her figure, though. She has more energy than anyone I know of."

The intrepid Japanese doctor performed a number of medical experiments in the Spacehab module ensconced in the shuttle bay. The action-packed mission also involved the deployment of the Spartan solar observing spacecraft and the Hubble Space Telescope Orbital Systems test platform. The latter was to perform tests prior to the Hubble's upcoming service plans.

By the end of her final flight on the shuttle, Chiaki had accrued in excess of 566 hours in space. Credited with writing almost sixty publications, Dr Chiaki Mukai has also been honoured by the Society of Japanese Women Scientists with an Outstanding Service Award in 1996. The US Congress had paid tribute to her achievements with the "Special Congressional Recognition" award a year earlier. In 1995 she was bestowed with the prestigious The De La Vaux Medal from The Federation Aeronautique Internationale.

Representing the NASDA agency she has travelled the world over delivering lectures and talks about her space flight experiences. In 2003 she visited the San Pedro Sula Children's Museum in Honduras with its newly opened planetarium built with a Japanese grant. She endeavoured to inspire new emerging generations in Latin America to dream about becoming astronauts. There is a good chance she will. Her energy and courage has taken her all the way from a hospital theatre to a laboratory in outer space.

More events In 1994

■ Flt Lt Jo Salter is posted to No. 617 Squadron RAF (Tornado GR1Bs), the RAF's first female fast jet pilot

■ Thousands dead in Rwanda massacre

1996

SVETLANA KAPANINA
(RUSSIA) 1968 –

"Siberian Angel." Beautiful, mother of two - and fiercely competitive in the air, Svetlana Kapanina is one of the best aerobatic pilots the world has ever seen

Svetlana Kapanina stuns audiences all over the world with her spellbinding performances, throwing different types of aerobatic aircraft through the air. In 2006 she captivated the 40,000 plus crowd at "Warbirds over Wanaka" with her precision low-level flying in Rob Fry's demonstrator Sukhoi Su-29.

Svetlana was born in 1968 in Shchuchinsk, Republic of Kazakhstan. Her birthplace is famous in Russian aviation folklore. According to an article in Aero Australia magazine, the province, 200 km south-west of Moscow, is known as the "Cradle of Cosmonautics", because the great Russian space scientist, Konstantin E. Tsiolkovskiy, carried out his life-long research there and wrote his book, "Dreams of Earth and Sky."

In 1987 she graduated from medical school as a pharmacist.

The following year she started flying in Kurgan, by 1991 she was a member of the Russian Aerobatic Joint Crew and by 1995 she had graduated from Kaluga aeronautical technical school. It looked as though she never intended to devote her life to flying. However, her hobby has turned into serious work as a professional aerobatic pilot. It did not take her long to join the world's elite.

She is supremely fit and trains within the Russian national team structure. Every year she attends the resident training camp at Borki Airport, near Moscow. Pharmacy has gone out of the window. Today she lives in Moscow with her kick-boxer husband and two children. She explained how untypical their jobs are to the outside world. She said to Aero Australia at the Wanaka event: "For a husband to have a wife who is a pilot I think it is something very different in Russia."

Svetlana has always been keen on sport. She spent years training as a gymnast. This discipline, which includes many hours on the trampoline, may have contributed to her success. She was invited to join the Russian Aerobatic Joint Crew in 1991. The same year aged 23, she became the Absolute Aerobatic Champion of Russia and in 1993 she won silver at her first foray into international contests; the European Aerobatic Championships. She was awarded the medal "For Service to the Motherland" in 1995 and "Award of Honour" in 2002.

She frequently appears at events with outright World Champion Aerobatic pilot, Jurgis Kairys, whose engineering and piloting skills were recognised when he was asked to work with the Sukhoi Design Bureau (SDB) to develop the Sukhoi Su-26, 29 and 31 series of aerobatic aircraft, which have dominated the Unlimited World Aerobatics Championships in recent years.

In 1983, a group of young enthusiasts at Sukhoi Design Bureau were encouraged to develop a new aerobatic aeroplane. The resulting two-seat Su-29, just 50kg heavier than the single-seat Su-26/31 models, has a carbon composite rear fuselage.

Svetlana demonstrated it at Wanaka. She said she found the control forces rather heavier than those in her own Su-31. She required extra cushioning on the seat in order to reach the controls. The two-seater is designed to be flown from the rear seat in order to provide a superior visual perspective for the pilot and to keep the centre of gravity near its aft limit to give improved pitch response, more control authority, lighter control forces and flatter spin characteristics.

Clad in a single-layer, fire-retardant flight suit, Svetlana refused to wear a protective helmet or gloves. She was linked to the airshow public address system, so that visitors could hear conversations between Svetlana in flight and Jurgis giving encouragement on the ground. Jerry Mead, the commentator, asked her whether she was enjoying the view. Although she had the busiest workload during her display, she said: "It is nice and exciting... gives bigger adrenaline."

Svetlana continually demonstrates that she is one of the best female aerobatic pilots ever.

The Fédération Aéronautique Internationale (FAI) website lists her as five times overall aerobatics World Champion: 1996, 1998, 2001, 2003, 2005; and twice overall World Air Games Champion: in 1997, 2001. She finished fourth overall (including men) in 2005. She was also overall World Air Games Champion in 1997 and 2001.

In 1997, she received the Paul Tissandier Diploma from the (FAI). The Paul Tissandier Diploma, established in 1952, is named after Paul Tissandier, the secretary general of the FAI from 1919 to 1945. It is awarded to those who have served the cause of aviation in general, and sporting aviation in particular, by their work, initiative, and devotion or in other ways.

In 2005 the FAI also awarded her the Sabiha Gökçen Medal for her outstanding achievement in winning a fifth consecutive title as Women's World Aerobatics Champion in 2005.

She has won a total of 38 gold medals in World Aerobatic Championships.

The FAI, added to that impressive collection, by presenting her with the FAI medal for "Best Pilot of the Century". She is also a flight instructor and active in training young people to fly light aircraft.

Svetlana is the first pilot ever to win a World Champion title more than twice. In June 2006, she became the first woman to be ranked at number two overall, including men. Kapanina has become a legend in her own lifetime. Before her, only Betty Stewart (USA, 1980, 1982), Petr Jirmus (CZE, 1984, 1986) and Catherine Maunoury (FRA, 1988, 2000) have taken the World Championship twice.

Svetlana also flew at the MAKS airshow in Russia 2007. President Putin gave a speech at the event. He said: "Russia, which has recently got some new economic advantages, is paying very close attention to high technologies." After his speech, a determined Kapanina approached him.

She told journalists that she had said to him that aviation needed more financial support. She said: "I told the president that we had the best planes in the world, that we still have the best pilots in the world. But we are on our knees now, in particular the sports aviation. We need financial aid to recover."

With such a champion highlighting the sport, it is likely to remain on the radar for some years to come.

Events In 1996

- Britain alarmed by an outbreak of "mad cow" disease
- Approximately 45 million people are using the Internet
- Dolly the sheep, the first mammal to be successfully cloned from an adult cell, is born at the Roslin Institute in Midlothian, Scotland.

1998
PATRICIA YAPP SYAU YIN (MALAYSIA) 1977 –

"The future belongs to those who believe in the beauty of their dreams."
Eleanor Roosevelt. Quoted in support of Malaysia's first female fighter pilot's campaign to become the country's first female astronaut

Patricia Yapp Syau Yin never expected to come first in a popularity contest organised by one of Malaysia's national television channels. She said afterwards: "I didn't expect to win. I thought the winner of such contests would be someone from a corporate background. I hope this will open the public's eyes, especially women, that we can do anything we want if we have faith in ourselves. Gender is not an issue anymore."

A firm believer in promoting women's rights, Patricia Yapp Syau Yin was born and raised in Sandakan, Sabah. Her parents had high expectations of their daughter, the second of their three children and hoped she would become a piano teacher. However, she had other plans and wanted to fly aeroplanes from a young age.

Her elder brother Ignatius inspired her when he joined Malaysia Airlines as a cadet when she was 16 years old. She was bent on becoming a pilot, too, and pursued her dream. She told the Malaysian Star in 2007: "Many women are afraid to even think of becoming a pilot, for fear of having to endure the gruelling physical training. Actually, flying is not judged by muscle strength. It is more of mental preparedness and determination.

"Since I was young, I knew this was what I wanted to do. The fact that my brother, was a pilot with Malaysia Airlines, was also one of the reasons for my determination." Her parents were reported to be initially concerned about her career choice, worrying that it was not a suitable job for a woman. However, her high achievements since have persuaded them otherwise and they are today proud of their headstrong daughter, who is now based in Kuantan with the Royal Malaysian Air Force (RMAF). She is Malaysia's only female fighter pilot and hopes to inspire other women to follow in her footsteps.

Patricia, callsign "Mulan," was the first woman in the world to become a MiG-29 fighter pilot. During her early years, Patricia, said she found the training tough. However, she received enormous support. She said: "My fellow pilots as well as my commanding officer Kol Lim Thian Hu from our RMAF 17th Squadron in Kuantan constantly encouraged me to keep on going."

She had joined the RMAF at 20 and, in 1998 early in her career was given the opportunity to get some hands on experience with the MiG-29 "Fulcrum'." She described the experience as "nerve-wracking." She told the Malaysian Star: "Words couldn't describe it. It's normal to feel nervous, and I knew it was something I had to overcome if I really wanted to be a fighter jet pilot." Years of experience have given her confidence. She is now keen to fly the Air Force's latest acquisition, the Russian Sukhoi Su- 30MKM fighter. She expressed her hopes: "As far as I know, no woman has ever piloted the `Flanker'. I hope I can be the first." This could put her in the air show circuit.

One of her many ambitions is to become a display pilot. A few years ago she started training with a small MD-3 aircraft and later progressed to bigger aeroplanes, such as the Pilatus PC-7 and Aermacchi MB339A. Her duties at the Langkawi International Maritime and Aerospace exhibition (Lima) 2007 were to oversee operations at her team's safety office, as well as do the ground handling at the static display area. She said: "Hopefully, I can become the country's first woman display pilot by Lima 2009."

One of the striking things about Patricia's story to date is the warmth she has engendered in women throughout her country. She has attracted powerful support for one of her public goals. She would like to become the first female astronaut in her country. Some of Malaysia's most influential women have come out in support of her campaign. She has obviously struck a chord in their hearts. Several powerful women have spoken up to say that Patricia has the "right stuff" to become an astronaut and that they hope that she will be given a chance.

Assistant Minister of Resource Development and Information Technology, Melanie Chia Chui Ket said the fact that Patricia is flying the sophisticated MiG-29 shows that she has the capability and potential to be an astronaut. She told Malaysia's Daily Express News that gender was no longer an issue. She said: "I would like to see more women step forward to do what they love. Difficulties are not insurmountable if one is resilient."

Former Sabah Women's Advisory Council chairman Datuk Adeline Leong said Patricia should be allowed to fulfil her dream even if this takes ten years. Sabah Energy Corporation chief executive officer Margaret Fung said those involved in selecting candidates for future space missions should take into account Patricia's qualifications, experience and suitability. She said: "If she [Patricia] has what it takes to be an astronaut, she should be given the chance. I hope it will be an objective and professional assessment in the event of screening potential candidates and that she will not be turned down just because she is a woman."

Another powerful voice fighting Patricia's corner is LDP Wanita party chief Datin Naomi Chong Set Mui, who issued a statement saying that she is impressed and proud of Patricia's achievement because she has already broken into the male-dominated arena as a fighter pilot with the RMAF. Naomi pointed out that Patricia's job is a demanding and dangerous one. The former Senator wrote: "She has already exhibited her capability and potential. If she meets all the stringent requirements, she should be given a chance to be the first Malaysian woman astronaut. Since we already have two male astronauts, the third slot should be offered to a woman to show that the Barisan Nasional government really walks the talk insofar as gender sensitivity and equity is concerned."

President of the Society for Caring Youth, Kota Kinabalu, Josephine Hadikusumo said: "All the great accomplishments in the world began with a dream. Unfortunately, our world is peopled with naysayers who are so grounded in what is, that they are unable to see what could be. But certainly Patricia is one who is able to perceive possibilities.

"I think it was John F. Kennedy who said 'some people look at the impossible and ask 'Why?' I look at the same thing and ask 'Why not? I believe in nurturing the dreams and dreamers in our society by putting our belief and support in them.'"

Hadikusumo told her countrymen to believe in and support Patricia, "because by believing in her, we give her the strength to achieve. And society as a whole will be the better for it. I look forward to seeing more young men and women rise up to take up the mantle of excellence."

Regardless of what happens Patricia intends to pass on her knowledge to younger people. She wants to teach eventually. She said: "When you are a pilot, you will be trained as an instructor and I'm looking forward to that. I'd like to share my experience with the younger generation and hope to see more women in this field in the future."

Events In 1998

- US President Clinton denies allegations of affair with intern, Monica Lewinsky
- Europeans agree on single currency, the euro.

1999

LT. COL EILEEN COLLINS (USA) 1956 –

How she followed her dreams and became the first woman shuttle commander

When I was a child, I dreamed about space - I admired pilots, astronauts, and I've admired explorers of all kinds. It was only a dream that I would someday be one of them. It is my hope that all children, boys and girls, will see this mission and be inspired to reach for their dreams, because dreams do come true."

On March 5th 1998 an ebullient Lt Col Eileen Collins spoke these words following the White House announcement of her appointment as the first woman shuttle commander. Attaining that post was the culmination of years of dogged determination and hard work.

Eileen Marie Collins was born on November 19th 1956 in Elmira, New York. She was fascinated by all things aeronautical, and dreamed of flying in one of the many sailplanes drifting overhead. Her interest evolved into a passion, stemming from watching Star Trek and reading about some of the trail blazing women in aviation, such as Amelia Earhart and the World War II female reserve service pilots. She would have been astounded to think that years later she would blast off from Cape Canaveral, wearing Amelia's actual scarf and carrying Bobbi Trout's flying licence on her first shuttle mission.

A young Eileen immersed herself in books about aviation covering all eras from the Wright Brothers, through the Second World War, to the booming jet fighters of the Vietnam conflict. Her parents often took to her to the local airport, allowing her to gaze at the succession of aeroplanes landing and taking off. Her family was unable to fund her desire for flying lessons, let alone college tuition. But this did not deter the resolute Eileen, who secretly planned a career in aviation.

Working at a pizza parlour enabled her to save the princely sum of $1000 she needed to obtain a pilot's license. She then drove to a local airport and enquired where she might learn to fly, and did just that. At nineteen the budding aviatrix knew full well that she needed to excel academically to stand a chance of achieving her lofty ambitions.

After graduating from High School in 1974 she attained an associate degree in mathematics and science from a local community college. This paved the way for a scholarship and two years at Syracuse University for a Bachelor of Arts in Mathematics and Economics. She went on to attend two further institutions, gaining a masters degree from each.

In 1976 Eileen discovered that the air force had officially opened up to train women pilots. The National Aeronautics and Space Administration (NASA) followed suit two years later, steering her towards her goal of becoming an astronaut.

In 1979, a year after she obtained her private licence, Eileen went straight from college to air force pilot training. She described the experience of training at Vance Air Force Base as "living in a fishbowl." It was a time when very few women were inducted into the pilot training programme, and those that did were under intense scrutiny. On graduating from Vance, the young air force pilot became an instructor on the T-38 trainer jet at the same base until 1982.

From 1983 to 1985 she served as aircraft commander and instructor on C-141 Starlifters assigned to Travis Air Force Base. She also served during the brief conflict in Grenada, earning the Armed Forces Expeditionary Medal as part of Operation Urgent Fury in October 1983. As a heavy lift jet transport pilot she amassed an impressive collection of medals during her service career, ranging from the Distinguished Flying Cross to a plethora of NASA Medals.

During her C-141 assignment she married fellow pilot, Pat Young. She then had to juggle family responsibilities with her aspirations of getting into NASA. From 1986 to 1989, she was assigned to the US Air Force Academy in Colorado as an assistant professor in mathematics and T-41 instructor pilot.

Eileen was selected for the astronaut programme while attending the Edwards Air Force Test Pilot School in California. She graduated in 1990. NASA then recruited her into the Astronauts Corps to be designated to full flight status in 1991.

Her passage through the innovative and exciting world of NASA was totally different from her public existence during her pilot training days. Women were becoming more accepted. The female mission specialists preceding her had performed well and in many instances had excelled in their zero-g support roles.

She performed a variety of roles in the shuttle programme during her gruelling training. Eileen was first assigned to the shuttle Orbiter engineering support team, soon moving on to the astronaut support team. The latter was responsible for pre-launch checkout,

Events In 1999

■ While trying to circumnavigate the world in a hot air balloon, Colin Prescot and Andy Elson set a new endurance record after being aloft for 233 hours and 55 minutes.

■ John F. Kennedy Jr. and his wife and sister in law are lost at sea when a plane he was piloting disappears.

final launch configuration and crew safety procedures. She had a stint sitting behind a bank of screens at mission control as spacecraft communicator. Eileen then transitioned to a number of related branch offices, managing systems, information and astronaut safety. She served as chief in all capacities.

Then came the actual shuttle missions. Her first as shuttle pilot on STS 63 Discovery was the first joint Russian-American space programme initiative. The Discovery rendezvoused with the Russian Mir Space Station on February 3rd 1995. The mission involved operating the Spacehab, retrieval of a satellite and a space walk. Eileen was consequently awarded the Harmon Trophy in recognition of her being the first female shuttle pilot.

She flew again as pilot on the Atlantis on May 15th 1997. This mission, STS 84, involved a return visit to the Mir Space Station. In addition to a few experiments, this mission was a four ton package delivery of much needed supplies for the ailing, orbiting Russian platform.

Eileen flew again as mission commander on her third outing, designated STS-93, on July 23rd 1999. This was the first time a woman had served as shuttle commander on the Columbia. The mission was to deploy the Chandra X-Ray Observatory telescope.

Tragedy struck. A later Columbia STS-107 mission, not flown by Collins, suffered a catastrophic failure on February 1st 2003. Damaged thermal tiles on the leading wing edge resulted in the disintegration of the Orbiter on re-entry, with the loss of all seven crew, including the first Indian female astronaut, Kalpana Chawla. As a result the entire shuttle fleet was grounded pending an investigation.

In 2005 the shuttle missions resumed with Eileen again at the helm as commander of the historical "Return to Flight" mission, designated STS-114. Launched in the Atlantis on July 26th for re-supplying the International Space Station, Eileen was the first to fly the Shuttle through a complete 360-degree pitch manoeuvre. This exposed the belly of the Atlantis to the ISS crew, enabling an inspection of its underside to identify possible damage to the thermal tiles, which had proved fatal on the Columbia. The mission was a success, with STS-114 returning to Edwards AFB, thankfully without incident. That was Eileen's final space flight.

She retired from NASA in 2006, citing the need to spend more time with her family. With her many trophies, medals and honorary accolades, Eileen is also an inductee of the National Women's Hall of Fame. She is also a member of several aviation and aerospace organisations, such as the US Space Foundation and the venerable "Ninety Nines." Since her retirement from NASA, she has been a space shuttle analyst, generally covering shuttle launches and landings for CNN.

It is estimated that Eileen had logged over 6,200 hours of flight time, and flown thirty different types of aircraft in the process. Some 800 of those hours had been spent in outer space.

Lt Col Eileen Collins dared to dream, quietly carving out an illustrious career through intellect and sheer natural ability. Like many of the predecessors who inspired her, she overcame each challenge with grace to join the ranks of respected pilots, successfully touching more than just the stars.

CAROLINE AIGLE (FRANCE) 1974 - 2007

The Eagle who soared further than anyone could have imagined. From fighter pilot to courageous mother, Caroline Aigle's story touched the hearts of many

Aged just 24, in 1999 Caroline Aigle was the first French female fighter pilot to receive the rosette that said she was capable of flying Mirage-2000-5 jets. At the time she was asked whether she could be called into service over Kosovo. She told the Times: "I talk about that with other pilots but I don't let it worry me. First I want to succeed in what I have undertaken."

In the event, the only battle she lost was to cancer, sacrificing her potential recovery for the life of her unborn child.

Caroline Aigle (which means "eagle" in French) was born in Montauban, France on 12 September 1974. She spent her formative years in Africa, as her father was posted out there, serving as a military doctor. Aged 14, she matriculated at the Lycée Militaire de Saint-Cyr (Saint-Cyr Military Academy), and stayed there for a further three years until she graduated. She went on to the Prytanée Militaire, which is an advanced military high school, finally attending the military academy wing of the prestigious École Polytechnique, France's top engineering school.

Between 1994 - 1995, she was stationed with the 13th Battalion of the elite mountain infantry, the Chasseurs Alpins. Her final year before she graduated was spent in the officer school (École de l'air) of the Armée de l'air (French Air Force). She graduated in 1997. She then opted for an air force career.

She was also a top sportswoman and became the 1997 French military triathlon champion. Two years later, she and her team won the triathlon world military vice-championship. In addition, she was a champion skydiver and free-fall parachutist. On 28 May 1999, she received her fighter pilot wings.

In 2000 she flew the Mirage 2000-5 in the squadron 2/2 Côte-d'Or in Dijon. After serving there for six years, she was sent to Metz to be in charge of flight security. She was promoted to Commandant (Major) in 2005 and altogether accumulated 1,600 hours flying. The European Space Agency was also interested in choosing her as part of its astronaut team.

In an interview given to online magazine "Au Feminin.com," Caroline spoke of her career. Like many of the women featured in this book, she was not looking for the glory of being 'the first' woman to fly as a fighter pilot in the French Air Force. She just wanted to fly. She said (translated): "My objective was to get my licence. The fact I was the first woman was secondary."

She said that the men accepted her, especially given that fighter pilots are generally young. According to Caroline, a fighter pilot at 35 is almost a veteran, so that sexism was not really an issue, given the generation present in her squadron. She said she was judged on her flying skills only.

She explained to her interviewer how she managed to cope physically with the challenges of her job: "I do a lot of sports and I go to bed early." She also talked of her passion for the aircraft she flew, which were state-of-the-art fighters.

Poignantly she said that a fighter pilot's career is short, "not more than fifteen years of flying." She spoke of her love for her family and dedication to her profession. She said she would like to see both men and women join up, but that numbers of applications for fighter pilots were on the decline. She attributed that partially to the high standards required to enter the profession and partly because many potential entrants were lured by other types of flying.

She was diagnosed with cancer in August 2007 and died suddenly on August 21 three weeks before her 33rd birthday. Her husband Christophe "Douky" Deketelaere was also a pilot and deputy leader of the Breitling jet team. They had two sons. Caroline was pregnant when the tumour was diagnosed. Her child was delivered by caesarean section, five-and-a half months into her pregnancy and fifteen days before her death. President Sarkozy honoured her with a posthumous Médaille de l'Aéronautique (Aeronautics Medal) on 2 October 2007.

A national hero, her country was devastated by her death. In an interview Christophe said, "She could not stop the life she had carried for five months. She told me: 'He has the right to have the same chances I had'." Her husband said that her pregnancy was "her final battle and she won." Before dying, she was able to see her son several times and hold him in her arms. He added: "She was heroic to the end."

Father Pierre Demoures celebrated her funeral mass. He was also a former fighter pilot and said: "The great lesson that Caroline gives us is the urgency to love. Not the urgency to fear, but the vital urgency to know that only love gives life. Man is made for life. This urgency can make love stronger and give life to a treasure amidst the most tragic events."

A strong and dedicated woman, Caroline had a brilliant officer's career in front of her. Her death touched millions of people in her native France and beyond.

The association of female fighter pilots 'Fighter Chicks' have a tribute to her on the home page of their website.

Here's a Toast

Our thoughts and prayers go out to the friends, family and squadron mates of the first French female fighter pilot, Major Caroline Aigle. She died of cancer on August 21st at the age of 32.

Major Aigle (Eagle in French...) was rated as fighter pilot in 1999 and served in that specialty until last year, logging 1,600 hours mainly on Mirage 2000. In the same time, she managed to be the mother of two babies, the last one born some weeks before her death. After a spell in a headquarters, she was due to take command of a squadron next year.

ww.fighterchicks.com

More events In 1999

- Nelson Mandela, first black president of South Africa, steps down, and Thabo Mbeki takes over

- War erupts in Kosovo after Yugoslavia's president Slobodan Milosevic clamps down on the province, massacring and deporting ethnic Albanians.

2001
VERNICE ARMOUR (USA) 1973 –

From police motorcycles to Operation Iraqi Freedom with the Marines – an inspiration to African American women

Born in Chicago Illinois in 1973, Vernice Armour was raised in Memphis Tennessee. She is credited as being the first female African American pilot to serve with the United States Marine Corps and America's first African American female combat pilot.

Attending the John Overton High School of Performing Arts, Vernice was an active member of a number of student bodies, including the mathematics honour society. She also found the time to be part of the National Honour Society as well as being elected class vice-president. She was also prominently involved in the musical arts. Her formative academic years brought together the many facets of Vernice Armour. Drawing upon her athleticism, intellect and drive to achieve whatever she set her mind to do, Vernice certainly possessed the early attributes of a future role model. The portents looked promising.

Following high school graduation in 1991, she enrolled at Middle Tennessee State University (MTSU). It was here that she would make her pioneering steps towards becoming an accomplished helicopter gunship pilot for the US Marines Corps.

Vernice would be inspired by many around her, none more so than by members of her own immediate family. The apt Armour name is hewn from the links of a powerful and sturdy military chain. Her grandfather was a marine and her father was a former major in the US Army Reserves. Her stepfather was also in the Marine Corps, having served a few combat tours during the Vietnam conflict.

So it was hardly surprising that Vernice enlisted in the army reserves whilst at MTSU. She then later joined the college based Reserve Officers' Training Corps (ROTC).

Taking a sabbatical from her sports science studies at MTSU, Vernice embarked upon her career in law enforcement, starting as an officer with the Nashville Sheriff's Dept of Corrections in April 1996. Accepting an invitation to the police academy, by December 1996, she was a fully fledged police officer serving on the Nashville Metropolitan Police Department. She then was to become the second woman, but first African American female, to serve on the motorcycle squad.

Graduation from MTSU beckoned in 1997, with a degree in sports science. She then served as a law enforcement officer in Arizona. Vernice then heard the cry from a jarhead drill instructor to be comissioned as a second lieutenant in the Marine Corps by December 1998. The feverish pace of events was just about to begin and Vernice was on the brink of making history.

Trading in her officer candidate dress blues for a one-piece flight suit, Vernice entered the world of marine aviation. She made time to make her first foray into the exciting world of aviation by taking private flying lessons the summer before she attended flight school while serving in the Presidents helicopter squadron.

Her initial training took place at the Naval Air Station in Corpus Christie, Texas followed by formal flight training at Pensacola Naval Air Station in Florida. She achieved her monumental wings of gold in July 2001, to become the first female of African American heritage in history to serve as a marine aviator. Ranking number one out of a class of 12 and of the last two hundred to graduate, she made the prestigious Commodore's List and was bestowed the Academic Achievement Award.

Graduating from flight school Vernice was stationed at Camp Pendleton near San Diego, California, transitioning into the formidable AH-1 Super Cobra gunship helicopter.

The Bell Textron Cobra gunship helicopter has a long history dating back to the Vietnam War. It was a time when the use of helicopters to support combat operations was still in its infancy. The AH-1 Huey Cobra, dubbed "Snake" by US Army pilots, cut its shark teeth in close quarter battle over the jungles of South East Asia. Starting out with a single jet engine, the sleek predatory fuselage was designed for speed and agility. It carried a variety of weapons from an integrated chin mounted mini-gun turret to rocket pods slung under stubby, angled winglets. The modern AH-1 Super Cobra is a completely updated beast of war, more powerful with greater range, and the ability to withstand considerably more punishment at the battlefront. Bristling with technology, it possesses an impressive armoury of weapons to bring to bear on land and air based adversaries. The Marine Corps allows only the most accomplished and courageous to fly their prized, redoubtable helicopter.

Vernice Armour was one of those pilots. Not content on being just a flyer, Vernice demonstrated her prowess on the athletic track and football fields at Camp Pendleton. She was named 2001 Female Athlete of the Year, and twice claimed the title of the Camp's annual Strongest Warrior Competition. Vernice also played as running back for the San Diego Sunfire women's professional football team.

The invasion of Iraq in 2003 prompted the storm clouds of war to gather that would eventually put her Super Cobra skills to the test. Vernice was one of 1,500 female marines deployed to the Persian Gulf as part of Operation Iraqi Freedom in March 2003.

Legislation had just been changed permitting women pilots to participate in actual combat operations. By then 29 years old, Vernice was part of the Marine Light Attack Helicopter Squadron 169, flying to support her fellow marines spearheading towards Baghdad. She achieved another distinction of being America's First African American woman combat pilot to serve in combat in any of the five branches of the US armed forces. Her deadly mission was to scout ahead of the advancing divisions and to engage enemy ground forces, thereby contributing to the toppling of Saddam Hussein's regime. She would eventually serve two combat tours of Iraq before being assigned to a liaison and equal opportunites role prior to leaving the Marine Corps.

Awarded numerous citations and medals for her gallant actions in combat, captain Vernice Armour left the US Marines in June 2007. A new calling presented itself to her by sharing with others the true essence of a goal inspired methodology drawn from her passionate experiences towards the pursuit of success as well as happiness. To achieve this end she established her own company VAI Consulting and Training, LLC assisting corporations, businesses, organisations and individuals to deal with the ever shifting business and social environments.

Vernice has also retained her ties with the heritage which allowed her to fulfil her dreams. She is a member of the East Coast Chapter of the Tuskegee Airmen Association. The Tuskegee Airmen were the first segregagted African Ameriacn fighter squadron deployed to escort the vulnerable US bombers during WW2. Flying their distinctive red tailed P-51 Mustangs they never lost a bomber during their countless escort missions. Vernice is also a member of the Bessie Coleman Foundation. Bessie Coleman was the first African American women who successfully battled prejudice to gain an official pilot's licence in 1921. The foundation was set up by African American women pilots in 1995 as a support network to encourage others to enter the world of aviation.

Vernice Armour represents the perfect role model for many of the emerging generations, men and women, irrespective of ethnicity. It was pure hard work and dedication that eased her passage into the complex cockpit of the AH-1 Super Cobra. Her talents and energies permitted her to ride the crest of a wave and she has now caught an even bigger wave in the pursuit of altruistic ambition. Standing on the shoulders of the early giants like Bessie Coleman and the Tuskegee airmen, Vernice Armour USMC has the firm foundations to pave the way for others to follow in her remarkable footsteps. She has all the hallmarks of becoming a giant herself one day.

Events In 2001

- The NEAR Shoemaker spacecraft touches down in the "saddle" region of 433 Eros, the first spacecraft to land on an asteroid.
- Space tourist Dennis Tito returns to Earth aboard Soyuz TM-31.
- NASA's Galileo spacecraft passes within 112 miles of Jupiter's moon Io.

POLLY VACHER (UK) 1944 –

Record-breaking pilot, who dedicates her flights to Flying Scholarships for the Disabled.

n 2007 British aviatrix Polly Vacher flew to 221 UK airfields in just over two months, battling typical British summer weather. Apart from not having "the terror of crossing the ice or Pacific" that she had experienced establishing her previous records, she says this challenge was the most demanding yet. Take this landing...

"I am standing in the middle of the runway; aim for me!" yelled the air traffic controller through the driving rain at Insch airfield near Aberdeen in the UK. "Aim for the yellow jacket, I will get out of the way." Although not all of Polly's landings were quite so dramatic during her "Wings around Britain" (WAB) flight in summer 2007, she says that the record was the most daunting she has set yet. She landed at all the airfields in the UK Jeppesen VFR Manual over two months to raise awareness for the charity Flying Scholarships for the Disabled' (FSD). This was the latest in a line of records she has set to help the organisation.

Polly Vacher was born in Oxfordshire in 1944. A gifted musician, she worked as a physiotherapist until 1968. She subsequently taught music and gradually became involved in fund raising for the disabled. A pivotal event came at the age of 45 when she took a tandem skydive to raise money. Another 245 jumps ensured she was well and truly hooked on air sports and she obtained her private pilot's licence in 1994 at the age of 52.

Shortly afterwards she and her husband moved to Australia. They flew together round the circumference of Australia, then on to Ayres Rock and Alice Springs and finally back across the Simpson Desert. This was an astonishing achievement for new pilots. That tour involved landing on dirt strips in the outback, and once on an island in the middle of the crocodile-infested Gulf of Carpentaria.

She went on to set several world records. From January to May 2001, she flew the smallest aircraft to be flown solo around the world by a woman via Australia and across the Pacific. She was flying her single-engine Piper PA-28 Cherokee Dakota G-FRGN, and the flight included a 16-hour segment from Hawaii to California, a distance of 2,066 nautical miles. Nine hours of the flight was in darkness. She had no trouble staying awake to make the frequent fuel, engine and position checks. She had followed the wingtips of the first person to fly from Hawaii to the mainland - Amelia Earhart - in 1935.

Four years later, between July and August 1997, Polly flew her first transatlantic solo flight. With 500 hours in her logbook and a freshly minted instrument rating, she flew alone across the North Atlantic to Boston and back. She met her husband in America and they flew together around the periphery of the United States and Canada. She then returned alone across the Atlantic, losing the lighting on her primary instruments half way.

Next up was her 'Wings Around the World' II (Voyage to the Ice)" flight, from May 6, 2003 to April 27, 2004. Polly flew 60,000 nautical miles in 357 days and raised £320,000 ($640,000) for FSD. This set several records. She became the first woman to fly solo over the North Pole in a single engine aircraft; the first woman to fly solo in Antarctica in a single engine aircraft and the first person to fly solo around the world landing on all seven continents.

Her last record-breaking flight in 2007 involved landing at 221 airfields, covering 19,000 nautical miles over 158 hours, and carrying 163 passengers, 96 of whom were disabled. It took 30 volunteers to support the effort. It did not help that summer 2007 was the UK's wettest ever, which meant Polly often visited up to nine airfields a day in order to meet the deadline. The longest flight was 2.5 hours – frequently she took off and landed again almost immediately, with the average flight being just 15 minutes. Additionally there were receptions at most places, as well as the logistics of getting passengers in and out of the aircraft.

Because of the weather, Polly frequently had to divert and "plan on the hoof," which made the whole venture exhausting. She would finish each day by writing her diary and tallying up the money raised by sales of her book, often not hitting the pillow until 1am, with a 6am start the following day. Unsurprisingly she caught a heavy cold by the last week.

According to Polly, there were other several priceless experiences on that trip – including landing at two of London's major airports – impossible under normal circumstances for a light aircraft. She says: "Heathrow and Gatwick made me proud to be British. I flew in late at night with Mandy Pantall, my husband and Philip Whiteman (editor of Britain's Flyer magazine) as guests. We were offered a 2220Z (11.20pm) slot for Gatwick and 2305Z for Heathrow (five past midnight)." Her diary details the chord her flight struck with the aviation community. At one point an air traffic controller was giving a British airline pilot instructions: " 'Monarch (tail number) – you will be delayed – there is a charity flight light aircraft.'" The pilot replied. "What's the charity?" Polly interjected: "Flying Scholarships for the Disabled.'" She writes: "We landed on this enormous runway and a surge of excitement filled the whole cockpit. As I took off the Monarch pilot said 'Good Luck for the rest of them – Polly.'"

They were passed to Heathrow and guided onto runway 09L. Polly writes: "I decided to savour the moment and instead of flying the ILS (Instrument Landing System) at 130 knots like we did at Gatwick where they were still very busy, I throttled back to 100 kts and put one stage of flap down and just enjoyed every moment...'I shall never see anything like that again in my life,' exclaimed Mandy. Mandy is such an enthusiast. She is the epitome of what FSD is about. She injured her spinal chord through a horse riding accident and although she can walk short distances with crutches, she is in constant pain. What an example. Her courage is very humbling."

So what makes this remarkable woman go to the lengths she does for FSD? The scheme was set up to help disabled people rebuild their confidence by learning to fly an aircraft. Each student completes a six-week residential course of training, which includes ground school and up to 40 hours of dual and solo flying in the USA and South Africa. Says Polly: "It is so rewarding to be involved. I find the scholars' courage humbling and inspirational."

Polly's book *Wings Around the World* about her record-breaking solo polar flight is an exciting and engaging read. It is available from her website www.worldwings.org and all her fees, plus a percentage of the publisher's profits go to support the charity she is so passionate about.

More events In 2001

- The unmanned aircraft RQ-4 Global Hawk flies from Edwards Air Force Base in the US to Australia in the longest flight undertaken by an unmanned aircraft.

- On September 11, four airliners, two each from American Airlines and United Airlines, are hijacked and crashed into the World Trade Center in New York, the Pentagon and a field in Pennsylvania, killing more than 3,000 people.

2003

YUE XICUI
(CHINA) 1949 –

The Major General who is inspiring the next generation of female Chinese military pilots

Since the Chinese Air Force recruited its first female pilots in 1951, China has trained several hundred women to fly aircraft. It is all a far cry from the early days when Li Xiaqing and Hilda Yan were turned away for being the wrong gender when they volunteered to help with the Second World War effort. Only Jessie Zheng managed to earn her wings. Today China boasts one of the largest complements of female military pilots in the world. Its air force has trained almost 400 women, 300 of whom managed to make it through the gruelling course.

It all started on March 8, 1952, International Women's Day. China's first batch of female pilots took part in a flyover of Tiananmen Square in Beijing. More than 7,000 people turned out to enjoy the spectacle, which was the first time women had flown aeroplanes over the capital. Chairman Mao Zedong praised them as "the pride of Chinese Women." The date is still regarded as the day women pilots were recognised in the military. In November 1951, they finished their classes and joined the Army.

lthough there will be no Chinese women on board China's Shenzhou VII spacecraft due to blast off late in 2008, they are cutting queues like never before. The future looks rosy for those with hopes of flying into orbit in the future. Major General Yue Xicui of the Air Force promised new recruits that: "They will also become a reserve force for the Chinese women taikonauts."

A distinguished veteran, Yue Xicui, a Han was born in Tai'an in the Shandong province in 1949. She joined the Chinese People's Liberation Army (PLA) Air Force in 1965 in its third intake of female pilots. According to chinavitae.org, she graduated from the Second Reserve Army School in 1966 and continued her studies until 1967, when she finished her training at the PLA, Services and Arms Air Aviation Division. By 1967, she was actually flying aircraft. She rose through the ranks to become deputy company commander, followed by deputy battalion commander. In 1971 she was promoted to squadron leader in the Guangzhou Military Region, based in Guangzhou. She also served as vice group leader and deputy director for the next thirty years until 2001.

She has flown as an aircraft commander since 1971. Her subsequent illustrious career is a remarkable achievement. In 1983 she became company commander for the PLA, serving the Guangzhou Military Region and the Wuhan Military District (Air Transportation Battalion) until 1987. That year she was promoted to deputy director, PLA, services and arms, Air Force, Air Aviation Division (Political Department). Between 1993 and 1995 she was a student at the CPC, Central Committee, Central Party School. In 1994, she became the first female deputy division commander of the nation's Air Force, where she served until 1997. By 1995, she took top place on a list of "10 Chinese Heroines."

Between 1997 and 2001 she worked as assistant of the Chief of Staff, PLA for the Guangzhou Military Region, Guangdong Province, in Guangzhou. Her political career was growing hand in hand with her military role and between 1997 to 2002 she was an alternate member, of the 15th CPC, Central Committee. She continued her role for a further five years as an alternate member of the 16th CPC, Central Committee until 1997. She also became deputy chief of staff of the Guangzhou Military Region in 2001, working for the political department of Guangdong Province.

In another first, on July 28th, 2003 Xicui became the first woman pilot to rise to the rank of major general of the PLA in Beijing. Described as a "meritorious pilot," she had 36 years of flying experience at the time of her appointment, with more than 6,000 hours in her logbook. She had also clocked up 1.2 million miles (2 million km) in her travels. Additionally, Xicui had completed 100 military training exercises and important missions, such as flight tests, rescue and relief operations, artificial rainfall and aerial seeding. She is widely respected worldwide and has visited many military and civil events and institutions throughout the globe. In 2006 she was at the Berlin Air Show, and met with US Air Force pilots.

In early 2008, the PLA Air Force announced that it would trawl the country looking for female pilots from senior high school graduates every three years, instead of every seven or eight years as has done for the past fifty years.

Senior Colonel Sui Guosheng, head of the Pilots' Recruitment Bureau, said that this intake would be the first group of female pilot cadets to be awarded with double BA degrees upon their graduation. Once selected, the students will spend four years in the Aeronautics University of the Chinese Air Force and be awarded a bachelor's degree in engineering. Following another year of advanced flight training, they will be granted a bachelor's degree in military science.

When the news came out Xicui was attending the annual session of China's top political advisory body. She is a member of the 11th National Committee of the Chinese People's Political Consultative Conference.

She told state news agency Xinhua: "It means that more Chinese women will have the chances of becoming pilots." She added that: "Actually, the Air Force has begun this year's selection of female pilot cadets from different parts of the country."

Today's young cadets have a chance of working on more active duties, such as air refuelling, airborne early warning and electronic reconnaissance. This is a far cry from their predecessors who were mostly assigned to crewing cargo aircraft, or navigation or telecom duties.

They will not, however, be on China's Shenzhou VII spacecraft, which will be launched from the Jiuquan Satellite Launch Centre in the north-western province of Gansu in 2008.

The taikonauts will leave their spacecraft for the first time.

There will be three men on board according to Qi Faren, a political advisor and former chief designer of Shenzhou spaceships. China successfully conducted its first manned space flight in October 2003, and plans to send a female taikonaut into space in three to five years.

This is likely to happen. Yue Xicui is proving already that it is possible for a woman to enjoy an astronomical career in the PLA Air Force today.

Events In 2003

- Space shuttle Columbia explodes, killing all 7 astronauts

- US and Britain launch war against Iraq

- Burmese opposition leader Aung San Suu Kyi again placed under house arrest by military regime

- Harry Potter and the Order of the Phoenix, the fifth instalment in the wildly popular series, hit the shelves in June and rocketed up the best-seller lists.

2003

KALPANA CHAWLA (INDIA/USA) 1962 – 2003

The star of India's space programme with a tiger's spirit

pretty much had my dreams, like anybody else and I followed them. People around me fortunately always encouraged me and said 'if that's what you want to do carry on,'" Kalpana Chawla, (with kind permission of the Montsu Foundation).

Dr Kalpana Chawla, the first female Indian astronaut, embodied the spirit of a tigress that neither growled, nor roared to be heard. She dared to defy the restrictive cultural traditions she grew up with, and realised her dreams. Kalpana knew from a tender age that she was destined to work in aeronautics. Her name Kalpana in the Hindi dialect means "creative imagination." In her wildest imaginings she may have dreamed of reaching for the stars, but poignantly not as a celestial being looking down on an earth that would continue to turn without her.

Kalpana Chawla was born in Karnal, Haryana, India on 17th March 1962. She was the youngest of four siblings and the third girl in a family influenced by the prevalent thinking that boys are to be celebrated, whereas girls are to be forgotten. It was time to shift this blinkered perception of women and their place in 21st century India. Kalpana unknowingly became a pioneer, not just by entering a profession dominated by men, but by challenging tradition. Her resolve and strength carried her forward and took her into outer space.

Her determination was perhaps derived from her parents' experiences as displaced Hindus, following the partition of India in 1947. Her entrepreneurial father went on to establish a successful business, never expecting that the same sort of drive would be reflected in his daughter.

As a child Kalpana was enchanted by the light planes and gliders she saw flying from the local airfield. Her father treated her and her brother to joyrides in the flimsy sailplanes and Piper Cub J3 equivalents, the Pushpaks that the club flew. This set her course for the path she wished to follow. She was also inspired by the industrialist JRD Tata and his first mail flights over India.

Kalpana's liberal-minded mother was a complete antithesis to her conservative father. She felt that her daughter should be able to pursue her own ambitions without impunity. Following high school graduation, Kalpana was the only girl to apply for a place at the Punjab Engineering College in Chandigarh to study aeronautical engineering. Many of her family and friends tried to talk her out of her wayward choice, but she refused to acknowledge the growing chorus of dissuasion, and enrolled successfully. She was one of only three women at the institution, and found time to be secretary of the Aeronautical and Astronautical Society.

She graduated with honours in July 1982, then asserted her independent streak by leaving India altogether for further tuition in the United States. This, too, caused her father great consternation, but greater shockwaves were yet to come.

She enrolled at the University of Texas in September 1982 and studied for a masters in her vocation of aeronautics. In 1983 she met Jean Pierre Harrison, a pilot and journalist, whom she married, much to her father's disapproval. Kalpana choosing her life partner without undergoing the formal consent process of an arranged marriage was another facet that distanced her from traditional Indian practices. Love marriages were not the done thing.

Undaunted, she obtained her postgraduate degree in 1984 and subsequently attended the University of Colorado. There she gained another masters, topped off with a PhD in 1988. In parallel with such a distinguished array of qualifications she embarked on training to be a pilot and earned her private pilot's licence. She loved the great outdoors and was passionate about hiking and the adrenaline rush she got from skiing and white water rafting.

She was recruited by the National Aeronautics and Space Administration (NASA)'s Ames research centre in California as a scientist in 1988. She then entertained thoughts towards applying for the astronauts' corps. This was despite the still raw Challenger Shuttle disaster. However, her taste for adventure fuelled her desire to free herself of the earth's gravitational pull, irrespective of the risks inherent in manned spaceflight.

Kalpana Chawla became a US citizen in 1990 and continued to add further flying licences to her CV. Following the route employed by budding airline pilots, she acquired a multi-engine FAA qualification. She also added her seaplane and multi-engine instrument ratings, followed by her instructor's certificate on both fixed-wing and gliders.

In 1992 she seized the opportunity to apply to NASA's astronaut corps following the reinstatement of the training programme. In 1993 she underwent a gruelling interview at the Johnson Space Center in Houston. In December 1994 she received the official call from NASA inviting her to join the shuttle programme.

Kalpana reported to the Johnson Space Center in March 1995 and joined her class of aspiring astronauts dubbed the "Flying Escargots." The name was coined by a French member of the class, an apt nickname given the 15 months of rigorous training they had to undergo (although this was not exactly at a snail's pace). Her acceptance on the space programme garnered a thawing of frosty relations with her family back in India.

She was asked in an interview about the people who most inspired her during the course of her cosmic journey. She responded by indicating explorers, teachers and making particular mention of Patty Wagstaff, who eventually became a champion aerobatic pilot. Kalpana highlighted the common theme of perseverance in all those who inspired her to pursue what she really wanted to do with her life.

She became a fully-fledged astronaut in 1996, and assumed a number of technical roles before being assigned to a shuttle mission. Her first shuttle ride was on the Columbia designated STS-87, making her the first Indian-American woman to fly in space. She was responsible for operating the robotic arm that released the Spartan satellite, which failed to deploy, necessitating its recovery. A later investigation found fault with the software and not her actions during the mission.

In between the hectic mission activities, Kalpana found the time to support the International Space School Foundation for promoting space to aspiring young would-be astronauts. The foundation gave her the opportu-nity to invite two students each year from her high school in India to participate in the space camp activities at the Johnson centre.

Her last and tragic flight was again aboard the Columbia on the ill-fated STS-107 mission, which flew on 16th January 2003. Israel's first astronaut was also on board. The flight went without a hitch until re-entry was attempted on 1st February 2003. The Orbiter had sustained damage to its thermal protection tiles on launch, exposing the compromised spacecraft to the extreme temperatures of re-entry. Kalpana Chawla and her six fellow crewmembers lost their lives as the Columbia broke up in the upper reaches of the atmosphere.

Kalpana's monumental achievement was embraced by India, and inadvertently set into motion a new cultural paradigm of thinking that maybe girls can do what boys can do. In honour of Kalpana's contribution to science, her family established the Montsu Foundation for the betterment of education and the environment, two of the many things she was passionate about.

The girl, who dared to be different, hailing from a small town in Haryana, used her talents to shape her own destiny. Kalpana politely acknowledged those who said she could not do as she chose, but instinctively followed her own heart and desires. She herself became a source of inspiration to those who now find it easier to voice their ambitions. The barriers are a lot lower; the glass ceiling a little more porous and the naysayers strangely silent....

More events In 2003

- Yang Liwei becomes the People's Republic of China's first man in space.

- Concorde makes its last scheduled commercial flight

Major Catherine Labuschagne (South Africa) 1979 -

Screaming high through the sky high above the heads of thousands of spectators, Major Catherine Labuschagne hurtled into history as the first woman to fly the Gripen 39-B fighter jet

Major Catherine Labuschagne was born on the 19th April 1979 and raised in Pretoria. She matriculated from Willowridge High School in 1997 and discovered the year that she left that the South African Air force had opened up to women and was training the first group of female pilots. She said: "I did not think twice about joining." She submitted her application and after a series of psycho-metric tests and a strict medical, she was accepted to join as a student pilot. She joined in May 1998 and her air force career began. She had three months of basic military training followed by three months on an officer's course. In the SAAF all pilots are officers.

She went on to spend two weeks of survival training that covered both land and sea. She arrived in Central Flying School in January 1999 at Langebaanweg on the West Coast with a course of about 30 other student pilots, who all studied ground school together. This was followed by an intense period of flying training on the Pilatus Astra, which included aspects such as close formation flying, low-level navigation and aerobatics. In June 2000 she received her wings as a qualified air force pilot.

Having qualified, she had to convert to the Impala, followed by a fighter orientation course combined with the Impala operational training course. The courses took three years, which

then qualified her as a fighter pilot. To become a fighter pilot she had to have completed the SA air force pilot's course, for which the maximum age is 28. After doing the operational training course, a pilot qualifies as a wingman until such time as he or she is ready to go on the flight leaders course. This requires a high level of hard work, dedication and commitment. Fighter pilots fly simulated operational sorties to maintain a high level of combat readiness.

In July 2000 Catherine joined the 41 Squadron at Waterkloof AFB, where she spent the next three years qualifying as a commander on the Cessna 208 (caravan) Kingair 200 and Kingair 300 mutli engine transport aircraft. during her stint there she qualified as an air traffic controller, which she still does whenever she possibly can.

In June 2003 with the support of Lt Col "Barries" Barnard she was given the opportunity to join her husband Major Jaco Labuschagne at 85 Combat Flying School Hoedspruit Air Force Base (AFB) where he was flying Impalas (MB 326). This was a huge step for the SAAF, since, although there were women flying transport aircraft and in the helicopter lines, at that point there were no female pilots in the fighter line. Like fellow female SAAF pilot, Phetogo Molawa, Catherine says she has never had any problems with gender issues. Her colleagues have always accepted her.

In September 2004 she was given what she calls "yet another amazing opportunity." She became the first female fighter pilot in the world to fly in the back seat of the Swedish built Gripen 39B fighter which will replace the SAF high speed fighters, the

Cheetah at 2 Squadron in late 2008. She said: "The event took place at the opening of African aerospace and defence exhibition (AAD) 2004. There was massive media hype around it." Catherine also flew the impala MK1 and Impala MK II until the end of 2005, when she moved on to the Hawk MK 120, which she still flies in preparation for the Gripen.

The kind of training the pilots undertake is fairly ruthless. According to an article in the SAAF's own magazine, in September 2005 Catherine took part in an electronic "war games" exercise, during which electronic warfare (EW) operators faced the elements. The squadron went out on to the scorching exposed Roodewal Bombing Range.

EW is an essential aspect of modern warfare that no Air Force can neglect, so every major air force will practise in some form. Catherine's squadron was no different and practiced using ground based Tactical Mobile Radar (TMR), an Automated System for the Capturing and Analysis of Radar Information (ASCARI), the manual annexure (MANEX) from which debriefings took place, the SA-8, Flapwheel, ZSU 23/4, Cactus AU and FU, an Open Loop Tracker and a Mobile Communication Unit (MCU).

A typical day consisted of several simulations, and started with a target reconnaissance sortie by a Cheetah C for accurate mission planning on where to attack the different weapon and radar systems. Attacks took place several hours later, starting with a two-ship Impala or Cheetah advance. The first priority of such a strike is to take out the Surface-to-Air Missile (SAM) sites, after which the command post can be destroyed.

The TMR "paints" the aircraft from about 40 miles out and acts as an early warning system that gives controllers the direction, airspeed and number of aircraft in formation. A controller inside ASCARI then warns the different weapon systems about the imminent attack. Weapon systems like the SA-8 SAM then go into a search mode in order to detect the target, get a lock-on and launch a missile.

Information from the ground troops is captured on fibre optic cables, while the pilots have to lay back their Heads-Up-Display (HUD) camera, so that their performance can be assessed. Videoconference technology was used to debrief the students. Catherine was the first woman to practice EW operations, flying alongside her husband on the simulated missions. She is reported to have conducted herself capably.

The entire operational training course is run over a period of a few months and covers both theoretical and practical phases dealing with aspects such as air combat manoeuvres (ACM), tactical flying, air to air and air to ground weapons delivery. Catherine said: "It is both physically and mentally demanding and with the arrival of the new aircraft I look forward to a rewarding and satisfying career. The opportunities are really endless." Despite the hard work her job entails, Catherine is clearly happy with her chosen profession and said: "I love what I do. I am very lucky."

2004
HANADI ZAKARIYA HINDI
(SAUDI ARABIA) 1977 –

The Saudi girl who wanted to be Queen of the skies

L
ike many a student pilot before her, Hanadi Hindi was desperate to kick her instructor out of the cockpit and fly solo. Knowing in her soul she was ready to take the aircraft up alone, she finally said to him: "Look even if I knew I would die by going solo, I have to do it." He let her go, and her world changed instantly. She said: "At that moment I decided to be a real pilot. I knew that this is my job, my dream. It made me feel 'Queen of the sky."

Hanadi Zakariya Hindi was born on 18th September 1977 into a close-knit large family in Mecca, Saudi Arabia. Her sisters are already married with children, but Hanadi decided she wanted to see the world. She loves to travel and studied English in college at Mecca before she took up flying. She had vague notions of becoming a teacher perhaps, but no solid career plans. Her father had wanted to be a pilot in his youth and encouraged his daughter to get her private pilot's licence. She obligingly went to neighbouring Jordan to train at the Middle East Academy for Commercial Aviation in 2002.

She found training at flying school challenging. She told World Aircraft Sales magazine in 2008: "I didn't dare make a mistake. I just wanted to show them I wasn't there as a hobby."

When she knew she was likely to fly solo, she notified her parents, who made the journey to her school to watch the key event, which became a turning point in her life. She said: "It was no longer my father's dream, it was mine."

At the time she had no idea she was the first and only Saudi female pilot, she had just gone to Jordan to get her licence. She glosses over the challenges she faced being the only woman at the school, but says: "Everywhere you go, you have to work much harder than the men. That gives me the push I need to do it. I have to be equal. It is my dream to be on an equal footing."

Saddened by the fact she was unlikely to get paid work in her own country, she was delighted when she had an invitation from Saudi's Kingdom Holding Company, owned by the philanthropic reformist HRH Prince Alwaleed bin Talal bin Abdulaziz Alsaud. She made headlines worldwide in 2004 when, aged 26 she was hired by Prince Alwaleed, a billionaire Saudi businessman and nephew of King Fahd, to fly for his firm. She said: "His Highness offered me the job as the first female pilot. It was the greatest opportunity I ever had. I thought that when I graduated I would not be able to find work in my own country. He has given me this chance."

Prince Alwaleed funded her advanced flying training. He told the Times in 2004: "Recruiting Captain Hindi as a pilot...is a major step in the employment of women and in their more active participation in Saudi society. The move transcends the traditional role of Saudi women who were previously confined to working in the health education and philanthropic sectors. I'm in full support of Saudi ladies working in all fields."

The Prince believes in supporting women, and in 2006 also backed jockey Alia Hayel Aboutaiyh Alhwaete all the way to the finishing post by supporting her when she took part in a gruelling 75-mile (120km) endurance race in Dubai.

Although she came in seventh of a field of 90, she was the first female Saudi jockey.

Hanadi earned her Jordanian commercial pilot's licence (CPL) and Instrument Rating in 2005. His Highness and members of the Saudi Embassy honoured her with a special presentation at the Kingdom offices. Prince Alwaleed said: "We are proud of Hanadi and what she has achieved. Her license has made us proud and I will continue to support her and her family in any way I can. I fulfilled her wish because it was within the banner of Islam. My message to any Saudi woman, who wishes to become a pilot, is to come forward and she will be supported by me."

Hanadi started training in the UK the same year to add a European JAA CPL to her ratings. She will go on to train on FlightSaftey's Hawker 800 simulator at Farnborough Airport in the UK. Once she has her type rating on the aircraft, she should be qualified as a first officer on Kingdom's Hawker 800 jet.

As a child, Hanadi had no idea that she would make the news as Saudi Arabia's first accredited female pilot. She takes her responsibilities seriously and said she keeps herself motivated by thinking of her family, friends and employer: "I promised the Prince I will not let him down. My colleagues are very supportive. Everyone is proud of what I am doing and offering support all the time."

Prince Alwaleed also mentioned the fact she is not allowed to drive in her country, but she can take the controls of a far more sophisticated machine. Women were banned from driving in Saudi Arabia in 1990. In common with all women in the kingdom, Hanadi's male family members drive her to work as she cannot drive or travel in a vehicle with a man who is not a family member. However, the Prince also said: "We should not talk about what women cannot do, we should talk about what women can do. Saudi women are able to do any job, a man can do, if not better."

Hanadi is determined to live up to her powerful sponsor and is keen to tell other women to live their dream. She said that her friends had been uncertain at first when she embarked on her flight training and feared that she might fail. However, now they back her all the way and are proud of her. She said: "They say 'you made this for us, you made it for your daughters in future." This kind of support galvanises her when she finds the training tough.

Hanadi is facing challenges that would be daunting enough for anyone, even without the extra pressures of international media attention. She is a young low-hour pilot flying alongside highly experienced captains for one of the world's wealthiest men. She is also undertaking some of the toughest training experienced by professional pilots, studying on her own in a foreign country. However, she remains cheerful and composed, especially when talking about the flying part of her career. She is obviously profoundly thankful to have the opportunity she is enjoying.

There are some serious perks ahead for her. The Prince has large aircraft in his fleet, including VIP variants of a Boeing 747-400. He will also have the first luxury version of the giant airbus A380, which he ordered at the 2007 Dubai Air show. Would Hanadi like to fly these jets? She laughed: "Of course, who wouldn't like to get in those cockpits? – even if only the jump seat."

Events In 2004

- Chechen terrorists take about 1,200 schoolchildren and others hostage in Beslan, Russia; 340 people die when militant detonate explosives.

- SpaceShipOne successfully makes her 3rd flight into space and proves to be a plausible option for space tourism.

- Enormous tsunami hits Asia; 200,000 killed.

2005
MANDY PANTALL
(UK) 1971 -
The disabled former wing-walker who helps others through aviation

Mandy Pantall is not averse to risk. A former wing-walker, ten years ago she was injured in a life changing accident. In 2005 she won a Flying Scholarships for the Disabled award and obtained her PPL. One year later, she threw in a steady job to co-found fly2help, a charity that helps disadvantaged people through aviation.

Born in Wiltshire in 1971, Mandy was an active teenager. She tried her hand for a while at flying gliders aged just 14, and loved being airborne so much that she signed up as a wing walker in the early nineties with the 'Cadbury Crunchie Flying Circus' wing-walking team. A horse riding accident in 1998 left her with spinal injuries and chronic pain. Consequently her life had to change in many ways. The accident crushed her spirit for a while and she did not work for five years. She writes on the fly2help.org website: "After the accident I was embarrassed by the 'new me', as I perceived it, and for years afterwards I avoided contact with many people. I had always been a 'doer' but I now felt like a mere spectator to the life I missed so much; everyday involved disappointment."

Things changed radically for her when in October 2004 a friend introduced her to the "Flying Scholarships for the Disabled" charity (FSD), set up in memory of Second World War fighter pilot Douglas Bader, who lost both his legs in an accident but continued flying. She was persuaded to apply for a scholarship and her confidence grew from there. She said: "I was completely overwhelmed, when.. I was told that I had been awarded one of these precious scholarships... I was in a state of shock, total disbelief, which finally turned to pride... and then back to disbelief... and back to pride... and, well, you get the picture. These people really seemed to believe in me... I kept asking myself 'why?' It was a scary thought, I couldn't let them down now, no matter how hard the challenges ahead, there was no backing out now, I had to do this."

In 2005 she was awarded a 'mini scholarship,' of ten hours flying. Because of her medication, she was not allowed to fly solo. However, something powerful shifted within her from the moment she took to the skies again. She said: "That feeling of freedom on my first flight unleashed so many physical and psychological restrictions that I had become so used to, I couldn't bear the idea of not continuing on to try and get my licence and the ultimate liberation." This led to a supervised withdrawal of her medication and a year of finding new ways to cope. She was determined to reapply to FSD in 2006 for another scholarship to get her chance to fly solo. To her utter disbelief, she was awarded a course at Goodwood, where, with the strong support from the Goodwood and FSD teams, she achieved her NPPL licence. She did not stop there. She earned her full PPL under her own steam.

She said: "The opportunity to prove my capabilities to both myself and others gave my life a new sense of purpose. Unbelievably, I began to move the boundaries I had lived within for the previous seven years, mentally, physically, emotionally and intellectually. There were no easy options with this; I had to find my own way to fight each challenge I came up against, of which there were many, but the bigger the challenge the greater the sense of achievement. It was incredible to find things out about myself that I never knew, while at the same time rediscovering positive aspects that I thought I had lost forever. I learned so much in so many ways. After many years of being told that I shouldn't or couldn't do things, I started to find a new self-belief and a feeling of 'Ability', not 'Disability'."

For Mandy the entire journey meant much more than simply learning to fly an aeroplane. It gave her the impetus to get her life back on track and she has chosen to channel this energy into helping others via the medium of flight. She said: "To be given the opportunity to reach for the sky can provide the psychological benefits that are often an intrinsic part of building a more positive future."

Ever one to rise to a challenge, her life completely turned around again after being recruited by former RAF fast jet pilot Phill O'Dell to help him launch the fly2help charity, based at Kemble Airfield, Gloucestershire. She took another risk and quit her job as a community support worker for the deaf, and became self employed to get the initiative off the ground.

fly2help aims to make a positive difference to people who are experiencing tragedy and trauma , many of whom fly under society's radar, such as families who are affected by long-term or life-limiting illness. These people in particular often spend most of their time in hospital wards rather than on family days out, or just enjoying time in their home doing things we all take for granted. They regularly miss out on the 'fun' and 'quality' aspect of family life. fly2help points out that such a situation affects everyone, especially when it is a child that is the ill family member. Siblings are also greatly affected; they miss out on time with their parents. Parents struggle to share themselves out equally and can then end up feeling guilty about a situation that is out of their hands. fly2help focuses on the whole family. A host of photographs of beaming faces on Mandy's office wall bear witness to the success of the enterprise.

There is no such thing as a 'typical' fly2help initiative, since the projects are geared towards individuals and families. Many of the best-known names in aviation have been happy to support the charity and fly2help are enormously grateful for all the support they are given. fly2help also works closely with several of its neighbours at the airfield and has instigated a scholarship scheme in partnership with Kemble Airport to introduce young people to aviation. Open to locals aged between 15-18, the scholarships last for a fortnight and include introductory flying tuition and aviation ground school. They are geared towards getting young people into the industry, so they are taken on site visits and meet with aviation professionals. They also have work placements in Air Traffic Control and maintenance / engineering workshops and are given a thorough overview of the many elements of the industry.

Mandy thrives on the challenges of building fly2help to the next level and said: "My whole life has been turned around. I wake each day with a sense of achievement and excitement for future challenges, whatever they may be, rather than the old overwhelming disappointment with life. I can now face new challenges head on and with relish rather than running scared. I would never have considered I could do a job like this one with fly2help, but this second chance has left me feeling like a different person... I AM a different person." It's time for fly2help to share more of these blue skies, adventures and smiles with those who need them most. For more information about fly2help, go to www.fly2help.org

Events In 2005

- **Pope John Paul II Dies. Benedict XVI becomes the next pope (April 24).**
- **NASA's Stardust mission successfully ends, the first to return dust from a comet.**

2006
SAIRA AMIN
(PAKISTAN)

The first woman in the Pakistan Air Force to take the prestigious Sword of Honour for best all round performance

t must have been a tough call on every level – academically, mentally and physically, but Saira Amin rose to the challenges presented to her in training to be named as best of the best in her year. In 2006, the young Pakistan Air Force aviation cadet made history by being the first woman to be awarded the coveted Sword of Honour for best all-round performance in any of the country's defence academies.

The prestigious award is given on the basis of overall performance in three disciplines: flying, academics and general service training. Saira excelled in all three. She also lifted the Asghar Hussain Trophy for her exemplary academic achievement.

The passing out parade of the 117th GD (P) course, which includes the second batch of three women pilots in the air force, was held at the Pakistan Air Force (PAF) Academy, Risalpur. With the induction of the three woman pilots, the number of woman pilots in the PAF had risen rose to seven, including the first four: Saba Khan, Nadia Gul, Mariam Khalil and Saira Batool.

Carrying a rifle and dressed in the same blue uniform as her male peers, Saira took part in the parade before family members, diplomats and other guests. She trained in MFI-17 Super Msuhak and T-37 jets and is checked out on other fighter jets.

She had spent a total of three years in training. Air Chief Marshal Tanvir Mahmood Ahmed, PAF chief of air staff, was on hand to witness the ceremony. He said that he was exceptionally proud to pass out the second batch of three female pilots, which included Saira.

He praised the PAF Academy for their high standards of training and commended the passion and endurance of the women for staying the course. He also mentioned that the young women were a source of inspiration for all Pakistani women.

He said: "As Air Power these days is the weapon-of-first-choice, the PAF will offer itself as a strong instrument of state in any future conflict. We shall come up with new and bold ideas; and train realistically and hard; by using modern training techniques. We shall be there, whenever the nation calls us-across the spectrum of conflict."

The PAF academy was all male for more than 55 years – and Saira and her classmates before her are proof that the changes implemented in 2005 when it opened its doors to women are positive ones. Women are now allowed to enrol on its aerospace engineering and fighter pilot programmes, and have proven their worth.

Saira's contemporary Saba Khan was one of the first four cadets to make it through the gruelling first stages of training. She told the BBC in 2005: "I always wanted to be a fighter pilot, and eventually with Allah's wish and the full support of my parents, I made it this far." She said the first newspaper advertisement seeking female cadets was like a dream come true.

Saira's achievement is a true victory for all her female peers. There is no special dispensation for gender. Women have to achieve the same performance levels as men. The air force academy is still male-dominated.

In many countries, there is a difficult transition period as women are integrated into the armed force combat units. In Pakistan the challenges of doing so have the extra dimension of cultural and religious sensitivities. The cadets are carefully segregated.

Saira would have marched shoulder-to-shoulder with the men during early-morning parade, but she and the other female pilots are separated for certain parts of the training, especially physical exercises.

Air Cmdr. Abid Kwaja, chief of the flight training college said: "In the initial part of the training we felt they (the women) were a little wanting in muscular power, which is needed to control the aircraft. They were put in the gym and given physical exercises, and within one or two months they came up to physical requirements. They are as good as the male cadets," he added. "There's no reason they can't become fighter pilots."

Saira joined an elite small group that has broken into the previously all-male bastion of Pakistan's armed forces. The women are all passionate about what they do. Flying Officer Gul told the Associated Press: "I want to fly fighter jets and prove that girls can equally serve our country in the best possible manner as men are doing." The dream could come true for her in the future. Depending on their abilities and the needs of the air force she could go on to fly PAF frontline fighter jets.

General Ahsan Saleem Hyat, vice chief of army staff, said the women had "shown the spirit and courage to rise above the ordinary and break new ground for others to emulate." He added: "If Pakistan is to rise to the height that it deserves ... both men and women of our beloved land must find equal space and opportunity."

After the initial intake Commander Abid Kwaja, chief of the flight training college said that three more women were due to get their wings in October, but the air force "will see how they perform before deciding whether to induct more female trainees." Saira was one of those three and certainly proved that the Air Force's confidence had been worthwhile.

The Daily Jang newspaper paid homage to Peshawari born Saira, who made history with the event. The fact that a female cadet outclassed her male colleagues in an institution like the PAF Academy Risalpur is a huge stride forward for women in Pakistan. According to the Daily Jang, her achievement proves that women can excel in fields that are traditionally dominated by males.

Saira's triumph has pushed another barrier for Pakistani women who wish to pursue careers in the PAF. Traditionally women in the air force were assigned to engineering detachments, working in medical services or serving in air traffic control as well as educational and administrative departments.

However now the next generation of women look set to perform pre-flight checks in the most sophisticated of fighters in the air force. More will be revealed as time goes on.

Events In 2006

- A group of scientists report finding the fossil of a 375-million-year-old fish that has early signs of limbs. The fossil suggests the missing link between fish and land animals

- Hezbollah, a Lebanese militant group, fires rockets into Israel. In response, Israel launches a major military attack, sending thousands of troops into Lebanon.

2006

NICOLE MALACHOWSKI (USA) 1974 –

Thunderbirds are go for the schoolgirl who passed over pop stars for the lure of an F-16

The perfect diamond formation of F-16s glinted in the sunshine over Southern England. The Thunderbirds were in town performing to the delight of a mesmerised British populace. The mystical Thunderbird motif emblazoned across much of the underside of each fighter had by now come alive, its wings igniting the surrounding ozone. Major Nicole Malachowski was steering the F-16 in the number three right wing position. Her spirited bird responded obediently to the subtle pressures and nudges to the throttles, nosecones and tail feathers close enough for her to reach out and touch…

Born in 1974, Santa Maria, California, Nicole Malachowski is a major in the United States Air Force. In March 2006 she became the first woman to fly with the Air Force Demonstration Squadron, famously known as the Thunderbirds.

Nicole was always fascinated by fighter planes. Her fondest and earliest memories stem from watching a venerable F-4 Phantom streak across the sky at an air show in California. Just five years old, an awestruck Nicole tracked the thundering warrior captivated by its raw throaty power, speed and redoubtable technology. It was then that she had made up her mind to become a fighter pilot.

Nicole's lineage is steeped in military history. Her grandfathers had served in the branches of the army and navy during Korea. Nicole's father was drafted into the army during the Vietnam era but remained Stateside. Her growing passion for fighter jets and the respect she had for the uniform meant that Nicole was almost preordained to fly for the air force. Unlike many of her peers gazing longingly at images of pop stars, Nicole had a detailed poster of an F-15 cockpit stuck to the ceiling of her bedroom. The dials, switches and display screens were memorized with her hands playing over them as she flew the fighter in her mind's eye.

Edging closer to her destiny, Nicole at the age of 14 moved with her family to Las Vegas, coincidentally the home of the Thunderbirds. It was during her school years that she announced her ambition to become a fighter pilot, ignoring those who told her that women would never be allowed to fly fast jets. As a cadet with the Nevada Civil Air Patrol, she flew throughout her high school tenure. By the age of 16 she had successfully soloed in an airplane. Graduating from high school in 1992 her aspirations of joining the fighter pilot fraternity were firmly within her sights. The signs and portents were encouraging for Nicole. Serendipity was to smile upon the budding aviatrix when just a year later the USAF opened up the jet fighter cockpit to women.

With her application submitted early, Nicole joined the US Air Force Academy studying for a graduate degree in management. She completed her tuition in 1996 and graduated among 200 of her classmates to achieve a Bachelor of Science degree. Resolute determination and hard grafting rewarded Nicole with the opportunity of flight training at Columbus Air Force Base in Mississippi. Embracing the chance to fly the T-38 Talon jet trainer, Nicole shone throughout the gruelling and challenging syllabus to become a fighter pilot, graduating fourth in her class. She even possessed the natural ability to withstand higher gravitational forces than any other of her fellow student flyers by never succumbing to unconsciousness. This in itself perhaps foretold that the very attractive former 1st runner up (2nd place) for Homecoming Queen was destined to fly more than just straight and level.

Wearing the silver wings with pride, Nicole, call sign 'FiFi,' then selected the deadly F-15E Strike Eagle as her fighter steed. She trained at the home of the Strike Eagle, Seymour Johnson Air Force Base in North Carolina. Following successful transition and time in the fighter, Nicole went on to serve as instructor pilot and flight commander with the 494th Fighter Squadron at RAF Lakenheath, England. As a consequence of Operation Iraqi Freedom, Nicole's squadron was deployed in the Gulf. She served a four-month combat tour enforcing no fly zones and supporting ground troops advancing through enemy lines.

It was during her time at RAF Lakenheath that she met her husband, Major Paul Malachowski. Flying from the backseat of an F-15 he serves as a weapons system officer or 'Wizzo'. It was Paul who encouraged Nicole to apply as demonstration pilot for the Thunderbirds.

Martin's single seat jet fighters is strikingly painted in a resplendent gleaming white, with bands of red and blue. The large Native American Thunderbird motif hugging the undersides singles them out as markedly different from their camouflaged cousins.

Leaving their Nellis roost, the Thunderbirds follow a demanding schedule with close to 88 performances around the country each year. The Thunderbirds have their own entourage of 130 enlisted support personnel tending to the planes and logistical requirements during the display season.

Nicole, now promoted to Major, debuted as Thunderbird number three at the opening show in Fort Smith, Arkansas in March 2006. She met all the challenges with flying colours. The trails of red white and blue tracking behind her precisely controlled F-16, thrilled crowds throughout her time with the Thunderbirds. Being the first woman ever to fly in an elite squadron in the US armed services, Nicole has garnered a legion of fans and well wishers inspired by her legendary accomplishments.

For her second season with the display team in 2007, Call sign 'FiFi' and her fellow flyers spun, dived and rolled through 22 states and 9 countries performing at 70 shows in total. The blistering demonstration of skilful aerial ballet was to celebrate the 60th anniversary of the USAF. This coincided with the European goodwill tour, which had taken the Thunderbird overseas for the very first time since 9/11.

Beginning in Ireland, Nicole and her fellow Falcon drivers hopped through Poland, Romania, Bulgaria, Italy and France, culminating in England and the largest air show in Europe, The Royal International Air Tattoo (RIAT). Such was their draw that the roads leading to RAF Fairford, the home of RIAT were jammed for several miles. Many abandoned their cars to view the breathtaking spectacle of Nicole and her top gun pilots gracefully lace the air with coloured smoke over the skies of Gloucestershire.

Nicole flew for the last time as Thunderbird three in the season finale of November 11th 2007 at Nellis AFB, Las Vegas. She has now handed the reins over to the second woman recruited by the Thunderbirds, Major Samantha Weeks. Another Strike Eagle pilot having chased Iraqi MiG-25's, Samantha flies the opposing solo Thunderbird Six position in her first year with the team.

For her astonishing achievements Nicole has been awarded numerous medals and citations. She was honoured by the International Forest of Friendship (IFOF) in Atchison, Kansas that was the birthplace of another pioneering aviatrix, Amelia Earhart. The IFOF was established by Fay Gillis Wells another legendary aviator, where trees are planted in the name of accomplished luminaries in aviation. Nicole is in good company as she shares the accolade with the likes of Charles Lindbergh and Chuck Yeager.

In March 2008 Major Nicole Malachowski was bestowed the honour of being inducted into the Women in Aviation International's Pioneer Hall of Fame. Approaching the rank of Lt Colonel, she has now been assigned to work in Washington D.C. in a Legislative Fellowship position as well as in a liaison capacity. Although this will take her away from flying for a few years, no doubt one day her name will grace the side of another fighter canopy together with her unique call sign of 'FiFi'.

Armed with 1,024 hours of stick time in the F-15E, impressive credentials and support, Nicole certainly had the right ammunition to hit a bullseye with the rigorous selection process. Fresh from her tour of Iraq, Nicole discovered the outcome of her application while on a vacation cruise in Russia with husband Paul.

The four star air force general on the other end of the line simply said: "I'd like to offer you a job" Those simple words marked the beginning of Nicole's two year attachment to the Thunderbirds aerobatic team. She had been awarded the number three right wing position in the four-ship diamond formation. Now an official member of the elite demo team she was summoned to Nellis Air Force Base, home of the Thunderbirds, to begin her training in 2005.

Nicole described the transition from the F-15 to the smaller agile F-16 at Luke Air Force Base akin to jumping from the cockpit of a Porsche to a Ferrari. The Thunderbird contingent of Lockheed

More events In 2006

■ Hezbollah, a Lebanese militant group, fires rockets into Israel. In response, Israel launches a major military attack, sending thousands of troops into Lebanon.

■ NASA's Stardust mission successfully ends, the first to return dust from a comet.

2006

LINDA MARY CORBOULD (AUSTRALIA) 1963 –

The achievements of Australian women pioneers in the early days of aviation made quite a splash in their time. Their male counterparts tried all they could to calm the waters disrupted by the new breed of aviatrix, without much success. Today Australia boasts several eminent female pilots, including Linda Corbould, the first female in command of a flying squadron.

Sydney's Nancy Bird fought against the endemic gender prejudice that existed during the 1930's to realise her dreams of becoming a pilot. In 1933 she learned to fly under the tutelage of pioneering aviator Charles Kingsford Smith. Later Nancy flew for the first air ambulance service operating from New South Wales. In 1950 she founded the Australian Women Pilots' Association with the motto of 'Skies Unlimited'. She remains one of the most respected living legends today.

Freda Thompson was another remarkable flyer, who in 1934 embarked upon an epic voyage in her brand new De Havilland Moth Major named 'Christopher Robin' from England to Australia. She battled weather extremes, near crashes and navigated over treacherous waters to finally alight at her flying club situated in her native Melbourne.

The ripples of their accomplishments did not fade over the years and certainly were instrumental in eroding the barriers, which kept women from sitting qualified in the cockpit.

Things are a lot different today in the land down under. Wing Commander Linda Mary Corbould of the Royal Australian Air Force (RAAF) represents a new breed of pioneer judged on merit alone. Linda in 2006 became the first female officer to take command of a flying squadron in the RAAF. Born in 1963, the Tasmanian always harboured the ambition to fly for the air force. Her passion stemmed from observing the polished display from the RAAF's Roulettes aerobatic team in Launceston. The Roulettes display team had been established in 1970 to celebrate the 50th Anniversary of the RAAF. Linda would have witnessed the Roulettes operating the Italian Macchi MB 326 jet trainer as opposed to the turboprops flown today.

Linda enlisted in the RAAF straight from high school at the age of 18. It was a time when the RAAF denied pilot training to women personnel. This, however, did not assuage her ambition to become a pilot in the military. She had joined hoping that the rules would relax during her tenure with the RAAF. Her very first role in the air force involved directing aircraft as an air traffic controller. She was also a keen parachutist, refining her sky diving skills to the extent of becoming a national champion. She went on to represent Australia at the 1985 international championships held in Turkey.

Then just five years later, Linda's prayers were answered. The restriction on women pilots in the air force had been lifted and training slots were opened on heavy transports. (However, the fighter cockpit remained an exclusive male domain with women still barred.) An elated Linda seized upon the opportunity to fly and managed to gain her wings to become the third female pilot in the RAAF. She then completed her transition to the Lockheed C-130 Hercules transport aircraft. The ubiquitous Hercules is the backbone workhorse transport aircraft of choice by not just the RAAF but also many air forces around the world.

Linda had flown the Hercules in a number of hotspots such as East Timor and Somalia as part of relief and peacekeeping missions implemented by the RAAF. In 2003 she was assigned as deputy commander of the C-130 detachment tasked to participate in the invasion of Iraq as part of the coalition war effort.

In a memorable night-time mission conducted on April 12th 2003, Linda flew at tree top level meandering low under constant threat of being targeted by missiles and ground fire during a perilous flight into Baghdad. Her mission delivered five tonnes of medical equipment to the city, which she later told journalists was particularly satisfying because it would relieve suffering. For her actions at planning and executing the

More events In 2006

■ **Israeli prime minister Ariel Sharon suffers a massive stroke; he is replaced by acting prime minister Ehud Olmert.**

■ **Kobe Airport, a controversial offshore airport in Kobe, Japan, opens for service.**

hazardous sortie through hostile territory she was awarded the Medal of the Order of Australia.

The RAAF's most senior female C-130 pilot had been tested in the heat of battle and proven herself to be a worthy deputy commander. In 2006 she officially became the air force's first woman commander by taking over the reigns of revamped No 36 Squadron RAAF. This exclusively transport squadron sports a long history dating back to March 1942 at RAAF Base Laverton where it was formed. The squadron has flown transport aircraft through most major historical conflicts such as World War Two, the Berlin Airlift, the Korean War and the Vietnam War.

Now as Commanding Officer, Linda had taken over the new squadron tasked with the privilege of flying a new plane. No 36 Squadron had entered the era of jet transportation thanks to a $2.2 billion order placed by the Australian government for the acquisition of four new Boeing C-17 Globemaster III aircraft. Linda's new aeroplanes are much larger than the C-130 Hercules and loaded with the latest technologies and automated systems. Smaller than a jumbo jet, the C-17 has a capacity four times greater than the still operational Hercules. The Globemaster III can also accommodate the larger tanks for rapid deployment in support of Australian ground troops and commandoes. The procurement of the C-17 Globemaster also means that the Australians no longer have to hire ageing Russian planes and American transports for their heavy lifting needs.

An official ceremony on 17th November 2006 at Richmond Air Base formally inaugurated 43-year-old Linda as the new commander of the newly formed No 36 Squadron. At the same event her command divested itself of the surplus Hercules, now handed over to another squadron. Prior to the ceremony Linda had already spent time in the United States learning to fly the new C-17 Globemaster III. She then had the honour of returning to the US to collect the first factory fresh C-17 from the assembly line at Boeing's plant in Seattle. Homeward bound she flew the C-17 along a trans-pacific route reminiscent of a similar aerial path taken by early pioneering aviators on their way to Australia.

Landing at Canberra on 4th December she was greeted by a host of dignitaries including Prime Minister John Howard, Defence Minister Brendan Nelson and a number of command staff representing the RAAF. Linda made a low pass in the C-17 before the tyres kissed the tarmac in a flawless touchdown before the attendant media. Disembarking, she carried with her a huge ceremonial key symbolic of the acceptance of the new transport plane.

Wing Commander Linda Corbould then flew the prized C-17 to its new home base at RAAF Amberley in Queensland to another rapturous reception. The welcoming committee of VIPs and base personnel watched the new jet-powered transport taxi through clouds of red smoke in lieu of the traditional fire hose spray. Following this fanfare, Linda's No 36 Squadron was expected to achieve full strength of four C-17 Globemasters III's together with a supporting complement of 170 personnel within 18 months.

Linda is also hopeful of achieving another first, by establishing an all female crew for just one flight in the C-17. Presently the RAAF has 13 women pilots in its ranks and many serve as navigators on the ageing F-111 fighter-bombers. However, no women fighter pilots serve with the air force despite all restrictions being lifted. It is only a matter of time before the next pioneering aviatrix comes along to make another splash in history and assume the title of another first in the RAAF.

HERCULES

The C-130 is a four engined, turboprop tactical transport plane designed and manufactured by America's Lockheed Martin Company.

The aircraft first flew in 1954 and was officially adopted by the USAF in 1956. Since then over forty different versions of the venerable transport plane have been procured by over fifty countries. The versatile Hercules has the capability of operating from unprepared runways and challenging terrain. The robust transport requires a short runway for take off and landing making it suitable for humanitarian missions as well as rapid troop deployment. The C-130 has found application in search and rescue, fire fighting and has been configured with an arsenal of machine guns and cannons serving as an orbiting gunship. The Hercules is a reliable aircraft with an excellent operational safety record given the 2,000 or so aircraft in service today. Because of its widespread use, losses of the C-130 serve as a grim indicator of the most troublesome hotspots

2007

PHETOGO MOLAWA (SOUTH AFRICA) 1986 –

"I would say it is a dream I developed in high school – to join the South African Air Force one day. I knew I did not want an office job. I did not want to die of boredom."

Phetogo Molawa first African female pilot in the South African Air Force

Second Lieutenant Phetogo Molawa realised a long-cherished dream when she became a co pilot on the Oryx helicopter in the SA Air Force. The fact that she happened to make history too was not her objective. She made her mark at the 2007 national conference on women in defence by landing her Oryx helicopter at the conference venue, the Saint George Hotel outside Pretoria.

Reports say that she flew her multimillion dollar chopper low past the crowds, then showed off her skills for the audience by taking off and repeating the performance. The Deputy Minister of Defence Mluleki George and senior SA National Defence Force (SANDF) generals, plus a large media contingent met her on the ground. She told the waiting journalists: 'it is excellent fun; I don't think there is anything better. I think it is the best thing ever." She is evidently thrilled about getting behind the controls of the large Air Force transport helicopter.

This was not the career her parents had envisaged for her when she was young. However, today they are bursting with pride that their daughter has got so far. Unsurprisingly, like mums everywhere, her mother had fears initially when Phetogo explained what she wished to do.

However, those fears have long dissipated and she is proud of her daughter's achievements. Phetogo says that she has the backing of her entire family. Although she has not yet flown them herself, they came up with her in an Oryx and were "very excited. More excited than I was."

Phetogo's story of how she got into the air force is simple. She went with her father to the local air force base and asked how she would go about applying.

When she got the news that she had got in she was delighted, but knew she had a long way to go. She entered the air force on 5 May 2004. One of only three women in a class of 18 men, Phetogo said her peers accepted her completely and gender was not an issue. She expects that she will be treated equally and that she will work to the same exacting standards as the men. Because of her generation, sexism tends not to be a big problem.

She had a year of intense ground school, followed by flying training. She says the most difficult things for someone coming new to the environment is that you are working in a different dimension and there are certain language protocols. She said: "That part gets easier, but there are different phases as you progress when it gets difficult. There are some aspects that are very challenging."

Phetogo waited until she had actually acquired her wings - on 7 December 2006, before she allowed herself to celebrate. All along she was certain that she wanted to fly a helicopter rather than a fixed wing aircraft.

She says that she prefers the helicopter because the aircraft is versatile and more challenging to fly than a fixed wing aircraft. She also loves the variety she experiences in her day-to-day work. She will continue her training until eventually rising through the ranks to join the command corps. "You'll never have the same thing twice, every day is a new challenge, and that is how I want to live my life, and the type of career I want to pursue," she said.

She still has to pinch herself to realise that she is actually living her dream. She said: "I do sometimes look at other pilots flying around me and think 'wow I can do that, too.' I feel very blessed that I have been able to follow the career I have and to have achieved so much at such a young age."

A real diplomat, Phetogo is invariably polite and enthusiastic with the press, aware that she is a role model for other young women. Although she also said: "I did not join the air force to be famous. I joined to be a pilot." She intends to use her position as a platform to encourage other young people to join the air force.

South Africa is not currently at war, but it has

Events In 2007

■ The entire span of an interstate bridge broke into sections and collapsed into the Mississippi River during evening bumper-to-bumper traffic

female soldiers deployed as part of United Nations and African Union peacekeeping operations on the African continent.

"In interacting in peacekeeping missions we are beginning to see the benefit of deploying women more so in addressing questions of gender-based violence," said the SANDF's most senior woman, Major-General Nontsikelelo Motumi. "We see women focusing more on the community needs. It's no longer only about what the warlords are doing and what they are up to but also about supporting communities," she added. However, enticing women into the military has not been easy.

In 2007 the defence force had almost reached its target of 30 percent women representation at the lower ranks. Of the 214 generals in the defence force, only 23 are females.

Female officers, such as Phetogo are likely to be sent to remote areas of the country to show young girls what horizons could be reached in a career with the military.

In an interview with AD ASTRA, Lt Phetogo Molawa said she was looking forward to fly her helicopter to highlight the achievements of women in the SANDF and said: "I am very excited to be an example of what women can achieve. My achievement in attaining my helicopter license belongs to all women in South Africa."

2007

MICHELLE GOODMAN RAF (UK) 1976 –

Racing against time, Royal Air Force helicopter pilot Flight Lieutenant Michelle Goodman demonstrated sheer courage under fire to rescue a mortally wounded rifleman with just fifteen minutes to live. For her gallant actions she became the first woman in the RAF to be awarded the Distinguished Flying Cross aged 31.

Born and raised in Bristol, Michelle Goodman developed an avid interest in aviation since attending air shows from an early age. She went onto study Aerospace Engineering at the University of Manchester. Michelle joined the Royal Air Force in 2000 and, according to the information held by the Ministry of Defence, she received her Initial Officer Training (IOT) at RAF Cranwell in Sleaford, Lincolnshire. Her initial flight training took place at RAF Shawbury, North Shropshire, which is dedicated to the schooling of helicopter aircrews.

As a pilot in training, Michelle would have qualified for her wings by flying the single engined Eurocopter Squirrel in addition to gaining experience on the Bell twin engine Griffin HT1 helicopter. Her operational assignment was to RAF Benson, Oxfordshire in 2004 joining 78th Squadron and flying EH-101 Merlin transport helicopters.

The EH-101 medium lift helicopter as operated by the RAF is a workhorse machine powered by three Rolls Royce jet turboshaft engines. A joint development venture between Britain's Westland Aircraft and Italy's Agusta, Michelle's steed was likely to have been manufactured in Yeovil, Great Britain. In its battle dress, the RAF Merlin bristles with a suit of electronic armour and counter measures. Some variants feature Forward-looking Infra-Red, allowing the pilot to cut through the haze and fog of the battlefield. Integrated chaff and flare dispensers distract and confuse heat-seeking missiles in addition to early warning threat detection systems offering further protection. A ring of mounted general purpose machines guns serves to reduce the helicopter's vulnerability during take off and landing from hostile territories.

In the heat and confusing farrago of battle with limited visibility the aircraft commander will make split second decisions based upon the intelligence at hand and the complexity of the mission ahead. Other considerations, such as the safety and responsibility of both crew and aircraft, influence the commander's decision to commit to a perilous undertaking. In June 2007 amid her two-month deployment tour in Iraq, Flight Lieutenant Michelle Goodman was forced to make such a judgement call.

On 1st June 2007, she was aircraft captain on a Merlin helicopter assigned to the Instant Reaction Team role (IRT) out of Basra Air Station. In the pitch black of night an alert came over the radios. A remote British location was under sustained mortar attack with one seriously wounded serviceman needing immediate evacuation. Earlier intelligence briefings suggested the high probability of a 'spectacular' attack in the Basra area with helicopters being targets of opportunity for the insurgents.

Armed with this knowledge and facing the prospect of flying into unfamiliar terrain crawling with unfriendlies, Flight Lieutenant Goodman quickly consulted her crew before entering the fray.

According to newspaper reports she said: "I think this could be a bit dodgy," when she informed them of the hazardous sortie in the offing. But all shared the same ethos of the IRT mission in providing unfailing support to the ground troops.

"I wouldn't have done it without asking them," she later told the Daily Mail newspaper. "This wasn't going to be a one-woman show. They all wanted to go, and they were all fantastically professional."

Michelle flew the Merlin low, attracting sporadic hostile fire and flying at speeds in excess of 160 mph. She used her night vision goggles to pierce through the pitch black of an almost moonless night. But her visibility was compromised by the vortex of swirling dust kicked up in the wake of her rotor wash engulfing the low flying helicopter.

"It was so thick, it was impossible to see where we were going. It was very dusty, so as we got to about 100 ft we started losing our reference points," she recalled. "The crew could see the ground and guided me down." With all

More events In 2007

- Palestinian and Israeli Leaders Pledge to Work Toward Peace

- Mega Millions sets a new world record for the highest lottery jackpot of US $370 million.

visual cues obscured and submerged in dust, her crew served as Michelle's eyes, but the flying expertise was all her own.

As they approached the simmering landing zone, the intensity of inbound enemy fire moved up a notch. Tracer fire peppered the rear of the fuselage impacting and ricocheting like angry wasps looking for something to sting. Michelle's helicopter would also be flying through a lethal corridor of head on covering fire from British artillery attempting to soften the landing zone. She successfully negotiated through the hailstorm of lead and exploding munitions to alight next to their casualty. It was a question of saving Rifleman Stephen Vause, 20, now being tended to by the medics from her aircraft.

Michelle maintained the helicopter light on its undercarriage, waiting in the midst of a barrage of mortar rounds exploding around the vulnerable Merlin and throwing up geysers of dust. The RAF Lynx flying cover overhead radioed in the impending threats as rocket propelled grenades and mortar fire walked closer to Michelle's aircraft.

Stephen Vause was soon stretchered aboard the Merlin, allowing Michelle to engage full military power from all three jet engines. More explosions impacted in the wake of the rapidly departing helicopter. Sensing a missile threat, the Merlin automatically discharged a salvo of counter measure flares to divert the incoming munitions away from the aircraft. All the while British artillery precisely pounded the area as Michelle dodged and evaded the formidable onslaught.

She arrived at the British Field Hospital fourteen minutes since taking the decision fly into the lead soup. Her gallant actions saved the life of the soldier who was mere moments from death.

In retrospect Michelle could have easily avoided risking both crew and aircraft. No doubt the loss of two RAF Benson pilots among five who perished when their Lynx helicopter was shot down over Basra City two years earlier was in the back of her mind.

"But if it was me lying down there," she said to the Mail reporter: "I'd like to think there was someone prepared to come and get me."

Upon hearing the news of her historic Distinguished Flying Cross (DFC) award, she said: "I am truly honoured to be awarded a DFC, but without both my crew and all the engineering support personnel, the rescue of the casualty would not have been possible. The helicopter IRT, whether in Iraq or Afghanistan, is regularly confronted with dangerous casualty extractions and all are dealt with in a professional and timely manner. This is not an award just for me, but recognises all the soldiers, sailors and airmen, who, day in and day out put their lives on the line for the British public to remain safe."

The DFC is one of the highest military decorations offered, second only to the Victoria Cross and Conspicuous Gallantry Cross. Michelle was presented with her medal on 7th March 2008 in an award ceremony held in London. At the same event a further twenty RAF personnel were also cited for exceptional courage on duty in Iraq and Afghanistan.

Flight Lieutenant Michelle Goodman's selfless motives were a testament to her leadership skills, flying aptitude and working in close partnership with her crew. Her actions also serve to demonstrate the excellent training provided by the RAF in honing the skills of their pilots and support personnel to make the right choices in the face of challenging adversity.

Michelle continues to serve with the 78th Squadron having completed three combat tours of Iraq flying the agile and very capable Merlin helicopter.

JENNIFER MURRAY
(UK) 1940 –

Sometime during your flight – reach out and touch the face of God for me, okay?
Sharon Wynne to Jennifer Murray

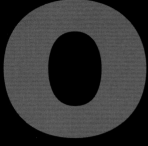

O n Thursday 11th January 2007, as most of her nation huddled round fires bemoaning their festive excesses, Jennifer stood frozen and crying at the spot where she had nearly died in a whiteout three years earlier. She and her flying partner Colin Bodill had landed again at their crash site, seventy miles north of the Patriot Hills in Antarctica and Jennifer promptly lost it. She said: "I wasn't prepared, I just burst into tears. Colin saved the key to the helicopter. I didn't know he'd kept in all this time. We buried it. It was very healing to go back there. I can visualise the whole scene. It was hugely nostalgic – it's a very spiritual place."

Her online diary that day noted: "The wreck of the helicopter was removed during the summer seasons of 2004 and 2005, sawn up into segments that could be carried in a Twin Otter and dumped in a landfill site in Punta Arenas. Nothing was left of that beautiful machine to mark the place. Now the key is there to mark the spot. I was really choked up as we buried it."

That reflective private moment marked a personal triumph for both.

Their epic journey had cost them far more than simply money. After their first attempt at the record was thwarted, the pair threw time and energy into ensuring they achieved their goal. Jennifer explained: "The challenge was unfinished business. It was hugely therapeutic for us to complete the journey. It was the only acceptable option."

That moment was the climax to a journey the young Jennifer Murray could never have imagined undertaking. Born in June 1940 in Providence, Rhode Island. Jennifer spent a lifetime in the Far East building up textile companies. She got her helicopter pilot's licence in 1994 aged 54. By 1997 she had earned her first world record, circumnavigating the globe with co-pilot Quentin Smith in a Bell 407 single engine helicopter the distance of 36,000 miles in 97 days. This earned her the current Guinness World Record for the first helicopter circumnavigation by a woman (accompanied by a male co pilot).

Her awards include: Rhode Island Aviation Hall of Fame Inductee 2005, The Gambia issued a postage stamp in her honour in 2004, Royal Aero Club - 1997 Silver Medal, 2000 Britannia Trophy, the Brabazon Cup, the Harmon Trophy and she has been inducted in the Ninety-Nines' Forest of Friendship. In 2008 Jennifer and Colin received the Frederick Feinberg Award from the American Helicopter Association, which is presented to the pilot(s) who have accomplished the most outstanding achievement during the previous calendar year. She has written two books about her experiences: "Now Solo" and "Broken Journey."

On 6th of September 2000, Jennifer became the first woman to make a solo flight around the world in a helicopter. The journey took 99 days. In 2003, Jennifer and Colin were almost killed during a record attempt to traverse the globe via both poles. However, the pair refused to give up and set off again four years later, this time on behalf of SOS Children's Villages.

Her record-breaking flights are always on behalf of charity – her round the world solo trip was for Operation Smile, which provides money for children with facial disfigurements to have simple surgery.

In May 2007 by now grandmother of five Jennifer and Colin finally conquered a pole-to-pole expedition in a Bell 407 single engine helicopter – a journey that had almost killed them in 2003. The pair kept a gripped public informed by posting regularly to the expedition website throughout the trip.

Completing the task involved huge amounts of planning and patience. They had to organise permissions and sponsorship. Bell Helicopters sponsored the trip heavily, lending the pair the jaunty red aircraft that was to take them around the world. Mike Blake, Bell's CEO said that when the pair approached him for sponsorship, he had been swayed by their motto 'You haven't failed until you stop trying.' "I kept on thinking about that," he said. "That's what did it for me."

This journey was enormous on every level and wonderfully detailed on their website. Jennifer described trying to relay information to the world from a base camp. "Colin has just brought me the satellite telephone and told me I will have to go out onto the airport apron by the Dash 8 airplane to get a signal. The wind is a constant 40 knots, howling across the bay with intermittent flurries of snow."

They grappled with an extremely tight time window in which they could travel to the North Pole, including cooling their already frozen heels in Eureka for nine days, waiting for a chance to get there. Jennifer said later: "I never accept anything that means 'stop.' I am a huge optimist. . There was never a time we thought we couldn't finish. We just thought we might not get to the North Pole. There is such a narrow window when you can get in. We knew we had to get in by the end of April. It was such a worry, we were hugely weather dependent."

She admitted that there were times when she was frightened. Her worst moment was between Igloolik and Iqaluit.

She wrote: "The skies were gloriously clear with light and variable winds. One hundred miles out and we could see low cloud to the south. But that was exactly what the weather charts had shown. Two hundred miles out and we were over low, misty, cloud. If we looked directly down we could just make out the ground. We called through to Iqaluit on our Iridium satellite phone, the tower assured us they had good VFR conditions: 'few clouds at 3,000, scattered at 4,400 and broken at 11,000.'

"Time passed. We were forty miles out of Igloolik, now forced up to 7,500 feet - strange phenomena all around. We were still getting wispy glimpses of rocks and ground. The outside air temperature was showing minus 10C – perfect icing conditions in cloud. We didn't want to risk descending through the misty gaps. Colin mirrored my thoughts – 'I don't like this,' he said. The tower was reporting that the weather had deteriorated, but still had a patch of blue to the NE. We looked in vain. As we knew only too well, dramatic weather changes are the norm in these high latitudes.

Jennifer described how grateful the pair were that Bell had insisted they took their instrument ratings. Colin looked at the murk in front of him and said: "'I'll set myself up for an ILS (Instrument landing systems) approach on runway 35.'" This time they were not practicing or keeping their skills up. Their aircraft was also in danger of icing over.

Jennifer advised the tower the pair were on seven mile finals. Collin kept calm and said: "OK, I'm descending at 700 feet a minute."

They found themselves in a vortex of white sludge. Jennifer wrote: "Those were the longest minutes – eyes fixated on instruments – mine constantly glancing at the torque meter – if that started rising it would mean icing – and then I would check for the flickering glimpses of the snow covered landscape directly below. At 1,000 feet above the ground, and perfectly lined up for the threshold of 35, we broke out of the last tendrils of cloud. Light snow had started to fall. The time was 7.15pm. Glorious, wonderful ground!"

One person for whom the trip had particular meaning was Karen Wynne, a teacher in Waco battling cancer. She asked Jennifer: "Sometime during that flight, reach out and touch the face of God for me, okay?" Sadly she died before the journey was over. But she received Jennifer's message to her: "In Antarctica I was able to do that. Karen, I have your 'bling bling' ribbon – which represents so many women fighting cancer - with me. It's now on the way to the North Pole and I'll be bringing it back to Waco and to you."

More events In 2007

■ Nicolas Sarkozy elected President of France

■ December: Benazir Bhutto former Prime Minister of Pakistan assassinated

2007

ASNATH MAHAPA (SOUTH AFRICA) 1980 –

The first African woman to fly for an airline in South Africa, Asnath Mahapa loves her job at South African Express and the joy she finds in flying

Like many of the young pilots in this book, Asnath Mahapa is making history inadvertently. Her primary objective is to fly for a living and she is working hard to ensure she does just that. At 23 she became the first female African beneficiary of South African Airways (SAA)'s level two cadet pilot training programme, and recipient of the airline's bursary scheme set aside for previously disadvantaged communities. She has loved the idea of flying for a living since she was 13 years old and living with her aunt and two sisters in Midrand. Her aunt would talk about a neighbour who was a pilot, sparking a fire in Asnath that has helped her pursue her goals.

Born in Ga-Matlala in Limpopo, Asnath grew up in Polokwane. She initially trained at a local field acquiring her private pilot's licence (PPL). Realising she wanted more out of her flying than a simple PPL she joined the South African Air Force, where she studied and accrued all her ground school exams towards her commercial licence (CPL). She accumulated 240 hours of flying and underwent the Force's military training.

Realising it would possibly be some time before she could actually fly more regularly and more often, she left the military and went to Port Elizabeth where she attained her commercial licence. This was partly funded by a legacy from her mother, who had died when Asnath was just 12 years old.

She said: "I got started on one of the improvement programmes and did my commercial training in Port Elizabeth." She had already put in a great deal of hard work before she got to the point where the airline hired her on to undertake her commercial training in 2003. She said in 2003: "Not many people get this opportunity and I am honoured to be chosen."

At the time a spokesman for the airline said: "We are very proud of Asnath's achievements and has the strongest confidence in her abilities and future prospects. We wish her luck in her training, her internship and the future."

SAA has created entry programmes to assist candidates who could have been disadvantaged because of historical reasons to meet the requirements on the level two programmes. The programmes are tailored to the individual candidates, who are coming into the airline with various skills and experience. It is a tough call. All candidates with a PPL or CPL qualification have to meet certain basic requirements, which include passes in mathematics, coupled with accounting, computer science or physical science. They also need English qualifications; to have obtained their PPL within 60 hours; and must be prepared to sign a training bond with SAA.

Once the candidates have been accepted, they go through rigorous selection processes and assessment tests. They are then sent for training to obtain an Airline Transport Pilot Licence (ATPL), which is frozen until the candidate has enough flying hours to be able to do the ATPL flying test.

Asnath joined South African Airlink and underwent conversion training to the BAe Jetstream 41, which carries about 30 passengers and is flown by SA Airlink at smaller airports. The training took place in the United States. Upon her successful completion of this conversion course, Asnath became a first officer on the Jetstream 41.

She is now accruing her hours at South African Express (SAX). She loves her job. Her family is extremely proud of her, too. For Asnath a great deal of the reward comes with the job itself. She said: "I love everything about flying. It is challenging every day. I have a different experience and it keeps me on my toes." She is passionate about the sights she sees out of the cockpit window and delighted that as a feeder airline, SAX does not fly at great heights. This enables her to enjoy the beauty of the land she overflies as well as the sunrise and sunsets she flies through.

She flies the Canadair Dash 8 -300 and loves the practicalities of her job. She never tires of using some of her skills. She said: "I love the feeling when you come into land. You would not get that every day if you worked in an office." If all goes well with her career, she would eventually like to join the main airline and fly larger aircraft, such as the Boeing 737-800. For now she is deeply content with her lot and says: "I am happy at SAX and like being a hands-on pilot."

According to Asnath, she has not experienced some of the gender issues that previous generations of women have had to contend with when they entered commercial flying service. Men and women fly and train alongside each other and Asnath says her peer group have accepted her as a fellow pilot.

In addition, she has promoted the level 2 scheme to other young African women. She cautions her peers not to run away from what was previously deemed to be "a man's industry." She said: "If you're passionate enough, you will succeed."

She was among the recipients of the Black Management Forum Limpopo Women in Excellence Awards in 2006. During his keynote address Sello Moloto, the Limpopo premier, encouraged women to fight for their own emancipation. She was also nominated for the Shoprite Checkers/SABC 2 Woman of the Year Award. She said: "It feels great to be one of the nominees.

"I hope that my nomination will not only be an inspiration to most girls but actually open doors to others, particularly in professions that were previously dominated by males."

More events In 2007

- Live Earth Concerts are held throughout 9 major cities around the world.
- Smoking in public and work places is banned in England.

SIZA MZIMELA
CHIEF EXECUTIVE, SOUTH AFRICAN EXPRESS
South African Express is one of the few world airlines with a female chief executive.

Siza Mzimela took the helm in October 2003. Prior to that she was the executive vice-president of global sales and Voyager at South African Airways (SAA). In charge of SAA's core business, she was responsible for SAA's overall sales functions.

She was involved in setting overall strategic direction for the sales and Voyager team and in actively managing and reducing costs. She was also responsible for positioning SAA as the carrier of choice in its market and maximising alliance relationships.

She has achieved her success in an industry, which is traditionally dominated by men, and was the first African woman to be appointed to SAA's leadership team.

Guided by her leadership, South African Express has recorded escalating profitability since inception. In addition, the airline continues to expand its footprint within the African continent to become the regional carrier of choice. Mzimela is currently the chairperson of the Airlines Association of South Africa (AASA) and is a South African Tourism (SAT) board member.

2008

Yi So-yeon
(South Korea) 1978 –

The Korean with a "wow" factor who hopes space will bring peace

At a press conference a day before her historic launch, an ebullient Yi So-yeon proclaimed she would shout 'Wow' in the weightless confines of the International Space Station (ISS). Smiling gleefully she also hoped her endeavours would foster greater ties with a certain kindred neighbour in the north.

The elfin Yi So-yeon, scientist and fresh-faced Ph.D student, became the first Korean to fly into space on 8th April 2008. She had hitched a ride on a Soyuz rocket as part of a scheduled transfer and exchange of personal to the orbiting International Space Station (ISS). The cost of Yi's space excursion was estimated to be $20 million, paid for by the South Korean government.

Born on 2nd June 1978, Yi So-yeon was raised in Gwangju Metropolitan City, the sixth largest city in South Korea. Schooled at Gwangju High School, So-yeon showed tremendous promise in the sciences and flourished academically. Later she would enrol at the prestigious Korea Advanced Institute of Science and Technology (KAIST) to gain both undergraduate degree and doctorate qualifications in biomechanical engineering. No sooner had the ink dried on her Ph.D certificate than So-yeon discovered herself whisked away to Russia for astronaut training.

She was selected in December 2006 as one of two finalists for a place to fly with the Russians en route to the International Space Station (ISS). The nationwide competition was open to any Korean national prompting 36,000 hopefuls to apply. The mammoth undertaking of whittling down the applications to a manageable shortlist of potential candidates was implemented through the state sponsored Korean Astronaut Program. The entire endeavour was under the auspices of the Korea Aerospace Research Institute (KARI). After months of interviews and tests, two members of the public were selected.

As successful finalists both So-yeon and her male counterpart Ko San, a computer engineer were despatched to Russia for intensive cosmonaut training. At 29 she would take the mantle away from Sally Ride as the youngest women to fly on a space bound mission. In a televised press conference an official from the Korean Ministry of Education, Science and Technology announced that Yi So-yeon had an assured seat on the imminent Soyuz mission. Women's groups commented that her selection was likely to be beneficial for the status of South Korean women.

Ko San served as back up to Yi, who was now thrust into glare of the media spotlight. Her entire experience from selection to training and eventual launch was televised to a captivated South Korean audience. With a sense of national pride So-yeon carried the expectations of a government now looking towards making inroads into the lucrative aerospace industry. So-yeon represented the first step for South Korea in its aspirations for developing its own spacecraft

and fledgling space programme. The country's eventual goal constituted of putting a man (or woman) on the moon by 2025.

When asked by journalists as to her reasons for becoming an astronaut, she remarked that she had a great deal of affection for science fiction films. She recalled watching as a child the many space heroine scientists depicted as both unflappable and accomplished in their field. So-yeon chuckled, confessing that she aspired to be just like those pretty and very 'cool scientists' that kept things together in the face of intergalactic adversity.

However on a more serious note, she was also very determined to convey the notion that women could be as equally good as men despite their perceived lesser physical strength. She explained that she hoped to demonstrate that women were as precise and methodical as any other male astronaut. Also during news conferences leading up to her launch she voiced her indebtedness to the Korean people and pledged to assist her country's development of its own space program.

Then on the morning of 8th April 2008, Yi So-yeon in the company of two Russian cosmonauts blasted off in the Soyuz rocket designated as flight TMA-12 from Kazakhstan's Baikonur space centre. Aboard were flight engineer Oleg Kononenko and Sergei Volkov, whose father was a famous cosmonaut during the former Soviet era. Both cosmonauts would be transferring to the ISS as relief crew for a six-month stint on the station.

During her ten day stay on the ISS orbiting platform she conducted a number of experiments and held interviews with the ever present Korean and wider media. She had carried with her some 1,000 fruit flies to investigate the effects of gravity on their behaviour. So-yeon also conducted an investigation on the influence of gravity on plant growth and changes to her physiology due to the weightless microgravity. South Korean food scientists managed to concoct a low calorie vitamin rich version of the traditional kimchi dish as a concentrate especially for Yi's discerning palate.

Following ISS regular crewmembers Peggy Whitson and Yuri Malenchenko aboard their Soyuz TMA-11 they readied for earth bound departure on 19th April. Their descent trajectory however was steeper than normal which subjected the occupants to significantly higher gravitational forces. It was estimate that they endured 10 times the earth's gravitational pull. As a consequence of the erroneous descent the Soyuz capsule landed 260 miles (418 km) off course in Kazakhstan. Although all three fortunately survived the unpleasant re-entry, So-yeon would be later hospitalised in Korea complaining of severe back pain. She was treated for a suspected dislocated vertebrae and later released to resume her research work with Korea Aerospace Research Institute.

Ms. Yi's mission will make South Korea the 35th country to send an astronaut into space since Russia first sent Yuri Gagarin into orbit in 1961. She makes South Korea the third country following the United Kingdom and Iran, to have a woman space traveller. That is well worth shouting "Wow" about.

Events In 2008

■ **British Airways Flight 38 a Boeing 777 lands short of the runway at London in the United Kingdom. Nine of the 152 people on board are treated for minor injuries, but there are no fatalities.**

WOMEN AT WAR

The Second World War was a time of great change in women's aviation all over the world. Female pilots seized the opportunity to be of service, despite some initial resistance from some of their male contemporaries. Ferrying units sprang up in the UK and the US, which saw the birth of women's auxiliary flying units. In Germany, Hanna Reitsch was reported to have flown in combat, while in Russia; there were entire female fighter squadrons.

ATA (UK)

The Air Transport Auxiliary (ATA) came about because in 1938, Gerard d'Erlanger, director of British Airways, foresaw a problem. Realising war with Germany would ground planes and aircrew, he suggested to the Parliamentary Under Secretary for Air, Harold Balfour, and the Director General of Civil Aviation, Sir Francis Shelmerdine, that the creation a pool of peacetime civil pilots who could employ their aviation skills in service of their country would be a sensible plan.

He was tasked with contacting holders of "A" (private) licenses with at least 250 hours of flying time, and to flight-test them with a view to recruiting them into the newly formed Air Transport Auxiliary (ATA). He got about a hundred responses. War broke out on September 3, 1939, just as the first of these men were arriving at a base in the west of England to be vetted.

D'Erlanger selected thirty. There were initially two ranks, second officer, for those whose abilities limited them to flying light single-engine aircraft, and first officer, for those with over 500 hours experience, and who could pilot twin-engine aircraft. They had a formal uniform and were given the urgent job of ferrying trainers, fighters, and bombers from storage units to RAF squadrons.

Since most of the ATA pilots were limited to flying light single-engine training aircraft, they had to take conversion courses. With its ever-increasing demand for ferrying services, the Under Secretary of State for Air proposed that the ATA open its ranks to women. This caused some cultural difficulties initially.

However, Pauline Gower, a commercial pilot with some 2,000 flying hours and a commissioner in the Civil Air Guard lobbied for change. It worked. In November 1939 she was asked to form a pool of eight women pilots to ferry Tiger Moths, which were small, slow single-engine open cockpit trainers. She was appointed commander of this first batch of women flyers. Like d'Erlanger, she would hold the post throughout the war.

On January 1, 1940, the ATA officially accepted the "First Eight" into service, which mushroomed into 166 by the end of the war. It was dangerous work. England was under aerial attack throughout most of the war and the Germans knew where most of the major aircraft factories were. Pilots were not instrument rated, so poor and changeable weather was a constant danger. Barrage balloons and friendly fire from anti-aircraft batteries were also a hazard, especially since pilots were not allowed to mark their maps in case they fell into enemy hands.

The ATA also hired foreign pilots from 30 other countries, particularly from the occupied nations in Europe. Anna Leska of Poland managed to snatch a Polish Air Force plane from an occupied airfield and fly it to Rumania. She made her way to England, where she joined the ATA.

In total pilots delivered over 300,000 aircraft, of 51 different types. There were 1,152 men and 166 women as well as 151 flight engineers, 19 radio officers, and 27 cadets. There were 120 male and 20 female fatalities. They were World War II's forgotten heroes. It took until 2008 before the British Government finally acknowledged their contribution and honoured the 115 surviving members with a special merit award.

NIGHT WITCHES (SOVIET UNION)

"Nachthexen," which means "Night Witches," was the nickname German fighter pilots gave to the female Soviet Air Forces 588th Night Bomber Regiment, later called the 46th Taman Guards Night Bomber Aviation Regiment. This women-only squadron was formed by Marina Raskova and led by Major Yevdokia Bershanskaya.

The regiment was aggressive, flying heavy bombing missions and precision target drops between 1942 to the end of the war. At its largest, it had 40 two-person crews. The women flew more than 23,000 sorties and reportedly dropped 3,000 tons of bombs. The squadron became the most highly decorated unit in the entire Soviet Air Force. Each pilot had flown more than 1,000 missions. Twenty-three of the women were awarded the Hero of the Soviet Union title. There were thirty-one fatalities as a result of combat.

They were given elderly aircraft in which to conduct their missions, flying in wood and canvas Polikarpov Po-2 biplanes, a 1928 design intended for use as training aircraft and for crop-dusting. The aircraft could carry a maximum of two bombs at a time, so the pilots had to fly several missions a night. Although their aeroplanes were obsolete and slow, they were easy to manoeuvre and the women exploited this. They also had the advantage of having a maximum speed that was lower than the stall speed of both the Messerschmitt Bf 109 and the Focke-Wulf Fw 190. This meant they were difficult to shoot down. One killer technique they employed was to shut down their engines near their targets and glide to the bomb release point, with only wind noise to reveal their location.

Women also flew elsewhere in the Soviet Air Force. Famous fighter aces Lilya Litvak and Ekaterina Budanova made their mark on the enemy and Olga Lisikova was one of the Soviet Union's biggest heroes during the war, although not honoured as such then. She flew 280 combat sorties, saving the lives of hundreds of wounded soldiers and officers of the Red Army. She flew on all fronts from the Barents to the Black Sea. During her career she delivered directly to the firing line, providing scores of tons of ammunition, medications, and provisions to those serving at the fronts. She eventually received four government awards for her efforts.

WASP (USA)

The Women's Air force Service Pilots, (WASP), came together via two individual groups, the Women's Flying Training Detachment (WFTD) and the Women's Auxiliary Ferrying Squadron (WAFS). These pioneering organizations of civilian female pilots flew military aircraft for the United States Army Air Forces during World War II. By the end of the war there were thousands of female pilots, freeing up the men for combat service and duties.

By the summer of 1941, both Jackie Cochran and Nancy Harkness Love had submitted proposals suggesting that women pilots could fly in non-combat missions to the Army Air Forces, the predecessor to the United States Air Force. The idea was to allow the men to concentrate on combat missions, while the women could ferry aircraft from factories to military bases. They also performed other duties, such as towing drones/aerial targets. Before Pearl Harbor, General Henry H. "Hap" Arnold, commander of the USAAF, had turned down both proposals outright. Eleanor Roosevelt did her best to intervene, but initially to no avail.

It was apparent by 1940 that war was on the horizon. Jackie Cochran went to England with 25 US women to volunteer and fly for the ATA. These were the first American women to fly military aircraft, crewing the Royal Air Force's fighters and bombers, such as Spitfires, Typhoons, Hudsons, Mitchells, Blenheims, Oxfords, Walruses, and Sea Otters. Many of them spent the entire war in the UK, but Jackie was determined to set up a similar organisation at home.

After Pearl Harbor, America was ready to accept women in the military. Commander William H. Tunner listened to Nancy Love when she took a civilian position with his command and asked her to draw up a proposal. He soon began using women to ferry planes from factory to airfields, which became the beginnings of the Women's Auxiliary Ferrying Squadron (WAFS). By mid-summer of 1942, General Arnold was willing to consider Cochran's proposal to use women as civilian instructor pilots. Cochran's and Love's squadrons were thereby established separately, as the 319th Women's Flying Training Detachment (WFTD) in Houston, Texas under Cochran, and the Women's Auxiliary Ferrying Squadron WAFS at New Castle Army Air Base in 1942 under Love. They later merged to form the WASP in July 1943.

The WASP was a unique corps of women pilots, each already possessing a pilot's licence. They were trained to fly "the Army way" by the US Army Air Forces. After completing months of military flight training, 1,078 of them earned their wings.

After their training, the WASP were stationed at 120 air bases across the United States, relieving male pilots returning from combat duty and assuming numerous other flight-related missions. They flew more than sixty million miles of operational flights and almost every type of aircraft flown by the USAAF during World War II.

They were not recognised as having done military service until the GI Bill Improvement Act of 1977, granting them the distinction of full military status for their service.

THE CHICK FIGHTER PILOTS ASSOCIATION (CFPA)

'We are a small group, but the point of the CFPA is not to set ourselves apart. We are, first and foremost, Fighter Pilots. That's our priority'.

The Chick Fighter Pilots' Association website.

In the early days of pioneering aviation a number of plucky women defied convention and forged a name for themselves as accomplished aviators. Feminine hands grappled with planes hewn from canvas, wood and much prayer to establish records still celebrated today. Unwieldy airframes aside, the minority of women flyers were pitted against the many male institutions reinforcing the ceilings with concrete and inhibiting their further progression.

Such women thrived on the fringes of aviation, tolerated but never fully accepted, more than anything feeling very isolated in their endeavours. Camaraderie of shared spirit would make that same impenetrable ceiling a little more transparent and perhaps instil some encouraging cracks.

After the adrenaline had ebbed away at the end of the first Women's Transcontinental Air Derby or 'Powder Puff Derby' in September 1929 Amelia Earhart, Bobbi Trout and host of other women pilots gathered under the bleachers of a public grandstand in Cleveland, Ohio. They came up with the concept of an organisation dedicated to the needs of licensed women pilots in the US. This was the birth of the Ninety Nines, which today enjoys many thousands of members from across globe.

Safety in numbers perhaps? More likely the numerical advantage of so many passionate aviatrixes and their unified voice resonating with enough passion to effect change. Decades later the same thing happened for the egg beaters shying away from the kitchen. Jean Ross Howard in 1955 made a bold statement by establishing the Whirly Girls. This fun group brought together women helicopter pilots from across the world. The Whirly Girls started with just 6 charter members at their first meeting or 'hovering' and today can boast a membership of 1,500 women representatives from 45 countries.

Fast forward to a day in 2005 when a group of women F-16 instructor fighter pilots serving in the United States Air Force were gathered at Luke Air Force Base. In the midst of saying goodbye to one of their own leaving active service, the six intrepid pilots had a light bulb moment during the farewell luncheon. As none had served operationally with another female F-16 pilot they came up with the idea of meeting once a month just to stay in touch. The Chick Fighter Pilots Association (CFPA) thus hatched into existence and word eventually spread attracting other scattered F-16 pilots to join. Today the CFPA not only encompasses women flying F-16's but other types such as the F-15 Eagle, F-117A Nighthawk and the A-10A Thunderbolt.

From informal monthly meetings, the CFPA has grown into a support network for serving member fighter pilots in the US Air Force. Strengthening ties, exchanging ideas and an esprit de corps in the context of flying fast jets binds the professional and social aspects of the CFPA. It's the hangout of choice for those wishing to share their experiences, catch up with friends and welcome new members. But who exactly are the Fighter Chicks?

'SHOCK', 'STAC', 'HAK' and 'Torch' represent some of the many thousands of personal call-sign names which US military aviators use to identify themselves. But all share the common bond of being part of the CFPA family, with some being the founding matriarchs of the sisterhood.

'SHOCK' a United States Air Force Academy graduate and F-16 driver is currently posted to the Academy as instructor. Like many of her compatriots she has seen through assignments in far flung locations such as Korea and Japan. Recently she served as an F-16 instructor pilot at her CFPA chapter home of Luke AFB. 'SHOCK' also took part in Operation Iraqi Freedom being awarded the Distinguished Flying Cross for her actions during that historic conflict.

From the sleek lines of the F-16 to the geometrically angular and sinister form of the F-117 Stealth Fighter. 'Kirby', a Holloman AFB Fighter Chick and pilot on the enigmatic F-117 took the time to whisper: "Between 2004 and the end of the F-117A Stealth Fighter's operational history in 2008, Kirby, Shaq and Cans became the first, and only, women to every fly the Nighthawk. As part of the 8th Fighter Squadron 'Black Sheep', they flew as wingmen, flight leaders, and instructor pilots. They were the 'Ladies of the Nighthawk'"."

Fighter Chick Major 'HARB' and her husband are the first couple to graduate together from the USAF Test Pilot School. The husband and wife team are assigned to the 416th Flight Test Squadron, Edwards AFB, California as F-16 test pilots. Major 'HARB' the second ever female test pilot, divides her time between pushing the F-16 to the end of its flight envelope and raising a three year old daughter.

The Fighter Chicks have also hit the headlines. 'FiFi' better known as Major Nicole Malachowski was the first ever woman to the fly with the Thunderbird demonstration team in 2006. Major Shawna Rochelle Kimbrell has the accolade of being the first ever F-16 pilot of African-

American heritage flying with the 555th 'Triple Nickel' Fighter Squadron.

Fighter Chicks also have an international flavour with 'Handles' flying an F-18C Hornet for the Canadian Air Force. Their appeal extends into other branch services of the US armed forces such as the pilots of the Marine Corps and navy. Civilian Fighter Chicks swell the numbers modestly through the Air National Guard and Reserves.

Embracing the Internet has made the world smaller for the Fighter Chicks, their web presence permitting the sisterhood to do more than just keep in touch. A gallery of hosted images places call signs to faces, vividly painting the operational picture of women pilots assigned to Stateside and overseas bases. The message board section invites members of the public to join the moderated forums. It acts as a platform for those interested in aviation and drawn towards making contact with actual fighter pilots without compromising operational security. Furthermore aspiring young

fighter chicks and those already in training can seek valuable advice from seasoned 'veterans'. The Fighter Chicks use the medium for general announcements and news, such as the all important periodic get together meetings in the traditional venue of Las Vegas.

Flight suits cut differently and hair a little longer than previous regulation length represents a testament to the tenaciousness of the few responsible for opening up one of the last bastions of male preserve, the fighter cockpit. Jackie Cochran may have flown an experimental fighter to clinch the Bendix race trophy in 1938, but it wasn't enough. In 1942 Jackie, in the company of Nancy Harkness Love, diligently established the Women's Air Service Pilots (WASP) to mitigate the anticipated pilot shortage during the war years. The capable WASP flew all types from pursuit fighters such as the P-51 Mustang to heavy bombers like the venerable B-17 Flying Fortress. However with cessation of hostilities in Europe the WASP were swiftly disbanded in December 1944. The new jet era of the post war years reinforced the lockdown of the fighter canopy to women.

A change of legislation in 1993 finally enabled qualified women pilots to compete on an equal footing with their male counterparts for coveted fighter placements. The first to successfully secure an assignment was Captain Jeannie Flynn call sign 'Tally'. She entered the history books in 1994 by becoming the first to fly the F-15E Strike Eagle. Today the US Air Force alone has 3,700 fighter pilots of which 70 are women.

The exclusive male domain is no more but shoring up the numbers of women serving as combat pilots will take some time. Integration and acceptance has been facilitated with the help of female pilots focusing on the mission parameters irrespective of earlier scrutiny. The novelty factor is yesterday's news and successive generations will compete more on merit and aptitude with gender issues relegated to history. A modern utopian prediction steadily edging closer to reality thanks to the altruistic and practical activities of contemporary pioneers. The CFPA demystifies the world of the fighter pilot to the average lay person and serves to inspire emerging generations, both male and female alike. In this respect the Fighter Chicks make the job of the air force recruiter a whole lot easier.

One thing will never change, the 'fighter 'trixes' of the CFPA will certainly remain as 'chick' members by association. But there's no denying that all have matured into eagles soaring high and ranked amongst the best of fighter pilots. Like the Ninety Nines and the Whirly Girls their future is assured to withstand the test of time.

■ Future 'Fighter Chicks' are always welcome, for further information please visit their nest at www.fighterchicks.com

Acknowledgements

Pictures

Liz Moscrop was principal picture researcher on this work and to the best of her ability has traced copyright, ownership and permission to use the images and attributed them accordingly. Given the wide-ranging and historical nature of much of the work, it has not always been possible to trace the creator of each photograph and she would like to thank the owners and remains at their disposal for future agreements.

Picture credits:

AirTeamImages Polly Vacher
Aviatrix Enterprises Bobbi Trout
Betty Skelton Frankman Betty Skelton
Canadian Air Force Deanna Brasseur
Captain Lucy Lupia Thereza de Marzo and Ada Rogato,
Dan Pimental Geraldine "Jerrie" Mock
Dassault Aviation Jacqueline Auriol
Etihad Aisha Al Mansoori and Salma Al Balooshi
Fiorenza di Bernardi Fiorenza de Bernardi
Getty Images Sabiha Gocken, Mary du Caurroy, Beryl Markham, Barbara Harmer.
Library of Congress (US) Helene Dutrieu Gobain LC-DIG-ggbain-08286, Harriet Quimby, LC-USZ62-15071, Ruth Nichols LC-DIG-npcc-17217, Katherine Stinson LC-DIG-ggbain-18208/LC-DIG-ggbain-18209, Blanche Stuart Scott GGBAIN loc.pnp/ggbain.12209, Raymonde de Laroche ID ggbain.20940, Marie Marvingt, LC-DIG-ggbain-05523, Anne Lindbergh LC-DIG-npcc-17645, Phoebe Omlie, LC 3b43433u.
Hill Air Force Base Yue Xicui, Willa Brown, Florence "Pancho" Barnes
Jennifer Murray Jennifer Murray
Jerusalem Post Yael Rom,
JetStarAsia Major Ana Gan, Chong Phit
Jo Kelland Jo Kelland
Judy Leden Judy Leden
Kingdom Holdings Hanadi Zakaria al-Hindi
Landspeed Productions Jeanna Yeager
Luftfart Museum Norway Gidsken Jakobsen
Malaysian Daily Star Patricia Yapp

Mandy Pantall Mandy Pantall
NASA Yi so-yeon, Shelia Scott, Sally Ride, Roberta Bondar, Marta Bohn Meyer, Mae Jemison, Kathryn Sullivan, Kalpana Chawla, Jacqueline Cochran, Fay Gillis Wells, Chiaki Mukai, Jerrie Cobb.
National Library of Australia, Freda Thompson, Nivedita Bhasin Nivedita Bhasin
Pakistan Air Force Sairi Amin
PA Photos Turi Wideroe
Patti Gully Li Xiapeng, Jessie Zheng, Hilda Yan
Patty Wagstaff Airshows Patty Wagstaff
Peter Finlay Svetlana Kapanina
RAF Museum Pauline Gower, Mrs Victor Bruce, Lettice Curtis, Hilda Hewlett, Hannah Reitsch, Diana Barnato Walker, Amelia Earhart, Anne Welch, Amy Johnson.
RAF Michelle Goodman
RIA Novosti Photo Library Valentina Tereshkova, Valentina Grizodubova, Svetlana Savitskaya, Marina Raskova, Lilya Litvak, Ekaterina Vaseline Budanova, Rosella Bjornsson, Rosella Bjornsson
Royal Australian Air Force Linda Corbould
Sanjay Rampal Chanda Budhabhatti, Liz Moscrop
Shock and Kirby Fighter Chicks
South African Air Force Phetogo Molawa, Katherine Labuschagne
South African Express Asnath Mahapa
State Library of New South Wales Nancy Bird, Jean Batten.
State Library of Queensland Lores Bonney
Suddeutsche Zeitung Melli Beese, Louise Thaden (also Hawker Beechcraft)
Texas Women's University Nancy Harkness Love, Jean Ross Howard
The Hindu Photo Archives Saudamini Deshmukh
Topfoto.co.uk Elinor Smith, Barbara Harmer, Michelle Goodman.
New York Public Library Elinor Smith, Bessie Coleman.
US Air Force ATA girls, Janet Harmon Bragg, Betty Huyler Gillies, Allison Hickey, Evelyn Bryan Johnson, Nicole Malachowski
Vernice Armour Vernice Armour
Zagreb Aeroclub Katarina Matanoviç
Zeppelin Museum Lady Mary Heath
US Navy Kara Spears Hultgreen
"Gunman" Caroline Aigle

Other thanks and acknowledgements:

Wherever possible we have spoken to the living members of our cast of 100. Otherwise, we have sourced reputable published source materials and are incredibly grateful to the following people and institutions for their support, enthusiasm and kindness:

Catherine Herrald Adams President, Whirly-Girls International, Heather Alexander, Intl Women's Air & Space Museum, Mohammed Fahad Al-Nafjan and Intisar Al-Yamani, Kingdom Holding Company, Vernice Armour, Luc Berger, Dassault Aviation, Nivedita Bhasin, Rosella Bjornson, Deanna Brasseur, Evelyn Bryan Johnson, Chanda Budhabhatti , Alison Chambers, Rebecca D. Danet TSgt - USAF, NCOIC, Public Affairs - Dept of the Air Force, Public Affairs & National Media Outreach, Fiorenza Di Bernadi, Dr. Peggy Chabrian, President Women In Aviation International, Peter Elliot Senior Keeper, Dept of Research & Information Services RAF Hendon (UK), Vadim Feldzer, Dassault Aviation, Fighter Pilot- Call sign 'Kirby' United States Air Force (USAF, Fighter Pilot - Call sign 'SHOCK' United States Air Force (USAF, Fighter Pilot-Call sign 'HARB', Major, United States Air Force (USAF, Fernand Francois, publisher BART International, Ana Gan, Michelle Goodman, Olav Gynnild, Norwegian Luftfahrt Museum, Rene Hackestetter, Jean-Pierre Harrison- Kalpana Chawla Foundation, Col. Mariette Hartley and Major Elize Beukes South African Air Force, Hanadi Hindi, Dileseng Koetle South African Airways, Helen Krasner, Dave Lam, Dawn Letson, Curator Special Collections, Texas Women's University, Lucy Lúpia Pinel Balthazar Alves de Pinho, Major Nichole Malachowski, USAF, Nanette Malher Aviatrix Enterprises, Pat Malone, GA Magazine, Kathryn Murano Rocheseter Science Museum New York, Russell Naughton , Tricia Nelmes British Women Pilots' Association, Louise Ann Noeth Landspeed Productions, Tim Orchard, British Airways Flying Club, Mandy Pantall, Tom Peaford, Major Scott Price, Flying Officer Kailash Rampal, Indian Air Force, Andrew Renwick, RAF Museum, Ian Seager, Yuri Shukost, Royal Australian Air Force, Grace Slater Australian Women Pilots' Association, Nicholas Smith- Ministry of Defence (UK) LF Media & Comms, Kathy Strawn Media Resource Centre, NASA, Khai Hua Tan JetStar Asia, Group Captain IR Tolfts - Ministry of Defence (UK) DACOS Media & Comms, Panay Triantafillides - Ministry of Defence (UK) DPR Publicity (Bureau), Celia Turner, Polly Vacher, Sonja Veljanovska , David Volenec , Patty Wagstaff, Roy Waterhouse, Turi Wideroe, Wanda Wideroe, 99s, Zagreb Aero Club

The Proud Supporter

AERO TOY STORE:
PROUD INDUSTRY SUPPORTER

This book would not have been possible without the support of Aero Toy Store and its founder and president Morris Shirazi (pictured right).

Shirazi and his team are well known among the business aviation community for their original thinking and determination to do things differently often by challenging the status quo – the very values that drove so many of the women recognized in this book.

The company is headquartered in Fort Lauderdale and was founded by Shirazi in 1993 as a side business to finance aircraft for upscale regulars of his Auto Toy Store, the venue for luxury, exotic and investment grade automobiles.

The company has grown into a global brand, owning an inventory of aircraft that range from smaller to medium-size jets, such as the Citation, Hawker and Lear, to the most luxurious large jets, like Falcon, Challenger, Gulfstream and Global Express.

With lifetime aircraft sales approaching the $3 billion mark, Aero Toy Store commands the title of largest pre-owned corporate aircraft dealer in the world – a goal that was achieved by educating and assisting its customers in making the best choice based on their operational requirements and personal preferences.

Additional locations to broaden the customer base include sales offices in Beverly Hills, Montreal and Monaco, with further satellite locations planned in Europe and around the world.

Very much an equal opportunities employer, Aero Toy Store applauds the tenacity of women in the aviation industry to have succeeded as they have over the past 100 years and supports the move to recognize those brave women of the past and encourage women of the present and future to reach new horizons.